Traditions of the Southeastern Conference

A Tailgater's Guide to SEC Football

Volume V

Chris Warner

Wagon Publishing

Perdido Key, Florida

Copyright 2020

ISBN:

978-0-9796284-6-7

Christopher Edward Warner

All rights reserved

"Tailgater's Guide" copyrighted

American Library of Congress

1st printing Vol. V

Layout and Cover Design by Jamie Welch; jamiewelch777.myportfolio.com

This title may be purchased in bulk for fundraising, sales or promotional uses.

For information, or to schedule a speaking event with the author, email him:

cewarner@mindspring.com

Table of Contents

Author's Note

Since this odyssey began in 2000, with the first publishing of *A Tailgater's Guide to SEC Football*, I have come into contact with tens of thousands of fans from across the Southeastern Conference. The nation's most powerful league has the most impressive fans!

Things have come full circle. In the 20 years this book has been in print, much has changed. My oldest daughter has enrolled at the University of Alabama, where she is a junior; and her younger sister is headed to Auburn in the fall, making my family quite mixed in terms of conference team allegiance and pride. In the tradition-rich SEC, this is not uncommon. Many families follow and cheer for more than one Southeastern Conference favorite, making their fall football experience particularly rich.

The visceral connection between Southerners and their SEC teams is evident. That is because there is nothing that can match the excitement of a live Southeastern Conference football game. From Athens to Baton Rouge and from College Station to Columbia and all parts in between, SEC football is always the hottest ticket in town and the driving cultural force of the waking community. Southerners love and live for their football Saturdays.

It is with these devoted, pigskin-loving Southerners in mind that we unveil this fifth edition of the ultimate tome on Southeastern Conference football history and tradition as well as the definitive, updated guide to the nation's toughest football subdivision.

Like its predecessors, this book is different than previous editions. There are new coaching and player profiles and updated records and statistics. Look for updated suggestions for golfing and shopping in each amazing campus town, as well as a trusted guide on where to go and what to do when you arrive, as well as the upcoming schedule for each school.

Road tripping in the SEC to some of college football's finest cathedrals and their supporting communities is always a memory-forging excursion. Make the most of the lasting Southern cultural experience with this fifth volume of the Bible of SEC Football!

Safe travels to you and yours, good luck to your team, and happy tailgating!
Bon appétit et laissez les bon temps roulez SEC fans!
Chris Warner
2020
Previous Editions of *A Tailgater's Guide to SEC Football*
2000 Volume I, 2004 Volume II, 2008 Volume III, 2013 Volume IV

Foreword

Tommy Casanova is one of the greatest college football players of all time. As an all-around athlete for the LSU Bengal Tigers from 1969-1971, he was a three-time All-American. Unable to play as a freshman due to NCAA rules, Casanova was perhaps precluded from becoming an unheard of four-time college All-American. Casanova appeared on the cover of the September 13, 1971, edition of Sports Illustrated, where he was touted as "The Best Player in the Nation." A consummate leader on and off the field, after football Casanova earned a medical degree and served in the Louisiana Legislature as a senator. Today, Dr. Casanova maintains a medical practice in his hometown of Crowley, Louisiana.

I am not and do not pretend to be a football expert. I am not particularly good at preparing or analyzing a game plan...X's and O's were never my forte'.

My college football experience was instinct and reaction—if you stopped for a split second to think you got beat for a touchdown, a missed block or a dropped pass. What looked exciting from the stands was really just mud blood and sweat. It was line up each play and try and beat the guy across from you. It didn't matter if he was big or small or fast or slow, an All-American or second team—my job was to beat him, and beat him soundly.

I did not care who he was, who he knew, how nice of a guy he was or what his mother thought of him. My teammates, each facing similar battles, were counting on me, just like I was counting on them. Individually and as a team we played for a school that we each had chosen, and that we each wanted to represent to the best of our abilities.

I think it is safe to say that my college football experience mirrors that of thousands of other young men so blessed. Young men who are better people today because of college football. For many, college football was the means to get an education, yet beyond the classroom an education of less formality was becoming part of our nature without us realizing it. While focusing on an upcoming opponent, we learned that preparation is important, and that it pays off; that practice and repetition make difficult things second nature; that discipline and self-sacrifice are essential components when working as a team; that 11 players of average ability working together can accomplish more than 11 "stars" playing without a common cause; that people do not demand that you always win, but that you always give your best; that you never stop to look at the size of the mountain, you just start climbing, then

scratch and climb as hard as you can until time runs out and more often than not you get to the top.

That for me is college football. It would be interesting to know what the experience of other college players has been in regard to the value of their formal education symbolized by its diploma versus the informal education the practice fields symbolized by arthritic joints. I know in my case the formal education opened many doors for me, but it's the informal education that helped me once inside.

Thomas H. Casanova, III, M.D.
LSU Tigers 1969, 1970, 1971

Preface

The Southern way of life is as endearing as the people who live it. In the South, customs, speech and actions depict a unique existence. However, there is perhaps no other defining trait of Southerners that best describes the way they approach and enjoy life than the manner in which they avidly ascribe to the Saturday fall phenomenon known as Southeastern Conference Football.

As a youngster I can remember my father's unbridled autumn anticipation for college football season to finally arrive, and the many SEC games that followed on television. During my earliest years I was transfixed by the unflappable, intrepid images of Alabama's Coach Paul "Bear" Bryant, clad in his iconic houndstooth hat. I can remember his commanding scowl that helped him realize more wins than any other college coach in college football's colorful and proud history. I recall SEC stalwarts Bo Jackson of Auburn and Herschel Walker of Georgia running through hapless defenses like runaway trains. These fledgling impressions have remained with me through the years, like etchings in the stone tablet of my mind.

As I grew older, during my teenage years, I learned to love and long for the excitement of watching the purple and gold Fighting Tigers of LSU pour exuberantly out of the tunnel in Death Valley in Baton Rouge. I found, after my first game in the old dugout arena, that Tiger football was Louisiana's Saturday night main event. It was intoxicating. The pure exhilaration that came from being inundated by the deafening roar of 92,000-plus bourbon-frenzied Mediterranean-blooded fans was nothing less than awe-inspiring to a young Cajun from a small Southwestern Louisiana town. I was hooked.

However, it was not until later, as a college boy at the Ole War Skule, that I would fully recognize and respect the many traditions the SEC member institutions so proudly embody. It was during my college days that I witnessed first-hand the indomitable spirit and fanfare of the other conference schools. After being weaned on these indelible football experiences, I came to realize, after graduation, in my early adulthood, that college football is the king of spectator sports, and that the SEC, without question, is its most beloved and storied domain.

This book is a dedication to the glory and accomplishment of the educators, coaches and athletes associated with the Southeastern Conference—in its past or present form. Spawned by my fondness for the American game of football and by my undying love of the SEC and all that it represents, I embarked on the task of writing about the total college football experience in the SEC. In doing so, I wanted to write a history of the conference, its earliest beginnings and how the game and the league—much like our country, evolved and changed over time. I wanted to write about each school and their proud traditions, their mascots and alma maters; their fights songs; their greatest coaches and players; and even their stadiums. I also wanted to include information on what to do while you were visiting each SEC college town—like where to eat and where one can enjoy an adult beverage or two, if so inclined.

The favored pastime of tailgating has become an art to avid SEC football fans. Good food and football games in the South go together like white and rice. Whether it's barbecue in Nashville, Ribs in T-Town or a bowl of spicy Cajun gumbo in Baton Rouge, a feast is always present before game time in the fun-loving SEC. Some fans might say that the pre-game warm-up is as big a part of the game day experience as the contest itself. I know this well having grown up in South Louisiana, where my family and friends always enjoyed well-prepared food. Inspired by my maternal grandmother's love for bringing people together with good Cajun food, tailgating has always been an opportunity to relive old times and to enjoy a cherished cultural pastime that has been passed down from one generation to the next.

For the benefit of your most untested taste buds, added to this one-of-a-kind tribute to the SEC schools are 14 authentic Cajun recipes my family and friends have enjoyed through the years. Each is easy to read and prepare and each is sure to please.

Enjoy the book and all of its varied contents! Use it to road trip like a pro and to learn and pass on the many proud traditions of the mighty Southeastern Conference.

Chris Warner
The Professor of Tailgating

A Brief History of Football in the South

Origins of the Game of Football in America

In 1820, students at the College of New Jersey, now Princeton University, participated in a soccer-like game, called ballown, in which they advanced the ball by punching it with their fists. Eastern colleges thereafter began competing in the game, which resembled soccer more than it did the modern games of rugby or football.

Other early forms of the modern game of football, derived from the rules of rugby, were played by college students during the late 1860's. Eventually, representatives of Harvard, Yale, Columbia, Rutgers and Princeton Universities met at Springfield, Massachusetts in 1876 and formed a new set of football rules and the Intercollegiate Football Association. The resulting combination of rugby and soccer became popular, and as time progressed, the new game of American football slowly evolved.

Prior to 1885, when the number of football players on the field was reduced to 11, the game was noticeably different. Prior to the rule changes of 1885, there were 25 members on each side. Further, the field of play was 300 feet by 500 feet and each goal post was 25 feet apart, connected by a crossbar ten feet above the ground. In this version, the ball was moved primarily by "scrimmaging," the process in which both sides massed together around the ball shoulder-to-shoulder, with their heads down, trying to push their opponents off the ball. During these early exhibitions, several thousand spectators were known to attend and watch the burgeoning spectacle.

Football – A Diversion from War

While the Ivy League's Rutgers and Princeton were playing the first collegiate football game in November of 1869, East Tennessee University, predecessor of the University of Tennessee, was still clearing the monument of debris left behind by the Southern and Northern armies—which had both used its campus buildings as hospitals during the war. Since East Tennessee had been somewhat sympathetic to the Union during the war it was rewarded among the first universities of the Old Confederacy to acquire land grand institution status (Morrill Act of 1862).

In the early 1890's in the South, most noteworthy colleges and universities were small and many were still recovering from the vast devastation and disheartenment of the Civil War some 25 years before. The epic conflict deeply divided the two separate populations of North and South; and the South, humbled mightily in defeat, had lost most, if not all of its former wealth and status.

College football in America emerged amidst the painful aftermath of this most debilitating Civil War. Our young country, once divided by its differences, was reunited by a bloody and costly ordeal. In many cases the struggle had even split families, pitting cousins and even brothers fighting against each other.

The South, subsequent to the capitulation of Lee's Army at Appomattox, was humiliated in defeat. War-torn and tattered, the region of Southern states was faced with the realization that its self-proclaimed sovereignty had been usurped by the Union and replaced with a bevy or corrupt and sometimes black, carpetbagger governments.

The emergence of the game of football allowed these sectional differences between the North and the South—ones that remained long after the war was over, to be momentarily forgotten, and in some cases reconciled, on the playing field. In light of this, football was one of the few ties that bound otherwise highly divergent national institutions with a common experience and point of reference.

Through organized competition on the gridiron, young men—especially those of the South, were able to once again, albeit in a different manner, prove their worth and their manhood; thereby regaining the self-pride and sense of purpose that the War Between the States had stripped from them. In the South, football emerged as a much-needed outlet of frustration and despair for both the players and the spectators. Each game represented a definitive opportunity to achieve victory and vindication—two things Southerners greatly longed for in the wake of the Civil War. Further, winning football games allowed Southern boys to erase many of the stinging transgressions they endured during the war and it provided much-needed hope for a successful, enjoyable life in the new South.

The Proliferation of the Game

The University of Kentucky was the first to play football in the South. Florida was the last. On April 9, 1880, football in the Southeast made its debut at Old Stoll Field at the University of Kentucky, then known as Kentucky A&M. Kentucky served as host to two visiting teams—Transylvania College and Centre College. Transylvania prevailed in that contest 13 to 0.

The Lexington Daily Transcript reported on the event, "An estimated 500 ladies and gentlemen watched the game. The head-on collisions between the players were equal to the explosion of Spanish bulls crashing into one another."

Kentucky A&M was enthralled by the game of football. They formed their own squad and issued a challenge to Transylvania for a best of three series slated for November 1881. Kentucky won the first game, but dropped the next two. The Knoxville Journal, in 1891, reported, "The fame of football is beginning to gain a foothold in Knoxville." By 1895, ten colleges from today's SEC were playing intercollegiate football.

As the number of colleges playing football spread like wildfire across the country and the South, new formations and plays were slowly introduced. In 1888, tackling below the waist was legalized. This particular rule change resulted in a significant increase in injuries. As other rule changes and new formations were added, the game became even more violent and dangerous to the players. Player safety in the early years was further jeopardized due to the lack of adequate protective equipment such as helmets, shoulder pads, etc. These were items that had not yet been conceived and introduced. During the early years, players were known to grow their hair long and bushy to cushion the fierce bodily contact that was experienced during play.

A game characterized by rough play from the onset, football appealed to the basic qualities of combat. Much like warfare, football effectively challenged each team to gain ground on the playing field through various and sundry methods. Brute force, daring sleight of hand and tactical maneuvers are techniques that are still employed by each side today. Because of this, football early on was a game of fierce bodily contact. Undoubtedly, the game's enormous past and current spectator appeal remains linked to its thrilling exhibition of strength, skill, speed and deception.

In addition to its rugged nature, a distinctive element of the game of football, even in its earliest years, was the social aspect of the event that made it especially enjoyable. In the beginning, it was customary that each game was preceded by an extravagant luncheon and then followed by a wild game and fish supper, in which both teams participated together. This practice marked the beginning of the beloved modern American college football pastime of enjoying food in a community setting...the undoubted predecessor of "tailgating."

Developed as a game to promote physical fitness and to foment competition between colleges after the Civil War, the gridiron quickly found favor among players and spectators. The game was a physical sport, played by only the toughest men on college campuses, and it was the alarming number of football-related injuries and fatalities that nearly resulted in the abolition of football and led to the forming of the National Collegiate Athletic Association in 1905.

The development of football in America occurred during the period subsequent to the Civil War known as the "Gilded Age," a term coined by the famous American author, Mark Twain. This era in American history is often referred to as America's joyous time of rebirth and renewal. During this epoch, an astounding post-Civil War industrial boom created unprecedented opportunities for wealth and prosperity for all young men in America. The emergence of football was another by-product of this innovative age that saw many technological advancements that changed the way Americans worked, lived and played. Football players during this era grew up in the world view of Horatio Algier. They believed that hard work and thrift would be rewarded with great success.

The Southern Intercollegiate Athletic Association (SIAA)

As football's popularity grew, so did the increasing need for an organizing body to help ensure fairness and consistency in the game. In 1894, William L. Dudley of Vanderbilt University promoted the establishment of the Southern Intercollegiate Athletic Association (SIAA) to "develop and purify" athletics among participating colleges and universities. The formation of the SIAA was welcomed by the schools since there was no existing organizing body at the time. The SIAA was the first major athletic conference in the United States.

The crowning achievement of the SIAA was that is wrestled control of college athletics from the students, placing it instead firmly in the hands of the school's administrators. Prior to the inception of the SIAA, football was a game that was controlled by underclassmen on the college campuses. As a result of this lack of organized leadership, the early game of football was rife with unfairness and inconsistencies.

At the time the SIAA was forming, many of the colleges in the South were already on their way to becoming million-dollar athletic programs. In an effort to combat this alarming trend, a constitution for the SIAA was drafted that drew heavily on the definition of "amateur" and "professional" athletes. Purification of the game of football was to be established through concise, delineated rules of player eligibility—an all-important aspect of the college game that has remained a fountain of controversy through the years. During the progressive years leading to World War I, the SIAA grew into a large conference that included both big and small institutions.

A "professional athlete" was strictly defined by the governing body, the SIAA, as "...somebody that used his athletic knowledge and skill for personal gain." The league's constitution stated that professionals were strictly forbidden from participating in the sport. Football players in the SIAA were required to have been students at the college or university they represented and they

had to register within 30 days of the beginning of school so as to prevent the proliferation of "ringers," talented football players who would earn money illegally by playing for several Southern football-playing schools. These "tramp athletes" were commonplace at the time in the South.

The hiring of star athletes by coaches, trainers and alumni of larger schools in search of a winning team was practiced due to the ease with which student athletes could transfer from one school to another without the loss of playing eligibility. Tramp athletes were known to have played for three or four schools simultaneously without ever attending classes. During the earliest years of football in the South it was even common to find coaches, such as LSU's A.P. Simmonds, a Yale graduate, in the school's lineup. During an 1894 game in Baton Rouge, Coach Simmonds scored the Bayou Bengals' only touchdown in a lopsided 26-6 defeat. In fact, it was not uncommon to witness a player compete for as many as eight years for the same school. This blatant practice was rampant in the South at the time.

Football's Brush with Death

By the turn of the century, in spite of the game's enormous popularity, concerns nevertheless materialized over the future of football in America. Brutality and foul play had so tainted the sport that President Theodore "Teddy" Roosevelt felt it necessary to prompt a serious national discussion about the debilitative nature of the game. Roosevelt's remarks were justified.

During the 1905 football season, the game's brutal nature, typified by mass formations such as the flying wedge, and gang tackling, resulted in 18 fatalities and 159 serious injuries on college football playing fields, as was reported by the influential football mind of Yale's Amos Alonzo Stagg in the Chicago Tribune that same year. President Roosevelt issued a statement to the representatives of Harvard, Yale and Princeton that it was "...up to them to save the sport of football by removing every objectionable feature." Roosevelt added that, "Brutality and foul play should be treated with the same summary punishment given to a man who cheats at cards."

Brutality and related fatalities had become a major concern among the playing institutions. Prior to President Roosevelt's landmark statements in 1905, the game of football had become a barbaric, and often deadly, game. According to John F. Stegeman, just a few years earlier in 1987, the football season had proved to be a rough one for the University of Georgia. One of Georgia's better-known football players, Vonalbade Gammon, was rendered unconscious by a blow he endured during the Bulldog's gridiron contest with Virginia. Interest in the game was so great among spectators and players that young Vonalbade was carried to the sideline and forgotten by his teammates, who were consumed with the task at hand—beating the Cavaliers. A doctor in the crowd who worried about Gammon's poor condition ordered him taken to a nearby hospital in an ambulance drawn by a horse. The Samaritan doctor's actions were in vain that day, however, for Gammon later died from his injuries the next day.

In light of this debacle, the Georgia legislature, via special session, voted to ban football within the state. However, before the bill ending football forever could be signed into law by the governor, the mother of the fallen boy pleaded in a last-minute letter to Georgia's Chief Executive to refrain from doing so (signing the bill), saying that, "It would be inexpressibly sad, to have the cause he (Vonalbade) held so dear injured by his sacrifice. Grant me the right to request that my boy's death should not be used to defeat the most cherished object of his life." The Governor of Georgia, consequently, did not sign the bill into law.

Following the 1905 season that saw an alarming number of fatalities and crippling injuries, a number of schools banned football altogether. Fearing additional unnecessary deaths, Columbia, Northwestern, and Stanford ceased playing until rule changes could be implemented that would make the game safer for its participants.

The NCAA

Compelled by Roosevelt's comments, Chancellor Henry M. McCracken of New York University called a conference of college representatives to the White House in Washington, D.C. in 1905, to consider whether or not college football should be reformed, or abolished. This initial meeting of delegates from 13 college football playing schools in early December 1905 spurred the creation of the organization that we today know as the NCAA. Rule changes were debated at the initial meeting and during a subsequent meeting on December 18th in New York City, the Intercollegiate Athletic Association of the United States, or IAAUS, was formed. The IAAUS was formally constituted in March 1906, and took its current name, the NCAA, or National Collegiate Athletic Association, in 1910.

The formation of the NCAA marked the beginning of a series of rule changes that would forever alter and rescue the game of football in America. The major focus of the deliberations in Washington, D.C. and New York centered on ending the typically rough, mass-formation plays, as well as the on-the-field fighting.

The rule changes of 1906 eliminated the less civilized aspects of the early game, such as making punches to the face of the ball carrier—a common

tackling practice, illegal. Other rule changes agreed upon by the fledgling NCAA related to legalizing the forward pass, establishing the current definition of an offensive line of scrimmage, making football look a lot less like rugby, and establishing the ten-yards-for-a-first-down rule.

The Forward Pass

"Fear not thy rivals, though for swiftness known;
Compare thy rivals' judgment and thy own;
It is not strength, but art, that obtains the prize,
And to be swift is less than to be wise.
-Homer, The Iliad

The biggest rule change in football occurred when the forward pass was legalized in 1906. Although it was not immediately used to its fullest extent, the pass forever changed the game's complexion. The forward pass opened up the game of football from its former heavy-handed, smash-mouthed approach of deliberate brute force, making room for further innovation and change. Specifically, the pass allowed for a natural progression toward a more open, quick-striking offense that was much more appealing to both participant and spectator. Being oblong in shape, and possessing an inherent tendency to spiral when lofted, the football was meant to be thrown.

The first team to use the forward pass was Wesleyen in a game against Yale in 1906. In spite of their innovative courage, Wesleyen still lost the game 21-0. However, St. Louis University's Head Coach Eddie Cochem used the forward pass extensively from 1906 to 1907. In 1907, St. Louis won all 11 of their games and led the nation in scoring by using the forward pass. Although Cochem demonstrated that the forward pass was an effective means for moving the football, it was nevertheless not universally embraced by college football coaches until later. "Three yards and a cloud of dust" would continue to be the favored method of moving the football for offensive coaches, in spite of the rule change, since there were penalties involved with incomplete passes.

In the beginning, there were restrictions placed on the passing game. For example, if the ball touched the ground, the ball became the other team's ball at the point where the pass was thrown. Put more simply, an incomplete pass was a turnover. Also, a pass completed in the end zone was a touchback for the defending team, and if the pass wasn't thrown within the hash marks, or if it hit an ineligible receiver, the ball went to the defending team.

Following the implementation of the forward pass and the slough of other rule changes, teams invented new offensive and defensive strategies. Tactics employing the pushing and pulling of the ball carrier, as well as the flying tackle, evolved. In spite of the rule changes of 1906, the number of fatalities from football continued to rise, reaching a tragic total of 33 deaths in 1908. The NCAA, prompted by this unsettling news, again convened to make further rule changes. The subsequent rule changes of 1908 by the NCAA resulted in a much safer game of football.

The 1908 rule changes mandated that seven men were required on the offensive line of scrimmage, thereby limiting the team's ability to assemble in mass formation. Additionally, pulling and pushing the ball carrier, interlocked interference, crawling on the ground and the "flying tackle" were barred from play. In 1909, the NCAA ordered even more changes. New rules stated that the points awarded for a field goal be reduced from four points to three points; during the following year, in 1910, the game was divided into four separate quarters instead of two halves.

During this progressive first decade of the 20th Century, football underwent significant changes. These major changes, culminating with the most prominent ones in 1912, forever changed the game of football and the manner in which it was played. This was so because the new rules promulgated during that year truly opened up the passing game for all teams.

The sweeping rule changes in 1912 stated that teams had four downs to make a first down, and that the length of the field would be 100 yards, instead of the previous 110. It was decided that the value of a touchdown would change from five to six points. Regarding the passing game, the new rules stipulated that all distance restrictions were to be removed from the game. A completed pass in the end zone thereafter was a touchdown and no longer a turnover like it was before; and finally, an incomplete pass was a loss of down and no longer a turnover.

These rule changes allowing for a more progressive passing game were the most significant in bringing the college game of football to its current level of play. The forward pass was implemented to remove the premium on weight and size and to develop greater possibility for speed, agility and cunning in the game of football. As a result of the full innovation of the pass, injuries were reduced, thereby creating a safer game for its participants.

Subsequent to additional 1912 rule changes, in the South, football continued to grow in popularity among colleges and universities. However, as time passed and competition increased, the rules of eligibility did not fit the diverging circumstances of both groups, big and small schools, resulting in a loss of the cohesion that had made the SIAA a former success. This turbulence led to the creation of the Southeastern Conference.

The Southern Conference

The Southern Conference was born on February 25, 1921, at a meeting in Atlanta, Georgia. After a short hiatus spawned by the critical years of World War I, 14 of the larger institutions from the 30 member Southern Intercollegiate Athletic Association reorganized to form the Southern Conference. Those charter members included Alabama, Auburn, Clemson, Georgia, Georgia Tech, Kentucky, Maryland, Missisippi State, North Carolina, North Carolina State, Tennessee, Virginia, Virginia Tech, and Washington & Lee. Athletic competition began in the fall of 1921. In 1922, seven more schools, Florida, Louisiana State, Mississippi, South Carolina, the University of the South, Tulane and Vanderbilt, joined the fold.

The stated purpose of the Southern Conference was "...to promote intercollegiate athletics in every form, and to keep them in proper bounds by making them incidental and not a principal feature of university life."

The Southern Conference was promoted by the larger state universities and land grant colleges, who were pushing for a new sanctioning organization. Although the SIAA was successful in wrestling the reins of college football from the players to the faculty, it had failed in its attempts to control and restrict player eligibility to constitutionally defined student athletes. Members of the newly formed Southern Conference wanted to increase control over player eligibility by disallowing freshmen from playing sports and by instituting a one year residency rule and a migrant rule. Additionally, the leaders of the conference schools wanted to definitely establish succinct measures to confine athletic activity strictly to amateurs.

The Southern Conference comprised larger state universities and land grant colleges, as well as smaller liberal arts colleges. Again, the diverging interests of the varying institutions within the conference caused dissension among the ranks. The larger schools wanted to push for a new sanctioning organization and to preclude freshmen from playing. Additionally, the bigger schools wanted to institute a one year residency rule and a migrant rule in order to increase eligibility requirements and to once and for all eliminate the proliferation of ringers and tramp athletes.

The major downfall of the Southern Conference was that it covered such a large geographical area. The conference's 23 members inhabited nearly the entire southeastern area of the United States from Maryland to Louisiana. This massive territory made management and travel difficult for the conference leaders and school members. Further, many of the schools held varying educational objectives. Some of the smaller, private liberal arts colleges were at a serious disadvantage from a resources standpoint, since the larger state universities and land grant institutions possessed more funding and support in their respective areas.

As a result of these inherent differences, regulations regarding the size of athletic squads, the number of scholarships, expenses of travel or the number of coaches employed could not be imposed on all conference members. Most important related to this was the implementation of a rule regarding the number of grants-in-aid a school was allowed to support.

Although there were a number of considerations that ultimately led the group of larger Southern universities to form a more compact, homogenous organization, it was mainly geographic concerns that prompted the shakeup of the Southern Conference. As a result, all 13 schools west of the Appalachians became charter members of the new Southeastern Conference.

Sportswriter O.B. Keller wrote in the 1933 Illustrated Football Annual the following statement regarding the eventual breakup of the Southern Conference and the forming of the Southeastern Conference: "Since the conclusion of the last football season there has been secession in Dixie. Rebellion, no less. One bright and sparkling day in December the old Southern Conference blew up with a detonation that shocked the natives as much as would the explosion of an under-nourished and water-logged firecracker...The old conference was too big and the geographical range too great for unity of thought and purpose. It stretched from the terrapin-infested shores of the Chesapeake and the bonded-bourbon depositories of Kentucky to the moss-hung oaks of Florida and Louisiana, and included 23 institutions of widely different scholastic and athletic standards. It was too unwieldy, everybody admitted."

The Southeastern Conference

"The Southeastern Conference is organized to form a more compact group of institutions with similar educational ideals and regulations in order that they, by joint action, increase their ability to render the services for which they were founded and for which they are maintained, by making athletics a part of the educational plan and by making them subservient to the great aims and objects of education and placing them under the same administrative control."

-Article II, Southeastern Conference Constitution, 1933

By the end of the roaring 1920's, several members of the Southern Conference had decided that a real change was necessary. However, the leadership of the 13 member institutions that chose to secede from the Southeastern Conference agreed that one thing needed to stay the same, and that was the ideal that athletics was part of the overall educational plan for colleges

and universities. The Southern Conference experimented with mild change during the early 1920's, but no positive results were ever realized from its actions. The leaders of the new conference felt that a more compact organization of institutions of "similar ideals" might make a difference in their operations and therefore bring about improvement in the fairness and consistency of the rules regulating athletic competition.

In February 1933, Dr. Frank L. McVey, President of the University of Kentucky and one of the South's leading educators, was elected first president of the Southeastern Conference.

The Southern Conference's 13 members west and south of the Appalachian Mountains all became charter members of the conference. These founding member institutions were Alabama, Alabama Polytechnic Institute (now Auburn University), University of Florida, Georgia Institute of Technology, University of Georgia, University of Kentucky, Louisiana State University, Mississippi State University, University of Mississippi, University of the South, University of Tennessee, Tulane University and Vanderbilt University.

The Sanity Code

Prior to the onset of World War II, the NCAA wanted badly to do something about the ongoing problem of universities recruiting athletes to specifically play football. However, the war rightfully captivated the attention and energy of the nation and funneled it to the most important goal of defeating the Axis Powers of Germany, Italy and Japan. As a result, the war considerably slowed the attempts of the NCAA to form a Sanity Code that would bring some semblance of order and fairness to the process in which universities garnered collegiate football players.

Subsequent to the war, the fact remained that any grant-in-aid for an athlete was still considered a violation of the amateur rule. In short, scholarships for athletes were illegal. In spite of this distinction, the practice of recruiting athletes to play football continued unabated, especially in the competitive Southeastern Conference. In 1935, prior to the start of World War II, the SEC began the practice of doling out athletic scholarships. Initially, each SEC institution was allowed to grant up to 125 athletes grant-in-aid scholarships for students who played football.

The NCAA took an immediate stand against this practice by the SEC, stating, "...the business of the colleges is education and not the entertainment of the multitude." The NCAA admitted that athletics contributed to the educational establishment, and that there was a need for athletics on college campuses. However, they also feared that the evolution of television and its revenue-generating capacity were going to make football a big business for colleges and universities. The Sanity Code made a futile last attempt at staying this imminent development.

In spite of the NCAA's objections, the SEC continued its rule of granting scholarships based on athletic ability, and that such grants did not make the recipients ineligible for competition. However, the early 1950's did witness the beginning of an attempt by the SEC to curtail the number of grant-in-aid a university could extend to football players. In 1953, 40 football grants were allowed by each school. In 1954, the number was increased to 55. In 1962, it was scaled back to 45 and in 1964 back to 40.

In 1953, following a confluence of conferences in the adoption of the practice of granting athletic scholarships, the NCAA finally capitulated. During that watershed year, the NCAA formally adopted the rule allowing the giving of athletic scholarships by universities. The following paragraph concerning financial aid was added to the NCAA's working papers:

"Any college athlete who receives financial assistance other than that administered by his institution shall not be eligible for intercollegiate competition. However, this principle shall have no application to assistance received from anyone whom the athlete is naturally or legally dependent."

The NCAA in 1953, by dropping the prohibition against aid to student athletes, went on official record in support of the idea that athletic participation had educational value comparable of any other course of study on a college campus. This measure marked the burgeoning movement of college football as a big business.

The arrival of television further solidified college football's financial prowess, and the SEC was no exception. College football on television in the South became immensely popular, since so many more fans were able to follow their respective state school teams. The advent of television brought the excitement and pageantry of college football into the comfort of every Southern home. College football, throughout its proud and storied history, had never been bigger.

Tulane University, Georgia Tech, and the University of the South eventually vacated the SEC, leaving the ten remaining founding member institutions. Tulane was a charter member of the SEC and left the league at the end of the 1965-66 academic year. The Green Wave football team competed as an independent from 1966 to 1996 when it joined Conference USA. In all sports besides football Tulane was a member of the Metro Conference from 1975 to 1995.

Georgia Tech, like Tulane, was one of the charter members of the Southeastern Conference in 1933, joining from its predecessor, the Southern Conference. Tech left the SEC after the 1963 season and became independent. Georgia Tech later joined the Metro Conference in 1975 for all sports but football for three years, 1975-1978. Tech would later leave the Metro to join the Atlantic Coast Conference in May of 1978.

Today, the Southeastern Conference comprises 14 schools representing 12 separate Southern states. Seven member institutions: Alabama, Arkansas, Auburn, LSU, Mississippi State, Ole Miss and Texas A&M, make up the Western Division. Another seven schools form the Eastern Division: Florida, Georgia, Kentucky, Missouri, South Carolina, Tennessee and Vanderbilt.

The conference got a facelift in 1990 (began playing in 1992) when Arkansas and South Carolina were added to the mix of schools. Further, a championship game pitting the two top teams from each division was implemented in 1992 in order to decide, on the playing field, a true conference champion for the first time during the league's history. In 2012, Texas A&M and Missouri were added, bringing the league's school total to an unprecedented 14 member institutions. Since these changes the new and improved SEC has outshined many of college football's preeminent conferences.

Introduction

The Southeastern Conference

A Tradition of Excellence

Legendary college football commentator Keith Jackson, in describing the SEC football experience, once aptly stated that "...there are few instances of alleged entertainment and relaxation that can match a college football game in stirring the deepest flames of partisanship and outright provincialism. And down South you can color that partisanship passionate!"

The irreplaceable "Voice of the Volunteers" on radio during the 1950's, George Mooney, once stated, "...No matter where I was broadcasting from, I found the fans in the South to be knowledgeable, fair – and yes, loud and frenzied. They are proud of their rich football heritage. And they are very proud of their schools, their teams – and the deep pride that goes with being from the South." Dan Jenkins simply summed up the popularity of the game of football in the South with the following statement, "To Southerners, football is as essential as air conditioning."

Long before the advent of the lucrative, media-driven, professional sports franchises, and television, there was simply college football. Prior to the onslaught of professional football in America after World War II, college football was the main outdoor spectator sport in the United States for nearly a century. Given this, it is no wonder then why the largest football playing venues in the country are college football stadiums.

In the days prior to television, hundreds of thousands of college football fans across the South listened to their favorite SEC football teams via radio. In those days, each school had its own announcer with a distinctive voice that all their fans could identify with. With the advent of television, college football has grown even larger in popularity. The competitive level of football played each fall in the SEC, and the millions of people who tune in each week to watch its marvelous display, are prime examples of this burgeoning American phenomenon.

The familiar ties of regional loyalty, along with the pomp and pageantry accompanying the game itself and all of its youthful trappings have made the SEC football experience like no other in the United States. The beautiful, often coquettish Southern belles dressed in their game day garb; the alma maters and the fight songs; the lively mascots; the rivalries; the reunion of lasting friendships; and the enjoyment of good Southern cuisine all make SEC football a special, cherished ritual in the South. Southern football is perhaps rivaled only by tailgating, and the beauty of it all is that the two pastimes go hand-in-hand in the tradition-rich Southeastern Conference.

Southeastern Conference football is the paragon of the college athletic experience. During its storied, 87-year existence, the SEC has evolved into the most impressive league of organized, intercollegiate gridiron competition in the history of the United States. No other American Football Bowl Subdivision (FBS) conference can boast of the many accolades and attendance records that the SEC currently holds. Further, the Southeastern Conference has produced more All-American football players than any other conference.

Each of the Southeastern Conference schools, at some point during their existence, has enjoyed success on either a conference or national level. Some of the schools have been so fortunate as to enjoy continued success at both levels. Alabama, Tennessee, Auburn, LSU, Ole Miss, Georgia, and Florida have all held at least once the lofty place atop the national polls at the end of the football season. In the modern era, the SEC has dominated this final poll.

In January 2013, the University of Alabama, under the leadership of Head Coach Nick Saban, hoisted their second-straight BCS National Championship (2012), their third in four years and the 14-team Southeastern Conference's unprecedented seventh-straight national football title! Alabama repeated

as National Champions in 2015 and 2017, continuing the SEC's amazing run in the post-modern era, to include an incredible nine championships in the last eleven years, with the only two reprieves coming to the Atlantic Coast Conference's Clemson in 2016 and 2018.

National Champions

2019 LSU (CFP)

2017 Alabama (CFP)

2015 Alabama (CFP)

2012 Alabama BCS

2011 Alabama BCS

2010 Auburn BCS

2009 Alabama BCS

2008 Florida BCS

2007 LSU BCS

2006 Florida BCS

2003 LSU BCS

This book is the story of the evolution of the organized game of football in the southeastern region of the United States from its earliest beginnings in the 19th century. Additionally, it is a tribute to the Southeastern Conference, in all of its past and present glory. Leading to the inevitable formation of the Southeastern Conference in 1933 and beyond, the text begins with a brief history of college football's inauspicious inception north of the Mason-Dixon Line. From there, the narrative chronicles the gridiron pastime's expansion to the Southern region, while paying tribute to the many cultural and human interests that propelled the college game during its formative years.

Close attention is paid to the manner in which the game evolved and changed tumultuously over time, and how the Southeastern Conference was conceived in an effort to bring order, fairness, and continuity to the game.

The unique histories and traditions of each of the member schools of the Southeastern Conference are included, along with other interesting, lesser-known campus and alumni-related facts, and trivia. The information contained within these pages should serve as a practical guide and reference source for the most avid Southeastern Conference football fan as well as a conversation piece and keepsake for the more sedentary enthusiast.

Road-tripping in the SEC is one of the true passions of the serious Southern football fan; and an annual reminder of the historical diversity and cultural strength of the nation's top football conference. It is for these latter fans this book is written.

This book is dedicated to all the Southern people who live for Saturdays in the fall, for those individuals who plan their business and personal engagements around their favorite team's football schedule; for those who always experience a rise in their body temperature when they enter the stadium; for those who shed a tear during the singing of their alma mater; and especially, for those who know all the words to their school's fight song. It is for the people who wake up early on Sunday morning after a win so they can read each and every one of the sports columns about the game they witnessed the day before. It is for all those who enjoy good company and good food in the parking lot before the game, as much, and if not more, than the food and company at a fancy restaurant. These things that we hold dear – all true SEC fans know and love, and look forward to each autumn. It's that time of year when the heated summer temperatures begin to fade and yield to colder days, when the leaves begin to change color, and when the youthful partisan spirit within us all crackles like the kindling of a well-planned winter fire.

The University of Alabama

At the University of Alabama no other tradition surpasses winning football games. The Crimson Tide of Alabama is historically the SEC's most successful football team. The thundering red elephants have attended more bowl games and have amassed more championships than any other Southeastern Conference school. The indomitable pride of Alabama's great football tradition was indelibly forged by the game's greatest Division 1-A coach, the legendary Paul "Bear" Bryant, a man whose noble legacy will outlive countless future generations of Alabama football fans. The Crimson Tide's modern-day success can be attributed to another great field general, Nick Saban, who has followed Bryant's innovative lead of bringing winning football to the beloved Capstone, earning his own treasured gridiron legacy and statue in tribute.

Nickname: Crimson Tide

In its earliest days, the Alabama football team was referred to as "The Varsity" or the "Crimson and White" after the school's colors. From this moniker, the players were nicknamed "The Thin Red Line" by sportswriters. "Thin Red Line" was used until 1906, when the term "Crimson Tide" was coined by Hugh Roberts, former Sports Editor of the Birmingham Age-Herald. Roberts first used "Crimson Tide" in his description of an Alabama-Auburn game played in Birmingham in 1907, (Auburn and Alabama began playing football in 1892 and met for the first time on Feb. 22, 1893, in Birmingham), the last football contest between the two schools until 1948 when the series was resumed. The game transpired upon a field of red mud; against a heavily-favored Auburn team; and in the end, the "Thin Red Line" of Alabama forced a 6-6 tie. From that day, "Crimson Tide" became the favored reference of Alabama fans. Former Birmingham sportswriter Zipp Newman popularized the oft-used moniker more than any journalist.

Founded: 1831

The state of Alabama was admitted to the Union in 1819. In 1827, Tuscaloosa, the state's capital at that time, was chosen as the birthplace of the University of Alabama. On April 18, 1831, the University enrolled 52 students. Initially, the campus consisted of only seven buildings; two faculty houses, two dormitories, the laboratory, the hotel (now Gorgas House), and the Rotunda.

By 1852, enrollment at the University of Alabama had more than doubled to 126. In 1860, Alabama became a military university, replete with military department and discipline systems established. In 1865, during the Civil War, Union Troops burned all but four of the University's fourteen buildings; the carnage included the President's Mansion, the Gorgas House, the Roundhouse, and the Observatory. The campus is noted for its many buildings constructed in the Greek revival style.

Location: Tuscaloosa, Alabama

The name "Tuscaloosa" is an Indian term meaning "black warrior." Antebellum mansions and Southern hospitality give the west Alabama city of Tuscaloosa the refined shine of a classic Southern community. Though Union Troops ravaged the city along the banks of the Black Warrior River, Tuscaloosa remained a Deep South antebellum antiquity. Another surviving landmark, the President's House, built in 1841, is a highlight of the University of Alabama campus. University life dominates Tuscaloosa's culture, especially during college football season, when Alabama fans young and old converge upon the Capstone and cheer on the Crimson Tide. Like most other Southern schools, Alabama began playing football in the early 1890's. The Athletic Department was officially formed in 1915.

Population: 100,000

Enrollment: 38,600

History:

Football came to the Capstone in 1892 via a youngster named Bill Little, who had attended Phillips Andover Academy in Massachusetts the year prior. Little's presentation of his football uniform, football, and cleated shoes served to warm his newfound Alabama colleagues to the game. In 1892, an Athletic Association and volunteers for a team were assembled and the University's first football team was formed. Subsequently, the "Thin Red Line" evolved into "The Crimson Tide." Money was collected to hire a coach and E.B. Beaumont was tapped for the job. Beaumont's tenure lasted four games of which Alabama won two.

First game:

Alabama's first football game was played against Birmingham High School on November 11, 1892, at Old Lakeview Park in Birmingham. Alabama won 56-0. The next day, November 12, 1892, Alabama lost to the Birmingham Athletic Club, 5-4. According to James B. Sellers, intercollegiate play started for the Tide on February 22, 1893, in Birmingham, when Alabama was thwarted by Auburn, 32-22.

Colors: Crimson and White

As early as 1892, Alabama uniforms were described as being white, with crimson stockings, accompanied by large crimson letters "U. of A." on their sweaters. Also, football players were known to wear crimson sweaters adorned with a white "A." There is no official historical reference linking Alabama to the colors crimson and white.

Mascot: Elephant

There are varying accounts as to why Alabama, a team with an aquatic moniker like "Crimson Tide" has an elephant for a mascot. However, two main theories prevail.

The least prominent is that in 1930, Rosenberger's Birmingham Trunk Company, whose trademark is a red elephant standing on a trunk to signify the luggage's durability, distributed red elephant good luck charms to the bowl-bound team members. When the large team emerged from the train in Pasadena with red elephant trinkets suspending from their luggage, media members made note, and a connection was born.

The more prominent explanation of how the Alabama Football Team became associated with the "elephant" relates also to 1930, when sportswriter Everett Strupper of the Atlanta Journal reported on a fan's exclamation, "Hold your horses, the elephants are coming!" as the eleven huge players rumbled on to the field. Strupper and other writers continued to refer to the Alabama linemen as "Red Elephants," the color of their crimson jerseys. That 1930 team, under the leadership of Coach Wallace Wade, posted a 10-0 overall record. The "Red Elephants" rolled over Washington State 24-0 in the Rose Bowl and were declared national champions.

Mascot Name:

"Big Al" is the name of Alabama's game day elephant mascot. His name was chosen in the late 1970's through a campus-wide contest.

Band Name: Million Dollar Band

The name was bestowed upon Alabama's band by W.C. "Camp" Pickens, an Alabama alumnus and football manager in 1896. Accounts of the story vary somewhat, but due to their fundraising prowess, the group was known as "The Million Dollar Band." Pickens, after a 33-7 loss to Georgia Tech, was asked by an Atlanta reporter, "You don't have much of a team, what do you have at Alabama?" Pickens replied, "A Million Dollar Band!"

Band Director:

Dr. Kenneth Ozzello (2003 – Present) has served the University since 1989.

Stadium: Bryant-Denny Stadium

Named for former Head Coach Paul "Bear" Bryant and former University President George Denny, Bryant-Denny Stadium is a first-class facility that compares with most professional venues. George Hutcheson Denny (1870-1955) served as President of the University of Alabama for nearly a quarter of a century. Denny Chimes and Bryant-Denny Stadium serve as a reminder of Denny's legacy at the University of Alabama.

Amidst homecoming festivities on October 4, 1929, Alabama's football stadium was presented by Governor Bibb Graves to University of Alabama President George Denny. Seating capacity at the time was an impressive 12,000. During the early years prior to the construction of Bryant-Denny, the Crimson Tide played on the quadrangle in Tuscaloosa until games were moved to University Field in 1915. In 1937, the first expansion of the stadium of 6,000 seats raised the capacity to 18,000. In 1950 additional expansions raised capacity to 25,000. In 1961, the grandstands climbed to 61 rows, raising capacity to 43,000 before being elevated to 60,000 in 1966. In. 1988, an upper deck was added to the west side of the stadium, raising capacity to 70,123.

The Alabama Legislature enacted a resolution to officially name the stadium Bryant-Denny Stadium at the annual A-Day game on April 10, 1976. In 1998, seating capacity at Bryant-Denny was increased when the East Stand upper deck was completed along with 81 luxury skyboxes, boosting capacity to 92,138. Paul Bryant compiled a staggering 72-2 record at Bryant-Denny. Every home Alabama football game since 1988 has been a sellout. Further additions (North Endzone 2006 & South Endzone 2010) including luxury skyboxes boosted seating capacity to 101,821, making Bryant-Denny the fourth-largest stadium in the Southeastern Conference and the seventh largest stadium in the United States.

First Game in Stadium: October 4, 1929 – Alabama 22, Ole Miss 7

First night game:

Alabama's season-opener against Spring Hill College in Mobile in 1940 was the Tide's first game under the lights.

Directions:

Coming from I-20/59, take either the McFarland Boulevard (U.S. Highway 82) exit and go North to University Boulevard or take I-359 into downtown Tuscaloosa. At 15th Street, I-359 becomes Lurleen B. Wallace Boulevard. At University Boulevard, turn right and travel east through downtown Tuscaloosa toward the center of the UA campus. The stadium is on your right.

Dining:

Buffalo Phil's— Right on "The Strip" (Tuscaloosa's main store-front road), "BPhil's" has excellent wings, cold drinks and an amazing buffalo chicken dip. 1149 University Boulevard, 205.758.3318. Opens at 11 a.m.

Rama Jama's at the Stadium – Charming old-style grill. Breakfast served here until 1:00 p.m. Monday-Friday and until 2:30 p.m. on Saturday. Juicy burgers, shakes and sandwiches. 1000 West Paul Bryant Drive, Tuscaloosa, 205.750.0901. Monday - Friday; 6:00 a.m. - 6:00 p.m.; Saturday; 7:00 a.m. - 3:00 p.m.

Glory Bound – Known for their fabulous gyros and pizza! A local favorite, GB offers many healthy alternatives. Brunch at 10 a.m. every weekend. 1301 University Boulevard, 205.349.0505. Opens at 11 a.m.

Night Life:

Gallette's/Campus Party Store – Conveniently located next to each other. Gallette's is one of the oldest and still one of the most popular of the Strip's bars. Decent dress accepted. 1021 University Boulevard, Tuscaloosa 1.205.758.2010. Opens at 6:00 p.m.

Innisfree Pub – An Irish Pub known for good food and much fun among the college crowd. 1925 University Boulevard. Opens at 11 a.m.

The Houndstooth – Sports Illustrated called this place one of America's best sports bars. Darts, Pool tables, many TV's, good food and cold libations. 1301 University Boulevard. 205.752.8444.

Accommodations:

Warner Lodge: Located 12 miles outside of town at Lake Tuscaloosa. Enjoy a true turn-of-the century style lodge experience with full amenities such as tennis, golf, swimming, and health options. Furthermore, the lodge is located next to the Westervelt Warner Museum of American Art, possessing an astounding collection. Rooms vary. 205.343.4215.

Nearest Hospital to Stadium:

DCH Health System

809 University Boulevard East

Tuscaloosa, AL 35404

205.759.7111

Bail Bondsman for Emergencies:

ASAP Bail Bonds

Tuscaloosa, AL

205.764.9541

Golf Courses:

Links at Tuscaloosa

1800 Links Boulevardmm Tuscaloosa, AL

(205) 247-9990

Ol' Colony Golf Complex

401 Old Colony Roadmm

Tuscaloosa, AL

(205) 562-3201 (Higher rated course)

Shopping:

Effie's Inc. – Ladies' clothing boutique nestled in the historic district of downtown. 404 Queen City Avenue, 205.345.1814.

Lucca – This women and ladies' retailer specializes in contemporary style. 2111 University Boulevard. 205.247.4910.

South – Unique Women's clothing. Suite 206. 1800 McFarland Blvd East. 205.469.9637.

Landmarks:

A must-see in Tuscaloosa is the Paul "Bear" Bryant Museum, located at 300 Bryant Drive on campus. It is a mecca of Southern college football centered on the SEC's most successful coach. The place is so revered by Alabama natives that suitors have been known to propose marriage to their girlfriends there. Open daily; 9:00 a.m. – 4:00 p.m. 1.205.348.4668. 1.866.772.BEAR (2327).

Denny Chimes - The slender 115-foot obelisk completed and dedicated in 1929, serves as the chief campus landmark. It is named in honor of George H. Denny, who served as President of Alabama from 1912-1936 and in 1941. The "Walk of Fame" at Denny Chimes has been an Alabama tradition since the spring of 1948. Etched into the base of Denny Chimes are the names of the men that have captained the Crimson Tide football team. It is located on the south side of the quadrangle adjacent to University Boulevard. Alabama is the only SEC school that honors its former gridiron captains in this way. Many consider the ceremony at Denny Chimes one of the most important Crimson Tide traditions. Denny Chimes is a classic example of Carillon Construction. The slender obelisk, or campanile, was completed and dedicated in 1929, and contains twenty-five bells. Denny Chimes is where since 1948, not only the namesakes—but also the hand and footprints of team captains—are etched into the tower's base—a unique gift for Crimson Tide posterity.

Coaches' Statues - In front of Bryant Denny Stadium are artistic tributes to two of college football's biggest coaching names: Paul Bryant and Nick Saban. National Championship years and teams are commemorated here on a tiny wall, along with their respective coaches.

Alabama Radio Broadcast Stations:

99.5 FM WZRR 690 AM JOX, 94.1 FM WZBQ, 105.5 FM WRTR

All-Time Record: 900-314-41 (.706)

Division Championships:

1992, 1993, 1994, 1996, 1999, 2009, 2012, 2014, 2015, 2016, 2018

SEC Championships:

27 1933, 1934 tied, 1937, 1945, 1953, 1961 tied, 1964, 1965, 1966 tied, 1971, 1972, 1973, 1974, 1975, 1977, 1978, 1979, 1981 tied, 1989 tied, 1992, 1999, 2009, 2012, 2014, 2015, 2016, 2018

National Championships:

15 (1925, 1926, 1930, 1934, 1941, 1961, 1964, 1965, 1973, 1978, 1979, 1992, 2009, 2011, 2012, 2015, 2017)

Undefeated Seasons:

Alabama has posted eleven unblemished records with the most victories coming in 2009 when they went 14-0 en route to their first modern BCS Championship.

Alabama Greats:

Coaches:

From 1892 to 1922, the University of Alabama went through a series of coaches...Eugene B. Beaumont, Eli Abbott, Otto Wagonhurst, Allen McCants, W.A. Martin, M. Griffin, M.S. Harvey, James Heyworth, W.B. Blount, Wallace Leavenworth, J.W.H. Pollard, Guy Bowman, D.V. Graves, Thomas Kelly, and Xen C. Scott.

Wallace Wade – (1923-1930) – (61-13-3) – (.790) - Alabama's football program settled down with the arrival of Wallace Wade, who coached the team to a 61-13-3 record through 1930. Under the direction of Coach Wallace Wade, for whom the road next to Bryant-Denny Stadium is named, Alabama became a national football power. He led the team to its first bowl game, the Rose Bowl in Pasadena, and to its National Championship in 1925 and to others in 1926 and 1930. After Alabama's defeat of Washington State 24-0 on January 1, 1931, Wade left the Capstone for Duke University. Wade was inducted into the National Football Foundation Hall of Fame in 1955. He died on October 6, 1986.

Frank Thomas – (1931-1946) – (115-24-7) – (.812) - A graduate of Notre Dame and a protégé of Irish legend Knute Rockne, Coach Frank Thomas' Crimson Tide teams secured Alabama's first Southeastern Conference title in 1933 and National Championships in 1934 and 1941. Six of his teams appeared in major bowl games, including three Rose Bowls. Four of Thomas' teams enjoyed undefeated seasons, including his 1934 and 1945 teams, which won Rose Bowl Championships. A young man named Paul "Bear" Bryant played end for Thomas from 1933 through 1935.

Harold Drew – (1947-1954) – (55-29-7) – (.600) - Under Harold D. "Red" Drew, Alabama was led to the 1953 SEC Championship. Between 1955 and 1957, the Crimson Tide faltered to 4-24-2 under the leadership of J.B. Whitworth. The glory days of Coach Bryant followed.

Paul "Bear" Bryant **–** (1958-1983) – (232-46-9) – (.810) - Undeniably the biggest cult icon to ever come out of the State of Alabama. The "Bear" was a simple man who knew the game of football like no other. Bryant died within months of retiring, at the age of 69. His lifetime record is 323-85-17 (.760). A native of Moro Bottom, Arkansas, born September 11, 1913, Bear had a 72-2 record in Tuscaloosa and an unblemished 25-0 record in Homecoming games. The Bear served as Alabama Athletic Director for a short time during his long career at the Capstone. As a player for Alabama, Bryant lost only three games. The "Bear" began his coaching career at Maryland in 1945. A year later he went to Kentucky where he coached for eight years. Kentucky had Adolph Rupp as basketball coach, so he moved on to Texas A&M for four years. In 1958, Bryant began his 25-year legacy at the University of Alabama. During that time Bryant won an amazing 232 games and six National Championships (1961, 1964, 1965, 1973, 1978, and 1979). To many older Alabama fans, there is only Bryant. His winning legacy remains. He died January 26, 1983.

Gene Stallings **–** (1990-1996) – (70-16-1) – (.800) – Born March 2, 1935, in Paris, Texas, after losing his first three games at Alabama, Coach Stallings won seventy games in seven seasons to average ten wins a year during his tenure as head man at the Capstone. A former player for Coach Bryant at Texas A&M, In 1958, Stallings joined Bear Bryant's first staff at the University of Alabama as a defensive assistant and was on the staff for Alabama's national championship seasons in 1961 and 1964. From 1965 to 1971 he was the head coach at his alma mater, Texas A&M, posting a 27-45-1 record and winning the 1967 Southwest Conference Championship. From 1972 to 1986 he coached defensive backs for the Dallas Cowboys and Coach Tom Landry, helping them win Super Bowl XII. In 1986 he became the head coach of the Phoenix Cardinals, posting a 23-34-1 record in almost four seasons. He landed the Alabama head coaching job in 1990. Stallings finished his seven-year career at Alabama with a 70-16-1 record and a unanimous 1992 undefeated, National Championship season. Stallings remarked, "The expectation level is high at the University of Alabama and it should be. What's wrong with people expecting excellence?"

Mike Shula **–** (2003-2006) – (26-23) – (.530) – Born June 3, 1965 in Baltimore, Maryland, he is the son of NFL Hall of Fame Coach Don Shula, and a former Crimson Tide quarterback (1984-1986). Shula's tenure can only be described as difficult. He took over the reins of the program from maligned Mike Price—the man who never coached a down at Alabama. The program was on NCAA probation. Shula had some big wins but in the end he could never beat Auburn, and that—and losing to Mississippi State—sealed his fate. His best year at Alabama was his third. That year, 2005, he went 10-2, landed the Tide on the cover of Sports Illustrated, and ended the season with a victory in the Cotton Bowl over Texas Tech. Today he is quarterbacks coach with the NFL's Denver Broncos.

Nick Saban – (2007-present) – (152-23) – (.868) - Nicholas Lou Saban was born on Halloween in 1951, in Fairmont, West Virginia and grew up southwest of Morgantown in Monongah. Saban is the modern-day standard bearer for winning football in Alabama and a defensive genius. He attended Kent State and played defensive back under Don James. Saban took the Alabama job prior to the 2007 season after leading the Miami Dolphins for two years (15-17) in 2005-2006 and previously coaching at LSU where he led the Tigers to a 2003 BCS National Championship. Before Baton Rouge Saban coached at numerous schools including Syracuse, West Virginia, Ohio State, Navy, Michigan State, Toledo, the Houston Oilers, and the Cleveland Browns. Before his first season Saban drew fanfare reminiscent of Bear Bryant when 92,138 Tide fans of the self-proclaimed "Saban Nation" jammed Bryant-Denny Stadium for the 2007 Spring Game. The previous attendance record was 51,117. The 92,138 mark is a national record for spring game attendance. The well-traveled Saban went 7-6 his first year at the Capstone, completing the slate with an Independence Bowl victory over Colorado. Since going 7-6 in 2007, his first year at Alabama, Nick Saban has rewritten the SEC record books in terms of championships won. An Independence Bowl victory that first season has been followed by six SEC Championships (2009, 2012, 2014, 2015, 2016, 2018) and five national championships (2009, 2011, 2012, 2015 & 2017). Saban is the only active coach to win national championships at two different schools (LSU 2003). His college coaching record is 243–65–1-(.788). In January 2013, a statue of a standing, clapping Nick Saban was erected on the commemorative plaza outside Bryant-Denny Stadium.

Players:

Johnny Mac Brown **–** (1923-1925) – A two-time All-Southern Conference player (the SEC wasn't formed until 1933), Brown is remembered for his role in Alabama's 20-19 win over Washington in the 1926 Rose Bowl. In that contest Brown was on the receiving end of what were at the time two long passes of 58 and 62 yards. The 58-yarder was thrown by Grant Gillis and the 62-yarder was lofted by Pooley Hubert. Brown's catches helped 'Bama to victory in that historic Southern college football conquest. Inducted into the College Football Hall of Fame in 1957, Brown is also a member of the All-Rose Bowl Team. The Dothan, Alabama native was known as the "Dothan Antelope" and he was the first of four brothers to play for the Tide. He died on November 15, 1974 in Beverly Hills, California.

Harry Gilmer – (1944-1947) **–** A native of Birmingham, Alabama, Gilmer is remembered as an early legend of Alabama football. Gilmer's talents at passing, running, tackling, returning kicks, and kicking forged a remarkable college football career at the Capstone. As an All-American and All-SEC player in 1945, Gilmer was voted MVP of the Rose Bowl after leading 'Bama to a 34-14 win over USC. His sixteen career interceptions rank second in Alabama history, while his 436 punt return yards earned during the 1946 season remain the best in Alabama history. In addition to interceptions and punt returns, in 1946 Gilmer also led the team in passing, rushing, and kickoff returns. Gilmer is a member of the College Football Hall of Fame. He died August 20, 2016.

Kenny Stabler **–** (1964-1967) – On Christmas Day, 1945, in Foley, Alabama, the man known by legions of Tide fans as "The Snake," Kenny Stabler, was born. Stabler is one of the most popular Tide stars to wear the Crimson and White. As colorful off the field as he was on, Stabler played on Alabama teams that compiled a 28-3-2 record. In 1966, he led Alabama to a perfect 11-0 season, including a 34-7 win over Nebraska in the Orange Bowl. In that victory over the Cornhuskers, Stabler completed twelve of seventeen passes for 218 yards and rushed for forty more while earning MVP honors. The SEC Player of the Year during his senior season, Stabler, along with Broadway Joe Namath, is a member of the Tide's All-Century Team. After college, Stabler was a first-round draft choice of the Houston Astros in the Major League Baseball draft, but turned it down to instead play football with the Oakland Raiders. Stabler was a second round draft choice, but he played like a first, notching four Pro Bowl appearances and the 1974 NFL MVP award. A member of the NFL All-Decade Team of the 1970's, he guided the Raiders to a Super Bowl victory in January, 1977. A former emcee and honorary Mullet Tosser of the Flora-Bama's Mullet Toss Weekend during the third weekend in April, Kenneth Michael Stabler passed away on July 8, 2015 in Gulfport, Mississippi. He was 69. Stabler once remarked, "There's nothing wrong with studying your plays by the light of the juke box."

Lee Roy Jordan **–** (1960-62) – Born April 27, 1941 in Excel, Alabama, Jordan is a former two-time All-American, and is considered the greatest inside linebacker in Crimson Tide history. Voted Alabama's Player of the Decade for the 1960's and to ESPN's All-time College Football Team in 1989, Jordan was enshrined into the NFL Hall of Fame in 1983. During his career at the Capstone, Jordan helped Alabama compile a 29-2-2 record. Jordan will perhaps best be remembered for his greatest single game – his unforgettable 1963 New Year's Day Orange Bowl performance against Oklahoma. In that 17-0 Alabama triumph, Jordan was credited with 31 tackles. Jordan was a first round draft choice (6th pick) in the 1963 NFL Draft by the Dallas Cowboys, where he stayed until he retired in 1976. With the Cowboys Jordan was a five-time All-Pro selection.

Joe Namath – (1962-1964) – The quarterback hailing from Beaver Falls, Pennsylvania is remembered as one of Alabama's brightest stars. Even though a knee injury limited playing time his senior year, Joe Namath was still instrumental in leading the Crimson Tide to a national title. The venerable #12 came off the bench in the 1965 Orange Bowl to complete eighteen passes for 255 yards and two touchdowns to earn Most Valuable Player honors in the Tide's 21-17 loss to Texas. An All-American and All-SEC choice at Alabama, Namath went on to an NFL Hall of Fame career with the New York Jets, highlighted by a Super Bowl III MVP performance in 1969. He tied with Ken Stabler, a later NFL MVP, for Alabama's Quarterback of the Decade for the 1960's. In 1985, Namath was inducted into the NFL Pro Football Hall of Fame. In three years as quarterback at the University of Alabama, Namath led the Crimson Tide to a 29-4 record, including three bowl appearances. He set Alabama records for pass attempts (428), completions (230), yards (3,055), and touchdowns (29). Despite the fact that Alabama lost the 1965 Orange Bowl to Texas, 21-17, Namath was voted the game's Most Valuable Player. While at Alabama Joe ran for 15 touchdowns and gained 628 yards on the ground for a combined total of 44 touchdowns and 3,652 yards.

John Hannah – (1970-72) – Hannah is considered by some to be the finest linemen to ever play the game. An All-American selection his senior year in 1972, Hannah was an All-SEC pick in 1971 and 1972. A member of Alabama's Team of the Century, he was selected to ESPN's All-time College Football Squad in 1989 and was also a member of Alabama's Team of the Decade in the 1970's. The recipient of the 1972 Jacobs Award, granted annually to the conference's best blocker, Hannah went on to a fabulous professional career where he was an All-Pro for several seasons. In 1991, he was named to the NFL Pro Football Hall of Fame. He is a member of the Alabama Sports Hall of Fame. Hannah is a native of Albertville, Alabama.

Johnny Musso – (1969-1971) – Born March 6, 1950 in Birmingham, Alabama, Musso is remembered by Tide fans as "The Italian Stallion." An All-American in 1970 and 1971, Musso was named the SEC Player of the Year in 1971, the same year he served as team captain. Remembered for his toughness, he is a member of Alabama's Team of the 20th Century, the All-Decade Team of the 1970's, and the Alabama Sports Hall of Fame. A former Academic All-American, Musso accounted for 2,741 rushing yards and 495 receiving yards and 38 touchdowns during his career. Musso is a member of the College Football Hall of Fame located in South Bend, Indiana. He was a third round draft choice in the 1972 NFL Draft and played professionally for the British Columbia Lions (CFL), the Birmingham Vulcans (WFL), and the Chicago Bears (NFL).

Sylvester Croom – (1971-1974) – An All-American and All-SEC selection in 1974, Croom, a native of Tuscaloosa, Alabama, was presented the Jacobs Trophy, given annually to the SEC's best blocker. A two year starter for the Tide, Croom played on Alabama squads that went a collective 32-4. Alabama won the SEC Championship all three of his playing years and won a National Championship in 1973. In 2003, Croom became the SEC's first black head football coach when he was hired by Mississippi State University to replace the retiring Jackie Sherrill. In 2007, he defeated his alma mater, 17-12.

Ozzie Newsome – (1974-1977) – Ozzie Newsome was voted Alabama's Player of the Decade for the 1970's, collecting 102 receptions for 2,070 yards and 16 touchdowns at Alabama. He averaged 20.3 yards-per-catch, still the SEC's best mark with a minimum of 100 catches. During his time at the Capstone, the Tide went 42-6, and won three SEC Championships. Newsome returned punts for Alabama averaging 7.5 yards on 40 returns. He went on to enjoy a 13-year NFL career after being selected as the Cleveland Brown's first round draft pick in 1978. He started 176 of 182 games for the Browns and was nicknamed the "Wizard of Oz" by his professional contemporaries. Newsome was named All-Pro in 1979 and 1984. In 1999, he was enshrined to the NFL Hall of Fame. He was born March 16, 1956, in Muscle Shoals, Alabama.

Dwight Stephenson **–** (1976-1979) – An All-American and All-SEC selection in 1979, Stephenson was voted the "Jacobs Trophy" winner, the award granted to the SEC's best blocker. Selected to Alabama's Team of the Decade for the 1970's, Stephenson, a Hampton, Virginia native, was also picked for the Quarter-Century All-SEC Team (1961-1985). Following his career at 'Bama, Stephenson played with the Miami Dolphins, where he was the 48th overall pick. In 1985 he was picked as the Walter Payton NFL Man of the Year award winner. He is a member of the 1980's NFL All-Decade Team.

Cornelius Bennett **–** (1983-1986) – A fantastic defender, Bennett is remembered as the first linebacker to win the Vince Lombardi Award. A three-time All-American from 1984-1985, Bennett was chosen as Alabama's Player of the Decade for the 1980's and a member of the All-Decade Team of the SEC for the 1980's. Indianapolis made him the second player picked in the 1987 NFL Draft after a senior year that included ten QB sacks, six forced fumbles, 21 tackles for loss, and two passes tipped, despite missing the first two games of season. He was a three-time All-SEC pick with 287 tackles, 16 sacks, 15 passes deflected, and three fumbles recovered. Bennett is a native of Birmingham, Alabama.

Derrick Thomas **–** (1985-1988) – A four-time All-SEC and All-American, Butkus Award winner, and NFL All-Pro linebacker, Thomas is remembered for his outstanding linebacker play while at Alabama. His quick feet and nose for the ball helped Thomas become Alabama's all-time game (5), season (27) and career (52) sack leader. During the 1988 season, Thomas led Alabama with 12 tackles for losses totaling minus 46 yards. He was one of the most feared defenders in the SEC and NFL during his playing years. A nine-time NFL Pro Bowl player, Thomas died less than a month after being paralyzed in a car crash on an icy road. Thomas was 33 at the time of his death in January 2000.

Jay Barker **–** (1991-1994) – The Trussville, Alabama native was a sophomore when he led the Crimson Tide to a National Championship in 1992. The winner of the Johnny Unitas Golden Award in 1994, Barker finished fifth in the Heisman Trophy balloting the same year. Barker completed his four-year career at the Capstone as the winningest quarterback in school history, posting a 34-2-1 record as a starter, completing 402 of 706 passes (.569) for 5,689 yards and 24 touchdowns. An All-American and All-SEC selection his senior year, Barker was the Birmingham News' SEC Offensive Player of the Year and was a finalist for the Davey O'Brien Award, given each year to the top quarterback in college football.

Shaun Alexander **–** (1996-1999) – The former 1999 SEC Player of the Year, Alexander notched three SEC and fifteen Alabama rushing records in addition to earning All-American honors his senior year. The Florence, Kentucky native who attended Boone County High School broke Bobby Humphrey's rushing record, becoming Alabama's all-time leading rusher with 3,565 yards (4.9 yards-per-carry) in four seasons. Alexander reached 1,000 yards faster than any other player in school history (after his seventh game) and he set 15 school records during his career, notching 15 100-yard games, 41 rushing touchdowns and 50 total touchdowns. During his senior year Alexander finished seventh in the Heisman Trophy balloting. In 2000, Alexander was drafted nineteenth overall in the first round of the NFL draft.

Julio Jones **–** (2008-2010) – Born February 3, 1989, as Quintorris Lopez Jones, "Julio," was rated as the top high school receiver in the country during his highly-publicized 2007 senior season at Foley High School in Foley, Alabama. At 6-4 220 pounds, Julio dominated the Lower Alabama high school ranks, as he had few physical equals. Possessing a 39-inch vertical jump and a 4.45 forty, Julio entered FBS (Football Bowl Subdivision) play at Alabama in 2008 as a true college freshman with a professional football repertoire. During his sophomore season with Alabama in 2009, he helped lead the Tide to an undefeated 14-0 season including a victory in the 2010 BCS National Championship Game. He was drafted by the Falcons with the sixth overall pick in the 2011 NFL Draft. Jones remains with the Falcons, where he is still regarded as one of the league's biggest receiving threats.

A.J. McCarron **–** (2010-2013) – A product of St. Paul's Episcopal School in Mobile, Alabama, McCarron was one of Alabama's greatest quarterbacks, leading the Tide to national championship victories over LSU in 2011 and Notre Dame in 2012, making him the first NCAA quarterback to win back-to-back titles since Matt Lienart of USC in 2003 and 2004. After a redshirt year, a year as a backup and three years as starter, McCarron in 53 games played was 686 for 1026 with 9,019 receiving yards and 77

touchdowns for 172 yards per game and a 66.8% completion rate. During his senior year he surpassed John Parker Wilson as Alabama's all-time leading passer, and finished second in the Heisman balloting. He was drafted in the fifth round of the 2014 NFL Draft as the 164th pick by the Cincinnati Bengals. In the pros, McCarron has done well as a backup. In 2018, he played briefly with Bills and the Raiders, until landing with the Houston Texans in 2019. He is married to former Miss Alabama and model, Katherine Webb, and they have two sons.

Derrick Henry **–** (2013 – 2015) – A four-year starter of Yulee High School in Yulee, Florida, as a running back Henry scored 153 touchdowns, and amassed a staggering record 12,124 rushing yards, eclipsing the previous state mark set by Ken Hall. At Alabama Henry showed signs early that he could carry the rushing load for the Tide, and in 2015 he brought home the heavy hardware starring in that magnanimous, leading role. After a 2014 season that saw him notch 990 yards on 172 carries, Henry in 2015, his junior year that proved to be his final for the Tide, rushed for 2,219 yards on 395 carries, scoring at least one touchdown in every game. During Alabama's 45–40 victory over Clemson in the 2016 College Football Playoff National Championship, he rushed for 158 yards on 36 carries with three touchdowns and became Alabama's all-time rushing leader, eclipsing Shaun Alexander's mark, in the process. The Heisman Trophy and Doak Walker Award recipient after that championship season, Henry was a second round pick (45th overall) by the Tennessee Titans in 2016. He was named the Alabama Player of the Decade 2010-2019.

Amari Cooper **–** (2012-2014) – The Miami native attended Northwestern High School where he was a favorite target of future-NFL quarterback Teddy Bridgewater. Cooper was recruited by Florida State, Miami, Ohio State and many others, but ultimately signed with the Tide. As a true freshman he played in 14 games and scored 11 touchdowns to go with 1,000 receiving yards on 59 receptions, proving to be one of the offense's most deadly deep threats, and a consensus All-SEC freshman performer. Over his last two years in Tuscaloosa Cooper caught 169 passes, with 124 coming during an All-American 2014 season that ended his collegiate career with 31 total touchdowns and the Biletnikoff Award, designating him the nation's top re-

ceiver. He was chosen the fourth overall pick by the Oakland Raiders in the 2015 NFL Draft and went to Dallas in 2018.

Quinnen Williams – (2016-2018) – Williams attended Wenonah High School in Birmingham, Alabama. He originally committed to Auburn but later signed with Alabama. Williams was one of the Tide's most dominating defensive linemen among a string of future pros recruited by Nick Saban, proving in many contests impossible to block. Williams played in 14 games as a redshirt freshman in 2017, logging 20 tackles and two sacks. Before the 2018 season, his third in Tuscaloosa, Williams, a redshirt sophomore, was named the Tide's starting nose guard. He went on to have one of the most acclaimed seasons for a defensive lineman in college football history. His 20 tackles for loss and eight sacks helped him claim the Outland Trophy given to the nation's best interior lineman. In January 2019, Williams, a consensus All-Conference and All-American, announced he would forego his final two years of eligibility and turn pro. He was drafted third overall in the 2019 NFL Draft by the New York Jets.

Great Bowl Games:

Alabama has appeared in 69 bowl games through the years. As of January 2020, their all-time bowl game record is 41-25-3 (.592).

2010, 2012, 2013 BCS National Championship Games: All winners for the Tide (Rose, Sugar and Orange)

2015 & 2017 National Champions: Played in the 2014 and 2018 Championship Games

1926 Rose Bowl:

It was January 1, 1926, when Alabama upset the University of Washington 20-19 in the Rose Bowl in Pasadena, California. At the time of the contest, Southern football, like most everything else in the South, was regarded as second rate. Most sportswriters laughed at the match-up between the powerful Huskies and the Tide. However, Alabama's Head Coach Wallace Wade was not daunted by the formidable task at hand. Wallace prepared his players in the locker room before the game by asking them to play for not just for themselves, or the state of Alabama, but for the South. He stated, "Southern football is not recognized or respected. Boys, here's your chance to change that forever."

"The greatest Southern football victory of all time was Alabama's Rose Bowl victory over Washington. It gained permanent esteem for Southern football."
– George Leonard

Auburn historian Wayne Flint explained the magnitude of Alabama's monumental win, "The Tide that went to Pasadena was not just Alabama's team, but the South's team," Flynt said. "They were reliving 100 years of sectionalism between the North and South. Fans were thinking 'this is just like Chancellorsville, just like Gettysburg.' Now we've got one more chance for Southerners to show them what we're made of. Alabama's victory was reported much as a victory at Gettysburg would have been. It was as if Southerners had proved something the South had been trying to prove since the Civil War, that we are as good as anybody else; and that given a level playing field, and the same number of players on the playing field, we can go out there and beat anybody, even the best the country has possibly produced."

Sports historian Andrew Doyle wrote in an article in The International Journal of the History of Sport, that Southerners "regarded the rest of the nation with a complex mixture of assertive pride and defensive hostility, and intersectional football gave full rein to both of these sentiments."

When Alabama defeated Washington, 20-19, in the 1926 Rose Bowl game, Doyle said its display of "masculine strength and virility...became proof that the martial prowess and chivalric grandeur of their mythologized ancestors (were) still alive in the modern world."

Additionally, in his interpretation of the event, Wayne Flint asked the compelling question, "Had Alabama lost badly in 1926, by forty points or more, would football have become the sort of important, defining experience that it became over the next five decades?" Flint answered his own question, "My answer is no, it would not have. Because the South would have just been proved yet again to be inferior in some other dimension in life, and what would have happened, I think, is the South would have found some other way to excel. It would have invested this kind of emotional energy and physical commitment to something else."

Fight Song:

"YEA ALABAMA"
Yea Alabama! Drown 'em Tide,
Every Bama man's behind you,
Hit your stride.
Go teach the bulldogs to behave
Send the yellow Jackets to a watery grave,
And if a man starts to weaken,
That's a shame
Cause Bama's pluck and grit have
Writ her name in Crimson Flame,

Fight on, fight on, fight on, men!
Remember the Rose Bowl we'll win then.
Go roll to victory, Hit your stride.
You're Dixie's football pride,
Crimson Tide

- Ethelred Lundy Sykes, 1926

Alma Mater:
Alabama, listen, Mother
To our vows of love,
To thyself and to each other
Faithful friends we'll prove.

Faithful, loyal, firm and true
Heart bound to heart will beat
Year by year, the ages through
Until in Heaven we meet.

College days are swiftly fleeting
Soon we'll leave thy halls
Ne'er to join another meeting
'Neath thy hallowed walls.

Faithful, loyal, firm and true
Heart bound to heart will beat
Year by Year, the ages through
Until in Heaven we meet.
So, farewell, dear Alma Mater,
May thy name, we pray,
Be rev'renced ever, pure and stainless
As it is today.

Faithful, loyal, firm and true
Heart bound to hear will beat
Year by year, the ages through
Until in Heaven we meet.
- Helen Vickers, 1908

Noteworthy Alabama Alumni:

Mel Allen, sports broadcaster, long tenured play-by-play announcer for the New York Yankees, (deceased)

Hugo Black, the Honorable, former Supreme Court Justice, (deceased)

Tom Cherones, director of "Seinfeld," semi-retired and teaches at the University of Alabama

Winston Groom, author of Forrest Gump and other books, currently lives in Point Clear, AL and Long Island, NY

Harper Lee, Pulitzer Prize winner for her 1960 novel, To Kill a Mockingbird, in 2007 awarded the Presidential Medal of Freedom by President George Bush (deceased)

Jim Nabors, actor (Gomer Pyle), Class of 1951, (deceased)

Howell Raines, former New York Times Executive Editor, author, currently a columnist with Conde Nast Portfolio

Sela Ward, Golden Globe and Emmy award-winning actress, former Alabama cheerleader and homecoming queen

Dr. E.O. Wilson, Harvard research professor and museum curator, National Medal of Science, Pulitzer Prize, recognized as one of the world's most talented entomologists

Kathryn Stockett, author, "The Help" 2009

Steve Shaw, head of SEC Football Officials, 2011-2019

Mark Childress, author, "Crazy in Alabama"

Joe Scarborough, host of "Morning Joe" on MSNBC, husband of Mika Brzezinski

Jimmy Wales, co-founder of Wikipedia

John M. McInnis, III, Owner, Flora-Bama Lounge & Package, Perdido Key, Florida

Claudia "Ladybird" Johnson, wife of President Lyndon B. Johnson, attended Alabama (deceased)

Bernie Madoff, Attended Alabama for one year, pledged Sigma Alpha Mu Fraternity

Timothy Leary, psychologist, writer and drug activist. Attended Alabama, was suspended for spending a night in the female dormitory (deceased)

2020 Alabama Football Schedule

Sept. 5 vs. USC (Dallas)

Sept. 12 Georgia State

Sept. 19 Georgia

Sept. 26 Kent State

Oct. 3 at Ole Miss

Oct. 10 at Arkansas

Oct. 17 Mississippi State

Oct. 24 at Tennessee

Oct. 31 OPEN DATE

Nov. 7 at LSU

Nov. 14 UT-Martin

Nov. 21 Texas A&M

Nov. 28 Auburn

University of Arkansas

Arkansas, the "Natural State," was once nicknamed the "Bear State" for a reason. The Ozarks are rife with hungry black bears! In light of this, it is no great mystery why the intrepid Davy Crockett became the area legend and folk hero that he remains today. People born and raised in "Hog Country" tend to stay close to home, and they enjoy passing along folklore about local animals, individuals, and events. Razorback football, much like the great outdoors, is a way of life in Arkansas, from the Ozarks to the Delta, and a common rallying point for Arkansans throughout the world. Within the last two decades, the "wild Razorback Hogs," with the help of the leadership of their departed favorite son, Frank Broyles, have emerged, since 1990, from the remnants of the Southwest Conference to become proud, seasoned members of the Southeastern Conference. In doing so, they have reentered national rankings and regained bowl invitations on their way to re-establishing one of the South's great football powers. Bringing with them an impressive Southwest Conference tradition, the Razorbacks have represented the league well during their formative years in the talent-laden SEC.

Founded: 1871

The University of Arkansas is the only comprehensive doctoral degree granting institution in the state. The Arkansas Legislature created the Arkansas Industrial Institution at Fayetteville under the conditions of the "Federal Land Grant Act of 1862." Students began attending classes in 1872. It is classified as a Carnegie II Research institution. The University of Arkansas in Fayetteville, although new to the Southeastern Conference, has enjoyed considerable success since entering the league in 1990.

Location: Fayetteville, Arkansas

The lush green hills of Fayetteville are home to a thriving college town. If Fayetteville's 3,110 acres of parks are not enough for the most enthusiastic nature-seeker, the northwest Arkansas city of 67,158 rests below the highest of the Ozark Mountains, and enjoys four distinct seasons. Initially settled in 1828, the city played host to both Union and Confederate soldiers during the Civil War. Today, the Arkansas academic hub is a recruiting ground for one of the South's most diverse economic engines—which includes retailing giant Wal-Mart, Tyson Chicken and Reynolds Aluminum, among other business and industry leaders.

Population: 209,889

Enrollment: 27,558

Nickname: Razorbacks

Arkansas athletic squads have not always been referred to as Razorbacks. During the university's earliest years, the Cardinal was its favored mascot. However, that changed in 1909, when Arkansas Football Coach Hugo Bezdek called his players "a wild band of Razorbacks hogs" after he led his team to a 16-0 thrashing of Louisiana State University on October 30, 1909. This newer, more ferocious, moniker gained favor quickly, and in 1910, the student body voted to officially change the school's mascot from the Cardinals to the Razorbacks.

Colors: Cardinal and White

The use of cardinal and white as official colors for the athletic squads at Arkansas can be traced to the earliest days of the athletic program when the school's mascot was the Cardinal bird. Cardinal Red was chosen as the official school color by student body vote in 1895. The two choices were cardinal and heliotrope (purple). Each color had its supporters, but cardinal triumphed in the end. White was added as a complementary color at a later date.

Mascot Name: The "Razorbacks"

Although students referred to the team as "the Razorbacks" as early as 1907, Coach Hugo Bezdek's line thereafter forever popularized the use of Razorback for the team mascot. The Razorback, known for its ridged back and tenacious wild fighting ability, had long been associated with the backwoods of Arkansas. The students loved the comparison, and the nickname stuck. In 1910, the student body voted to change the university mascot from the Cardinal to the Razorback.

The live mascot tradition at the University of Arkansas dates to the 1960's and many hogs have represented the school well through the years. "Tusk," a 380-pound Russian boar which resembles a wild razorback hog, is the current official live mascot. He is kept on a local farm and only leaves his home to attend all Arkansas home football games and other select events. The University of Arkansas also has a family of uniformed mascots. "Big Red," who is also known as the "Fighting Razorback," is the traditional mascot for the university. He attends all athletic events. "Sue E" is the female hog and "Pork Chop" is fittingly the kid mascot. Further, "Boss Hog" is a nine-foot inflatable mascot that joined the mascot family during the 1998-99 football season.

Band: The "Razorback Marching Band"

Renowned as "The Best in Sight and Sound" the Razorback Marching Band is one of the oldest college bands in the United States. Formed in 1874, as the "Cadet Corps Band" as part of the military art department, the band participated in all the formalities of the Military Art Department, and played for football games, pageants, and commencement exercises. In 1947, following steady post World War II growth, the Cadet Corp Band was divided into the three current bands, a football band, a concert band, and an R.O.T.C. band. In 1956, the band adopted the modern name "Marching Razorbacks." In 2006, the Razorback marching band was awarded the prestigious Sudler Trophy, the highest honor bestowed upon a collegiate marching band.

Band Director: Benjamin Larenzo

Stadium(s):

The Razorbacks have traditionally split their home games between Fayetteville, the site of the main University of Arkansas campus, and Little Rock, the capital and largest city of the "Natural State." Razorback Stadium in Fayetteville was built in 1938 and currently holds 76,000 fans. It is located next to the main university campus. War Memorial Stadium in Little Rock was built in 1948 and holds 54,120 people. It is located in the central part of Little Rock near the Fair Park Boulevard Exit from I-630.

The University of Arkansas trustees, citing financial reasons, voted in February of 2000 to move most of the school's home football games to its Fayetteville campus stadium. The Razorbacks still play in Little Rock, but the vote dimmed hopes for an expanded War Memorial Stadium. The board voted 9-1 to give Little Rock just two games each in eleven of the next 15 seasons. In 2018, it was agreed that the Hogs would play once at War Memorial every other year.

Beginning in 1932, Arkansas split its home games between its Fayetteville campus and Little Rock. Convenience was a key; until recently, there was no four-lane road into Fayetteville from the rest of the state. Since 1948, Little Rock and Fayetteville each have annually hosted at least three Razorback games, except there were only two at Little Rock in 1954 and at Fayetteville in 1985. University of Arkansas officials have stated that freshmen retention rates suffered when only three games were being played annually on the campus.

Stadium: Donald W. Reynolds Razorback Stadium

Stadium Capacity: 76,000

Built as a United States Work Progress Administration project with a capacity of 13,500, Razorback Stadium was dedicated on October 8, 1938, during a home contest against Baylor. Prior to the 1938 dedication of Razorback Stadium, the Hogs played in a stadium constructed in 1901, on land now occupied by the Mullins Library and the Fine Arts Center. The primitive structure

had room for 300 spectators along with a fence around the outside. The first of many expansion projects of Razorback Stadium began with the arrival of John Barnhill as Athletic Director in 1947. Barnhill was successful in realizing the construction of another 2,500 seats for the north end of each side of the stadium. In 1950, a new press box was built and 5,200 more seats were added on the west side.

A 5,200-seat east complement was erected in 1957. More additions were completed in1965 and 1969, increasing seating capacity to 42,678 prior to 1985. On September 27, 1969, Arkansas played its first game on Astroturf at Razorback Stadium. Arkansas took to the playing surface change kindly, defeating Tulsa 55-0. The field reverted to natural grass in 1995. On November 11, 1989, the first game with lights was played in Razorback Stadium. Arkansas defeated Baylor that first night by a score of 19-10.

Donald W. Reynolds Razorback Stadium underwent a major expansion and renovation completed prior to the 2001 season. The $110 million project, which included a $20 million gift from the Donald W. Reynolds Foundation, saw the capacity of the stadium increased from 51,000 to 72,000, but that may not be the most noticeable improvement. The concrete and steel below the stands has been completely enclosed with a brick and glass façade. The new look rivals that of many of the newer Major League Baseball stadiums. In addition to covering the steel and concrete, the concourses are wider, and concession areas and restrooms have been replaced.

The east concourse is "Championship Alley" with displays of conference championships, the 1964 National Championship, and every football letterman. The south end zone concourse is "All-American Alley' and is dedicated to Razorback All-Americans. The west concourse is "Bowl Alley" with tributes to each bowl team.

Other than the façade covering, the other most noticeable addition is the enclosure of the south end zone, which features chair-back seating and the addition of approximately 7,300 total seats with space for an additional upper deck that would push the capacity to 80,000.

Other major additions include an expanded press box and the addition of luxury suites. Sixty-eight suites were added, bringing the total to 132, and the stadium's capacity includes 8,950 club seats. Other additions include the 15,000 square foot "Bob and Marilyn Bogle Academic Center" and the 3,800 square foot Wilson Matthews "A" Club, both on the east side where an upper deck, which seats 6,500 was added along with enclosed premium club seating. During the 2000 season, a 30x107-foot SMARTVISION LED video screen, one of the largest video boards at any sports venue in the world, made its tantalizing debut in the north end zone. In 2007, the field at Razorback Stadium was named "Frank Broyles Field, and in 2012, the video screen was nearly doubled in size, to 38 feet x 167 feet.

In 2017, the Broyles Athletic Center was demolished as part of a $160 million renovation and stadium expansion, which added 4,800 seats and new premium seating to the north end zone, boosting stadium capacity from 76,000 (with use of the south end zone top bleachers) to over 80,000. On August 5th, 2019, Arkansas reverted to natural grass as the playing surface, replacing the turf installed under Coach Bobby Petrino in 2009.

Directions:

Coming from the U.S. 71 Bypass, take either the Cato Springs Road or the 6th Street exit. If traveling from U.S. 71 North from I-40, take Exit 43 and continue on 6th Street (Highway 62). Head north on Razorback Road from 6th Street into Fayetteville.

Tailgating:

Tailgating at Reynolds Razorback Stadium is always a treat; nestled in the verdant, rolling hills of the Ozarks, the bucolic setting is the perfect backdrop for a college football game. Hog enthusiasts encourage visiting fans to tailgate

near the Bud Walton Arena while they do their best to surround the enemy throughout the expansive campus.

Stadium: War Memorial Stadium

Stadium Capacity: 53,727

For over fifty years, War Memorial Stadium has served as the Razorbacks' venue for games in Little Rock. With a current capacity of 53,737, the stadium was christened in 1948, with a capacity of only 31,500. The stadium's original capacity was expanded from 31,500 to 53,727 and the original grass field replaced during the 1960's. The stadium went to an artificial surface along with a complete lighting system in 1969. Subsequent artificial turfs replaced older ones in 1974 and 1984. However, in 1994, War Memorial Stadium returned to a natural grass playing field.

Record Crowd:

55,912 on September 19, 1992 - Alabama 38, Arkansas 11

First game in stadium:

September 18, 1948 - Arkansas 40, Abilene Christian 6

Directions:

War Memorial Stadium is located in War Memorial Park, west of downtown Little Rock. Take Fair Park Boulevard and exit north off of I-630, looking for the Stadium Drive Exit.

Tailgating:

In recent years Arkansas fans have begun the practice of commandeering the War Memorial Golf Course as their exclusive tailgating area. When Hog fans converge on War Memorial the course fairways become virtual tent cities of cardinal and white.

Dining in Fayetteville:

Hog Haus Brewing Company – Wonderful two-story location, 11,000 square feet, at the corner of Dickson and West Street. The only operating brewery in Northwest Arkansas, the brewery is visible from both floors. Salads, burgers, pizza, pasta, fish and more. Also, the Hog Haus is the only place in Northwest Arkansas to buy beer-to-go on Sundays. 430 West Dickson Street, Fayetteville, AR. 1.479.521.2739. Tuesday – Saturday: 11:00 a.m. – 11:00 p.m.; Sunday: 11:00 a.m. – 10:00 p.m.

Penguin Ed's Bar-B-Q – The Razorbacks' tradition for barbecue! Family owned and operated for over 15 years. Slow, hickory-mesquite-cooked meats: pulled pork, brisket, ham and polish sausage make this place the best for mouthwatering B-B-Q in Northwest Arkansas. Claims to have one of the largest penguin collections in America! Three locations: 2773 East Mission Boulevard, Fayetteville. 1.479.587.8646. 230 South East Avenue, Fayetteville. 1.479.521.3663. 6347 West Wedington Drive, Fayetteville. 1.479.251.7429.

Nightlife:

Infusion - 416 West Dixon Street. DJ/Karaoke/Good times. Opens at 7 p.m.

Piano Bar - 230 West Dixon Street. Live, Dueling Pianos. Opens at 7 p.m.

Accommodations:

Inn at Carnall Hall – This former dormitory building for women built in 1906, is now a 50-room boutique hotel that houses a first-class restaurant, Ella's. Located on the southwest corner of Maple Street and Arkansas Avenue, this modern inn offers stately rooms with king size beds and Jacuzzi tubs. High-speed Internet access and room service are available. 465 Arkansas Avenue, Fayetteville. 1.479.582.0400.

Nearest Hospital to Stadium:

Washington Regional Medical Center

3215 North Hills Boulevard

Fayetteville, AR 72703

479.463.1000

Bail Bondsman for emergencies:

Mountain Man Bail Bonding

479.273.3506

Golf Courses:

Razorback Park Golf Course

2514 West Lori Drive

Fayetteville, AR 72704

479.443.5862

Stonebridge Meadows Golf Club

3495 E Goff Farm Road

Fayetteville, AR 72701

479.571.3673

Shopping:

Dickson Street downtown has a great collection of specialty, antique, jewelry and eclectic retail shops. Enjoy the manicured flowers at the Downtown Square.

Records:

All-Time Record: 684-472-40 (.571)

Southwest Conference All-Time Record: 226-194-15

Bowl Appearances: 39

Bowl Record: 13-23-3 (.333)

SEC Championships: None

Radio:

103.7 FM

920 AM KABZ

102.9 FM KARN

Arkansas Greats:

Coaches:

Hugo Bezdek - (1908-1912) - (29-13-1) – (.670) - Bezdek was the first full-time paid football coach at the University of Arkansas. Bezdek led the Cardinals in 1909 to a breakthrough 7-0 season that included wins over collegiate powerhouses like LSU and Oklahoma. Arkansas scored 186 points in its seven game span that year while allowing only 18 points.

John Barnhill - (1946-1950) – (22-17-3) – (.560) - Prior to taking the job at Arkansas, Barnhill coached for General Bob Neyland at Tennessee. While Neyland served in World War II, Barnhill coached his team in Knoxville. Barnhill's tenure in Fayetteville marked the resurgence of a proud winning tradition at Arkansas, as before his hiring, Arkansas endured nine straight losing seasons. Barnhill was loved by Razorback fans for recruiting Smackover's Clyde Scott, an eventual silver medalist in the 1948 Olympic Games. He died October 21, 1973.

Frank Broyles - (1958-1976) – (144-58-5) – (.708) - Broyles arrived at Arkansas after serving one year as head coach at Missouri. Broyles' stern leadership energized the Hogs and helped them win a national championship in 1964. A principal figure in Arkansas athletic history, Broyles led the Razorbacks on the gridiron for 19 seasons. During that time he coached Arkansas

greats like halfback Jim Mooty and receiver Lance Alworth. He served as Athletic Director, a position he held at Arkansas long after coaching, until the end of 2007, upon his retirement. Broyles brought Arkansas into the modern age, the Southeastern Conference and the international spotlight for its world-class facilities. Broyles once remarked after being asked if he would like football coach Ken Hatfield as much if Arkansas lost half its games. He replied, "Sure I would. I'd miss him, too." He died August 14, 2017.

Lou Holtz **-** (1977-1983) – (60-21-2) - (.720) – Holtz is one of college football's greatest coaches. Known for his elite motivational tactics, Holtz played linebacker at Kent State in 1956 and 1957. In 1960 he was an assistant at Iowa, beginning a long and prosperous career. He coached at William & Mary, Connecticut, South Carolina and Ohio State before taking the head coaching job at William & Mary in 1969. In 1972 he took the North Carolina State job before bolting to the NFL for a 3-10 year with the New York Jets in 1976. In 1977, he took the Arkansas job. That year the Razorbacks were ranked no higher than fifth in the Southwest Conference in any preseason poll, but none of the sportswriters had factored in the ability of Lou Holtz. During that first year as the head coach of the Razorbacks, Holtz shocked the college football world with a brilliant campaign that culminated in the Orange Bowl in Miami in 1978. During that magical season the Hogs finished 11-1, defeating Oklahoma in the postseason by the score of 31-6; and finishing third in the polls. Adding greatly to the Holtz mystique was the fact that prior to the Orange Bowl, Holtz suspended the Hogs' top two ball carriers and a leading receiver for

disciplinary reasons. In spite of the tough decision by their coach, the Hogs rolled over the heavily-favored Sooners. As a result, Holtz became a national hero overnight for his strong moral conviction and his unflappable coaching style. Holtz left Fayetteville in 1984 and went on to coach at Minnesota and Notre Dame, where he won a national championship in 1988, and at South Carolina, in 1999, where he helped rebuild a once-proud program. The Follansbee, West Virginia native was born February 6, 1937 and raised in East Liverpool, Ohio. He is a sought after motivational speaker and magician. On May 1, 2008, he was inducted into the College Football Hall of Fame.

Ken Hatfield - (1984-89) - (55-17-1) – (.750) - Hatfield was the head coach at the Air Force Academy when he returned to his alma mater to bring much-needed life back to the program. He did this by winning four games in the fourth quarter, and by winning seven during his inaugural, pivotal, 1984 campaign. In 1985, Hatfield directed the Hogs to an improved 10-2 record, edging Arizona State in the Holiday Bowl post-season. In 1986, Hatfield led the Hogs to their first victory over the Texas Longhorns in Austin in over 20 years, in addition to a 14-10 victory over Texas A&M, which led to an Orange Bowl invitation. During Hatfield's last season, he led the Razorbacks to the Cotton Bowl with a stingy defense typified by the determined play of standouts Wayne Martin and Steve Atwater. Hatfield also coach at Clemson and Rice University, compiling a career college coaching record of 168–140–4.

Houston Nutt – (1998-2007) - (75-48) – (.640) - A Little Rock, Arkansas native, Nutt was recruited by Arkansas and Alabama as a quarterback. After playing two years at Arkansas under Frank Broyles and his successor, Lou Holtz, Nutt transferred to Oklahoma State where he played and graduated. Like his former coach, Nutt took over as head football coach for the Hogs in 1998, and elevated the Arkansas football program to unprecedented heights. Prior to coaching at Arkansas, Nutt was a head coach at Murray State and Boise State. Under his tutelage the Hogs went to two Southeastern Conference Championship games in 2002 and 2006. Houston Nutt left the Arkansas program in turmoil before the end of the 2007 season, days after he defeated the eventual SEC and National Champion, LSU Tigers in Death Valley in Baton Rouge. Nutt took the head coaching job at the University of Mississippi, where he coached four seasons, posting a 24-26 overall record, going 10-22 in league play. Today he is a CBS college football analyst.

Bobby Petrino – (2008 – 2011) - (34-17) – (.666) – Petrino is known as a talented yet troubled coach, having seen success and failure at both the college and pro levels. He coached quarterbacks for the Jacksonville Jaguars in the NFL in 2000 and was their offensive coordinator in 2001. In 2002, he was Auburn's offensive coordinator before taking the Louisville head coaching job, a position he held until coaching for the Falcons for a season, in 2007. He landed at Arkansas in 2008. After four successful years in Fayetteville—his last two seasons were 10-3 and 11-2, respectively, Coach Petrino was dismissed by the University of Arkansas in the spring of 2012 for not disclosing an "inappropriate relationship with a female employee," tarnishing an otherwise solid coaching effort, and sending the Arkansas Football Program into an incontrovertible tailspin. His overall record at Arkansas was a 34-17, 17-15 in SEC play. He was head coach at Western Kentucky in 2013, and coached a second stint at Louisville from 2014 to 2018, a post he held from 2003 to 2006. Petrino's overall college coaching record is 119-56. In 2007, he was 3-10 during a failed, abbreviated NFL season as the Atlanta Falcons head coach. Following his abrupt, unexpected departure in 2011, Arkansas Football went a combined 37-62 from 2012-2019, under the leadership of John L. Smith (2012), Brett Bielema (2013-2017) and Chad Morris (2018-2019).

***Sam Pittman* –** (2020 – present) – (0-0) – A native of El Reno, Oklahoma and graduate of Pittsburg State University where he earned an education degree, Sam Pittman was a well-traveled offensive line coach before he worked as the associate head coach and offensive line coach at the University of Georgia under head coach Kirby Smart. After playing football for Pittsburg State from 1980 to 1983 he served there as a graduate assistant. After a high school and junior college coaching career spanning eight years, in 1994, Pittman got his first major college gig coaching offensive line for Northern Illinois. He coached offensive line for seven Power Five schools, spanning more than 25 years: Cincinnati (1996), Oklahoma (1997-98), Western Michigan Assistant Head Coach (1999), Missouri (2000), Kansas (2001), Northern Illinois (again 2003-2006), North Carolina (2007-2010, 2011 Assistant Head Coach), Tennessee (2012), Arkansas (2013-15 Assistant Head Coach), Georgia (2019 Assistant Head Coach). Known as an excellent offensive line coach and recruiter, Pittman is undefeated as a head coach.

Players:

Lance Alworth **-** (1959-1961) - Alworth is considered one of the greatest athletes in Razorback history. The 1960-61 All-American from Brookhaven, Mississippi is both a College and Pro Football Hall of Fame member. A great all-around player for the Hogs, Alworth, nicknamed, "Bambi," for his slender build, grace and uncanny leaping ability, led the team in 1961 with 18 receptions for 320 yards and three touchdowns to go along with 110 rushes for 516 yards and five touchdowns for a 4.7 yard-per-carry average. During the 1961 season, against the University of Tulsa, Alworth returned seven kicks for 136 yards. On the season, Alworth had a total of 28 returns for 336 total yards. In his career at Arkansas, he totaled 690 yards on 51 returns. He was the 8th overall pick in the first round of the 1962 NFL Draft. He is a member of the Mississippi and Arkansas Athletic Halls of Fame.

Clyde Scott **-** (1946-48) - Nicknamed "Smackover" for his hometown namesake of Smackover, Arkansas, Scott rushed for 1,463 yards during his career, which was a school-best mark at the time. During the 1948 season, Scott rushed 95 times for 670 yards, for a 7.0 yard-per-carry average. Scott was the first Razorback to win a medal at the Olympic Games, winning a silver medal in the hurdles in 1948. Scott's jersey, #12, was retired following his graduation. He died January 30, 2018.

Joe Ferguson **-** (1969-1972) – An Alvin, Texas native, who played his high school ball in Shreveport, Louisiana at Woodlawn High School, Ferguson is perhaps the greatest quarterback in Arkansas history. He holds numerous individual Arkansas records, setting the Hogs' mark for the most plays in a single game – 56 against Texas A&M in 1971, 52 passes, five rushes, and one touchdown. He holds the record for the most pass attempts by a Razorback in a single game – 51, also against Texas A&M. On that great outing Ferguson posted 345 yards passing on thirty-one completions and one interception. That same year he was named Southwest Conference Player of the Year. During his Razorback career, Ferguson completed 327 of 611 passes for 4,431 yards. Ferguson was drafted in the third round of the 1973 NFL Draft by the Buffalo Bills. He played for other NFL teams, including Tampa and Indianapolis before retiring and coaching at Louisiana Tech University.

Steve Little **-** (1974-1977) - Little is considered the greatest kicker in school history. A two-time All-American, Little owns school marks for the most points scored by a kicker with 280. He still shares the NCAA record for the longest field goal with a 67-yarder against Texas in 1977, during his senior year. Little attempted more field goals that any kicker in school history, 89, and made 52, the schools' second highest total, seven of which were over fifty yards.

Brandon Burlsworth **-** (1994-1998) - An All-SEC offensive guard in 1997 and 1998, Burlsworth was named a first-team All-American selection by The Football News. After redshirting in 1994 after walking on to the Arkansas Razorback football teams, Burlsworth earned a scholarship for his outstanding work ethic in the weight room. After providing a backup role on the Hogs' offensive line during the 1995 SEC Western Division Championship campaign, Burlsworth nabbed a starting job during the spring of 1996 and never again relinquished the guard position he held for the remainder of his career. Burlsworth started thirty-four consecutive games for the Razorbacks, including the Florida Citrus Bowl on New Year's Day in 1999. Burlsworth's leadership helped the Razorbacks during the 1998-99 season score more points than any other since 1970 and produce more yards than any since 1989. In addition to his many athletic talents, Burlsworth was a good student, earning a bachelor's degree in marketing in 1997, and began his master's studies in business administration. In December 1998, Brandon Burlsworth became the only Razorback football player to earn a master's degree before he played in his final game. Tragically, two weeks after being drafted by the Indianapolis Colts organization in the 1999 NFL draft, Brandon Burlsworth's great young life was ended in an automobile accident.

Cedric Cobbs **-** (2000-2003) - A Little Rock, Arkansas native, Cobbs was one of the most recruited running backs in the country. A smooth rusher possessing size and speed, Cobbs is remembered by Hog fans as one of the University of Arkansas' brightest football stars. As a true freshman in 1999, Cobbs posted the then-best rushing performance ever by a Razorback freshman. That record has since been eclipsed by Darren McFadden. Nevertheless, Cobbs rushed for a team-leading 668 yards on just 116 carries, despite splitting time with senior Chrys Chukwuma. Cobbs caught eleven passes for sixty yards and returned twelve kickoffs for 328 yards. His all-purpose yardage total of 1,056 was the second highest over by a Hog freshman. A Doak-Walker Award candidate prior to his sophomore season, Cobbs separated his shoulder against Alabama in the third game and missed the remainder of the season. Cobbs returned in 2001 and continued to battle injuries over the next three seasons, but still led all Hog rushers, finishing with 3,018 yards in 46 games played. He

was drafted by the New England Patriots in the fourth round of the 2004 NFL Draft and was later traded to the Denver Broncos.

Matt Jones **-** (2001-2004) - Born April 22, 1983, in Dermott, Arkansas, Jones is remembered as one of the league's best all-around big athletes. At Northside High School he was the quarterback of the football team and a sprinter on the track team. At 6'6", 235 pounds, and a sub 4.5/40, Jones was a large moving target who was tough for opponents to catch, much less hit. He held the conference record for the most career rushing yards as a quarterback, rushing 382 times for 2,535 yards and twenty-four touchdowns. Possessing a huge stride and surprisingly nimble athleticism, Jones led the Arkansas team at quarterback and also played on the basketball team. A four-year letterman at quarterback, Jones finished his with 5,857 yards, 53 touchdowns and 30 interceptions. He gained 8,392 yards in total offense and was responsible for 77 touchdowns, shattering the previous Razorback all-time records set by Clint Stoerner. As a senior he completed 151 of 264 passes for a career-high 2,073 yards and 15 touchdowns and rushed 83 times for 622 yards and six scores. At the NFL combine Jones wowed everyone, running a 4.37/40-yard dash; a 39.5 inch vertical leap; and a ten foot nine inch broad jump. He was drafted as the 21st pick overall by the Jacksonville Jaguars in the First Round of the 2005 NFL Draft, where he played for four seasons from 2005 to 2008.

Shawn Andrews **-** (2001-2003) – A native of Camden, Arkansas, Andrews was a unanimous 2003 All-American selection at offensive tackle (Associated Press, Sports Illustrated, Walter Camp, ESPN, American Football Coaches, Football Writers Association, Sporting News), and one of the most dominant line forces in all of college football during his three years as a starter at Arkansas. Andrews wore a size 17 shoe and a size 54 jersey. He destroyed opponents at the point of attack with his superior size and strength. Andrews bypassed his senior season after a stellar 2003 campaign to enter into the 2004 NFL draft, where he was the 16th overall pick in the first round by the Philadelphia Eagles. He was a Pro Bowl Selection in 2006 and 2007.

Darren McFadden **-** (2005-2007) - Born August 27, 1987, in North Little Rock, Arkansas, Darren McFadden is remembered as Arkansas' greatest football player and one of the

SEC's most electrifying athletes. At Oak Grove High School in Little Rock, McFadden played a variety of positions from tailback to quarterback to even safety on defense. After his senior season he was named a Parade Magazine All-American and the Arkansas High School Player of the Year while also receiving the Landers Award given to the state's top football player. McFadden was one of the most gifted athletes to ever grace the SEC gridirons. His freakish abilities and extraterrestrial physique astounded players, coaches, and observers alike—Darren McFadden was a phenomenon personified—a great athletic gift to the Arkansas Razorbacks and the Southeastern Conference. In an abbreviated career, he set numerous Arkansas records. Among these are the most rushing yards in a single game (321 versus South Carolina), the most rushing yards in a single season, and the most career rushing yards (4,485 in thirty-seven games), which is second only to the great Herschel Walker in SEC standings. Furthermore, he's only the second Hog running back to rush for more than 1,000 yards in three consecutive seasons. A three-time All-SEC and two-time consensus All-American, McFadden was twice the runner-up for the Heisman Trophy balloting, in 2006 and 2007. McFadden was named the SEC Offensive MVP in 2006 and the Sporting News 2007 Player of the Year. He twice won the Doak Walker Award (2006 & 2007), with Ricky Williams of Texas and he being the only two players to ever double up on the accolade. On November 3, 2007, McFadden tied the SEC single-game rushing record (Frank Mordica, Vanderbilt, 1978 vs. Air Force) with 321 yards rushing in a win against South Carolina. McFadden was the fourth pick by the Oakland Raiders in the First Round of the 2008 NFL Draft.

Felix Jones - (2005-2007) - Born May 8, 1987, in Tulsa, Oklahoma, Felix Jones attended Booker T. Washington High School where his senior year he was a blue-chip running back, leading the Hornets to the state championship game. Jones signed with the Hogs where he became one of its brightest offensive stars, an elusive return man and the principal backup to two-time "Doak Walker Award" winner Darren McFadden. Jones used his ample playing opportunities to his full advantage, managing seven yards per-carry his first two years as a Hog running back while winning first-team All-SEC honors as a kick returner; where he excelled at making people miss and then outrunning them. In 2007, Jones improved as a running back, averaging 8.7 yards-per-carry with 1160 total yards and eleven touchdowns. In his 38-game, abridged Arkansas career, Felix Jones rushed for 2954 yards and 20 touchdowns for a whopping 7.6 yard-per-carry average, while logging 1744 kick return yards on 64 returns for an impressive 27.3 yard average. Jones was the 22nd pick by the Dallas Cowboys in the first round of the 2008 NFL Draft.

Hunter Henry **–** (2013-2015) – A native of Little Rock, Arkansas, and son of a four-year Arkansas Razorback starter, Mark Henry, Hunter attended Pulaski Academy where he was a standout all-around football player, a consensus Parade All-American and a highly-sought after college football recruit. Henry played multiple positions at Pulaski—offensive tackle, wide receiver and even defensive end, demonstrating uncanny athleticism and toughness, before signing with Arkansas in 2013. In three seasons he caught 116 balls for 1661 yards and nine touchdowns—four coming during a terrific freshman season. In 2015, as a junior, Henry made one of the biggest plays in Arkansas Football history. On 4th and 25 in overtime against Ole Miss, Henry caught a pass from quarterback Brandon Allen and before being taken down flipped the ball to running back Alex Collins—who picked it up and ran for a 31-yard gain for a first down, setting up a game winning score. That year Hunter received the John Mackey Award for best tight end in the nation, leading Arkansas to its first-ever back-to-back bowl game victories. A consensus All-American, the super-talented Henry was selected by the San Diego Chargers as the 35th overall pick in the early second round of the 2016 NFL Draft.

Alex Collins **–** (2013-2015) – A native of Fort Lauderdale, Florida, where he lettered in football, track, basketball and lacrosse at Plantation High School, Collins, the 2013 Broward County Male Athlete of the Year, signed with the Arkansas Razorbacks. Remembered as one of many great modern Arkansas running backs, Collins was an electric ball carrier with sprinter speed and an unrivaled shiftiness. He started from day one as a true freshman and in total played in 38 games with only 14 starts, totaling 3,703 yards and 36 touchdowns on 271 carries. Named the2013 SEC Freshman of the Year, he joined former Arkansas great Darren McFadden and Georgia great Herschel Walker by opening his super career with three straight 1,000-yard rushing seasons, reaching 500 yards rushing before his 90th carry in each of his three seasons. His 3,703 rushing yards and 17 100-yard games are second in Arkansas program history. Collins was only the 14th player in league history to rush for 3,500 yards or more. He was drafted 171st overall by the Seattle Seahawks in the fifth round of the 2016 NFL Draft.

Retired Jerseys:

Only two jerseys have been retired by the Arkansas football program. Interestingly, one of those jerseys was "un-retired" for four years, but neither of the two jerseys will ever be worn by a Razorback football player again. Following the fantastic career of Clyde Scott during the latter portion of the war-torn decade of the 1940's, the Arkansas' Athletic Department chose to retire his #12. Twenty-five years after the retiring of Scott's jersey, a young high school kicking phenom by the name of Steve Little was being heavily recruited by Arkansas. Little required Scott's #12 as his jersey number and the Hogs requested permission from Scott to allow Little to wear his coveted #12. Scott gave his consent and the rest is Arkansas Razorback lore. Little went on to become the greatest Arkansas kicker of all-time as a two-time All-American selection. Once Little's career at Arkansas was completed, #12 was again retired.

Sadly, in 1999, the Arkansas Athletic Department retired the jersey of former Razorback great Brandon Burlsworth. A former All-American and All-SEC standout (1997-1998) offensive guard for the Hogs, Burlsworth was an unbelievable success story. A former walk-on, Burlsworth built himself into a great college offensive lineman through hard work and determination. Drafted in the third round of the 1999 NFL draft by the Indianapolis Colts, Burlsworth was killed in a car crash two weeks later, stunning the entire Razorback community. Head Coach Houston Nutt recommended to Athletic Director Frank Broyles that Burlsworth's #77 be retired. Frank Broyles agreed forthwith, and Burlsworths' locker remains intact today as a tribute to his memory as a complete football player and student athlete.

Great Bowl Games:

Cotton Bowl: January 1, 1976; Arkansas 31, Georgia 10

Cotton Bowl: January 1, 1965; Arkansas 10, Nebraska 7

Orange Bowl: January 2, 1968; Arkansas 31, Oklahoma 6

Hall of Fame Bowl: December 27, 1980; Arkansas 34, Tulane 15

Holiday Bowl: December 22, 1985; Arkansas 18, Arizona State 17

Cotton Bowl: January 1, 2000; Arkansas 27, Texas 6

Independence Bowl: December 31, 2003; Arkansas 27, Missouri 14

Liberty Bowl: January 2, 2010; Arkanas 20, East Carolina 17

Cotton Bowl: January 6, 2012; Arkansas 29, Kansas State 16

History and First Game:

In 1894, students at Arkansas petitioned the Board of Trustees to designate 2.5 acres on campus as football and baseball grounds and to provide monies for its upkeep. The students were successful in acquiring the land for their stated purposed, but were unsuccessful in their fundraising attempts to garner money for upkeep of the grounds.

In 1893, an Athletic Association was formed at the University of Arkansas in order to "...foster and encourage the growing interest in which the student body is manifesting in the development of the physical man." The association comprised the Athletic Club, the Baseball Club, the Football Club, and the Tennis Club. The sole responsibility of the Football Club was to provide one exhibition game per fall season.

The first football team at Arkansas was formed in 1894 by John C. Futrall, manager and coach. For the following 19 years, Futrall was Chairman of the Athletic Committee or manager of the football team – and often both. In those days, the playing field was a simple dirt patch and the players were described as "thugs, pug-uglies, and roughnecks" by the local press. The first Arkansas squad abused nearby Fort Smith High School twice before stepping up to legitimate college competition in the form of the University of Texas. The Longhorns ripped the Razorbacks in Austin, 54-0 in their first intercollegiate contest. Over time, the schedule was expanded to include more contestants and the 1902 squad finished 6-3. However, until 1908, the Razorbacks' coach was an unpaid volunteer. The first full-time football coach at the University of Arkansas was Hugo Bezdek. Bezdek, you might recall, is responsible for giving the Razorbacks their name.

Traditions:

The Senior Walk:

The Senior Walk is the longest tradition at the University of Arkansas--not in years, but in miles. Started in 1905, the Senior Walk contains over 120,000 graduates' names which have been etched in the campus' sidewalks. Unique among American universities, Senior Walk now stretches over five miles.

Old Main:

One of the oldest buildings in the State of Arkansas, Old Main is considered "the symbol of higher education in Arkansas." Old Main houses the Fulbright College of Arts and Sciences, its honor program, and five academic departments. Old Main was constructed between 1873 and 1875 as part of a land grant for the State of Arkansas. Originally the structure was known as University Hall. It was designed by John Mills Van Osdel, a Chicago architect, while construction was carried out by the firm of William Mayes and Oliver. In 1873, the University of Arkansas purchased Van Osdel's plans for the University Hall at the University of Illinois at Urbana-Champaign, which was demolished in 1938, and erected an identical structure on its campus. The contract to build the Hall was signed by the superintendent of public instruction, Joseph Carter Corbin, who was the highest elected African American official in Arkansas during Reconstruction. Most of the building materials used in Old Main came from local areas, because the nearest river port was 60 miles away and the nearest railroad was 150 miles away. The red exterior bricks were fired from clay dug on campus in kilns west of Old Main. The brown sandstone used for the foundation and basement was also quarried from the near building site. The five-story structure contained 2.6 million bricks when constructed.

Razorback Walk:

Razorback Walk is a walk lined by Arkansas Razorback fans that funnels the players to the stadium from where they exit the team bus. The players leave the bus and walk through the crowd offering high-fives and shaking hands, while the crowd elicits partisan chants and cheers. The Razorback Walk is the brain-child of former head coach Houston Nutt, who started it in 1998. "We want all the fans to be there in numbers greeting us at the stadium and wearing their red," Nutt said of the now much-anticipated stroll. In 1999, the Arkansas fans turned out in droves that stretched from the Tyson Poultry Science building to the front doors of the Broyles Athletic Center and down the access road from the north end of the stadium. The newfound tradition has spread quickly at Arkansas, evidenced by the fact that the Razorback Walk is practiced by fans at away games as well.

A Proper Hog Call:

The familiar chant of "Woo Pig Sooie" is known universally as the Hog Call, and it is one of the more unique and exuberant among its league counter-

parts. However, there are versions of the Hog Call, along with different spellings. A properly executed hog call is composed of three "calls," slowly raising one's arms from the knees to above the head during the "Woo."

Traditionalists argue an eight second "Woo." The fingers should be wiggled and the "Woo" should build in volume and pitch as the arms rise. Upon completion of the "Woo" phase, both arms are brought straight down with fists clinched as if executing a chin-up while yelling, "PIG." The call is finished by thrusting the right arm into the air, fist clinched, all the while exclaiming with great pride, "Sooie!"

A full Hog Call – the kind one will always hear victorious Razorbacks execute after contests – requires two more Hog Calls, followed closely by the "Razor-Backs" yell, in cadence with the pumping motion of the right arm after the third "Sooie" in synch with the break between "Razor" and "Backs." In order, the full and proper Hog Call is:

Woooooooooooooooooooooooo. Pig Sooie!
Woooooooooooooooooooooooo. Pig. Sooie!
Woooooooooooooooooooooooo. Pig. Sooie! Razor Backs!

Fight Song:

Hit that line, Hit that line, Keep on going, Move that ball right down the field.
Give a cheer, Rah! Rah! Never fear, Rah Rah
Arkansas will never yield. On your toes Razorbacks to the finish.
Carry on with all your might.
For it's A-R-K-A-N-S-A-S for Arkansas, Fight, Fight, Fi-i-ight!

The Fight Song used today at the University of Arkansas was written in the late 1920's, and its author is unknown. It is played at every home Razorback football game. Head Football Coach Houston Nutt, during his tenure, established a related, new tradition for Arkansas Football. After victorious home games the Arkansas players and coaches sing the fight song to the adoring student section.

Alma Mater:

Pure as the dawn on the brow of thy beauty,
Watches thy soul from the mountains of god,
Over the fates of thy children departed
Far from the land where their footsteps have trod.
Beacon of hope in the ways dreary lighted;
Pride of our hearts that are loyal and true;

From those who adore unto one who adores you,
Mother of Mothers we sign unto you.

In 1909, Brodie Payne, an alumnus of the University of Arkansas, submitted his original lyrics to an ongoing competition to find a university song and won first prize. Henry D. Tovey, director of the Glee Club at the time, set the song to music. In 1931, the University College Song Association in New York reviewed a collection of 500 college tunes, and the Arkansas Alma Mater was judged to be one of the 25 best college songs of the United States.

Noteworthy Arkansas Alumni:

Meredith Boswell, Hollywood set designer (Apollo 13, The Grinch)

Admiral Vernon E. Clark, former Chief of U.S. Naval operations

Jimmy Johnson, football coach, University of Miami, Dallas Cowboys, sports analyst

Jerry Jones, businessman, owner, Dallas Cowboys, member 1964 National Champs

Charlie Jones, NBC sportscaster

J. Walter Keller, developer of the human heart pacemaker

Robert Mauer, developed fiber optic technology

Thomas "Mack" McLarty, III, White House Chief of Staff for President Bill Clinton

Pat Summerall, NFL broadcaster

S. Robson Walton, chairman, Wal-Mart stores

Donna Sum Whitworth, former Miss Arkansas and Miss America

TJ Holmes, CNN anchor

Charles Portis, author of "True Grit"

Wiley Branton, former Dean, Harvard Law School

Joe T. Ford, founder, CEO, Alltel

Ed Wilson, President, FOX Broadcasting

Mark Pryor, United States Senator

Mike Beebe, Arkansas Governor

Rodney Slater, U.S. Secretary of Transportation

2020 Arkansas Football Schedule

Sept. 5 Kent State

Sept. 12 at Notre Dame

Sept. 19 at Mississippi State

Sept. 26 vs. Texas A&M (Arlington)

Oct. 3 Charleston Southern

Oct. 10 Alabama

Oct. 17 LSU

Oct. 24 OPEN DATE

Oct. 31 Tennessee

Nov. 7 at Auburn

Nov. 14 Ole Miss

Nov. 21 ULM

Nov. 28 at Missouri

Auburn University

Since its inception, Auburn University has been one of the SEC's most successful institutions–in both academics and athletics. Nestled in the northeast central part of the State of Alabama, deep in the heart of Dixie, Auburn is a leading Division 1-A research facility in the United States. Auburn graduates annually rank among the nation's best and brightest in science, engineering, and mathematics, and like its SEC brethren, Auburn has enjoyed its share of national championship success in football through the years. Called by poet Oliver Goldsmith "the Loveliest Village on the Plain," Auburn's sprawling, vibrantly landscaped campus makes it an attractive gem among the SEC schools. And whether you consider yourself a War Eagle, a Tiger, or a Plainsman...you're still an Auburn fan! Today, Auburn's rich football tradition is embodied by its current coaching namesake, Gus Malzahn, a crafty play caller who despite mixed results has thrice defeated his nemesis Nick Saban—which is more than any of his SEC and national coaching counterparts.

Founded: 1856

The university traces its beginning to the East Alabama Male College, a private liberal arts institution whose doors opened in 1859. From 1861 to 1866 the college was closed because of the Civil War. The college affiliated with the Methodist Church before the war. Due to financial straits, the church transferred legal control of the institution to the state in 1872, making it the first land-grant institution in the South to be established separate from the state university. It became the Agricultural and Mechanical College of Alabama. Women were admitted to Auburn for the first time in 1892, and in 1899, the name of the institution changed to the Alabama Polytechnic Institute. In 1960, the school acquired a more appropriate name, Auburn University, a title more in keeping with its location, size, and complexity.

Location: Auburn, Alabama

Judge John J. Harper, of Harris County, Georgia, founded the Town of Auburn in 1836, foreseeing the small village seated in the Piedmont as a potential

centerpiece for education, religion, and the arts. The land on which Auburn rests was opened to settlement in 1832, with the Treaty of Cussetta. The first settlers, led by Judge Harper, came in the winter of 1836, mainly from Harris County Georgia. Auburn was incorporated in February 1839, covering an area of two square miles. By that time, churches had been established, and a school was built and had come into operation. In the mid-1840's, separate schools for boys and girls were established in addition to the primary school. This amalgam of educational institutions led to a rapid influx of families from the planter class into Auburn in the 1840's and 1850's. By 1858, of the roughly 1,000 free residents of Auburn, some 500 were students.

Population: 63,973

Enrollment: 27,287

Nickname: Tigers

It is often misunderstood that Auburn has three nicknames: Tigers, War Eagles, and Plainsmen. However, Auburn has only one nickname, The Auburn Tigers. The nickname "Tigers" comes from a passage in Oliver Goldsmith's poem "The Deserted Village," published in 1770, "where crouching tigers wait their hapless prey…" The term "Plainsmen" comes from a line in the same Goldsmith poem, "Sweet Auburn, the loveliest village of the Plain…" Since Auburn's earliest athletes were men from the plains of Alabama, it was only natural for newspaper reporters to shorten the expression to "Plainsmen."

"War Eagle!" is Auburn's battle cry. The "War Eagle" cry rings out at sporting events, pep rallies, alumni meetings, or anywhere Auburn people gather. The legend of the Auburn War Eagle is interesting. The story goes that an Auburn student who fought in the Civil War was wounded at the "Battle of the Wilderness" in Virginia, which was regarded as a most gruesome clash. The Auburn student was wounded in the fighting and was left forlorn on the battlefield. After mustering the strength to awaken in spite of his injuries, the student discovered that only he and a baby eagle had survived the tumult. The young Confederate soldier made his way back to Auburn, with the baby eagle in tow. The soldier became a professor at the university and the eagle would also gain fame. The soldier and the eagle attended Auburn's first football game in Atlanta's Piedmont Park, and as legend has it, subsequent to Auburn's first touchdown the eagle broke from the clutches of its newfound master and soared high above the playing field. Auburn fans saw this and began to chant the now familiar battle cry "War Eagle!" The old bird died at the end of the game, in which Auburn won 10-0.

Colors: Burnt Orange and Navy Blue

Auburn's colors of burnt orange and navy blue were chosen by Dr. George Petrie, Auburn's first football coach, based on those of his alma mater, the University of Virginia.

Mascots: Golden Eagle and Aubie

Auburn University has two mascots. One is the golden eagle and the other is the costumed Tiger named "Aubie." Aubie, who has stalked the sidelines for Auburn since 1979, has nine times been named the #1 mascot in the country by the University Cheerleading Association, the most recent coming in 2016. Aubie originated as a cartoon character drawn by Birmingham Post-Herald artist Phil Neel for a football game program in 1959.

Auburn has enjoyed the company of seven golden eagles since the first perished in 1892. Students of Auburn's Veterinarian School donate their time to look after the popular bird while funds for its upkeep are generated by students and friends of the university. Auburn's current golden eagle is War Eagle VIII. The bird, which is nicknamed "Aurea," has been the official mascot since November, 2019. War Eagle VIII has talons that can squeeze with a grip of 450 pounds-per-square inch. To put that fact into its proper perspective, the average person has a grip of about 20 pounds-per-square inch.

Band: The Auburn University Marching Band

Auburn University's Marching Band (AUMB) was the 2004 recipient of the prestigious Sudler Intercollegiate Marching Band trophy. With 375 members, the band traces origins to 1897, when M. Thomas Fullan submitted to then-president Dr. William Broun that the drum corps accompanying cadet drills be replaced with a full instrumental band. The Auburn University Marching Band performs pre-game and half-time shows at all home football games and travels to most away games. A smaller pep band composed of AUMB members supports the Auburn Tigers at all away games the full band does not attend.

The band has marched in three inaugural parades including for Presidents Harry Truman (1949), George H. Bush (1989), and George W. Bush (2005). Unlike most college marching bands across the country, the Auburn University Marching Band does not have a nickname. It is the only band in the SEC that does not.

Director of Bands: Dr. Corey Spurlin

Stadium: Jordan-Hare Stadium

What is now Jordan-Hare Stadium was first opened and dedicated on November 30, 1939, at the Auburn-Florida game. That first stadium held 7,500 seats and consisted of what is now the bottom part of the lower west stands. Renamed "Cliff Hare Stadium" in 1949, 14,000 seats, the present lower-east stands, were added, raising the capacity to 21,500. Shug Jordan became the head coach in 1951, and the stadium underwent three major expansions in fifteen years. More than 40,000 seats, nearly half the stadium's current capacity, were added while Jordan was coach.

In an impressive demonstration of admiration and respect, Cliff Hare Stadium became Jordan-Hare Stadium in 1973, making it the first stadium in the country named for an active college coach—"Shug" Jordan. Clifford Leroy Hare, a member of Auburn's first football team, President of the old Southern Conference, and longtime chairman of Auburn's Faculty Athletic Conference, is also honored in the naming of the stadium. The later success of the Pat Dye-coached Auburn teams of the 1980's brought about the addition of the east side upper deck in 1980, as well as the luxury suites in 1987. These 1980's additions made it the largest stadium in the State of Alabama until the 2006 expansion of Alabama's Bryant-Denny to 92,158. A 2004 expansion extended the east upper deck by an additional section on each end, adding more luxury suites and additional seating, allowing for its current maximum capacity of 87,451. On November 19, 2005, the playing field at the stadium was named Pat Dye Field, honoring the school's former championship coach. Jordan-Hare has been referred to by The Sporting News as "College Football's Grand Canyon" and the "epitome of what the college football experience is all about."

Stadium capacity: 87,451

First Game in Stadium: November 30, 1939; Auburn 7, Florida 7

Directions:

The stadium is located on the campus of Auburn University. It is buffered on the west by Donahue Drive, on the north by Thach Avenue, and on the south by Roosevelt Drive.

From Montgomery: Take I-85 North towards Auburn. Travel approximately forty-nine miles, and take Exit 51 (Auburn). Turn left off the exit ramp on Highway 29 (College Street) and then turn left at the second light (Donahue), approximately 3.5 miles from I-85.

From Birmingham: Take U.S. Highway 280 East approximately 110 miles. Make a right onto Highway 147, and follow it five miles to Auburn. Turn on Donahue.

From Atlanta and Atlanta Hartsfield Airport: Take I-85 South towards Montgomery. Travel approximately 103 miles, and take Exit 51 (Auburn). At the end of the ramp, bear right onto College Street. Travel another 3.5 miles. Turn left at the second light (Donahue).

Dining:

Niffer's Place – An Auburn staple and community favorite since 1991. Fun, casual dining for the family with an extensive menu of great food at reasonable prices. Niffer's daily burger specials are the best in Auburn. 1151 Opelika Road, Auburn 1.334.821.3118. Open daily 11:00 a.m. until...full bar available.

Jim & Nick's BBQ – Laid back Barbecue joint known for slow-cooked meats, cheese biscuits, burgers, salads and classic sides. 1920 S. College Street, Auburn, 334.256.5197.

Night Life:

The Hound – Rustic-chic bar with a simple New American menu, an extensive bourbon selection & many craft beers. 124 Tichenor Avenue, Auburn. 334.246.3300. Opens at 11 a.m.

Sky Bar – Live music, karaoke, drink specials in a casual, collegiate atmosphere with a dance floor and roof deck. Close to stadium. 136 West Magnolia Avenue, Auburn. 334.821.4001. Opens at 8 p.m.

Accommodations:

The Hotel at Auburn University and Dixon Conference Center – This modern establishment located in the university's core has 243 beautifully adorned guest rooms and three presidential suites. The facility boasts a full caterer and their own gourmet restaurant—Ariccia, which gets its name from Au-

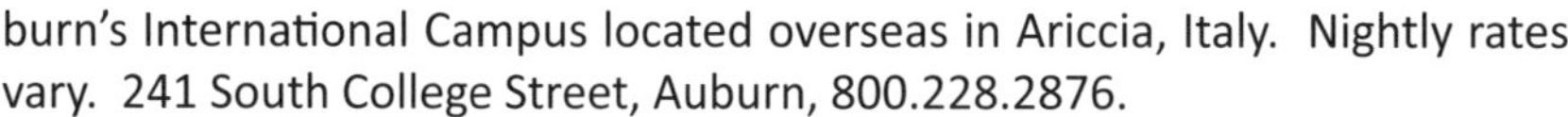

burn's International Campus located overseas in Ariccia, Italy. Nightly rates vary. 241 South College Street, Auburn, 800.228.2876.

Tiger Suites Condo Hotel – These are luxury condo hotel units; one and two bedroom units are available, furnished with fully equipped kitchens, located near the Auburn campus and within walking distance of the stadium. 430 West Glenn Avenue, Auburn Reservations – 1.334.466.5348. 1.877.462.8276.

Golf Courses:

Auburn University Club

1650 Yarbrough Farms Boulevard, Auburn, AL 36832

334.821.8381

Auburn Links at Mill Creek

826 Shell Toomer Parkway, Auburn, AL

(334) 887.5151

Shopping:

Ladies will love the eclectic, trendy Auburn shopping scene. Options include:

Therapy, 150 East Magnolia

The Private Gallery, 140 North College Street

Ellie, 113 North College

Records:

All-Time Record: 772-441-47 (.631)

Division Championships:

1997, 2000, 2004, 2010, 2013, 2017

SEC Championships:

7 (1957, 1983, 1987, 1988 (tie w/LSU) 1989 (tie w/Alabama & Tennessee), 2004, 2010, 2013,

National Championships: 1957, 2010

Bowl Record: 22-13-2 (.594)

Great Bowl Games:

1937 Bacardi Bowl: Sometimes referred to as the Rhumba Bowl or the Cigar Bowl, it was Auburn's first bowl trip and the only bowl game to ever be played outside of the United States. Auburn and Villanova fought to a 7-7 tie in Havana, Cuba on New Year's Day in 1937. Auburn's first All-American, Jimmy Hitchcock, scored the Tigers' only touchdown of the game on a 4-yard run.

1938 Orange Bowl: Auburn 6, Michigan State 0.

1954 Gator Bowl: Auburn 33, Baylor 13.

1984 Sugar Bowl: Auburn 9, Michigan 7.

1998 Peach Bowl: Auburn 21, Clemson 17.

2003 Capital One Bowl: Auburn 13, Penn State 9.

2005 Sugar Bowl: Auburn 16, Virginia Tech 13. Auburn completes a perfect season, 13-0, but somehow falls short of a national title, as the BCS is unkind.

2007 Cotton Bowl: Auburn 17, Nebraska 14.

2011 Fiesta Bowl BCS National Championship: Auburn 22, Oregon 19. Auburn completes a perfect season in Glendale, Arizona, claiming its second national championship.

2014 Rose Bowl BCS National Championship (2013): Auburn falls to Florida State 34-31 in a disappointing thriller

2018 Music City Bowl: Auburn 63, Purdue 14

Radio Commentators:

Jim Fyffe – (1981-2003) - A native of Paintsville, Kentucky, Fyffe was the Auburn Football Play-By-Play Announce for 22 seasons until his death on May 15, 2003. Fyffe was a fabulous announcer—one that was remembered well by Auburn fans for his titillating, trademark call, "Touchdown Auburn!" Fyffe also called Auburn Basketball games for 22 years, and was known to say, "hello" to an Auburn player's home town following a slam dunk. As good as a broadcaster Fyffe was, he was an even better human being, and he is still revered by legions of the Auburn faithful for his clarity of voice, his uniqueness and his undying love for Auburn University.

Rod Bramblett – (1965-2019) - A 1988 graduate of Auburn University, Bramblett was the lead announcer for Auburn baseball for 11 seasons before succeeding the late Jim Fyffe as lead announcer for Auburn football and men's basketball on June 23, 2003. Bramblett and his wife Paula were killed in a car accident in Auburn, Alabama, on May 25, 2019.

Andy Burcham – A part of Auburn radio broadcasts for over 30 years in various capacities, Burcham was named the lead announcer for Auburn football, men's basketball and baseball, in August 2019.

Auburn Tiger Radio Broadcast Station: Auburn, 97.7 FM WKKR

Auburn Greats:

Coaches:

John Heisman – (1895-1899) – (12-4-2) – (.666) - The legendary coach for which college football's top individual accolade is named. Auburn is the only school where John Heisman coached to also have a Heisman Trophy winner. Heisman left Auburn for Clemson and then Georgia Tech, where he lost ten of 15 meetings with Auburn. Heisman once instructed his players, "Gentlemen, it is better to have died as a small boy than to fumble this football," as well as "Don't cuss. Don't argue with the officials. And don't lose the game...When you find your opponent's weak spot, hammer it! And finally, when in doubt, punt!" He died October 3, 1936 in New York, New York.

Mike Donahue – (1904-1906, 1908-1922) – (99-35-5) – (.712) - "Iron" Mike Donahue, as he was known, won 99 games in two different stints as Auburn's head coach, tying him with Pat Dye for second on the all-time Auburn victories list. Donahue coached Auburn for a total of 18 years, and his 1913 SIAC Championship team not only went undefeated at 8-0, but they also did not allow a single point. He also coached at LSU and Spring College. He died December 11, 1960 in Baton Rouge, Louisiana.

Ralph "Shug" Jordan – (1951-1975) – (178-83-8) – (.666) - Auburn's all-time winningest coach; Jordan led Auburn to 19 winning seasons in 25 years, seven top ten rankings, 12 bowl victories and an SEC Championship. Four times he was named the SEC Coach of the Year. He was also named National Coach of the Year after leading Auburn to its National Championship in football in 1957. To most Auburn fans who knew him, Jordan is remembered as a true sportsman who handled both victory and defeat with uncommon grace. He died July 17, 1980 in Auburn, Alabama.

Patrick Fain Dye – (1981-1992) – (153– 62-5) - (.707) - Pat Dye, who coached at Auburn for 12 years from 1981-1992, won four SEC Championships. A Blythe, Georgia native, and former assistant under legendary Alabama Coach Paul "Bear" Bryant, Dye was an even 6-6 against Auburn's arch-nemesis, Alabama. He brought Auburn's "home" game with Alabama to the Auburn campus on December 2, 1989, which ended up a 30-20 victory for Auburn. Subsequent to Dye bringing the Iron Bowl to Jordan-Hare, Auburn won five straight home games against Alabama, until the 1999 season, when the Tide finally beat the Tigers on their home turf for the first time. A former Georgia player, Dye was voted into the College Football Hall of Fame in 2005.

Terry Bowden – (1993-1998) – (47-17-1) – (.720) - The son of Florida State legend, Bobby Bowden, the enigmatic Terry Bowden was both loved and hated during his Auburn coaching days. Bowden coached a total of six seasons on the Plains. However, Bowden only coached in six games for Auburn during his final year in 1998. Bowden resigned and was replaced by "Brother" Bill Oliver after notching an unacceptable 1-5 record to start the season. In 1993, the first-year head football coach led Auburn to its first undefeated, eleven-win season. Unfortunately for Bowden, that year Auburn was suffering through its first year of NCAA probation that prevented the Tigers from playing on television and in post-season bowl games. Nevertheless, the eleven wins in 1993 were the opening act of a record-setting 20-game winning streak for Auburn, a mark that still stands today. Bowden later served as the head football coach at the University of Akron, after a short stint at the University of North Alabama, and in 2019, he took an unpaid graduate assistantship at Clemson University, while pursuing a master's degree.

Tommy Tuberville – (1998-2008) – (85-40) – (.680) – Born September 18, 1954, in Camden, Arkansas, Tommy Tuberville revived Auburn's tradition-rich football program by making them a perennial competitor for the Southeastern Conference title. A former free safety at Southern Arkansas University in Magnolia, Arkansas, Tuberville was known as a daring competitor who occasionally used trick plays and various sleights of hand. Tuberville became Auburn's 25th head football coach in November, 1998. He led Auburn to three Western Division championships and one outright SEC Championship. Prior to coaching at Auburn, Tuberville coached at Arkansas State, Miami, Texas A&M and the University of Mississippi from 1995-1998, where he forged a reputation as a "riverboat gambler" for his irresistible penchant for going for it on fourth down. In 1997,

during his Ole Miss tenure, he was named the Associated Press SEC Coach of the Year. Tuberville was the recipient of the 2004 Walter Camp and Paul "Bear" Bryant Coach of the Year awards for Auburn's perfect 13-0 season. Known as a great recruiter of assistant coaches and a brilliant defensive strategist, he is the only coach in Auburn history to beat in-state rival Alabama six straight times. After Auburn, Tuberville coached at Texas Tech and Cincinnati. In 2019, he ran for the United States Senate in Alabama.

Gene Chizik **–** (2009-2012) – (33-19) – (.634) - The Tarpon Springs, Florida native is remembered for his undefeated 2010 national championship run led by Heisman Trophy recipient Cam Newton. Chizik played college football for Coach Charley Pell at Florida and was a graduate assistant at Clemson from 1988 to 1989, working with the outside linebackers. At Clemson he coached in the 1988 Citrus Bowl and the 1989 Gator Bowl, under secondary coach Bill Oliver. His first coaching job was as the defensive ends coach at Middle Tennessee State from 1990 to 1991. He served as the defensive coordinator and secondary coach for Central Florida from 1998 to 2001. Chizik landed at Auburn next, where he served as the defensive coordinator and secondary coach from 2002–04 under Coach Tommy Tuberville. His 2004 defensive unit led the country in scoring defense, giving up 11.3 points per game, and the total defense ranked 5th. He garnered the 2004 Broyles Award, which is given each year to the top assistant coach in the nation. In 2005, Chizik was hired by Texas to serve as their co-defensive coordinator, assistant head coach, and linebackers coach. At Texas, the team won the 2005 NCAA Division I-A national football championship by defeating USC in the 2006 Rose Bowl. After Texas, Chizik landed his first head coaching job at Iowa State, where he went a questionable 5-19 overall in two years. At Auburn, Chizik was a mixed bag. An undefeated national championship season sandwiched between two 8-5 seasons was complemented by a disappointing (3-9, 0-8) 2012 season. It proved to be his last on the Plains, where he finished with a 15-17 SEC record. His overall head coaching record is 38-38 (.500). After Auburn he served as the defensive coordinator at North Carolina. Today he is a college football analyst for the SEC Network.

Guz Malzahn - (2013 – present) – (62-31) (.666) – Malzahn served as Auburn's offensive coordinator from 2009 to 2011, and importantly, during its unforgettable, unblemished 2010 national championship run. For the accomplishment he received the distinguished Broyles Award recognizing the top assistant coach in college football. The red hot Malzahn

left Auburn in 2011 to become the head coach at Arkansas State University, taking over for departed head coach Hugh Freeze, who left for the University of Mississippi. Malzahn coached one season at Arkansas State, leading them to a 9-3 record and a Sun Belt Conference championship. Prior to his stints at Arkansas State and Auburn, Malzahn served as offensive coordinator at the University of Arkansas and the University of Tulsa, respectively. Malzahn is the author of the acclaimed book and instructional video titled "Hurry Up No Huddle – An Offensive Philosophy." Many college and pro coaches have adopted aspects of Malzahn's offensive strategies. He is recognized as the originator of the "Wildcat" formation, which became famous during his year with the Razorbacks, which is a variation of the forgotten single wing. In his first season as coach on the Plains, Malzahn took the Tigers to the National Championship Game, dropping a thriller to Florida State. Since 2013, despite a mixed bag of results, his three victories over Nick Saban (Iron Bowl) are a feat no other league coach can claim.

Players:

Jimmy Hitchcock – (1930-1932) – Born June 28, 1911, Hitchcock was known as the "Phantom of Union Springs." Hitchcock was Auburn's first All-American in 1932. He was an offensive triple threat as a passer, runner, and punter who led Auburn to the 1932 Southern Conference Championship. Against Tulane in 1932, Hitchcock returned an interception sixty yards for an Auburn touchdown and later returned an errant punt snap sixty-three yards for a second score. Duke Head Coach Wallace Wade said of him, "Hitchcock is the finest all-around back ever to play against any of my teams." Hitchcock also received All-American honors in baseball and played briefly in the Major Leagues after leaving the Plains of Auburn. Hitchcock, inducted into the National College Football Hall of Fame in 1954, passed away June 23, 1959.

Tucker Frederickson – (1962-1964) - A Hollywood, Florida native, Frederickson was a standout fullback and defensive back for Auburn. A consensus All-American, Frederickson was "Player of the Year in the South" in 1964, while finishing sixth in Heisman Trophy balloting. A two-time winner of the "Jacobs Trophy" for his blocking, Frederickson ended his stellar gridiron career at Auburn with back-to-back plus-100 yard rushing games against Georgia and Alabama. Frederickson was the first player chosen in the 1965 NFL draft, by the New York Giants (1965-1971) and is remembered as one of Auburn's greatest football players. He was elected to the College Football Hall of Fame in

1994. "Tucker Frederickson is about the finest football player I have seen," said the legendary Paul "Bear" Bryant.

Terry Beasley **–** (1969-1971) – Born February 5, 1950, in Montgomery, Alabama, Beasley was a receiver for Pat Sullivan from 1969 to 1971. Considered the greatest to play the position at Auburn, he was All-SEC and All-American during his career. Terry Beasley hooked up with Heisman-winning quarterback Pat Sullivan for over 2500 passing yards and nearly 30 touchdowns. Sullivan and Beasley still hold Auburn's all-time passing and receiving record. In his career, Beasley totaled 141 receptions and was selected as the 19th pick in the first round of the 1972 NFL Draft by the San Francisco 49ers. He was elected to the College Football Hall of Fame in 2002.

Pat Sullivan **–** (1969-1971) – Born January 18, 1950, in Birmingham, Alabama, Sullivan is remembered as the 1971 Heisman Trophy winner. He was also an All-American, All-SEC, and the SEC Player of the Year in 1970 and 1971. Sullivan threw for over 6,000 yards and 53 touchdowns during his career on the Plains. He ran for 18 touchdowns and led Auburn to a 26-7 record from 1969 to 1971, played in three bowl games, and beat Alabama twice. He is emembered by Auburn fans for his masterful 351-yard performance in the Gator Bowl over Ole Miss. He is considered Auburn's greatest quarterback, posting a 26-7 record under his direction. Sullivan was the first college player from the State of Alabama to win college football's highest individual honor. He played six seasons in the NFL for Atlanta and Washington. Sullivan passed away December 1, 2019.

Bo Jackson **–** (1982-1985) – Born November 30, 1962 in Bessemer, Alabama as Vincent Edward "Bo" Jackson, the 1985 Heisman Trophy winner is remembered as Auburn's greatest football player. Named a consensus All-American and All-SEC performer in 1983 and 1985, Jackson rushed for more than 4,300 yards with a 6.6 yard-per-carry average. During his career on the Plains, Jackson scored 43 touchdowns, and totaled 4,303 career rushing yards, averaging 113 yards-per-game. Jackson holds the Auburn single-season record for rushing yards with 1,786 in 1985, scoring 17 rushing touchdowns in the process. In the pros Jackson starred for the Los Angeles Raiders as their first pick in the 1986 NFL Draft, and also was

a rare two-sport professional, as he played baseball in the major leagues for the Kansas City Royals. He was named an All-Pro in both sports. Jackson is considered one of the greatest athletes to ever play American college football. In 1983 and 1985 he was named an All-American, and received the Sugar Bowl MVP and Liberty Bowl MVP awards. Number "34" became synonymous with "Bo Knows" in 1990, when the popular NIKE advertising campaign promoted a cross-training shoe bearing Jackson's name, further solidifying his already great athletic legend. Later that year he suffered a career-ending hip injury. Jackson remains one of the State of Alabama's biggest cultural icons. His 4.10 forty time at the 1986 NFL combine is still a record. In 2013, ESPN named Jackson "The Greatest Athlete of All-Time," over Jim Brown.

Kevin Greene – (1981-1984) – Born July 31, 1962 in Schenectady, New York, Greene is remembered as an over-achieving and tenacious linebacker/defensive end. After being cut once, Greene walked on at Auburn a second time, made the team, and lettered at defensive end during the 1983 and 1984 seasons. He totaled 69 career tackles as an outside linebacker and 11 sacks his senior year when he led the Southeastern Conference. Known for his patented, terrorizing "bull rush," Greene, a 5th round steal, went on to become an All-Pro in the NFL, playing for the Los Angeles Rams' organization, the Pittsburgh Steelers, the San Francisco 49ers and the Carolina Panthers. He was a five-time Pro Bowl player during his fifteen-year professional career and is third on the NFL all-time sacks list. In 1995, he hit future NFL Hall of Fame Quarterback Brett Favre so hard he spit blood. Greene received a Criminal Justice degree from Auburn and had two brief stints in World Championship Wrestling. Today he is a linebackers coach for the Green Bay Packers.

Tracy Rocker – (1985-1988) – Born April 9, 1966 in Atlanta, Georgia, Rocker made history at Auburn in 1988, when he was the first player from the SEC to win both the Outland Trophy and the Lombardi Award. Blessed with great size and speed for a down lineman, Rocker was a three-time All-SEC player and two-time All-American. Rocker is the premier defensive lineman in Auburn football history. From 1985-1988 Rocker logged 199 solo and 155 assisted tackles for 354 total tackles. Rocker led all SEC linemen in tackles as a freshman and his trench talents helped Auburn to a pair of SEC titles in 1988 and 1989. He was drafted in round three (pick 66) in the 1989 NFL Draft by the Washington Redskins. Today he is a defensive line coach for the South Carolina Gamecocks.

Frank Sanders – (1991-1994) – A native of Fort Lauderdale, Florida, Sanders was a standout tight end for the Tigers. After leading the SEC in receiving yards per game and breaking Auburn's single-season receptions record, the incomparable Sanders was named first-team All-American by the Associated

Press, the Football Writers Association, and Scripps Howard. He caught 58 passes for 910 yards and seven touchdowns during his senior year in 1994. Sanders finished his Auburn career second in total receptions with 121, receiving yardage with 1998, and receiving touchdowns with fifteen. He was a second-round draft pick by the Arizona Cardinals in 1995.

***Terry Daniel* –** (1991-1994) – A consensus All-SEC and All-American as a junior, Terry Daniel had the best year ever by an Auburn Tiger punter. He finished the 1993 season with an impressive 46.9 yards-per-punt average. During that season Daniel booted 16 punts over 50 yards, three over 60 yards, and a career-best of 71 yards. Daniel was more than just a distance punter. The Valley, Alabama native landed eleven punts dead inside the twenty-yard line, including a forty-nine yard effort against Alabama that was downed at the six and led to a safety. In October 1993, Mississippi State Coach Jackie Sherrill accused Daniel of filling the football he punted with helium...he was later cleared of any wrongdoing.

***Carnell Williams* –** (2001-2004) - Born April 21, 1982, in Gadsden, Alabama, Carnell "Cadillac" Williams was one of the smoothest running backs in SEC history, cruising to 3,831 rushing yards during his four-year career. A national recruit coming out of Etowah High School in Attalla, Alabama, Williams originally committed to Tennessee. He changed his mind at the last minute and signed with Auburn after an intense in-house visit with Coach Tommy Tuberville. Possessing uncanny speed and tremendous start and stop capability for a back his size, Williams was difficult to stop for opposing SEC defenses—especially since he was paired with Ronnie Brown—another eventual first-rounder he shared the backfield with throughout his career on the Plains. Brown's carries limited Williams', and had he not had to share time with another professional grade talent he may have caught Bo Jackson as Auburn's all-time leading rusher. Williams was drafted as the fifth pick overall in the 2005

NFL Draft by the Tampa Bay Buccaneers. He was subsequently named the "AP NFL Offensive Rookie of the Year" that same year, amassing 47 votes of the national panel of fifty sportswriters and journalists covering the NFL. He played pro ball for seven years before retiring. He is currently the Auburn running backs coach.

Cam Newton **–** (2010) – The Atlanta native is one of Auburn's greatest and notorious football players. He is the third player to be awarded the Heisman Trophy, win a national championship, and be the first overall pick in the NFL draft all in the same one-year span, joining Leon Hart (1950), and Angelo Bertelli (1944); he is the only one to earn NFL Rookie of the Year, as it did not exist until 2002. Originally a Florida Gator under Urban Meyer in 2007 and 2008, Newton encountered trouble and transferred to Blinn College in Texas, where his team won a national junior college football championship in 2009. In 2010, Newton was recruited by Gene Chizik and he transferred to Auburn. On the Plains he became the third player in major college football history to pass for 30 touchdowns and rush for 20 touchdowns in a single season. Newton led the Auburn Tigers to a 14–0 record and 2010 National Championship Title. He was the recipient of the 2010 Davey O'Brien National Quarterback Award, the Maxwell Award and the Walter Camp Player of the Year winner. The Associated Press and Sports Illustrated first team All-American was also named Offensive Player of the Year by the AP and Scout.com. He was the first overall pick by the Carolina Panthers in the 2011 NFL Draft. In his NFL debut, Newton became the first rookie quarterback in NFL history to throw for 400 yards in his regular-season opener, breaking Peyton Manning's long-held rookie record.

Greg Robinson (2011-2013) **–** The Raceland, Louisiana native was a standout football player on both sides of the ball and a prodigious track athlete at Thibodaux High School before signing with Auburn. Robinson was rock solid for the Tigers and his steady, dominating play was pivotal in helping them to an unforgettable SEC and National Championship run. After a redshirt year, Robinson assumed a starting role in eleven games at left tackle in 2012. In 2013, he started every game and was a leader of one of Auburn's greatest

championship teams—one that won on two amazing last-second plays—against Georgia and Alabama. That Auburn Tiger team finished 12-2 after winning the Iron Bowl on an unlikely failed field goal return for a touchdown. The Tigers won the SEC Championship against Mizzou but lost to Florida State in the national championship in the Rose Bowl in Pasdadena, California. Robinson was drafted by the St. Louis Rams second overall in the first round of the 2014 NFL Draft.

Kerryon Johnson - (2015-2018) – The Madison, Alabama native is remembered for play reminiscent of his unparalleled pigskin namesake. Named Mr. Football in Alabama in 2014, and later a member of the USA Today All-American team, Kerryon was an elusive runner with deceptive power and speed. During his first year on the Plains Johnson was a backup to Peyton Barber, a future NFL running back. In 2016, as a sophomore, he started six games before giving way to a surging bull, Kammryn Pettway. In 2017, Johnson became the Tigers' primary rusher, amassing three times the carries of any other back. He surpassed the century mark in ten of 12 regular season games for 1391 yards on 285 carries with 18 touchdowns. He had 233 yards from scrimmage against a #2-ranked Georgia team as well as rushing and receiving touchdowns in the season finale against Alabama. He ended his Auburn career with 2,494 rushing yards, fourth most in school history. He was drafted the 43rd overall pick in the second round by the Detroit Lions in the 2018 NFL Draft.

Daniel Carlson (2014-2017) – A graduate of the Classical Academy in Colorado Springs, Colorado, Carlson signed with Auburn and Head Coach Gus Malzahn as a highly-touted high school kicker. As a four-year starter for the Tigers he became the SEC's all-time leading scorer. At 6-5, Carlson is much taller than most kickers, but his height never hindered his stellar performance on the Plains, something Auburn fans could always count on. Carlson refused to miss an extra point. He made 198 of 198 PAT's and 92 field goals on 114 tries for 80.7%. His 474 points are the most in league history; and third among NCAA kickers in that lofty category. Carlson was drafted by the Minnesota Vikings 167th overall in the 5th round of the 2018 NFL Draft.

Retired Jerseys:

Bo Jackson's #34, Pat Sullivan's #7, and Terry Beasley's #88, are retired Auburn jersey numbers.

History:

1892 turned out to be an eventful year for Auburn University. It was the year Auburn played its first football game, as well as the year that women first attended the university. The first gridiron contest in Auburn history was the handiwork of Dr. George Petrie, a faculty member in the Agricultural and Mechanical College in 1892. Petrie organized and coached Auburn's first football team, and is responsible for scheduling Auburn's first football game, a 10-0 victory over the Georgia Bulldogs in February 1892. Professor Herty of Georgia and Professor Petrie of Auburn met each other during graduate school at Johns Hopkins University, so Herty wrote to Petrie with the idea of the game, and the rest is college football history. After the game was played, Auburn publicized the contest as "the first college game in the Deep South." Georgia asserted the same distinction for its contest with Mercer on January 30, 1892.

For years some of Auburn's primary rivals – Georgia, Tennessee, Georgia Tech, and Alabama – never made it to the Plains. Auburn's "home" games with these schools were played in Montgomery, Mobile, Columbus, Georgia, and Birmingham. All that changed in 1960. Prior to 1960, the Auburn-Georgia game was played in Columbus, Athens, Atlanta, Macon, or Savannah from 1892 through 1959. In 1960, the Bulldogs traveled to the Plains and lost, 9-6. From 1906 until 1970, Auburn and Georgia Tech played 53 consecutive times in Atlanta – before the Yellow Jackets finally gave in and came to Auburn, to lose 31-7. In a series that began in 1900, Tennessee finally played at Auburn in 1974, losing 21-0.

Traditions:

Auburn-Georgia - "The Deep South's Oldest Rivalry" – Auburn and Georgia began their series on February 20, 1892 (Auburn won 10-0) at Piedmont Park in Atlanta and has been played almost every year since. 1996's quadruple-overtime win by Georgia was the 100th meeting in the contentious series. The Tigers and the Bulldogs have played every year since 1898 with the exception of 1943, when Auburn did not field a team due to World War II.

***Auburn-Alabama* –** Referred to as the "Iron Bowl" because of the State of Alabama's heritage in the steel business, these two SEC Western Division teams enjoy one of the South's most intense rivalries. The game is such an event among Alabama circles, that family members taking opposite sides have been known to cease communication between one another during the week preceding the game. These two state teams first clashed in February 1893, at Lakeview Park in Birmingham, Alabama. Auburn won that initial meeting between the two schools and the rivalry was on. However, after the 1907 meeting between the two schools, the annual match-up was abolished due to a petty squabble over travel expenses and who would referee the game. This feud lasted for 41 years. In 1947, it took a resolution by the

Alabama House of Representatives to get the two teams to resume playing one another.

Tiger Walk – An Auburn tradition which began in the early 1960's when Auburn players walked from Sewell Hall to the football stadium and fans lined Donahue Drive to wish them luck. Over the years the Tiger Walk has grown into a major part of game day at Auburn. Tiger Walk is two hours before kickoff of every home game.

The Tiger Trail of Auburn – Representing a bond between the city and the university, this walk of fame comprises twenty-six granite plaques bearing the names of distinguished Auburn men and women recognized for their contributions to the institution's prestige.

Toomer's Corner - Situated on the corner of College Street and Magnolia Avenue, Toomer's Corner has long been the gathering place for Auburn athletic celebrations. This legendary locale is in the center of town, where the Auburn University campus meets the City of Auburn. Some of the best lemonade in the South is served within Toomer's Drug Store. Also, after any football win, and significant victories in other sports, Auburn students and citizens alike join forces and "roll" the boughs and limbs of the massive oak trees at Toomer's Corner with toilet paper. Some of the zanier celebrations can leave Toomer's Corner looking like a winter wonderland. Sadly, in 2013, University of Alabama fan Harvey Updyke Jr. was sentenced to spend six months in jail and five years on supervised probation after pleading guilty to the poisoning of the Toomer's Corner oaks, a crime he strangely revealed as a caller on the Paul Finebaum Radio Show in Birmingham, Alabama. His probation terms include being forbidden from the Auburn campus or any Auburn sporting event—which means no more Iron Bowls for Mr. Updyke. Auburn is currently replanting Toomer's Corner with new oak trees. As of August, 2019, Mr. Updyke owed Auburn University over $800,000 in compensatory damages, and had paid $6,646.50.

Fight Song:

"War Eagle!"

"War Eagle, fly down the field
Ever to conquer, never to yield.
War Eagle, fearless and true,
Fight on you orange and blue,
Go, Go, Go...
On to vict'ry, strike up the band.
Give 'em hell, Give 'em hell
Stand up and yell, Hey!

War Eagle, win for Auburn
Power of Dixie Land!

Alma Mater:

"On the rolling plains of Dixie
'neath the sun-kissed sky,
Proudly stands, our Alma Mater
Banners high.

To thy name we'll sing thy praise,
From hearts that love so true,
And pledge to thee our
Loyalty the ages through.
We hail thee, Auburn, and we vow
To work for thy just fame,
And hold in memory as we do now
Thy cherished name.
Hear thy student voices swelling, Echoes strong and clear,
Adding laurels to thy fame Enshrined so dear.
From they hallowed halls we'll part, And bid thee sad adieu,
Thy sacred trust we'll bear with us The ages through.
We hail thee, Auburn, and we vow, To work for they just fame,
And hold in memory as we do now Thy cherished name.

Composed by bill Wood, 1942, Revised 1960

Noteworthy Auburn Alumni:

Timothy D. Cook, CEO, worldwide operations for Apple Computer

Rowdy Gaines – A 1982 graduate, Olympic gold medalist, world record holder, and TV sports commentator

John Hilburn, Ph.D. – President, Microcomputersystems, Inc., Baton Rouge, LA (microcomputersystems.com), Built the Mars Rover computer processor

Fob James – A 1957 graduate, James earned All-American honors as a running back for the Tigers. Moreover, James went on to enjoy a successful business career, founding DP Industries, and he was twice elected Governor of Alabama (1979-1983,1994-1998)

Don Logan – A 1966 graduate, Logan is CEO and President of Time, Inc.

Carl Mundy – A 1957 graduate, Mundy retired after serving as Commandant of the United States Marine Corps. (More than 100 Auburn graduates have served as generals or admirals in the United States armed forces)

Walter Merritt Riggs, President of Clemson University, 1910-1924, "Father of Clemson Football"

Ashley Crow, American movie and television actress

Miller Reese Hutchison, 1897, Inventor of the electric hearing aid

General Holland Smith, USMC General, "Father of modern U.S. Amphibious Warfare"

Joe Gilchrist, 1965, Founder of the Flora-Bama, co-author, "Bushwhacked at the Flora-Bama"

2020 Auburn Football Schedule

Sept. 5 Alcorn State

Sept. 12 vs. North Carolina (Atlanta)

Sept. 19 at Ole Miss

Sept. 26 Southern Miss

Oct. 3 Kentucky

Oct. 10 at Georgia

Oct. 17 Texas A&M

Oct. 24 OPEN DATE

Oct. 31 at Mississippi State

Nov. 7 Arkansas

Nov. 14 UMass

Nov. 21 LSU

Nov. 28 at Alabama

Louisiana State University (LSU)

Louisianans have long been known for their uncompromising "joie de vivre," or "joy of life." Weekend festivals throughout the state are a common thread within the Louisiana cultural fabric. These festivals showcase the food, music, and fun Louisianans enjoy year-round. As a result of their zest for living "the good life," people from the Bayou State live differently from the rest of America and the South. This is due in large part to the fact that the population of Louisiana consists of an amalgam of both French and Spanish influences – two of the three empires that held the Louisiana territory prior to the Louisiana Purchase in 1803. This cultural diversity comprises a state community that enjoys the best of what each group has to offer within an environment conducive to having a good time. After all, "Laissez-les bon temps roulez!" or "Let the good times roll!" is the motto of the fun-loving French Cajuns from South Louisiana. Therefore, it only seems fitting that Louisianans look forward to Saturday nights in Tiger Stadium with unbridled anticipation. Not only is an LSU football game another chance for Louisianans to see their venerable Tigers play – it's also a huge tailgating party, complete with the trappings of a Louisiana festival – good food, friends, and fun! Recently, a favorite son of the Bayou State, Ed Orgeron–the irascible, irresistible Cajun come home—has brought great pride to the State of Louisiana, just like his successful predecessors, Nick Saban and Les Miles. In the modern era LSU has produced some of the National Football League's biggest and brightest stars.

History of LSU: Pronounced "Ellesshoe," 1860, Pineville, Louisiana

In 1853, the Louisiana General Assembly established the Louisiana State Seminary of Learning and Military Academy near Pineville, Louisiana. The university opened January 2, 1860, with Colonel William Tecumseh Sherman as superintendent. The school closed in 1863 because of the Civil War. The Seminary reopened its doors in October of 1865, only to be burned in October 1869. In November of 1869 the school resumed its exercises in Baton Rouge, where it has since remained. Land for the current campus was acquired in 1918 and construction started in 1922. Formal dedication of the present campus occurred on April 30, 1926.

William Tecumseh Sherman, who served as a General for the Union Army during the Civil War, was the first Superintendent/President of the university. Initially torn between the North and the South, Sherman sided with the Constitution of the United States and left the post in Pineville, Louisiana to assume a command in the Union army at the start of the Civil War. Sherman's fondness for the Ole War Skule softened his hard-lined stance toward the

Confederacy. Remarkably, at the request of General Sherman, whose troops sacked and burned much of the rest of the Deep South, the Louisiana State Seminary, as well as many Louisiana homes and cities, were spared by Union troops during the Civil War. As a result, many of Louisiana's most beautiful antebellum homes and plantations survive today.

LSU's strong military heritage earned it the nickname "Ole War Skule." "Ole War Skule" was a popular reference to Louisiana State University at the turn of the 20th century, as was the term "Old Lou." Three LSU presidents were generals in the armed forces. Until 1969, ROTC was mandatory for all entering freshmen, and during that time LSU produced as many officers for World War II as West Point, Annapolis, or Texas A&M.

Location: Baton Rouge, Louisiana

Baton Rouge is the heart of plantation country in the South. The bustling industrial city contains the largest concentration of plantation homes in the South along the Mississippi River corridor. And the name, Baton Rouge? It means "red stick," and it refers to the Indian custom of using a red stick, or baton to mark the boundary between two Indian tribes. To most Louisianans, Baton Rouge is simply LSU. The state's flagship university calls Baton Rouge its home and its sports teams – especially football – inspire unparalleled loyalty among its most rabid fan base. Baton Rouge is also a great venue for popular rock bands, such as the area's homegrown sound of Better Than Ezra, which got its start in Red Stick in the late 1980's. One Better Than Ezra song, titled "This Time of Year," was written on the way to an LSU-Ole Miss game in Oxford.

Population: 225,000

Enrollment: 31,500

Nickname: Fighting Tigers

The nickname was drawn from the legendary Confederate battalion, Robert E. Lee's "Louisiana Tigers," who distinguished themselves during the Shenandoah Valley Campaign in Virginia. This elite fighting regiment, which was made up of New Orleans "Zouaves" and Donaldsonville "Cannoneers" was so renowned for their ferocity during battle that even fellow Confederate troops were reluctant to fight alongside the licentious lot. During the fall of 1896, Coach A.W. Jeardeau's team posted a perfect 6-0 record, and it was in that fourth gridiron campaign that LSU adopted the Tiger moniker for its team.

Colors: Purple and Gold

The inception of LSU's colors of purple and gold are linked to the Louisiana carnival known as Mardi Gras. In 1893, LSU played its first football game against Tulane University of New Orleans. Upon arrival in the Crescent City, LSU coaches realized that LSU's gray uniforms were drab in comparison to Tulane's green uniforms. This prompted the LSU coach to purchase purple and gold ribbons at a nearby store to adorn the Tiger uniforms. Because of Mardi Gras, the store had plenty of purple and gold material (Mardi Gras colors are Purple, Gold, and Green).

Mascot: Royal Bengal Tiger

The Bengal tiger, or Royal Bengal tiger, is a subspecies of tiger found in Bangladesh, India, and also in Nepal and Southern Tibet. It is the second largest of the cat family and the most common tiger subspecies. The Bengal tiger lives in a variety of habitats, including grasslands, subtropical and tropical rain forests, scrub forests, wet and dry deciduous forests, and mangroves. It is the national animal of India and Bangladesh.

Mascot Name: Mike the Tiger

Named after the original Tiger trainer, Mike Chambers, tradition dictates that for every growl by Mike before a football game, the Tigers will score a touchdown that night. The current Mike the Tiger, Mike VII, is cared for by the students at the LSU School of Veterinary Medicine and lives in a 15,000 square foot gallery environment featuring a large live oak tree, a waterfall, and a stream flowing from a rocky backdrop. Mike VII is a Bengal-Siberian mix. He lives in the new, multi-million dollar "cage" adjacent to the Pete Mavarich Assembly Center on the LSU campus. Mike VII was born September 13, 2016. Mike I was purchased with $750 in student contributions in 1936, from a Little Rock, Arkansas zoo. Since the 1950's, Mike the Tiger has been portrayed by a costumed student who appears at most LSU sporting events. In August of 2007, "Costumed Mike" appeared on a This Is Sportscenter commercial with LSU graduate and NBA superstar, Shaquille O'Neal.

Band: Golden Band from Tigerland

This 325-member marching band performs at all LSU home football games, all bowl games, and selected away games. It represents Louisiana State University at other functions as one of its most recognizable student and spirit organizations. The John Phillip Sousa Foundation awarded the LSU Band the 2002 "Sudler Trophy," the highest honor a college marching band can receive. The LSU band was influenced by the United States military and former Governor Huey Pierce Long. In 1893, LSU established its own eleven-mem-

ber Cadet Band. By the 20th century the Cadet Band became a marching unit. Tours throughout the state and regular Mardi Gras displays became band traditions.

The band held its first halftime performance in 1924. By the 1930's Huey Long took interest in the band, setting it on a unique path to national prominence among college outfits. He hired Castro Carazo, an orchestra leader of the popular New Orleans Roosevelt Hotel, as bandmaster. Long ordered a change in dress code for the band. He provided them with new uniforms to add color and style to their anticipated halftime displays.

Band Director: Damon Talley (2019 – present)

Stadium: Tiger Stadium

Stadium Capacity: 102,321

Named for the team's mascot, it is known as "Death Valley" to LSU opponents. The stadium opened in 1924 with only 12,000 seats. East Stadium was constructed in 1926; West in 1932; North in 1937 (46,000); South in 1957; an addition was completed above the West side in 1978 (78,000). During the 2000 football season, Tiger Stadium's capacity was expanded to 92,600 seats. Completion of the South End Zone upper deck expansion added 70 "Tiger Den" suites, over 3,000 club seats and over 1,500 general public seats to increase the capacity of Tiger Stadium to 102,321, making it the fifth-largest college football stadium in the country. When Tiger Stadium is filled on fall Saturdays it is more populous than fifty of the state's sixty-four parishes (counties). Former LSU head coach Les Miles said of Tiger Stadium, "Our stadium is called 'Death Valley' because it is where visiting teams' winning hopes come to die."

Tiger Stadium is known for its intimidating atmosphere, as game preparation normally culminates with a massive outdoor tailgating party attended by more than 150,000 fans. Architecturally its many arches resemble the famed Roman Coliseum. Unlike most football fields, where the yard lines ending in "0" are marked, Tiger Stadium marks the yard lines ending in "5." Tiger Stadium still uses the classic double-posted, "H-style" goal posts, one of only three colleges to do such. Historically, LSU wins over 80 percent of its night games.

Record Crowd: 93,374 November 3, 2012 vs. Alabama

First Game: 1893 vs. Tulane (0-34) at New Orleans

First Victory: 1894 vs. Natchez AC (36-0) at Natchez, Mississippi

First Game Played in Tiger Stadium: November 25, 1924: Tulane 13, LSU 0

First Night Game in Tiger Stadium:

October 3, 1931: LSU defeated Spring Hill 35-0

The Campanile:

Often referred to as "the tower" or "the clock or bell tower," it is the memorial granted by the students and the people of Louisiana to those 1,447 Louisianans who lost their lives during World War I. The names of these patriots are engraved on a bronze plaque inside the rotunda of the obelisk. Dedicated in 1926, the 175-foot tower was designed by Theodore Link and today it serves as the campus' chief landmark. It was erected with funds coming from public donations led by the American Legion Post Number 58 and an appropriation by the Louisiana legislature totaling $226,225. A clock at the top of the tower once chimed; however, today it is silent. Legend has it that if an LSU coed kisses her beau at the stroke of midnight in front of the bell tower then he is the one that she will marry. Many LSU married couples claim to have engaged in this age-old campus tradition and ritual.

Huey Pierce Long and the Ole War Skule:

Huey P. Long, former flamboyant Louisiana governor from 1928-1932, is remembered by Louisianans as "LSU's most ardent and vociferous fan" in Professor T. Harry Williams' timeless Pulitzer-Prize winning, biographical tribute titled, Huey Long. A native Louisianan, Huey wanted LSU to have a bowl football stadium, and a winning program like the other national football powers of the day. However, university officials said what the university really needed was a dormitory. The clever, undeniable Huey learned that the federal government would pay for classroom and dormitory buildings through the

Works Progress Administration. In light of this, Long sought and discovered an architect who would design a football stadium with dorm rooms in it. The Tiger Stadium dormitory dwellings were still being used into the 1990's.

Long, infamous for wearing wacky purple and gold outfits on game day, was such an LSU fanatic that he often filled in as drum major and led the LSU band around campus and onto the football field. On occasion, he was known to act as de facto head coach and recruiting coordinator--much to the chagrin of figurehead Coach Russ Cohen.

Long is credited with creating and funding LSU's first true athletic department. The quintessential demagogue, Long was once quoted as saying, "I don't fool around with losers," and "LSU can't have a losing football team, because that will mean that I am associated with a loser!" If it were not for Huey Long, one could argue LSU would not have turned the corner so soon; and become a prominent, modern football school with an impressive stadium, and such a colorful, storied history.

Long fell victim to an assassin's bullet at the height of his power in 1935. The then-U.S. Senator and de facto Governor of Louisiana is rumored to have spoken these last words while dying in a hospital bed in Baton Rouge, "...My God, my God, I have so much left to do. Who will look after my darling LSU?" Huey Pierce Long was 42 at the time of his death.

Directions:

Coming from the East-Take I-10 West, exit Dalrymple Drive. Take a right towards the south and follow Dalrymple through campus and turn right onto North or South Stadium Drive.

Coming from the West-Take I-10 East, exit Nicholson Drive to the left and follow Nicholson to Tiger Stadium on your left side in about four or five minutes.

Coming from the South-I-10 is the eventual route. Follow signs to Baton Rouge via East or West I-10.

Coming from the North-Take I-110 South to I-10 East, exit Dalrymple Drive. Take a right towards the south and follow Dalrymple through campus and turn right onto North or South Stadium Drive.

Dining:

The Chimes Restaurant and Tap Room – Located next door to The Varsity Theater at the North Gates entrance to LSU, the Chimes has some of the best food in town with one of the broadest menus...something for everyone. The crawfish etouffee' is excellent, over sixty beers for your selection, and a wine cellar. Fresh blackened, broiled, or fried seafood. 3357 Highland Road, Baton Rouge 1.225.383.1754 New location at 10870 Coursey Boulevard, Baton Rouge 1.225.296.4981 Monday – Saturday; 11:00 a.m. – 2:00 a.m.; Sunday; 11:00 a.m. – 11:30 p.m.

T.J. Ribs – This popular eatery has been around for years and is loaded with LSU memorabilia—including Billy Cannon's "Heisman Trophy." The baby back ribs are worth stealing. Other than beef, pork, and sausage dishes, T.J.'s also features salads and burgers. Enjoyable family environment with kids' menu. 2324 South Acadian Thruway, Baton Rouge 1.225.383.7427 Monday – Sunday; 10:30 a.m. – 10:30 p.m.

Night Life

Walk-Ons Bistreaux & Bar – Located in the shadow of Tiger Stadium at the intersection of Burbank & Nicholson. A popular meeting place for students, faculty, and alumni, the establishment was opened by two former LSU basketball walk-ons and is all about LSU sports! It has numerous TV's, tasty sports bar food, many beers on tap, and a great socializing atmosphere. 3838 Burbank Drive, Baton Rouge 1.225.757.8010 Monday – Saturday; 11:00 a.m. – 2:00 a.m.; Sunday; 11:00 a.m. – 12:00 a.m.

Fred's – A Tigerland tradition for over four decades! Mark Fraioli has rocked this spot with live music, cold beer and libations since the beginning. Look for the expansive circus tent on game weekends. 1184 Bob Pettit Boulevard, Baton Rouge, 225.766.3909. Millions and millions served. Opens 8:00 p.m.

The Varsity Theatre – Located on Highland Road at the North Gates entrance to LSU, next to The Chimes. Opened in 1991, this refurbished historical theatre is Baton Rouge's best venue for live music and retro dancing. Popular before and after LSU football games. 3353 Highland Road, Baton Rouge. 1.225.383.7018.

Accommodations:

Lod Cook Hotel – Located overlooking the LSU lakes on sorority row, the beautiful inn offers first class accommodations in the heart of the campus. This is where Shaquille O'Neal stays when he's in town. Ask for his personal Mega-Suite when he's not using it—a spacious room replete with a whirlpool, large-screen TV and Shaq's signature 8-foot "super king" sized bed. 1.866.610.COOK or 1.225.383.COOK

Nearest Hospital to Stadium:

Ochsner Medical Center

17000 Medical Center Drive, Baton Rouge, LA 70816 225.752.2470

Bail Bondsman for Emergencies:

Bad Boyz Bail Bonds

1.225.229.7218

Golf Courses:

LSU Golf Course

Address: Nicholson Drive, Baton Rouge, LA 70808 (view of Tiger Stadium)

Phone: (225) 578-3394

Copper Mill

2100 Coppermill Blvd., Zachary, LA 70791

(225) 658-0656

Shopping:

Tanger Outlet Mall in Gonzales between New Orleans and Baton Rouge has many stores, as does the upscale Perkins-Rowe development at Perkins and Bluebonnet. Chimes Street near the Gates of LSU has shops of interest.

Records

All-Time Record: 753-395-47 (.656)

Bowl Appearances: 45

Bowl Record: 23-21-1 (.511)

SEC Championships:

(11) 1935, '36, '58, '61(tie), '70, '86, '88 (tie), '01, '03, '07, 11

SEC Western Division Championships:

(9) – 1996, 1997, 2001, 2002, 2003, 2005, 2007, 2011, 2019

National Championships:

(4) 1958, 2003, 2007, 2019

62-0: The score that LSU has beaten its former arch-rival Tulane on three separate occasions – 1958, 1961, and 1965

22-0: LSU's records against the University of Louisiana at Lafayette, formerly known as the University of Southwestern Louisiana (USL).

Great Bowl Games

1947 Cotton Bowl: LSU 0, Arkansas 0. (Often referred to as the "Ice Bowl")

1959 Sugar Bowl: LSU 7, Clemson 0. LSU wins National Championship.

1966 Cotton Bowl: LSU 14, Arkansas 7. LSU shocks the second-ranked Razorbacks.

1996 Peach Bowl: LSU 10, Clemson 7. LSU clinches fifth ten win season in history.

1997 Independence Bowl: LSU 27, Notre Dame 9. Tigers avenge regular-season loss to Irish.

2000 Peach Bowl: LSU 28, Georgia Tech 14

2002 Sugar Bowl: LSU 47, Illinois 34

2004 Sugar Bowl: LSU 21, Oklahoma 14 (BCS National Championship)

2005 Peach Bowl: LSU 40, Miami 3

2007 Sugar Bowl: LSU 41, Notre Dame 14

2008 BCS National Championship, New Orleans: LSU 38, Ohio State 24 (BCS National Championship)

2011 Cotton Bowl Classic: LSU 41, Texas A&M 24

2019 Fiesta Bowl: LSU 40, UCF 32

2020 Peach Bowl CFP Semifinal, Atlanta: LSU 63, Oklahoma 28

2020 National Playoff Championship Final, New Orleans: LSU 42, Clemson 25 (2019 season)

LSU Greats

Coaches

Dr. Charles Coates **–** (1893) - The Johns Hopkins University graduate founded the football team and coached only a single game, resulting in a loss. The academic hall in the quadrangle housing the Speech Department bears his name. Coates reportedly drove nails into the bottom of his players' shoes since they had no cleats. He was the third professor at LSU to hold a Ph.D. A chemist, he was known for his research on sugar chemistry. He died December 27, 1939 in Baton Rouge.

Gaynell Tinsley **–** (1948-1954) – (35-34-6) – (.507) - Tinsley was a two-time All-American end for the Tigers in 1935 and 1936. The Haynesville, Louisiana native led the Tigers to three straight SEC Championships by playing both ways from 1934-1936. The 1936 LSU team finished the year ranked #2 in the country. Tinsley was drafted in the second round of the NFL draft in 1937 by the Chicago Cardinals. Tinsley later returned to LSU to coach the Tigers from

1948-54. Tinsley's 1949 team at LSU finished 8-3, and ended the season ranked #9 overall. He died July 24, 2002.

Bernie Moore **–** (1937-47) – (89-39-6) – (.671) - The Carson-Newman graduate led LSU to SEC championships in 1935 and 1936. Under Moore's tutelage, the Bengal Tigers did not lose an SEC game until his third year as head coach. Moore led the Tigers to three consecutive Sugar Bowls, an Orange Bowl, and a Cotton Bowl berth. He was the head track coach at LSU as well, from 1930-1947, and the track stadium at LSU is named for him. The trophy going annually to the best all-around athletic program in the SEC is named for him. He died November 6, 1967 in Winchester, Tennessee.

Paul Dietzel **–** (1955-61) – (46-24-3) – (.651) - Dietzel was 31 when he began coaching LSU in 1955. His Tigers became the 1958 National Champs, earning him National Coach of the Year honors. Dietzel was affectionately referred to by Tiger fans as "Pepsodent Paul" for his sparkling white smile. He is remembered for his coaching genius that produced a platooning system for the Tigers that rotated three teams on and off the field to compensate for the Tigers' lack of depth, and the inhibiting substitution rules of the day. The White Team, the Go Team, and the "Chinese Bandits" were all used by Dietzel to win ball games. The platooning system allowed Dietzel to play 35 to 40 players in each game, thereby keeping his players fresh. Dietzel later served as head coach and athletic director at South Carolina, from 1966 to 1974, and later as the athletic director at LSU, from 1978 to 1982. Dietzel was a trustee and past President of the American Football Coaches Association. He died September 24, 2013 in Baton Rouge. He was 89.

Charlie McClendon **–** (1962-1979) – (137-59-7) – (.692) - By posting winning records in 16 of 18 seasons, "Cholly Mac," a graduate of the University of Kentucky where he played for Bear Bryant, became the winningest coach in LSU history. McClendon's 18 years at the post are the longest tenure of any LSU head football coach. Born October 17, 1923, in Lewisville, Arkansas, he is remembered as LSU's most successful coach in terms of games won, but he was berated by fans for losing to his famous nemesis in Tuscaloosa, Paul "Bear" Bryant. Despite the constant jabs, McClendon led LSU to two Sugar Bowls, two Cotton Bowls, two Bluebonnet Bowls, two Orange Bowls, two Sun Bowls, a Tangerine Bowl, a Liberty Bowl, and a Peach Bowl. Coach McClendon, throughout his long career at LSU, had 14 teams play in bowl games. Fifteen of his teams finished in the AP Top 15 during his tenure. In 1970, Coach Charles "Cholly Mac" McClendon was honored as "National Coach of the Year." Charles McClendon died December 6, 2001 in Baton Rouge. He was 78. He was inducted into the National College Football Hall of Fame in 1986. After LSU, McClendon became the executive director of the Tangerine Bowl, now renamed the Citrus Bowl, from 1980 to 1981. He was the president of the American Football Coaches Association in 1979 and executive director from 1982 to 1994. The Charles McClendon Practice Facility at LSU was named in his honor on September 9, 2002, nine months after his death on December 6, 2001. His death came just two days before LSU won its first outright SEC title in 15 years. At midfield at Tiger Stadium from a wheelchair before his passing, McClendon offered,"My final coaching point...remember...responsibility means your actions."

Jerry Stovall – (1980-1983) – (22-21-2) – (.511) – After finishing second in the Heisman balloting and a standout NFL career with the St. Louis Cardinals, Jerry Stovall returned to LSU, as an assistant for head coach Charles McClendon. Stovall became LSU's head coach as an emergency hire in 1980, after new head coach Bo Rein died when his plane mysteriously depressurized and disappeared over the Atlantic Ocean. Stovall had the tall task of following in the footsteps of LSU's winningest football coach. With a 22-21-2 overall record at LSU in four years from 1980-1983, Stovall had an up-and-down LSU tenure, finishing 7-4, 3-7-1, 8-3-1, and 4-7. Only one of Stovall's teams appeared in the final AP poll, the 1982 squad. That team finished the season ranked #11 after it beat #4 Florida, #8 Bear Bryannt and Alabama and #7 Florida State and Bobby Bowden, earning them a spot in the Orange Bowl where LSU lost 21-20 to a #3 Nebraska team led by Tom Osborne. In 1982, Stovall was named the National Coach of the Year by the Walter Camp Football Foundation. Stovall left LSU after four seasons and was later the athletic director for Louisiana Tech University from 1990 to 1993.

Bill Arnsparger – (1984-1986) – (26-8-2) – (.750) - Born December 16, 1926, Arnsparger's hiring by athletic director Bob Brodhead breathed a healthy dose of fresh air into the LSU athletic program. A former pro coach with the Miami Dolphins, each of Arnsparger's teams at LSU played in bowl games. Unfortunately, all three post-season games, two of which were against Nebraska, were losses. His 1986 team finished 9-3 overall and 5-1 in the SEC to win the conference. Arnsparger succeeded on the field but he did not possess the political clout necessary to keep his job. He left LSU after the 1986 season and took the athletic director's job at the University of Florida. It was in that capacity that Arnsparger later hired a young football coach from Duke University, Steve Spurrier, the SEC's most successful modern-day coach.

Mike Archer – (1987-1990) – (27-18-1) – (.598) - In 1987, 31-year old Mike Archer, the youngest Division 1-A head coach in America, took over for Bill

Arnsparger and coached four years at LSU. A Miami, Florida native and 1976 graduate of the University of Miami, Archer was a star defensive back and punter for the Hurricanes. Born July 26, 1953, in State College, Pennsylvania, Archer coached seven years as secondary coach at Miami under Coach Howard Schnellenberger. Archer left Miami in 1984 to become the defensive coordinator at LSU. When Archer was selected many felt he was too young and had too little experience. He was chosen over many named candidates, including Steve Spurrier. Archer's first two years were memorable, culminating in a 1988 SEC Championship, but after that things fell apart. After LSU, Archer coached at Virginia and Kentucky before spending seven years with the Pittsburgh Steelers. Later he was the defensive coordinator for the Kentucky Wildcats and the defensive coordinator for the North Carolina State Wolfpack and a slew of other college and professional teams. He coaches linebackers for the Tampa Bay Vipers of the XFL.

***Gerry DiNardo* –** (1995-1999) – (33-24-1) – (.578) - In 1995, DiNardo came to LSU during a down time in the school's storied football history. Following Curley Hudson Hallman's four-year tenure in which he notched a disappointing 16-28 record, DiNardo landed at LSU from Vanderbilt to bring respectability to the program. DiNardo was pivotal in bringing LSU Football back to greatness by teaching the program how to win again. A graduate of Notre Dame, and the son of a Bronx beat cop, DiNardo won early with Hallman's recruits but during his last two seasons in Baton Rouge his luck and his talent ran out. In five seasons DiNardo posted a more than respectable record at the helm for the Tigers, his biggest win coming in October 1997 when the Tigers defeated Steve Spurrier's #1 ranked Florida Gators in an unlikely 28-21 upset in Tiger Stadium. After a short and unsuccessful stint as a head coach in the failed XFL, DiNardo took the head coaching job at Indiana University, a post he left in 2004. A former ESPN radio analyst, today DiNardo is a restaurateur.

***Nick Saban* –** (2000–2004) – (48-16) – (.750) - Born October 31, 1951, in Fairmont, West Virginia, Saban is remembered for bringing LSU its second national championship in football at the end of the 2003 season. In late 1999, prior to the 2000 football season, Saban was named the 12th LSU head football coach during the SEC era that began in 1933, and the school's 31st overall. Saban succeeded interim head coach Hal Hunter, who took over for a fired Gerry DiNardo. A graduate of Kent State where he was a three year letterman as a defensive back, Saban paid his dues by coaching defensive backs at his alma mater under Don James, briefly at Syracuse, West Virginia, and for Earl Bruce at Ohio State. In 1983, Saban went to Michigan State and served as defensive coordinator under George Perles for five seasons. In

1988 and 1989 Saban coached the secondary for the Houston Oilers. He assumed his first head coaching position at Toledo in 1990, producing a 9-2 record on the season. In 1991, Saban returned to the NFL for four seasons as Cleveland's defensive coordinator, making the Cleveland Browns' defense one of the NFL's best stop units. In 1995, Saban took the head coaching job at Michigan State where he coached for five seasons, ending with a best 9-2 record in 1999. Described as a "no-nonsense" type coach, Saban is known as a hard worker, a steadfast defensive instructor and a consummate recruiter of talent. In his first year in Baton Rouge Saban went 8-4, culminating with a 28-14 victory over Georgia Tech in the Peach Bowl. In 2001, he built on his earlier success by leading LSU to it first SEC Championship since 1988 with a climactic come-from-behind victory over the Tennessee Volunteers in the SEC Championship Game. In 2002, LSU finished as SEC Western Division Co-Champs and in 2003 LSU repeated as SEC Champions with a 34-13 victory over Georgia and went on to defeat Oklahoma 21-14 in the Sugar Bowl in New Orleans for the BCS National Championship, its first since 1958. Saban left LSU on Christmas Eve 2004 to become the head coach of the Miami Dolphins. Today he is the Alabama head football coach, a post he has held since 2007. "Play for 60 minutes," is one of Saban's favorite motivating lines.

Les Miles – (2005-2016) – (114-34) – (.800) - Born November 10, 1953, in Elyria, Ohio, Les Miles enjoys the distinction of having the best start of any LSU football coach. A graduate of the University of Michigan and disciple of Bo Schembechler, Miles coached at Colorado, Michigan and the Dallas Cowboys prior to his head coaching gig at Oklahoma State. Miles took over LSU in 2005, in the catastrophic wake of two of the nation's most destructive hurricanes, Katrina and Rita, and was the first SEC coach to lead his team to the SEC title game during his first season. Despite the storm distractions, Miles led his team to an 11-2 record, with a 40-3 Peach Bowl victory over a ninth-ranked Miami Hurricane team. The only setbacks that season came against Tennessee at home and against Georgia in the SEC Championship Game. The 2006 season was equally successful win-wise for Miles and the Tigers. LSU finished the season with an identical 11-2 record, punctuated by a 41-14 drubbing of 11th-ranked Notre Dame in the Sugar Bowl in the New Orleans Superdome. The

2007 Sugar Bowl was the first one played in the indoor arena since the destructive 2005 hurricanes ravaged the Crescent City. In 2007, Miles led LSU to its third national championship by going 10-2, with losses to only Kentucky and Arkansas. He led the Tigers to victory in the SEC Championship Game against Tennessee by a score of 21-14. The Tigers defeated Ohio State in the National Championship in New Orleans by a score of 38-24. Miles is the only LSU coach to lead his team to three straight ten-win seasons. From 2005 to 2016, Les Miles, a.k.a. "The Hat," amassed a 114-34 (.80) overall record, a 62-38 SEC record, two SEC Championships and a National Championship. Miles, much like his predecessor, Charlie McClendon, had trouble beating Alabama, and was fired after the fourth game of 2016, a loss at Auburn. In 2019, he took the head coaching job at the University of Kansas, going 3-9 in 2019. His overall college coaching record is 145-64 (.698).

Ed Orgeron – (2017-present) - A native of the Bayou State, Ed "Bebe" ("Bay-Bay") Orgeron was born and raised in Cajun Country—Larose, Louisiana, a small town on Bayou Lafourche, in Lafourche Parish, near Grand Isle and the Gulf of Mexico. An over-achiever bent on his cultural namesake of hard work and perseverance, Orgeron has overcome personal problems and a mountain of obstacles to reach the pinnacle of college football. He attended South Lafourche High School in Galliano, Louisiana with future NFL QB Bobby Hebert, where they played on the school's 1977 State Championship team. Orgeron signed with LSU but transferred after his freshman year to Northwestern State in Natchitoches, Louisiana. His career began in 1984 as a grad assistant at Northwestern State. In 1985, he coached defensive line at McNeese State in Lake Charles, Louisiana. In 1986 and 1987 he was an assistant strength coach at Arkansas under Ken Hatfield. In 1988, he got his first taste of big-time football, landing with the University of Miami and Coach Jimmy Johnson, coaching defensive line for four years, continuing with Johnson's successor, Dennis Erickson. During this time the Hurricanes won two national championships and Orgeron recruited and coached eight All-Americans—including three first round NFL draft choices Russell Maryland, Warren Sapp and Cortez Kennedy. In 1991, his Miami career ended in turmoil. Personal problems unmanaged resulted in him taking a leave of absence. Orgeron returned home and credits his father for helping him get his life in

order. He returned to coaching in 1994, as a volunteer at Nicholls State University. In 1995, he landed at Syracuse University, under Coach Paul Pasqualoni, where he coached D-Line for three years. Orgeron credits Pasqualoni for giving him a much-needed second chance at coaching. In 1998, Orgeron was hired by USC Coach Paul Hackett to coach defensive line. After Hackett's firing, Orgeron was retained by new Coach Pete Carroll. Carroll and Orgeron won two national championships and Orgeron became recruiting coordinator, where he won 2004 National Recruiter of the Year honors, the same year he took the head coaching job at Ole Miss, replacing David Cutcliffe. Oxford from 2005 to 2007 was a humbling experience for Orgeron, and Rebel fans. Not yet ready for the big time, Ed's three-year ride in Rebel Town came to a thankful end. He went a hapless 10-25 overall; and 3-21 in SEC play. In 2008, Orgeron coached D-Line for the New Orleans Saints, a position he held for a season. In 2009, he took a job under Tennessee Head Coach Lane Kiffin, serving as associate head coach, recruiting coordinator and defensive line coach. In 2010, Orgeron followed Kiffin back to USC and took over as interim head coach in 2013, after Kiffin's firing. Orgeron wanted the USC job, and felt he deserved it, but it was not to be. In January 2015, he landed on LSU's staff under troubled head coach Les Miles, as a defensive line coach. On September 25, 2016, after the fourth game loss to Auburn on the road, Orgeron was named interim LSU coach after Miles was fired. Known as a player's coach and a tireless, fiery recruiter with a booming, gravelly voice, and a penchant for the unexpected motivational ploy, Orgeron in three years at LSU, has amassed an enviable win-loss record and a trophy case full of accolades. Orgeron's 2019 LSU Team, which some say is college football's greatest, went 15-0 and won the College Football Playoff in the Superdome against Clemson and Dabo Swinney, 42-25. Clemson, prior to the contest, had won 29 straight games. Orgeron post-season was named Associated Press Coach of the Year, Eddie Robinson Coach of the Year, granted the George Munger Award, the Paul "Bear" Bryant Award and was SEC Coach of the Year.

Players

Yelberton Abraham "Y.A." Tittle – (1944-47) - The Marshall, Texas native committed to play for the Texas Longhorns in Austin. However, after a dorm-room visit in Austin, Texas from LSU Assistant Coach Red Swanson, Tittle packed his bags and left for Baton Rouge. Tittle used his athletic ability to lead the Tigers to their first win over Alabama in over thirty years in 1948, bringing with that victory national acclaim to LSU. Tittle completed his eligibility in Baton Rouge as the Tigers' all-time leading passer, a mark that would later be broken as passing offenses became popular in the college game. Tittle went on to an illustrious pro football career with the New York Giants, where he was

named the league's Most Valuable Player on three separate occasions. The bare-headed photo of a bloodied and battle-tested Tittle on his knees is as iconic as the age in which he played. He is a member of the NFL Hall of Fame. Y.A. Tittle passed away October 8, 2017.

***Billy Cannon* –** (1956-1959) - Born in Philadelphia, Mississippi on August 2, 1937, Cannon's legs led the Tigers to their first national championship in 1958. Known for his toughness and resolve, Cannon possessed unparalleled rushing skills. Gifted with size and speed, Billy Cannon was the prototypical running back during an era of college football that had few true sprinters. Cannon, in his prime, could run a sub 4.5 forty-yard dash; which was rare. Cannon's gridiron talents set him apart from his SEC and national counterparts, and his exploits on the playing field were the stuff of legend. The Baton Rouge native's timely run into Bengal Tiger and college football lore came during the 1959 season when he returned a punt eighty-nine yards against Ole Miss to catapult the Tigers to a 7-3 victory. Mississippi Head Coach John Vaught had this to say about Cannon's magical romp, "Outside the Louisiana Purchase in 1803, many Cajuns consider Billy Cannon's touchdown run the greatest event in state history." For his accomplishments on the football field, Billy Cannon was named the 1959 Heisman Trophy recipient. During his career in Tigertown, Cannon scored 19 touchdowns and rushed for 1,867 yards on 359 carries, for an average of 5.2 yards. Following his 1959 Heisman Trophy-winning season, Cannon's jersey, #20, was retired to the LSU Football Hall of Fame. Possessing movie star looks, Cannon once remarked, "I don't understand why guys get upset if a girl turns them down. Just move on to the next one!" His LSU jersey #20 is retired. He was the first pick in the 1960 NFL Draft and played for the Houston Oilers, Oakland Raiders and Kansas City Chiefs for eleven seasons. After the NFL he built a successful real estate business only to see it crash with the market. After turning to alcohol, then counterfeiting, to cope, Cannon found himself a felon, and later, after a short prison sentence, a new beginning as the resident dentist and medical director at Angola State Penitentiary. A statue outside Tiger Stadium bears Cannon's playing likeness. In 2015, Cannon co-authored and published a book about his life, "A Long, Long Run," with Charles deGravelles. Cannon died May 20, 2018. He was 80.

Tommy Casanova **–** (1968-1971) - Born July 20, 1950, Casanova was a consensus All-American for LSU in 1969, 1970, and 1971. He is remembered by many as LSU's greatest all-around football player. Known for his versatility, Casanova played on both sides of the ball as a running back and kick returner, as well as a three-time All-American safety during his career as a Tiger. From 1969-1971, he intercepted seven passes, rushed for 302 yards on 72 carries for five touchdowns, returned 44 punts for 517 yards and returned 17 kickoffs for 334 yards. He was renowned as a fearless competitor both on and off the field and remains one of a handful of three-time First Team All-Southeastern Conference performers at LSU, joining the likes of David Browndyke (1978-89), Kevin Faulk (1996-98), Dalton Hilliard (1982, 1983, 1985), and Tommy Hodson (1986-89). He was the 29th pick in the second round of the 1972 NFL Draft, playing for the Cincinnati Bengals for six seasons. He was invited to three Pro Bowls, and was named an All-Pro in 1976. A former state senator, he is a medical doctor in his hometown of Crowley, Louisiana. In 1995, Casanova was named to the National Football Foundation Hall of Fame.

Kevin Faulk **–** (1995-1998) - Born June 5, 1976, in Lafayette, Louisiana, Faulk was a 1996 and 1997 All-American, LSU's All-Time Leading Rusher, and the SEC's All-Time All-Purpose Yardage Leader (6,833) his senior year. As primarily a tailback for the Tigers, Faulk rushed for 5.3 yards-per-carry and 46 touchdowns. The Carencro High School graduate finished his career in Baton Rouge second on the All-time SEC rushing list, behind Herschel Walker. During his career for the Bayou Bengals, Kevin Faulk averaged 20.9 carries, 856 in 41 total games and 111.2 yards rushing-per-game (4,557 in 41). A four-year starter, Faulk graduated in three and a half years. Faulk was selected in the second round by the New England Patriots in the 1999 NFL draft. The consummate third down back won three Super Bowl rings with the Pats and is now a member of Ed Orgeron's staff at LSU.

Matt Mauck **–** (2001-2003) - The Jasper, Indiana native spurred the Tigers to a huge upset victory over the second ranked Tennessee Volunteers in the 2001 SEC Championship Game during his non-traditional freshman season. A former professional baseball player, Mauck was 22 when he made an impromptu appearance and earned "MVP" honors in the 2001 SEC Championship Game. Remembered for his ability to make plays with his feet and for his ability to read defenses, Mauck earned the starting job in 2002. In 2003, he led LSU to its first National Championship in 45 years in a 21-14 victory over Oklahoma in the Sugar Bowl at the New Orleans Superdome. Mauck threw for 2,825 yards and 28 touchdowns during his last year in an LSU uniform. His 18-2 record as a starter is the best winning percentage for an LSU quarterback. Mauck skipped his senior season at LSU to enter the 2004 NFL draft. He played with the Broncos and the Titans before retiring to a career in dentistry after receiving his M.D. from the Colorado School of Dentistry.

Jacob Hester **–** (2004-2007) - A Shreveport native, Jacob Hester attended Evangel Christian Academy where he was the 5-A Offensive MVP in 2002, leading his team to the state championship game his senior year. Remembered as a gritty runner who could be relied on for the tough yards, Hester is one of LSU's most popular modern players. Bucking the stereotype of the conventional SEC tailback, Hester was considered a quintessential throwback player for his deliberate, hard-churning rushing style. Hester fumbled twice in his LSU career--once as a freshman--on his first carry, and once as a senior, losing one to the opposition. In 2004, he played in every game, starting once, recording nine tackles and notching 123 rushing yards. In 2005, he again played in every game, with his best coming in the Peach Bowl victory over Miami, running for seventy yards on thirteen carries. Hester broke out as a junior when he started at tailback and fullback, totaling 269 receiving yards on 35 passes and ran for 440. As a senior during LSU's second BCS National Championship season, Hester again started, mainly at tailback, rushing 225 times for 1103 yards and 12 touchdowns, in addition to notching 14 catches for 106 yards and a touchdown. Hester, an avowed Elvis Presley fan, is the third cousin of former Hall of Fame, Pittsburgh Steelers quarterback Terry Bradshaw. In 2008 he was a third round pick of the San Diego Chargers. Today he is a radio personality.

Glenn "Putt" Dorsey **–** (2004-2007) - Born August 1, 1985, in Baton Rouge, Louisiana, East Ascension High School graduate Glenn Dorsey became the most decorated football player in LSU history, collecting the grand slam of 2007 college football awards: The Bronko Nagurski Award (best player), the Outland Trophy (interior lineman), the Lombardi Award (lineman/linebacker), and the Ronnie Lott Trophy (best defensive impact player). As a freshman in 2004, Dorsey started three games, logging 18 tackles. On his first collegiate snap he recovered a fumble against Oregon State. In 2005, he started one game, but worked in the four-man defensive line rotation, totaling 28 tackles and three sacks. In 2006, Dorsey was the anchor of the Tiger defense, finishing the All-American season third on the team with 64 tackles, including 8.5 for losses and three sacks despite regular double-teams. Dorsey opted against going pro after his junior year, although many felt he was a legitimate first day pick. He came back to LSU a consensus pre-season All-American and team leader. His huge presence during the season, despite nagging injuries, helped the Tigers become one of the country's staunchest defensive units, giving up a nation's third-best of 288 yards-per-game. After his senior, national championship season, Dorsey was named the SEC's Defensive MVP and was again a consensus All-American. As talented as Glenn Dorsey was on the football field for LSU, he is remembered as a better person, and one of the most popular players in Tiger history. His message to youth groups makes sense: "Dream Big." After LSU, Glenn was the fifth pick overall in the 2008 NFL Draft. He played for Kansas City for five years and with San Francisco for three.

Matt Flynn **–** (2004-2007) - A Tyler, Texas native, Flynn bided his time in 2005 and 2006, waiting behind starter JaMarcus Russell until he got his own shot as a senior to lead the Tigers during the 2007 season. A heady player with great leadership ability, Flynn was the perfect fit for the Tigers' second BCS Championship run, and as a result he drew many comparisons to another LSU quarterback named Matt (Mauck) from the 2003 BCS Championship season. As a redshirt sophomore Flynn started in the Peach Bowl against Miami in the place of an injured JaMarcus Russell and led the Tigers to a 40-3 thrashing of the Miami Hurricanes and was named "MVP." After a quiet junior year Flynn stepped into the lead role for the Tigers and never looked back, completing 183 passes for 2,233 yards en route to the Tigers' second BCS National Championship. During his senior year Flynn engineered comebacks against Alabama, Auburn, and Florida. In the National Championship Game against Ohio State in New Orleans, Flynn completed 19 of 27 passes for 174 yards and four touchdowns, again earning "MVP" honors. He was drafted by the Green Bay Packers in the seventh round of the 2008 NFL Draft and was a member of the Packers when they won Super Bowl XLV over the Pittsburgh Steelers.

Patrick Peterson **–** (2008-2010) - The Pompano Beach native was one of LSU's most electrifying cornerbacks and return specialists and is one of its most impressive pros. Possessing lightning-fast speed and acceleration for his size, Peterson wowed college fans during his final year in Baton Rouge with amazing all-around ability. During that fantastic season Peterson earned consensus All-SEC and All-American honors, winning SEC Defensive MVP, and the Jim Thorpe and Bednarik awards in the process. Peterson elected to forego his senior season and was the fifth pick overall in the 2011 NFL draft by the Arizona Cardinals. In 2011 he had the most punt return yards by a rookie in the history of the NFL, 699. He was a member of the Pro Bowl in 2011, 2012, 2013 and 2014.

Odell Beckham, Jr. **–** (2011-2013) - Born in Baton Rouge the son of an LSU track athlete and standout Tiger football player, Beckham attended Isidore Newman High School in New Orleans, where he played youth soccer and lettered in football, basketball and track, foreshadowing a stellar all-around football performance at LSU and in the National Football League, where to-

day he remains one of the game's most electrifying receivers. Beckham and another Louisiana receiver, Jarvis Landry, teamed up at LSU and broke numerous receiving records, but it was Beckham's all-around return abilities and penchant for one-handed catches that set him apart from his in-state counterpart. As a true freshman he hauled in 41 catches for 475 yards. As a sophomore he caught 43 balls for 713 yards and had two punt returns for touchdowns. As a junior he broke out with 59 catches for 1,152 yards and received the 2013 Paul Hornung Award given to the nation's most versatile football player. He was drafted 12th overall by the New York Giants, where he played for five seasons. In 2016, he became the fastest NFL player to 200 career receptions and 4,000 receiving yards. In 2019, he rejoined his old teammate, Jarvis Landry, with the Cleveland Browns.

Leonard Fournette – (2014-2016) - The New Orleans native who grew up in the 7th Ward attended St. Augustine High School where he was a standout four-year starter at track and football, foreshadowing one of the greatest running performances in NCAA history. In his high school freshman season Fournette rushed for over 2,500 yards and drew the attention of LSU Coach Les Miles, who made him the first freshman at St. Augustine to receive a scholarship offer from LSU. Fournette was perhaps the last of the great backs to play toward the end of an era of tough running football. He possessed great size and strength to complement his amazing speed and his outlier blend of alacrity and power is a fabled "Goldilocks Zone" for running backs—meaning at his top speed he becomes a weapon capable of inflicting great damage on opposing defenses. In his three years in Baton Rouge he amassed 3,830 rushing yards and 40 touchdowns, with 1,953 coming during his sophomore season, which saw him dismantle Auburn's defense in Baton Rouge in a scintillating daytime display of speed and power. That fantastic year Fournette averaged 167 yards per game, making him the nation's top rusher.

After a disappointing junior season beset by injuries, Fournette turned pro where he was signed fourth overall by Jacksonville in the first round of the 2017 NFL draft.

Devin White – (2016-2018) – A product of North Webster High School in Springhill, Louisiana, just shy of the State of Arkansas, Devin White was a terrific running back and linebacker for the hometown football team, rushing for over 5,000 yards and scoring 81 touchdowns. Devin loved running the football, and LSU was known for its great running backs. Possessing rare speed for someone weighing 245 pounds, Devin settled instead on linebacker at LSU to fill a need at the position; and the rest is history, as he grew into one of the most dominant linebackers for the Tigers in many years, despite his devout country upbringing. Devin grew up riding and training horses. When he left Springhill for LSU he took his horse Daisy Mae with him; and it was a good move, because she brought him much luck during his time in Tiger Town. White played mainly on special teams and as a backup linebacker as a freshman. During his sophomore season he broke out, logging a league-best 133 tackles at middle linebacker. As a junior he added another 123 tackles with three sacks and 12 tackles for loss, serving as the leader of the defense and a team leader along with junior quarterback transfer Joe Burrow. Devin finished his LSU career with 286 tackles and was given the Butkus Award after his junior season and went pro, where he was chosen as the fifth pick overall by the Tampa Bay Buccaneers in the 2019 NFL Draft after logging a 4.4 forty-yard dash at 6-1 255 pounds.

Joe Burrow – (2018-2019) - A native of The Plains, Ohio, a sleepy, rural enclave where he attended Athens High School, Burrow was named Mr. Football for the State of Ohio in 2014, and signed with Ohio State. At OSU Burrow redshirted and assumed a back-up role to starter J.T. Barrett; to his chagrin, for the next two seasons. It seemed his chance would never come. Burrow, the consummate competitor, undeterred, entered the transfer portal and landed at LSU before the 2018 season, where second-year Coach Ed Orgeron was looking for an offensive spark, a new offense, and a return to championship football. In unknown transfer Joe Burrow, Orgeron found both Messenger and Messiah, as Burrow's leadership example, skill and unprecedented

moxie revolutionized the struggling Tiger offense, making LSU champions and him a conference, college and Tiger football legend.

The son of a football coach and the youngest of three boys, Joe's two older brothers and his father played football at Nebraska, and his Dad coached in the college ranks for years. In 2018, Burrow was LSU's starting quarterback for 13 games, notching a 10-3 mark. He led the Tigers to five wins over Top 25 teams, including four ranked in the Top 10, and a gritty, come-from-behind victory over UCF in the Fiesta Bowl. He became the first player in LSU history to throw for 2,500 yards and rush for at least 350 yards in a season, completing 219-of-379 passes for 2,894 yards, 16 touchdowns and only five interceptions; he added another 399 rushing yards and seven touchdowns on 128 carries. 2019 proved even bigger for Burrow. No one imagined how big it would be.

Prior to the 2019 campaign, Coach Joe Brady, a former Saints analyst, was brought in to revamp the LSU offense from a traditional pro style to the elusive spread with Run-Pass-Option elements. Burrow, familiar with many of the concepts from his days at Athens High School, was like in everything else football-related—a quick study. The Tigers ripped through an early schedule that included top-ten Texas on the road and a revenge game against the Florida Gators in Baton Rouge. Sitting at 8-0, the Tigers traveled to Tuscaloosa to take on Alabama—the team that had beaten them an unconscionable seven straight times. In what many considered the first of many "Heisman Moments," Burrow led the Tigers to an improbable 46-41 victory over the Crimson Tide. The Tigers finished the season 12-0, winning the West and appearing in the SEC Championship Game in Atlanta, a game they won in convincing fashion over Georgia, with Joe named Offensive MVP. On December 14, 201,9 Joe Burrow was awarded the Heisman Trophy, making him the second LSU Tiger to win the game's most prestigious award. LSU, a #1 seed, played Oklahoma, a #4 seed, in the first round of the NCAA Football Playoff. The Tigers torched the Sooners 63-28, setting up a championship game with the undefeated Clemson Tigers, who had won 29 straight games. The teams met in New Orleans, Louisiana on January 13, 2019. Like he did all year, Burrow led the Tigers in victory, notching an unforgettable 42-25 win, and placing himself and his teammates prominently in the annals of college football history as one of its greatest, if not greatest, team. In addition to the coveted Heisman, Burrow won every accolade that could be bestowed upon him, including the Manning Award, the Davey O'Brien Award, the Maxwell, Walter Camp and a host of prestigious others. He was the first pick in the 2020 NFL Draft.

History:

LSU football began in 1893, under the direction of Dr. Charles E. Coates, a chemistry professor from Baltimore, Maryland. When Coates arrived in Baton Rouge in the early 1890's, he was surprised football had not been established. He issued a request for a football team in the fall of 1893. Coates remarked that "some mighty good-looking prospects" reported. Coates was assisted in his efforts by a young professor of entomology and zoology who had learned the game of Canadian rugby prior to coming to LSU. This young gentleman's name was Harcourt A. Morgan, who went on to become President of the University of Tennessee and a member of the first Board of Directors of the Tennessee Valley Authority. Dr. Coates drove nails into his players' shoes in order for them to have cleats during their inaugural season. The Tigers went 0-1 that first year, losing to eventual arch rival Tulane. By 1896, the Tiger football schedule had increased to six contests, with LSU winning all of them.

The first night game in Tiger Stadium was played in 1931. Night football increased the attendance at LSU games and allowed tailgating to become a day-long, anticipated event. Legend has it that the Tigers play better in Tiger Stadium at night than they do in the daylight. In the four decades from 1960 to 2000, LSU recorded a night time winning percentage in Tiger Stadium of over 80 percent.

LSU was the first school to have a female dancing squad to join their football team on the field and perform at halftime. The Golden Girls were overnight copied by all the universities in the SEC.

Traditions:

One of the most important traditions at LSU is when the Tiger Band arrives at the stadium after its normal tour through campus and lines up on the field just minutes before kickoff. The band, amidst a stirring drum roll, marches ceremoniously onto the gridiron, playing the fan favorite tune of "Hold that Tiger" and posting a four-corner salute to the fans already seated in the north, south, east, and west stadium sections. Among the pre-game activities is the tradition of the Tiger Golden Girls snapping their head to the right to face the flag at the end of the first line of the "Star Spangled Banner." When the pre-game preparations are completed, the crowd buzzes in anxious anticipation of the stadium announcer, Dan Borne,' saying, "It's Saturday night in Death Valley, and here come your LSU Tigers!" as the muscle-bound purple and gold Tigers pour out of the tunnel.

The Boot:

LSU and Arkansas play every year for a sectional trophy named "The Boot." The Boot is a 24-carat gold trophy in the shape of the states of Arkansas and Louisiana that forms a boot. This new tradition between the two Western Division schools began in 1996, in an attempt to stimulate competition. The shiny metal trophy always rests on the previous winner's sideline during the game since the victor of the yearly contest always earns ownership of the Boot, as well as bragging rights for the following year.

Chinese Bandits:

The term "Chinese Bandits" started when Coach Paul Dietzel recited a line from the old Terry and The Pirates comic strip which described Chinese Bandits as the "most vicious people in the world." During their prime, the Chinese Bandits were featured in Chinese masks for a layout in Life Magazine. In 1980, the LSU band revived the traditional practice of the Bandit tune being played when the LSU defense stops any opponent's drive. It persists today.

The Earthquake Game:

October 8, 1988, is known as the "Night the Tigers Moved the Earth." LSU struggled all night against a tough Auburn team. The visitors from the Plains had held the Tigers scoreless on the night, while Auburn had only managed two field goals. With just 1:41 left to play, on fourth and nine from the Auburn eleven, Tommy Hodson zeroed in with Eddie Fuller in the back of the end zone for a tying touchdown that catapulted LSU to a 7-6 victory. The play caused such an explosion from the rabid crowd of 79,341 that the tremor caused by the vibrations registered on a nearby campus seismograph in the LSU Geology Department. The seismograph recordings for the game revealed a large track of ink that registered at 9:32 p.m., at the exact moment of the winning touchdown by LSU. In May 1994, the memorable moment in Tiger football history was featured in a "Ripley's Believe It or Not!" segment circulated to newspapers throughout the world.

The Rag:

The Rag was the traditional item that was symbolic of victory in the LSU-Tulane rivalry for many years. A flag decorated partly in LSU's colors of purple and gold, and the other partly in the green and white of Tulane, it was customarily held for one full year by the wining school until the next game the following season. The whereabouts of the storied flag are unknown.

LSU Alma Mater

-Lloyd Funchess and Harris Downey
Where stately oaks and broad magnolias shade inspiring halls,
There stands our dear old Alma Mater to who us recalls
Fond memories that waken in our hearts a tender glow
And make us happy for the love that we have learned to know,
All praise to thee, our Alma Mater, molder of mankind,
May greater glory, love unending, be forever thine.
Our worth in life will be thy worth, we pray to keep it true
And may thy spirit live in us, forever LSU.

Hey Fightin' Tigers!

Hey! Fightin' Tigers! Fight all the way!
Hey! Fightin' Tigers! Win the game today!
You've got the know-how, you're doin' fine,
Hang on to the ball as you hit the wall
And smash right through the line.
You've got to go-o-o! For a touchdown, Ru-u-un! Up the score!
Make Mike the Tiger stand right up and roar. ROAR!!!!!!
So give it all of your might as you fight tonight,
And keep the goal in view-Vic-to-ry for LSU!

Hot Boudin & Cold Cush Cush!
"Hot Boudin! Cold cush cush! Come on Tigers! Push! Push! Push!"

This short, rather colloquial cheer is a favorite among Cajun Tiger fans. Boudin is a spicy Cajun delicacy resembling a sausage that is created by encasing ground pork, rice, and seasonings. Cush-cush is fried cornmeal mush served hot with syrup or in milk.

Noteworthy LSU Alumni

Elizabeth Ashley, actress with Evening Shade

James Carville, Political Consultant, Commentator

Edwin Washington Edwards, four-term governor

Kevin Griffin, Better Than Ezra lead

Steve Scalise, U.S. Congress, Republican Whip

Lolo Jones, U.S. Olympian, track athlete

Stephen E. Ambrose, "Band of Brothers" author, deceased

General Claire Chennault, Founder/Commander of the world renowned World War II "Flying Tigers," deceased

Bill Conti, Academy Award Winner, Composer/Conductor for The Right Stuff

Lod Cook, Retired Chairman and CEO of ARCO

Max Faget, NASA Engineering & Development Director

Carlos Roberto Flores, former President of Honduras

Hubert Humphrey, former Vice President of the United States (1964-1968), deceased

John J. Lejeune, WWI Marine Corps Commandant, Camp Laverne, NC

Russell Billiu Long, Former Senator, Chairman, U.S. Senate Finance Committee, deceased

General Troy Middleton, 8th Army Commander, held Bastogne, Battle of the Bulge

Shaquille O'Neal, NBA Star, Actor, Entertainer

Rex Reed, New York Author & Critic

D.M. Waghelstein, Operator, USMC Recon, USAF Pararescue, U.S. Special Operations, co-author "The Tiger Among Us"

James Andrews, M.D., Founder of the American Sports Medicine Institute

Alex McCool, Manager of the NASA Space Shuttle Projects Office in Huntsville, Alabama

Richard M. Weaver, Professor of English at the University of Chicago, Author of "Ideas Have Consequences"

Blaine Lourd, Founder & CEO, Lourd Capital, Beverly Hills, CA, Author of "Born on the Bayou"

2020 LSU Football Schedule

Sept. 5 UTSA

Sept. 12 Texas

Sept. 19 vs. Rice (Houston)

Sept. 26 Ole Miss

Oct. 3 Nicholls State

Oct. 10 at Florida

Oct. 17 at Arkansas

Oct. 24 Mississippi State

Oct. 31 OPEN DATE

Nov. 7 Alabama

Nov. 14 South Carolina

Nov. 21 at Auburn

Nov. 28 at Texas A&M

Mississippi State University

Amidst a rustic backdrop of the gentle, rolling, red-dirt and tall pine-tattered hills of north-central Mississippi rests Mississippi State University, home of the mighty Bulldogs. Mississippi State, in spite of its bucolic setting, has long enjoyed its place as a football school among its more urban SEC counterparts. Possessing a lively and resilient fan base, Starkville is a special place for football games where the Bulldog brethren can leave opponents' ears ringing with the near-deafening, continuous clanging of industrial-sized cowbells. Today, the Bulldogs are led by one of the league's more colorful characters, Mike Leach, who landed in Starkville via Washington State and Texas Tech. For each home football game, Mississippi State University's Scott Field transforms, to the delight of every Mississippi State football fan, and to the chagrin of every visiting opponent, into the dreaded "'Dawg Pound," where every foe is in for the fight of their life!

Founded: 1878

The university started as the Agricultural and Mechanical College of the State of Mississippi, a national land grant institution established after Congress passed the Morrill Act in 1862. The school was created by the Mississippi Legislature on February 28, 1878, to complete "...the mission of providing training in agriculture, horticulture, and the mechanical arts...without excluding other scientific and classical studies, including military tactics." The first students arrived in the fall of 1880 with General Stephen D. Lee as the first president of the college.

By 1932, the school was renamed the Mississippi State College, and later, in 1956, its name was changed to its present moniker, Mississippi State University. Today Mississippi State University is the second largest land grant institution and one of the top 100 Division 1-A research facilities in the country. The buildings and grounds of the University comprise over 4,200 acres including the campus, farms, pastures, and woodlands of the Mississippi Agricultural and Forestry Experiment Station.

Location: Starkville, Mississippi

Founded in 1831, the town of Starkville was initially referred to as "Boardtown" for its extensive sawmilling operations. Subsequent to its chartering in 1837, the town was renamed for Revolutionary War hero General John Stark. Starkville is the county seat of Oktibbeha County (pronounced ahk-TIB-a-ha). Oktibbeha is an Indian word meaning "bloody water" i.e., "maroon." Once known as the "Dairy Center of the South," Starkville's economic composition has evolved over the past several years into a diverse conglomeration of education, industry, service and retail trade. Starkville is located 125 miles northeast of the capital city of Jackson; 23 miles west of Columbus; and one hour south of Tupelo, Mississippi, the birthplace of "The King of Rock N' Roll," Elvis Aron Presley.

Population: 25,352

Student Enrollment: 21,622

Nickname: Bulldogs

As with many other institutions, Mississippi State's teams have answered to other nicknames through the years. Mississippi A&M's first football teams were referred to as "Aggies." The college first became Mississippi State College in 1932, and the nickname "Maroons," known for the club's uniform colors, gained acceptance. Bulldogs became the official title for State's teams in 1961; soon after the school was granted university status. References to school athletic teams as Bulldogs date back to the early twentieth century, as the moniker had been used interchangeably with both "Aggies" and "Maroons" since 1905.

Colors: Maroon and White

The origin of maroon and white dates to before the turn of the 20th century. On November 15, 1895, the first Mississippi State team was preparing for a road trip the following day to Jackson, Tennessee to play Southwest Baptist College, now Union University. Given every college was expected to have its own uniform colors, the student body at Mississippi State requested the team choose a suitable combination. Considering the selection an honor, the team deferred the decision to its captain, W.M. Matthews. Accounts report Matthews summoned maroon and white as the school's colors, which it has used since.

Mascot: English Bulldog

Mascot Name: Bully

The official mascot of Mississippi State is an American Kennel Registered English Bulldog given the inherited title of "Bully." Use of the bulldog as an official game mascot began in 1935, when Coach Major Ralph Sasse, on orders from his team, traveled to Memphis, Tennessee to acquire a bulldog. Sasse returned with Ptolemy, a gift of the Edgar Webster family. A littermate of Ptolemy became the first mascot named "Bully." Sadly, Bully was hit by a bus in 1939, ending his short career as MSU mascot. Days of campus mourning ensued, as Bully lay in a glass coffin for all to witness and pay their last respects. A half-mile funeral procession accompanied by the Famous Maroon Band and three ROTC battalions went to Scott Field where Bully was buried under the bench at the 50-yard line. The event was such a spectacle that Life Magazine covered it. Other Bullys have since been buried near campus dorms, fraternity houses, and the football stadium.

The current Bully, who has served since 2015, is "Bully XXI, Cristil's Golden Prince" or just "Jak." His care is entrusted to the professionals of MSU's College of Veterinary Medicine and students in the Pre-Veterinary Medical Club. There are three Bully student mascots, two students who receive a $500 per semester scholarship and an alternate Bully who is on standby if needed as a replacement. As a member of the MSU Spirit Group, Bully entertains the Bulldog faithful on football game days and at other sporting events.

Band: Famous Maroon Band

The oldest university band in the South, the Famous Maroon Band was first a military band when it was established in 1902, when Mississippi State was still a military college.

The name "Famous Maroon Band" was coined in the 1930's after an incident that led to the 40 members of the band being called the "Famous Forty." During an A&M vs. Alabama football game, the bands participated in a band contest with the winner taking home a trophy. Unbeknownst to the Alabama band, the A&M band had new, non-military themed uniforms. After the A&M band performed first, to thunderous applause, the Alabama band refused to play. The band still has the trophy on display in the band room and the forty members of the band were thenceforth nicknamed the "Famous Forty." Later, during the 1930's, a sportswriter referred to the band as the "Famous Maroon Band" and the moniker was born.

Director of Bands: Elva Kaye Lance (2002-present; first female director)

Stadium: Davis Wade Stadium at Scott Field

Built in 1914, Scott Field was named in honor of Don Macgruder Scott, an Olympic sprinter and one of the University's first football stalwarts (1915-1917). Scott competed in the 1920 Olympics in Antwerp, Belgium in the 800 meters.

The nation's second-oldest on-campus Division 1-A football stadium (Georgia Tech Bobby Dodd) has been refurbished and expanded four times during its history. Expansion occurred during 2001-2002 bringing the stadium capacity to 55,082. This significant project included fifty skyboxes, 7,000 upper deck seats, and 1,700 club-level seats. The $30 million building effort was funded largely by a generous donation made by the late Floyd Davis Wade, Sr. of Meridian, Mississippi. The stadium was named in his honor.

In 1986, an additional 9,000 seats were added to Scott Field's capacity. This construction project, which brought the stadium to a capacity of 40,656, was funded without the use of appropriated state funding. Earlier building efforts in 1936 and 1948 increased seating capacity to 35,000 seats. These projects provided the basic concrete grandstand structure. In the summer of 1997, a multi-million dollar Sony JumboTron was installed in the north end zone. Scott Field's playing surface is Prescription Athletic Turf ("PAT") and includes an underground drainage and irrigation system.

A $75 million expansion, finished in August 2014, increased capacity to 61,337, enabled new concessions and restrooms, and unveiled a new west side concourse. Part of the expansion included sealing the north end zone and installing a large HD video board, similar to the one in the south end zone which replaced the JumboTron that was installed in 1997.

The first Division 1-A football game played after 9/11/2001 was at Scott Field between the Mississippi State Bulldogs and the South Carolina Gamecocks. The game was broadcast by ESPN.

Stadium Capacity: 61,337

First Game:

On Thanksgiving Day, November 26, 1892, a group of faculty members at Mississippi A&M College met a select group of pupils for a game of the new sport known as "foot-ball." Football was brought to A&M by educators and graduates from the Eastern colleges. In the beginning, the game was played mainly by students. In 1885, A&M joined the Intercollegiate Athletic Association, signaling the beginning of competitive football for the Bulldogs.

During October 1895, W.M. Matthews organized a true college team and arranged a game at Southwestern Baptist University (Union University). Football made its inaugural debut when Matthews, a student from the state of Texas, organized and coached the Bulldogs during their first season. On November 16, 1895, the Bulldogs played in Jackson, Tennessee against Southwestern Baptist University. Disappointingly, the Bulldogs were welcomed to the ranks of college football with a resounding 21-0 defeat.

First Game in Stadium:

October 1914; MSU-54, Marion Military Institute-0

Directions:

Coming from the East on Mississippi Highway 12:

Continue past Mississippi Boulevard (MSU North Entrance Road).

Go under bridge and turn left onto Mississippi Highway 12.

Immediately exit onto Collegeview Street and make loop under bridge.

Go to first stop sign (Barr Avenue).

Stadium will be across the intersection.

Coming from the West on Mississippi Highway 12:

Exit onto Collegeview Street and turn right.

Go to first stop sign (Barr Avenue).

Stadium will be across the intersection.

Coming from the East or West on Mississippi Highway 82:

Mississippi Highway 82 intersects with Mississippi Highway 12 from either direction.

Follow directions stated above for Mississippi Highway 12.

Tailgating:

Tailgating activities are centered in "The Junction," a large grassy knoll area south of the stadium. Though named in honor of Starkville's railroad history, MSU alumni remember this area as "Malfunction Junction." Tailgating areas are available after 5:00 p.m. on the day before a weekend or holiday game, or five hours before the start of a game that occurs on a weekday. Garbage should be sealed in plastic bags and left for collection. MSU follows all local ordinances and state laws regarding alcohol. Charcoal grills are allowed, but your neighbors would prefer those that are battery operated. Only small weighted tents (12-by-12 feet maximum) may be erected in "The Junction." Areas must be cleared by 7:00 a.m. the day following the game.

The Bulldogs' football team and the Famous Maroon Band make their "Dawg Walk" through "The Junction" two hours prior to kickoff of each home game. The MSU cheerleaders and spirit squad also hold a pep rally in "The Junction" as part of pregame spirit activities.

Dining:

BIN 612 **–** Offers a unique dining experience through a variety of Italian dishes complemented by Southern American style. Dishes are delicious and well-prepared and served in a lively atmosphere with efficient service. Almost exclusively non-processed, food is served fresh. Great bar area and outside dining patio. 612 University Drive, Starkville 1.662.324.6126. West of stadium. Tuesday – Thursday; 11:00 a.m. – Midnight; Saturday; 3:00 p.m. – 1:00 a.m.

The Little Dooey **–** Considered by locals and alumni as the best barbecue in Oktibbeha County. Find out why the ESPN game day crew always eats here! 100 Fellowship Street, Starkville 1.662.323.6094. Monday – Saturday; 11:00 a.m. – 9:00 p.m.

Night Life:

Mugshots Grill & Bar **–** Laid back burger spot with salads, sandwiches and beers. 550 Russell Street, Starkville, MS 39759. Opens 11 a.m. 662.324.3965.

Accommodations:

Hotel Chester **–** Listed on the National Register of Historic Places. Located downtown within walking distance of restaurants and shops. Full made to order complimentary hot breakfast served each morning. Early reservations for game weekends strongly suggested. 101 North Jackson Street, Starkville 1.866.325.5005; 1.662.323.5005.

Nearest Hospital to Stadium:

Oktibbeha County Hospital

400 Hospital Road, Starkville, MS 39759

1.662.323.4320

Bail Bondsman for Emergencies:

A Bail Bonds Man

Starkville, MS

1.662.324.2020

Golf Course:

MSU Golf Club

1520 Old Hwy 82 E

Starkville, MS 39759

(662) 325-3028

Shopping:

Downtown Starkville boasts a variety of boutiques and specialty shops. Shopping centers include Cotton Crossing, Starkville Crossing and College Park.

Records:

All-Time Record: 569-585-39 (.493)

Division Championships: SEC Western Division 1998

SEC Championships: 1 (1941)

National Championships: 0

Bowl Record: 13-10 (.565)

1937 Orange Bowl, Miami, FL Duquesne-13, MSU-12

1941 Orange Bowl, Miami, FL MSU-14, Georgetown-7

1963 Liberty Bowl, Philadelphia, PA MSU-16, North Carolina State-12

1974 Sun Bowl, El Paso, TX MSU-26, North Carolina-24

1980 Sun Bowl, El Paso, TX Nebraska-31, MSU-17

1981 Hall of Fame Bowl, Birmingham, AL MSU-10, Kansas-0

1991 Liberty Bowl, Memphis, TN Air Force-38, MSU-15

1993 Peach Bowl, Atlanta, GA North Carolina-21, MSU-17

1995 Peach Bowl, Atlanta, GA North Carolina State-28, MSU-24

1999 Southwestern Bell Cotton Bowl Classic, Dallas, TX Texas-38, MSU-11

1999 Chick-fil-A Peach Bowl, Atlanta, GA MSU-17, Clemson-7

2000 Sanford Independence Bowl, Memphis, TN MSU-43, Texas A&M-41 (Overtime-"Snow Bowl 2000")

2007 AutoZone Liberty Bowl, Memphis, TN MSU-10, UCF-3

2010 Gator Bowl, Jacksonville, FL MSU-52, Michigan-14

2011 Music City Bowl, Nashville, TN MSU-23, Wake Forest-17

2013 Liberty Bowl, Memphis, TN MSU 44, Rice 7

2017 Tax Slayer Bowl, Jacksonville, FL MSU 31, Louisville 27

Radio Commentators:

For years Jack Cristil served as the unwavering "Voice of the Bulldogs," until his passing in 2014. Jim Ellis took over for the departed Cristil, calling football and basketball, and was replaced in 2017 by Neil Price, who allowed Ellis to concentrate on baseball.

MSU Bulldog Radio Broadcast Stations:

Listen to Bulldog games on 107.9 FM WFCA

Bulldog Greats:

Coaches:

Allyn McKeen – (1939-1948) – (65 wins-19 losses-3 ties) – (.764) - Coach McKeen led the Bulldogs to their first bowl victory in 1941, a 14-7 victory over Georgetown in the Orange Bowl. State finished ninth in the final Associated Press' poll that year. Subsequent to State's first bowl win, McKeen earned "SEC Coach of the Year" honors for the Bulldogs' 1940 season, leading them to a 10-0-1 overall record, 4-0-1 league record and their only SEC title. He died September 13, 1978 in Montgomery, Alabama.

Emory Bellard – (1979-1985) – (37 wins-42 losses) – (.468) - A graduate of Southwest Texas State, Coach Bellard is best remembered by State fans for leading the Bulldogs to one of its biggest victories in school history, a 6-3 defeat of #1 ranked Alabama in 1980, a game played in Memorial Stadium in the state's capital of Jackson, Mississippi. State finished 9-3 and ranked 19th nationally in 1980. Under Bellard's direction, State returned in 1981 to go

6-1 versus ranked opponents and climbed to a lofty #7 ranking in the polls, its highest ranking in school history at the time. He died February 10, 2011 in Georgetown, Texas.

Jackie Sherrill **–** (1991-2003) – (75 wins-75 losses-2 ties) – (.500) - Hired December 9, 1990, Sherrill, a protégé of SEC coaching legend, Paul "Bear" Bryant, coached at Washington State (1976), Pittsburgh (1977-1981), and Texas A&M (1982-1988) prior to his arrival in Starkville. A native of Duncan, Oklahoma, Sherrill mentored coaches Jimmy Johnson and Dave Wannstedt, among others. On October 1, 1992, Sherrill's Bulldogs handed Florida's Steve Spurrier one of his worst SEC losses before the largest home-opening crowd in Scott Field's history, 33,886 spectators--a record which has since been shattered. The 24th ranked Bulldogs humbled the 13th ranked Gators 30-6. On November 16, 1996, MSU defeated eighth-ranked Alabama 17-16 in Starkville for the Bulldogs first home victory over the Crimson Tide. Sherrill's 1998 team won the SEC Western Division Championship.

In 1999, Sherrill's Bulldogs finished 10-2 after defeating Clemson 17-7 in the Peach Bowl in Atlanta. In 2000, Sherrill led his team to an 8-4 record and a dramatic 43-41 win against his former Texas A&M team in the Independence Bowl (the "Snow Bowl"). In 13 seasons at MSU, seven at Texas A&M, five at Pittsburgh, and the lone year at Washington State, Sherrill compiled a 180-120-4 (.600) record. At the time of his retirement at the end of the 2003 season, Sherrill was fourth among active Division 1-A coaches in wins behind Joe Paterno, Bobby Bowden, and Lou Holtz. Sherrill was replaced in December 2003, by Sylvester Croom, the SEC's first black head football coach. He is a studio analyst for FOX Sports.

Dan Mullen **–** (2009 – 2017) – (69-46) – (.608) – Mullen served as one of Mississippi State's better and longer-lived head coaches, lasting nine years in Starkville and winning over 60 percent of his games while proving to be a capable program manager. He attended Ursinus College in Collegeville, Pennsylvania, lettering two years at tight end. He graduated in 1994 with a Bachelor's Degree in Exercise and Sport Science and went to Wagner College, where he coached wide receivers and earned a Master's Degree in Education in 1996. Before State, Mullen served as offensive coordinator at the University of Florida and served earlier alongside Urban Meyer at Utah, where he was quarterback coach of the Utes during their undefeated 2004 season. During that stint he developed quarterback Alex Smith into the number one overall pick in the 2005 NFL Draft. In his first season at Mississippi State in

2009, his team went 5–7 against one of the toughest schedules in the nation. In 2010, his Bulldog team went 9–4 overall and 4–4 in the SEC, including victories over Georgia, Florida, Kentucky, and Mississippi; and the four losses came to top-12 ranked teams. Mississippi State capped off the 2010 season by defeating traditional power Michigan in the 2011 Gator Bowl 52–14, and achieved a #15 ranking in the final AP poll. In 2011, Mullen's Bulldogs went 7-6, followed by a 2012 showing of 8-5. His 2014 team finished 10-3 and second in the SEC West. !n 2017, after an 8-4 season, he left for Gainesville, where he was named head coach of the Florida Gators.

Mike Leach – (2020-present) – (.000) – A native of Susanville, California, Leach played tight end two years at Cody High School for legendary head coach John McDougall, winning a state championship. Leach did not play college football. Instead, he attended BYU and graduated with honors, and later Pepperdine, where earned a Juris Doctorate. Known for his disarming sense of humor, an open penchant for pirates, and for designing prodigious offenses, Leach's hire was a breath of fresh air in Starkville. Leach is a good coaching instructor, evidenced by the list of respected coaches who have flourished in his ranks.

Considered an offensive guru, he is known for winning most of the games he's supposed to; and for pulling the occasional upset. He has had mixed results at a couple of less than premier stops. Leach's spread offense relies on an accurate passer and he has coached successful quarterbacks--like Kentucky's Tim Couch, into a No. 1 NFL draft pick. Leach was named the 1996 Division II Offensive Coordinator of the Year by American Football Quarterly magazine, for helping Hal Mumme lead Valdosta State to a 40-17-1 record. Before Valdosta, Leach and Mumme met at Iowa Wesleyan College in 1989. From 1989 to 1991 Leach served as offensive coordinator and line coach for an offense that led the NAIA in passing yardage one season and finished second the other two. Iowa Wesleyan quarterbacks passed for more than 11,000 yards in Leach's three seasons and broke 26 national records. Before Mumme, Leach made coaching stops at Cal Poly-San Luis Obispo in 1987, College of the Desert in 1988 and in Pori, Finland, where he served as a head

coach in the European Football League in 1989. Leach cut his teeth at Valdosta State and Kentucky, where he was offensive coordinator under cohort Hal Mumme. Under Mumme he pioneered his patented "Air Raid" system and broke 42 SEC and 116 Kentucky offensive records. He later coached at Oklahoma under head coach Bob Stoops, and at Texas Tech, where he became head coach in 2000, and was named the 2008 Big 12 Coach of the Year, prior to his departure in 2009, with an 84-43 record. At Washington State, from 2012-2019, Leach went 55-47, his best year coming in 2018, when he went 11-2 and beat Iowa State in the Alamo Bowl. As a head coach, Leach took 16 of his 18 teams to bowl games, winning seven. His overall head coaching record with Texas Tech & Washington State is 139-90. He made a cameo appearance on the fourth season of the TV show "Friday Night Lights," posing as a loon at a gas station who implores to high school coach Eric Taylor to "swing your sword" and "find your inner pirate." The holder of a master's degree in coaching from the United States Sports Academy, he sleeps with a Viking axe at his bedside. He is undefeated in Starkville.

Players:

Jackie Parker **–** (1952-1953) – A versatile quarterback considered by many of the Bulldog faithful to be the most valuable athlete to wear the maroon and white. Parker still holds many MSU records including the only Bulldog to throw for a 100 percent completion rate in a game, 9-for-9 against Ole Miss in 1953. He holds State's scoring record in a season with 120 points in 1952. In 1952 and 1953, he was named the SEC's Most Valuable Player by the Nashville Banner. Parker was an outstanding professional football player in the Canadian Football League and was named to the CFL Hall of Fame in 1971. He became a member of the "College Football Hall of Fame" in 1976. Parker died of cancer in November 2006 in Edmonton, Canada at the age of 74.

Dwight Douglas "D.D." Lewis **–** (1965-1967) – A native of Knoxville, Tennessee and youngest of 14 children, overlooked by his hometown Tennessee Vols, D.D. became the leading tackler on Bulldog teams that were unproductive in the wins column during his career. As a linebacker, D.D. was a two-time All-SEC player and named an All-American after his senior year. Drafted by the Dallas Cowboys in 1968, he was a durable, consistent tackler and team leader for the Cowboys, appearing in five Super Bowls. In 2001, D.D. was inducted into the College Football Hall of Fame.

David Smith **–** (1968-1970) – Smith finished his career as MSU's All-Time Leading Receiver with 162 career catches and a total of 2,168 receiving yards. He played in 29 games for an average of 5.6 catches-per-game. Smith set State's all-time single-game receiving mark on October 17, 1970, with a 215-

yard performance with twelve catches and two touchdowns versus Texas Tech in Jackson's Memorial Stadium. Smith's marks were impressive as he only played for three seasons. His 14 catches against Ole Miss in 1969 was a record that stood until 1995 (Eric Moulds).

Walter Packer – (1973-1976) – On completion of his Bulldog career, the Leakesville, Mississippi native was MSU's all-time career rushing yardage leader with 2,820 yards. Packer played in 42 games, averaging 5.8 yards-per-carry. The Bulldogs won 28 games in four years while he was in Starkville. He was selected by his fellow students as Mr. Mississippi State University in 1975. In 1977, he was an 8th round draft choice of the Atlanta Falcons.

Johnie Cooks – (1977-1981) – A Leland, Mississippi native, Cooks was an All-American linebacker for the 'Dawgs in 1981. He was a first team All-SEC player in 1980 and 1981. In 1981, Cooks was named the Birmingham Touchdown Club's Most Valuable Player and the United Press International's SEC Defensive Player of the Year. The Baltimore Colts selected Cooks with the number two pick in round one of the 1982 NFL draft. Following his college career, the MSU Hall of Fame and the Mississippi Sports Hall of Fame member spent six years with the Baltimore Colts and three seasons with the New York Giants, helping them win a Super Bowl in 1990, before finishing with the Cleveland Browns in 1991.

Kent Hull – (1979-1982) – The Pontotoc, Mississippi native was one of the finest offensive linemen to wear a Bulldog uniform. Hull earned four football letters playing center during his Bulldog career. He was an All-SEC performer who went on to star with the Buffalo Bills as one of the most durable linemen in NFL history. Hull played in 121 straight games at center for the Bills where he was a four-time All-Pro, played in four consecutive Super Bowls, and made three Pro Bowl appearances. He is the only Bulldog to play in the Super Bowl and the Pro Bowl. He died October 18, 2011 in Greenwood, Mississippi. He was 50.

Don Smith – (1983-1986) – A Hamilton, Mississippi native, Smith is State's all-time total offensive yardage leader with 7,097 total yards, playing quarterback for the Bulldogs in 39 games for a 182 yards-per-game average. Smith was selected as the Most Valuable Player in the 1987 Senior Bowl in Mobile, Alabama, the second MSU Bulldog to win the award. He was the 51st overall pick in the second round of the 1987 NFL Draft. He played for two years with Tampa Bay, a year with Buffalo and a year with Miami in 1991. He caught a career high 21 passes for 225 yards in 1990, while also returning 32 kickoffs for 643 yards. He scored the Bill's first touchdown in Super Bowl history in Super Bowl XXV for the Bills in what was the final carry of his career.

Eric Moulds – (1993-1995) – A Lucedale, Mississippi native, Moulds was known as an explosive open field runner with reliable hands and excellent concentration, enabling him to make difficult and aerobatic catches in heavy traffic. He ranks third on the school's career receiving list with 118 catches for 2,022 yards. Mould's 17.1 yard average-per-catch ranks sixth on State's all-time receiving list. He started 23 of 31 games and holds the MSU record for the most catches in a game–15 for 183 yards against Tennessee in 1995. Moulds was the 1994 Division 1-A kickoff return champion with a 32.8 yards-per-return average. Drafted 24th overall in the first round by the Buffalo Bills in the 1996 NFL draft, Moulds led AFC receivers with 1,368 receiving yards in 1998. He played 12 seasons in the NFL before retiring in 2007.

Fred Smoot – (1999-2000) – A Jackson, Mississippi native, Smoot was a standout, silky smooth cornerback for the Bulldogs who possessed cover skills. Smoot was selected as an All-SEC player both of his years as a Bulldog. He is considered one of the most colorful characters to wear a Bulldog uniform. A walking quotation book, Smoot provided Bulldog and SEC fans a steady dose of witty, insightful commentary on his website, www.Smootsmack.com. Smoot once said, "Three fourths of the world is covered by water and the rest is covered by Smoot!" The two-year starter for the Bulldogs was an All-American junior college transfer from Hinds Community College. Smoot recorded ten interceptions for the 'Dawgs. He was a second round draft pick of the Washington Redskins during the 2001 NFL draft.

Jerious Norwood – (2002-2005) – Born July 29, 1983 in Jackson, Mississippi, the speedy Norwood graduated from Brandon High School in Brandon, Mississippi. The 2005 "Conerly Trophy" winner—an award granted to the state of Mississippi's best college football player—Norwood finished his Bulldog career its leading rusher in school history with 3,222 yards. His best performance was his 180-yard rushing performance against the Florida Gators during his junior year in 2004. The Bulldogs won in dramatic fashion that day, capped by a 37-yard run by Norwood to seal the victory with 32 seconds remaining. Jerious was the only Bulldog to gain more than 200 yards in three different games.

Josh Robinson **–** (2011-2014) – Robinson is revered as one of State's greatest running backs during a resurgent time for the gridiron Bulldogs. A native of Bogalusa, Louisiana, the diminutive 5-8 Robinson made up for his lack of height with bullish power, speed and quickness—which always made him difficult to tackle. Robinson teamed with talented quarterback Dak Prescott, forming a formidable duo that was difficult for defenses to stop. After redshirting his first year Robinson appeared in 12 games as a sophomore, rushing 55 times for 335 yards. The next year he added 78 carries for 459 yards, setting things up for a breakout junior year. That year—2014—turned out to be one of State's best in many seasons, and Robinson helped paved the way to the team's success with 1,203 yards rushing on 73 carries, including a 197-yard effort against LSU and a 198-yard strike against Kentucky. He was drafted 205th overall by the Indianapolis Colts in the sixth round of the 2015 NFL Draft.

Dak Prescott **-** (2011-2014) - Prescott is remembered as one of State's and the league's greatest dual threat quarterbacks. A native of Sulphur, Louisiana where he attended Haughton High School, Prescott redshirted and played sparingly in 2012 as a backup to Tyler Rusell. In 2013, Russell experienced a concussion early in the season and thereafter Prescott was the signal caller. In 11 games he completed 156 of 267 passes for 1,940 yards with ten touchdowns. During his senior season Prescott led the Bulldogs to a memorable 10-2 record, its first #1 ranking in school history and to the Orange Bowl. His 3,449 yards passing during his senior season is a Mississippi State record. His 107 total touchdowns placed him fourth in SEC history in that category, and he finished third overall in total yards. He holds 38 separate Bulldog records. After his senior season he was awarded the Connerly Trophy and was drafted 135th in the fourth round of the 2016 NFL Draft by the Dallas Cowboys. At the completion of the 2016 NFL season he was named NFL Rookie of the Year.

Jeffery Simmons – (2016-2018) - The Lasalle Parish, Louisiana native played at Noxubee County High School where he was highly recruited as a five-star talent. In his three seasons in Starkville Simmons forged a surly reputation as a serious run-stopper with potential big play ability. As a freshman he logged 40 tackles with three for loss. As a sophomore, he added 60 more with 12 for loss and five sacks. As a junior, Simmons' name was a feared commodity, and it helped him notch 63 total tackles with 18 for losses with two sacks. He was drafted 19th overall by the Tennessee Titans in the 2019 NFL Draft, despite tearing his ACL while training for the combine. He made his NFL debut in week 7 against the Los Angeles Rams, recording four tackles and a sack in the 23-20 win.

Traditions:

Cowbells:

The most noteworthy symbol of Mississippi State University is the infamous cowbell. Despite years of repeated attempts to banish their use on game days, diehard Bulldog fans still loudly cheer on their 'Dawgs with the distinctive, ringing sound of industrial-sized cowbells. This practice continues despite the fact that a 1974 SEC rule outlaws the practice at all games. Bulldog cowbells are especially noisy against non-conference opponents.

The origin of the cowbell as a fixture of Mississippi State sports tradition remains nebulous. The best records have cowbells gradually introduced to the MSU sports scene during the late 1930's and early 1940's, coinciding with the Mississippi State Football's Golden Age.

The most popular legend is that during a home football game between State and arch-rival Mississippi, a jersey cow haplessly wandered onto the playing field. Mississippi State whipped the Rebels that Saturday, and State College students adopted the cow as a good luck charm. Students continued bringing a cow to football games for a while, until the practice was discontinued in favor of bringing just the cow's bell.

Whatever the origin, it is certain that by the 1950's cowbells were common at Mississippi State games, and by the 1960's were established as the special symbol of Mississippi State. The cowbell's popularity grew most during the long years when State football teams were rarely successful. Flaunting this anachronism from the 'Aggie' days was a proud response by students and alumni to outsider scorn of the university's "cow college" history.

In the 1960's two State professors, Earl W. Terrell and Ralph L. Reeves, obliged some students by welding handles on the bells so that they could be rung with convenience and authority. By 1963, the demand for these long-handled cowbells could not be filled by home workshops alone, so at the suggestion of Reeves, the Student Association bought bells in bulk and the Industrial Education Club agreed to weld the handles. In 1964, the MSU Bookstore began marketing these cowbells with a portion of the profits returning to these student organizations. The cowbells can still be purchased today at the MSU Bookstore.

'Dog Walk:

The Bulldogs' football team and the Famous Maroon Band make their "Dog Walk" through "The Junction" two hours prior to kickoff of each home football game. The Bulldogs are greeted by thousands of fans clanging their cowbells and cheering on the Dogs as they proceed to the stadium.

The "Egg Bowl:" Since Thanksgiving Day in 1927, Mississippi State and its long-time, in-state archrival, Ole Miss, have played what amounts to the "Egg Bowl" in the Magnolia State. According to William George Barner III, who wrote a book titled Mississippi Mayhem chronicling the boisterous beginnings of the "Egg Bowl," the rivalry has a great story behind it.

The 1927 inaugural "Golden Egg" game was proposed by members of Sigma Iota, an Ole Miss honorary society, in an effort to temper the 1926 post-game exploits of some of the overzealous and unruly fans involved on both sides. The game in 1926 saw a series that had been dominated by Mississippi State; the Bulldogs had won 18 of the last 23 contests.

Ole Miss won a hard-fought 7-6 contest that fateful day. After, a throng of Ole Miss fans banded together on the west side and rushed triumphantly onto the field toward the object of their destructive desire, the goal posts, while Mississippi State "Aggie" supporters on that side of the field stood calmly and sang their alma mater. However, on the east side, matters were not as stable, and cooler heads did not prevail, as many of the disgruntled Mississippi State fans brandished cane bottom chairs raised high over their heads and sought after the Rebel revelers hell-bent on tearing down their goal posts. Many fights ensued.

As described in an article by the Memphis Commercial Appeal by Ben Hilbun, who later became President of the Starkville campus, "The phantom of victory, that for thirteen years eluded Ole Miss, returned to the bearded Berserkers...and they won over A&M, their traditional rivals, 7-6." "Ole Miss students fought for the goal posts," he added, "but were restrained." The Mississippian, Ole Miss' student newspaper, replied that the Aggie chair brigade who defended their goal posts "came to the field with malice afterthought...with the intent of staging a 'free for all'..."

Ole Miss and Mississippi State students, shocked by injuries to spectators, vowed that it should never happen again. The resulting agreement between the two student bodies was the "Golden Egg," a trophy that would cool the heated battle between the two bitter in-state rivals. Because the trophy was shaped in the likeness of the more standard, rounded, ball of the day, it came to be called the "Golden Egg."

That initial meeting of the two schools in 1927 for the "Golden Egg" ended in a 20-12 victory for Ole Miss. However, unlike the previous year's contest, the game ended with a much dignified ceremony celebrating the participants and the winners. As agreed upon prior, the schools sang their alma maters. Ole Miss, the victor, sang first, followed by State. After the serenading was complete, the two team captains, the presidents of the two student bodies, and the leaders of the two schools met at the 50-yard line. There, B.M. Walker, President of Mississippi State, presented the first "Golden Egg" trophy to Ole Miss Captain Applewhite. Applewhite was then carried off the field by a score of students.

Today, the "Golden Egg" remains one of the most treasured prizes of either school. Symbolizing the football supremacy in the State of Mississippi, the trophy is engraved annually with the score of each preceding year's game. It rests in a place of great honor at both schools. During the years in which there was a tie, the trophy would return to the previous winner's school for the first half of the year and then it would go to the other school for display.

Fight Song:

"Hail State"

Words and music by Joseph Burleson Peavey, 1939

Hail dear 'ole State!
Fight for that victory today;
Hit that line and 'tote that ball;
Cross the goal before you fall,
And then we'll yell, yell, yell, yell!
For dear 'ole State we'll yell like hell!
Fight for Mis-sis-sip-pi State,
Win that game today!

Alma Mater:

"Maroon and White"
Words by T. Paul Haney, Jr.
Music by Henry E. Wamsley

In the heart of Mississippi,
Made by none but God's own hands,
Stately in her nat'ral splendor
Our Alma Mater proudly stands;
State College of Mississippi,
Fondest mem'ries cling to thee,
Life shall hoard thy spirit ever,
Loyal sons we'll always be.

Chorus:
Maroon and White! Maroon and White!
Of thee with joy we sing;
Thy colors bright our souls delight,
With praise our voices ring.

Tho' our life some pow'r may vanquish,
Loyalty can't be o'er run;
Honors true on thee we lavish
Until the setting of the sun;
Live Maroon and White for ever,
Ne'er can evil mar thy fame,
Nothing us from thee can sever,
Alma Mater we acclaim.

Noteworthy Mississippi State Alumni:

Marsha Wedgeworth Blackburn, United States House of Representatives, Tennessee's 7th District

Eugene Butler, publisher and founder of The Progressive Farmer, forerunner of Southern Living

Fred Carl Jr., founder, President, and CEO of Viking Range Corporation, Greenwood, Mississippi

John Grisham, novelist, retired attorney, avid MSU baseball fan

Toxey Haas, founder and CEO of Mossy Oak, West Point, Mississippi

Hunter Henry, former CEO, Dow Chemical

E.B. McCool, one of the founders of the Holiday Inn hotel franchise

G.V. "Sonny" Montgomery, United States Congressman (Montgomery G.I. Bill, 1984)

Hartley Peavey, founder and owner of Peavey Electronics, Meridian, Mississippi

Janet Marie Smith, former president of Turner Sports and Entertainment Development

John C. Stennis, former United States Senator, (deceased)

Brad Watson, author, 2002 National Book Award finalist

Cynthia Cooper, Worldcom whistleblower, 2002 "Time Magazine Person of the Year"

Troy H. Middleton, World War II Corps Commander and LSU President

G.V. "Sonny" Montgomery, former U.S. Representative and author of the Montgomery G.I. Bill

Amy Tuck, Mississippi Lieutenant Governor

Ronnie Parker, Pizza Inn Founder

Jerry Clower, Comedian (deceased)

2020 Mississippi State Football Schedule

Sept. 5 New Mexico

Sept. 12 at North Carolina State

Sept. 19 Arkansas

Sept. 26 Tulane

Oct. 3 Texas A&M

Oct. 10 OPEN DATE

Oct. 17 at Alabama

Oct. 24 at LSU

Oct. 31 Auburn

Nov. 7 Missouri

Nov. 14 at Kentucky

Nov. 21 Alabama A&M

Nov. 26 at Ole Miss

The University of Mississippi "Ole Miss"

Distinctively Southern in its flair for good food, beautiful coeds, and hospitality, Oxford holds a special place among its urban counterparts in the SEC. A college town containing the quiet seclusion of any small Southern town, Oxford is where people from all walks of life come to gain enlightenment and education at the University of Mississippi. Affectionately known by family as, "Ole Miss," the University of Mississippi is the quintessential Southern college experience, and one of the last great vestiges of the Deep South. The tradition of SEC football runs deep at the University of Mississippi. Like so many of its SEC brethren, Ole Miss has too enjoyed its reign at the top of the national polls. Legendary Coach Johnny Vaught led Ole Miss to the 1960 National Championship, whetting the appetite of the Rebel football fan base like never before. Since that magical time in the days of Rebel lore, Ole Miss has represented the SEC as one of the nation's finer football programs. Under first-year Head Coach Lane Kiffin, the Ole Miss faithful are hopeful of a post-modern return to gridiron glory in the nation's toughest sub-conference, the SEC Western Division.

Founded: 1844

The University of Mississippi was chartered February 24, 1844. It began educating 80 students in Oxford four years later, in 1848. For 23 years (1848-1871) Ole Miss was the state of Mississippi's only public higher institution of learning. Mississippi's flagship university during that period, Ole Miss established the fourth state-supported law school in the nation in 1854, and was one of the first schools in the United States to offer an engineering degree, also in 1854. Additionally, Ole Miss was one of the first schools in the South to admit women (1882) and the first school to hire a female faculty member (1885).

"Ole Miss"

The University of Mississippi gained its famous nickname over a hundred years ago, in 1896, when it was selected in a student contest held to designate the name of the new student yearbook. The term "Ole Miss" was recommended by Miss Elma Meek, an Oxford native. The name "Ole Miss" became an ingrained aspect of the institution and today remains a treasured note of the University's rich and storied history.

Nickname: Rebels

The name "Rebels" as Ole Miss' official athletic moniker first began in 1936. Submitted by Judge Ben Guider of Vicksburg, it was one of five entries submitted to various Southern sportswriters for a final selection from among over two hundred suggestions. The promotion was sponsored by the student newspaper at the time, The Mississippian. The sportswriters chose the nickname of "Rebels" by a vote of 18-3. The late Judge William Hemingway of the University Athletic community commemorated the event with the statement: "If 18 sportswriters wish to use Rebels, I shall not rebel, so let it go Ole Miss Rebels."

The late Frank E. Everett, Jr., B.A. 1932, LLB 1934, described the meaning of "Ole Miss" best when he wrote: "There is a valid distinction between The University and Ole Miss, even though the separate threads are closely interwoven. The University is buildings, trees, and people. Ole Miss is mood, emotion, and personality. One is physical, and the other is spiritual. One is tangible, and the other intangible. The University is respected, but Ole Miss is loved. The University gives a diploma and regretfully terminates tenure, but one never graduates from Ole Miss."

Location: Oxford

Nestled among the rolling hills of northern Mississippi the sleepy little town of Oxford thrives. Once home to author William Faulkner, the historical ties to this old Southern enclave are as strong as the boughs of the hundred year-old magnolias that drape its rhythmical, undulating landscape. John Grisham, another author, lives much of the year near Oxford, although he is a graduate of Mississippi State.

Population: 19,393

Enrollment: 23,639

Colors: Cardinal and Navy (Red and Blue)

In 1893, when Ole Miss' original football team was preparing for a five game season, Dr. A. Bondurant, organizer, manager, and coach, later recalled: "The team had much discussion as to the colors that should be adopted, but it was finally suggested by the manager that the union of the crimson of Harvard and the navy blue of Yale would be harmonious, and that it was well to have the spirit of both of these good colleges." And hence, the red and blue were adopted by the university as its official colors.

Old Mascot name: Colonel Rebel

An ephemeral source of modern social contention and public consciousness, the likeness of "Colonel Reb" first appeared in the Ole Miss Yearbook in 1938, as the leading illustration in the publication referred to as "The Rebel Number." Due to incessant pressure from social justice warriors and political correctness, in 2003, the University of Mississippi banned Colonel Reb and his likeness from appearing inside Vaught-Hemingway Stadium. Chancellor Rober Khayat asserted that Colonel Reb was related to "nothing that Ole Miss does," and therefore, had no place inside the university setting. This abrupt change was met without fanfare. To the contrary, fans accustomed to the mascot were enraged.

For years the Old South vestige, "Colonel Rebel" represented Ole Miss as the quintessential caricature of the old Southern gentleman. Today, he remains "officially dead" according to the university, but nevertheless his likeness can be found on aging fan apparel and merchandise. Colonel Reb is a distinguished-looking chap with a bushy white moustache and beard. His ensemble includes a tailed suit with an old-fashioned ribbon tie, flowered lapel, cane and two-gallon hat. Subsequent to his jettisoning, a brief campaign to choose a new mascot was held. Nevertheless, this initial movement proved to be fruitless, as few alumni and fans could bear the thought of losing their longtime visual identity.

New Mascot: The Rebel Black Bear

In 2010, Ole Miss students voted and chose a new mascot. The special election did not allow the option of renaming Colonel Reb as the official mascot, even though the anachronism still held support among the rank and file student population. The voting selections were reduced to 11 candidates: Hotty and Toddy, a black bear, a blues musician, a cardinal, a "fan-atic," a horse, a land shark, a lion, the Mojo, a riverboat pilot, and a titan. The committee polled Ole Miss students, faculty, staff, alumni, and season ticket holders about three finalist mascots: Rebel, The Black Bear, based on the legend that Theodore "Teddy Bear" Roosevelt refused to shoot a bound black bear in Mississippi; the Rebel Land Shark; and Hotty Toddy, from a popular cheer. The committee selected Rebel, The Black Bear, as the new on-field mascot. The University of Mississippi reclassified the Colonel Reb trademark as historical, yet still retains ownership. In October 2017, Ole Miss Chancellor Jeffrey Vitter announced another mascot change—"The Landshark," although the university acknowledged it will still be known as the Rebels. The change was verified by a student vote resulting in 81 percent support for the new moniker. The term Landshark originated in 2008, and was adopted by the football team's defensive unit. Since, Ole Miss athletes have celebrated big plays by putting a hand to their forehead, imitating a shark's protruding dorsal fin. The new mascot, the Landshark, was unveiled in 2018.

Stadium: Vaught-Hemingway

Located on the southeast section of the Ole Miss campus, historic Vaught-Hemingway is home to the Rebel football team. The Stadium, known in its beginnings as Hemingway Stadium, was erected in 1915, when students of the University of Mississippi pitched in to help build the grandstand at its present site. The effort to build the stadium was a federally-funded project lasting three years. Stadium capacity after the initial construction was listed as 24,000, an impressive figure for the day. In 1950, the stadium was expanded with the addition of an 80-yard long press box. In 1970, Astroturf was added.

1971 saw the insertion of custom blue fiber glass seating to the west side stands. The east side received a similar seating upgrade in 1973. Aluminum bench bleachers were added to the end zones in 1980 to bring the stadium's capacity to 41,000. During the summer of 1984, the Astroturf was removed from the field and was replaced with Prescription Athletic Turf. The summer of 1998 saw another major facelift for Vaught-Hemingway Stadium. A new press box was constructed along with new aluminum sideline seating, restrooms and concession stands, in addition to a new club level seating section for 700 people.

Further renovations continued in the summer of 1990, when lights were added to the stadium. Later for the start of the 1997 season, a Sony Jumbotron screen and a scoreboard/message center was added. Construction on the east side of the stadium was completed prior to the 1998 football season, which included a Rebel Club seating section with an enclosed lounge area. In 2002, construction replaced the south end zone bleachers with a rounded bowl, adding luxury boxes and covered club seating in an upper deck, as well as new general admission seating for students and season ticket holders; these renovations expanded seating by nearly 10,000, giving Vaught-Hemingway an improved capacity of 60,580. In August 2011, the school announced Forward Together, a new capital campaign that would seek to build a new basketball arena and expand the stadium. Phase 1 of the campaign added 30 luxury suites and 770 club level seats. New stadium lights, a sound system, and 2 new video boards were added. Stadium capacity was increased, accomplished by closing the north end zone.

In 2012, Ole Miss announced the start a new tradition, a bell tower in the north end zone that rings before kickoff to let fans know the game is starting; and after an Ole Miss victory. The most recent stadium expansion, finished in 2016, completed the stadium's bowl shape and added 3,458 additional seats. This brought the stadium's capacity to 60,580, making Vaught-Hemmingway the largest stadium in the State of Mississippi.

The stadium's name honors two great University of Mississippi men. Judge William Hemingway (1869-1937) was a professor of law and a long-time chairman of the University's Committee on Athletics. The football stadium bore his name until October 16, 1982, when John Howard Vaught saw his namesake juxtaposed with Hemingway's, and the stadium was officially renamed Vaught-Hemingway Stadium. As head football coach at Ole Miss, Vaught posted an overall record of 190-61-11, and led the Rebels to their only fully-recognized National Championship, in 1960.

Stadium Capacity: 60,580

Band: "Pride of the South"

The University of Mississippi Band, or "Pride of the South," has provided outstanding performances in concert and in support of Ole Miss athletic events since its organization in 1928. Outside the Marching Band there are several "Pep Bands" formed from members of the "The Pride of the South." These pep bands perform for numerous functions, like pep rallies, before each home game. Another extension of the Ole Miss Band is the Ole Miss Basketball band. The basketball band supports the Rebel and Lady Rebel Basketball teams at all home games after football season, as well as traveling to the SEC and NCAA tournaments. The Ole Miss Band comprises students from many diverse courses of study.

Band Director: David Wilson, 28 years of service to the University

First Game: November 11, 1893

Ole Miss 56, Southwest Baptist University of Jackson, Tennessee 0

History:

Ole Miss began playing football in 1893, completing a five-game schedule with four wins and a loss, with the first three victories coming by shutout. Dr. Alexander Bondurant, a Latin professor and proponent of athletic competition at the collegiate level, organized the first Rebel football squad and the first athletic association. Bondurant served at Ole Miss for years as manager of the football team. According to James "Bobo" Champion, during the fall of 1893, Ole Miss' first year playing football, the University Magazine wrote: "The athletic fever has now taken full possession of the University...and the time is already here when in order to rank high in college or society, one must join the running crowd and play on the football team."

First Game in Stadium:

October 1, 1915 Arkansas Aggies 10, Ole Miss 0

Directions:

Coming from East or West: Take Highway 6 and head north on Old Taylor Road. Head north until you reach University Avenue. Turn left and go over bridge. Entry to campus is also available on Coliseum Drive. Head north until you reach fraternity row. Turn right on fraternity row.

Coming from the North or the South: Take I-55 to Batesville, then take Highway 6 to either Coliseum Drive or Taylor Road. Also, from the North or South, take Highway 7 to Highway 6. Take Highway 6 to either Coliseum Drive or Old Taylor Road.

Accommodations:

Downtown Oxford Inn & Suites **–** Only a stone's throw from the picturesque Courthouse Square, this refurbished hotel is in the heart of downtown Oxford and a short stroll from the university. The hotel features regular rooms or suites ranging in price. 662.234.3031.

Dining:

Ajax Diner **-** Soulful grub and drinks in a funky, casual atmosphere in the heart of the Square. Voted Oxford's "Best Plate Lunch," "Lunch" and "Casual Dining." Fried pickles, Mom's meatloaf, veggie plates, and chicken and dumplings are featured. Get your comfort food here. 118 Courthouse Square, Oxford. Monday through Saturday 11:30 a.m. to 10:00 p.m. 1.662.232.8880.

City Grocery **–** The Chef John Currence creation has been the culinary epicenter of Oxford since 1992. Treat yourself to a unique, upscale dining experience. 152 Courthouse Square, Oxford. 1.662.232.8080.

Nightlife:

Proud Larry's Restaurant & Spirits – Go hybrid...by day, Larry's is a great place for a hot meal featuring pasta dishes, salads, and burgers. The spinach and artichoke dip is the best in Mississippi! By night, Larry's becomes a true hot spot featuring live music, including local and regional bands. 211 South Lamar Boulevard, Oxford 1.601.236.0500.

The Library **–** One of the best venues for talented local bands and performers. Attracts a younger crowd...déjà vu of your college years! Open for lunch during the day. Also, experience The Library Sports Bar which fills the void of the true sports bar on the Square. 120 South 11th Street, Oxford. 1.662.234.1411.

Golf Course:

The Ole Miss Golf Course

147 Golf Course Road, Oxford, MS 38655

Shopping:

Hit the Historic Downtown Square and fall in love with the quaintness of the Old South with a darling arrangement of antique, book, jewelry, clothing and specialty shops for the more discriminating tastes.

Records:

All-Time Record: 671–524–35 (.560)

Bowl Appearances: 34

Bowl Record: 24-13 (.649) *Highest in the Southeastern Conference

SEC Championships: Six

1947 (9-2), 1955 (10-1), 1962 (10-0), 1954 (9-2), 1960 (10-0-1), 1963 (7-1-2)

National Championships: Three

1959 (10-1) (SEC Team of the Decade) (Berryman, Billingsley, Dunkel and Sagarin), 1960 (10-0-1) (Football Research, National Championship Foundation and Williamson), 1962 (10-0) (Litkenhous).

Vacated Wins:

On February 11, 2019 Ole Miss announced the vacation of all wins from the following years: 2010, 2011, 2012 and 2016. In 2013, all wins except the Music City Bowl, and in 2014, all wins except the Presbyterian game were vacated. These vacations were made in retribution for former head coach Hugh Freeze's improprieties regarding the recruitment of football players.

Ole Miss Greats

Ole Miss has eleven former players and coaches in the College Football Hall of Fame:

1951 Bruiser Kennard

1965 Charlie Conerly

1973 John Cain

1974 Barney Poole

1979 John Vaught

1984 Doug Kenna

1987 Thad "Pie" Vann

1989 Archie Manning

1991 Parker Hall

1995 Jake Gibbs

1997 Charlie Flowers

Coaches:

Harry Mehre **-** (1938-1945) - (39-26-1) - (.590) – A native of Huntington, Indiana, Mehre was educated at Notre Dame. Mehre's tenure at Ole Miss was highlighted by several impressive victories, including notable triumphs over Vanderbilt in 1939—the school's first ever, LSU in 1938—its first in eleven years, and the first win against Tulane in over 25 years, in 1941. Mehre coached at Georgia from 1928-1937, spanning the Southern and Southeastern Conferences. His overall coaching record was 98-60-7. Mehre served as head coach of the NFL's Minneapolis Marines in 1923, posting a record of 4–5–2.

John Vaught **-** (1947-1970) - (190-61-11) - (.725) – Born May 6, 1909, in Olney, Texas, Vaught coached the Rebels from 1947-1970, leading Ole Miss to six SEC titles: the 1959 Dunkel System National Championship, the 1960 Football Writers of America, Dunkel System, and Williamson System national championships, the 1962 Litkenhous Ratings National Title, and a position of both regional and national prominence over 24 years. During his career as head coach at Ole Miss,

the former high school valedictorian, Vaught led the Rebels to an impressive 18 bowl game appearances, with a 10-8 record. He is remembered by Rebel fans as their greatest coach. Vaught said, "I'd do anything for Ole Miss." Vaught was elected to the College Football Hall of Fame in 1979 and in 1982 Ole Miss renamed its stadium in his honor. Johnny Vaught died February 3, 2006, in Oxford, Mississippi. He was 96 years old.

Tommy Tuberville **–** (1995-1998) – (25-20) – (.555) - A Camden, Arkansas native, Tuberville attended Southern Arkansas University, where he lettered in football as a safety for the Muleriders and played two years on the golf team. He received a B.S. degree in physical education from SAU in 1976. He coached at Hermitage High School in Hermitage, Arkansas before he was an assistant coach at Arkansas State University. He landed at the University of Miami next, beginning as graduate assistant and ending as defensive coordinator in 1993, winning the national championship three times (1986–1994). In 1994, Tuberville replaced Bob Davie as defensive coordinator under R. C. Slocum at Texas A&M University. The Aggies went 10–0–1 that season. In 1995, he took over for the Rebels in what was his first head coaching job. Despite NCAA sanctions that reduced scholarships, Tuberville, in 1997, was named SEC Coach of the Year in year three, after going 8-4, gaining the nickname, "Riverboat Gambler" for his anything goes attitude. After winning three of four seasons in Oxford, Tuberville took the Auburn head coaching job at the end of the 1998 season. He later coached at Texas Tech and Cincinnati.

David Cutcliffe **-** (1998-2004) - (44-29) – (.602) - On December 2, 1998, after serving 17 years at the University of Tennessee as an assistant coach, David Cutcliffe took over as Ole Miss' 34th head football coach. A Birmingham, Alabama native known for a keen offensive mind, he replaced departing head coach Tommy Tuberville, and compiled a 39-22 overall record and competed in four bowl games. During his initial five years with the program, Cutcliffe won at least seven games in each of his first five years in Oxford, the only coach in school history to accomplish such a feat. Cutcliffe, who coached Peyton Manning at Tennessee and then Eli Manning at Ole Miss, brought pride back to the University of Mississippi and its faithful fan base. The 2003 season produced Cutcliffe's best year as head coach, ending with a share of the SEC Western Division Championship and a bowl win over Oklahoma State in the Cotton Bowl, allowing the Rebels to finish with an impressive 10-3 record. Cutcliffe left the Rebels at the end of the 2004 season and took an assistant coaching position with Tennessee, a school he had previously assisted. Today he is the head coach at Duke University, a position he has held since 2008.

Lane Kiffin **–** (2020 – present) – (0-0) - Born May 9, 1975, in Lincoln, Nebraska, Lane Monte Kiffin was hired by Ole Miss to reclaim respectability lost from the painful Hugh Freeze debacle. A named and pedigreed coach with an impressive body of work, Kiffin is known as a heady play caller, with a penchant for the unexpected—both on and off the field. He is the son and namesake of long-time NFL defensive coach, Monte Kiffin. Kiffin has coached at Alabama as an assistant under Nick Saban and as a head coach at Tennessee (7-6) Southern Cal (28-15) and Florida Atlantic (26-13). His overall head coaching record is 61-34. Kiffin attended high school at Bloomington Jefferson High School in Minnesota in 1994. He signed with Fresno State University and was a backup quarterback before giving up football his senior year to serve as a student assistant coach under position coach Jeff Tedford. Kiffin graduated in 1998 and worked as a grad assistant at Colorado State for a year before working quality control at the Jacksonville Jaguars for a season. A year later he was coaching tight ends under Pete Carroll at USC from 2002 to 2006. In 2007, he became the youngest-ever NFL coach when Al Davis tapped him to lead the Raiders. Kiffin's NFL tenure was short. He lasted a little over a season, posting a 5-15 record. After the NFL, Kiffin landed in Knoxville in 2009, where his tenure again was short-lived, and not without controversy, posting a 7-6 record. In 2010, he took the head coaching job at Southern Cal, where he coached three full seasons before being fired on a plane in New York after an unlikely loss to Syracuse, in 2012. Thereafter he landed the offensive coordinator position at Alabama under head coach Nick Saban, where he helped the Tide to the 2014 national championship. From 2017-2019 Kiffin went 11-3, 5-7 and 10-3 at Florida Atlantic, in three years for an overall mark of 26-13. He is undefeated at Ole Miss.

Players:

Charlie Conerly **-** (1941-1947) – Born September 19, 1921, the Clarksdale, Mississippi native is remembered as one of the SEC's greatest football players. A standout tailback at Ole Miss during the war-torn years of 1941 and 1942, Conerly spent three years as a Marine during World War II. Upon his return to Oxford after the war in 1946, Conerly became the Rebels' quarterback in the newly formed T formation. Conerly captained and quarterbacked Mississippi to a 9-2-0 record in 1947, when the school won its first SEC Championship and beat Texas Christian 13-9 in the Delta Bowl. Conerly went on to become an NFL star joining the New York Giants in 1948 and was named Rookie of the Year. "Chuckin' Charlie" as he was called, retired from the NFL in 1961. As a pro, he completed 1,418 of 2,833 passes for 19,488 yards and 173 touchdowns, impressive passing statistics during an era in football that had not yet fully embraced passing. Conerly is the namesake of the football award, the Conerly Trophy, granted annually to the top college player in the State of Mississippi. Conerly died February 13, 1996 in Memphis, Tennessee at the age of 74.

***Elisha Archibald "Archie" Manning* -** (1968-1971) - The SEC's most favorite son, Archie Manning is Ole Miss' most famous college football star. The Drew, Mississippi native was a two-time All-American Quarterback (1969-1970). He finished fourth in Heisman voting in 1969 and third in 1970 and was the second overall selection by the New Orleans Saints in the 1971 NFL draft. Manning played for the Saints from 1971 to 1981, for the Houston Oilers from 1982 to 1983, and for the Minnesota Vikings from 1983 to 1984. During his career at Ole Miss, Manning passed for 31 touchdowns and rushed for another 25. In Birmingham, Alabama in 1969, in a valiant, losing effort to SEC power Alabama, Manning performed admirably, accounting for 540 total yards and three touchdowns, completing 33 passes for 436 yards while rushing fifteen times for another 104. Manning is remembered by Ole Miss and SEC fans for his on-the-field toughness and his indomitable competitive spirit. In 1971, in a losing Gator Bowl effort, Manning displayed unquestionable courage by playing with a broken left arm with the aid of a makeshift plastic sleeve. Despite his injury, Manning managed 95 yards rushing and 180 yards passing against Auburn. Archie's son, Peyton, was a standout quarterback for the Tennessee Volunteers while his younger son, Eli, also a quarterback, enrolled at Ole Miss prior to the 1999 season. Like their famous father, both went on to the NFL, where they won Super Bowls.

John Fourcade **-** (1978-1981) - A 1979-80 All-SEC quarterback, Fourcade holds the Rebel record for the most total offensive yards in a career at 6,713, breaking Archie Manning's record. Fourcade, a native of Gretna, Louisiana on the West Bank of the Mississippi, at Marrero's Arch Bishop Shaw High School, holds the record for the most plays, at 1,275, and the most rushing touchdowns, with 22. A tough, physical football player who enjoyed competing, Fourcade was the most valuable player of the 1982 Senior Bowl after passing for 115 yards and running for 33 yards and two touchdowns. After Ole Miss Fourcade went on to a pro career in the Canadian Football league with British Columbia in 1982, with Memphis in the now defunct USFL in 1984, and with the New Orleans Saints (NFL) from 1987-1990. In 2016 he was the coach of the New Mexico Stars of American Indoor Football.

Kent Austin **-** (1981-1985) – A Natick, Massachusetts native, Austin is the all-time leading passer in Ole Miss history with 6,184 total passing yards while completing 566 of 981 passes for 31 touchdowns. Drafted in the 12th round by St. Louis in the 1985 NFL Draft, in 1986, Austin began a lengthy Canadian professional football career in Saskatchewan, where he played from 1987-1991. Austin later played for British Columbia in 1994, Toronto in 1995, and Winnipeg in 1996. He was the 1989 Grey Cup MVP, a CFL Western All-Star, and also a CFL All-Canadian All-Star in 1990. Since 2003, he coached for a number of Canadian Football League and American college football teams, including Ole Miss as its offensive coordinator (2008-10), Cornell and Liberty.

Wesley Walls **-** (1985-1988) – A native of Batesville, Mississippi, Walls played high school ball at South Pontotoc High and Pontotoc High School. He began his career at Ole Miss at defensive end. For his senior season, he was moved to outside linebacker and added tight end to his duties to serve as a rare, two-way contributor. He excelled in the dual role with 36 receptions for 426 yards and three touchdowns to reap All-American and All-SEC honors in 1988. The engineering major achieved academic All-SEC honors as a junior. A second-round selection (56th pick) by the San Francisco 49ers in the 1989 NFL draft, Walls played for the New Orleans Saints, the Carolina Panthers and the Green Bay Packers, competing professionally for 14 seasons and was a five-time Pro Bowler. He was elected to the College Football Hall of Fame in 2014.

Kristofer (Kris) Mangum **-** (1994-1996) - The Magee, Mississippi native attended Magee High School and is the son of John Mangum, a defensive tackle for the Boston Patriots from 1966-1967, and the brother of John Mangum, Jr., a cornerback for the Chicago Bears. Mangum graduated from high school in 1992 and first enrolled at the University of Alabama. During his freshman year at Alabama, Mangum played in eight games mainly on special teams.

He was part of the 1993 Sugar Bowl and national champion Alabama team of 1992. In 1993, Mangum transferred to the University of Mississippi and sat out a season. A first team All-American, Mangum caught 74 passes for 729 yards (9.9 yard average) and four touchdowns. He ended his college football career ranked 14th all-time in receptions at Ole Miss, collecting 74 catches for 729 yards during three seasons. As a junior in 1995, he was a first-team All-Southeastern Conference selection, while making nine starts. During his senior season in 1996, Mangum made 29 catches for 264 yards and 2 touchdowns and was a first team All-SEC pick. Mangum led the SEC with 36 catches for 391 yards and two touchdowns, the most receptions by a Rebels tight end since Wesley Walls established the mark in 1988. Mangum was drafted in the seventh round of the 1997 NFL draft by the Carolina Panthers as the 228th overall pick. He was with the Panthers for ten years, six of which he spent backing up former Ole Miss tight end Wesley Walls.

Eli Manning **-** (2000-2003) - The New Orleans, Louisiana native attended Isadore Newman High School. He is the final offspring of the SEC's "Favorite Son," Archie Manning, who starred at quarterback for Ole Miss and head coach Johnny Vaught during the 1960's. A consummate collegiate quarterback, Manning drew favorable comparisons to both his older brother and father throughout his publicized tenure in Oxford. Rebuffing LSU, Tennessee, and the other SEC schools for his services, the youngest Manning chose his father's alma mater to earn an education and to play football. During his SEC career, Eli started 36 games and played in 42, throwing for 10,119 yards and 81 touchdowns, making him Ole Miss's all-time passing leader. Manning holds 45 different school records and was named the 2003 SEC Offensive Player of the Year by the Associated Press. At the end of the successful 2003 campaign in which Eli led Ole miss to a 31-28 Cotton Bowl victory over Oklahoma State in January 2004, he was named one of the prestigious 15 scholar-athletes by the National Foundation and College Hall of Fame. In the spring of 2004, Eli was the first pick in the

first round by the San Diego Chargers in the NFL draft, but was traded to the New York Giants. Eli spent 16 years with the organization. In his third season with the Giants, in 2007, he led them to victory in Super Bowl XLII, and was named the game's Most Valuable Player. He and his brother Peyton are the only brother combination to play quarterback in the Super Bowl and the only brothers to win Super Bowl MVP awards, doing so in successive years.

Terrance Metcalf **-** (1997-2001) – Born January 28, 1978, in Clarksdale, Mississippi, Metcalf, considered one of the nation's top high school offensive line prospects, signed with Ole Miss and became one of the school's most impressive offensive linemen. At left tackle Metcalf started all but six games of his fantastic five-year career in Oxford. Metcalf did not allow a sack during his junior or senior seasons, and for that he was respected. He was a consensus First-Team All-American during his senior year when he started eleven games and earned second-team All-American honors as a sophomore. As a freshman he started all 12 games. He is the Ole Miss bench press record holder with a 500-pound lift. Metcalf entered the NFL as a third round selection (93rd overall) of the Chicago Bears in the 2002 NFL Draft.

Deuce McAllister **-** (1997-2000) – Born December 27, 1978 in Lena, Mississippi, McAllister is considered one of Ole Miss' greatest all-around backs. McAllister ended his Ole Miss playing days with 18 school career, season, and single-game records. Blessed with incredible size and speed, McAllister, a Morton High School graduate, finished his career with 3,060 rushing yards on 616 rushing attempts for 37 touchdowns, 15 100-yard rushing games and 246 total points scored. McAllister was a talented punt and kick returner for the Rebels, evidenced by his 4,889 career all-purpose yards. The first player in Rebel history to record three consecutive seasons with at least 1,000 all-purpose yards, McAllister was a first round draft choice by the New Orleans Saints in the 2001 NFL draft. He was given the nickname "Deuce" by his father, as he is the second child in his family.

Patrick Willis **-** (2003-2006) – The Bruceton, Tennessee native graduated Hollow Rock Bruceton Central High where he was a two-time All-State selection at linebacker, Regional MVP and West Tennessee Player of the Year. Remembered as one of the most physical defensive players to don a Rebel jersey, Willis signed with Ole Miss and played in all 13 games as a true freshman, logging 20 tackles. As a sophomore in 2004 he played in 10 of 11 games recording 70 tackles with 11 for losses. For the effort he received honorable mention All-SEC honors from the Associated Press. Willis broke out as a junior. After making 128 tackles (90 solo) in just ten games started he was a unanimous First-Team All-America pick by College Football News and the All-America Football Foundation. He was named a consensus First-Team All-

SEC player by a host of other publications including The Sporting News. Willis also earned the 2006 Conerly Trophy, and the Butkus Award. After running a 4.3 forty-yard dash at Pro Day, Willis was a first-round pick (11th overall) by the San Francisco 49ers in the 2007 NFL Draft and was named the 2007 NFL Defensive Rookie of the Year and was invited to the Pro Bowl.

Michael Oher **–** (2005-2008) – Oher is remembered as a dominant offensive lineman with a story as big as his agile frame. The son of a broken Memphis, Tennessee home, he found a second family, and a second chance, in the Tuohy's, who happened to be members of the Ole Miss family. Although the NCAA had doubts about the legitimacy of Oher's recruitment, he nonetheless started in ten games as a guard during his first season, earning first-team freshman All-American honors. After shifting to left tackle for the 2006 season, he was named to numerous pre-season All-Conference and All-American teams. Oher was named a second-team Southeastern Conference offensive lineman after his sophomore season and a first-team SEC offensive lineman after his junior season. On January 14, 2008, Oher declared he would enter the 2008 NFL Draft. Two days later he announced his withdrawal from the draft to return to Ole Miss for his senior season. After the 2008 season, Oher was recognized as a unanimous first-team All-American, and graduated with a degree in criminal justice in the spring of 2009. He was drafted 23rd overall by the Atlanta Falcons in the 2009 NFL Draft. A film inspired by his life, "The Blind Side," based on the book by Michael Lewis, was nominated for an Oscar as "Best Picture" along with Sandra Bullock as "Best Actress" for her portrayal of Leigh Ann Tuohy, the wife of Sean, a former Ole Miss Basketball standout, sports commentator and restaurateur.

Peria Jerry **–** (2005-2008) – The powerfully quick Batesville, Mississippi native is remembered as a dominant presence on the defensive line for Ole Miss. After a quiet freshman year, in 2006, Jerry battled through injuries to play in eight games, starting six. He made starts at end, tackle and nose tackle, totaling 22 on the season with a tackle for a loss and a sack. In the spring he received the Jeff Hamm Memorial Award for the most improved defensive player. He moved from tackle to end and emerged as the starter. 2007 saw Jerry named Second Team All-SEC by the Associated Press and he started all 12 games at defensive tackle and was ranked sixth in the SEC in tackles for loss with 14. In 2008, Jerry was named to the All-SEC First Team by the SEC coaches and to the All-SEC First Team by the nation's news media and was named to the Associated Press All-America First Team. He was drafted in the first round (24th overall) by the Atlanta Falcons in 2009.

Robert Nkemdiche **–** (2013-2015) – The Loganville, Georgia native played at Grayson High School where the USA Today All-American was regarded as

one of the best players in the country, as a three-sport letterman in football, basketball and track. A behemoth at 6-3 285, he played both defensive end and running back for Grayson, demonstrating agility and quickness despite his size. Robert hit the ground running for Coach Hugh Freeze as a true freshman in Oxford—not as a running back—but as a defensive lineman, playing in 11 games with 10 starts, amassing 28 tackles and a sack on the season, with six for loss, earning freshman All-SEC playing honors. As a sophomore in 2014 Robert added another 27 tackles at defensive tackle, with three for loss. That year the Rebels led the country in scoring defense with a 16 point per game average and defeated the Alabama Crimson Tide and Head Coach Nick Saban. In 2016 as a junior, Robert led a team that again defeated Alabama, making it the first from Ole Miss to do so. He had 26 total tackles with seven for loss and three sacks, making him a finalist for numerous national accolades, including the Lombardi Award, and was named First-Team All-SEC. He was drafted 29th overall by the Arizona Cardinals in the first round of the 2016 NFL Draft.

Laremy Tunsil **–** (2013-2015) - A native of Lake City, Florida, Tunsil attended Columbia High School where he lettered in football and track. A consensus five-star recruit, he chose Ole Miss over a litany of suitors that included every major college program, and every SEC school. As a true freshman in the SEC Laremy Tunsil started at left tackle on day one—making him a true anomaly in the modern college football world; and was named freshman All-SEC by the Associated Press and a Freshman All-American by The Sporting News. As a sophomore Tunsil started 11 games and was again named All-SEC. In June 2015, prior to his junior season, Tunsil was involved in a bitter family dispute with his stepfather that produced allegations of impropriety on the part of Ole Miss in the form of illegal benefits to Tunsil. Coach Freeze benched Tunsil for the first seven games as a precaution. He was reinstated for the Texas A&M game and Ole Miss finished the season with a Sugar Bowl victory over Oklahoma State, in which he scored a two-yard touchdown. Tunsil was the first pick in the first round of the 2016 NFL Draft, signing with the Tennessee Titans.

Chad Kelly **–** (2015-2016) – Kelly is remembered as one of Ole Miss's more competitive championship quarterbacks, possessing a game as spunky as his off-field demeanor. Due to disciplinary issues, Kelly attended St. Joseph's Collegiate Institute in Tonawanda, New York. A four-time Punt, Pass and Kick competition National Champion, he is the son of the younger brother of former NFL quarterback Jim Kelly of Buffalo Bills fame. A top-ranked, highly-recruited dual threat quarterback coming out of high school, Chad signed with Clemson. He redshirted at Clemson during his first year. As a freshman in

2014 he played in five games and was dismissed due to unbecoming conduct; and he landed at East Mississippi Junior College for the 2015 season. In his lone sophomore season with the Lions he started 12 games and threw for 3,906 yards with 47 touchdowns and eight picks en route to a JUCO National Championship. Coach Hugh Freeze recognized Chad's budding talent and signed him in December 2014. In 2015, Kelly threw for 4,042 yards and 31 touchdowns, leading Ole Miss to a 10-3 season. He was the first Ole Miss quarterback to steer the Rebels to victories over LSU, Alabama and Auburn in the same year, with the win against Bama coming in Tuscaloosa. His 465 passing yards against Auburn are a Rebel record, which eclipsed the mark set by Archie Manning. In 2016, Kelly again started for the Rebels and threw for 2,758 yards and 19 touchdowns. However, in early November his season was cut short after suffering ACL and meniscus injuries. In his abbreviated Rebel career he threw at least one touchdown in 22 straight games. His 12 300-yard games are the most in school history. He was selected by Denver in the 2017 NFL Draft as the 253rd pick in the 7th round. Kelly was the last player chosen in the NFL Draft that year, earning him the dubious badge of: "Mr. Irrelevant."

Traditions/History:

The Walk of Champions – Two hours before kickoff, the team walks down the sidewalk that goes through "The Grove," a ten acre grassy plot shaded by oak trees at the center of campus fans congregate in for tailgating. The Ole Miss faithful fight for position on both sides of the sidewalk and greet the players with loud cheers.

Roy Lee "Chucky" Mullins Courage Award – This award is presented each spring to Ole Miss' top defensive player, who then has the distinguished honor of wearing Chucky's #38 the following football season. Mullins died in 1991, the result of a tragic football-related accident. He is remembered for his dedication to the game and for his steadfast courage. Chucky, in the face of overwhelming adversity, once stated, "No matter how bad things seem, never give up..." and "You'll never know how much God means to you, till tragedy hits and friends come through."

Egg Bowl – Ole Miss, and its long-time, in-state, arch-rival, Mississippi State, since Thanksgiving Day in 1927, have played what amounts to the "Egg Bowl" in the Magnolia State. According to William George Barner III, who wrote a book titled Mississippi Mayhem chronicling the boisterous beginnings of the Egg Bowl, the rivalry has a great story behind it. The 1927 inaugural "Golden Egg" game was proposed by members of Sigma Iota, an Ole Miss honorary society, in an effort to temper the 1926 post-game exploits of some of the

overzealous and unruly fans involved for both sides. The game of 1926 saw a series that had been dominated by Mississippi State. The Bulldogs had won 18 of the last 23 contests. Ole Miss won a hard-fought, 7-6 ball game that fateful day. After the game, a throng of Ole Miss fans banded together on the west side and rushed triumphantly onto the field toward the object of their destructive desire–the goalposts. Mississippi State "Aggie" supporters on that side of the field stood calmly and sang their alma mater. On the east side, matters were not as stable, and cooler heads did not prevail, as many of the disgruntled Mississippi State fans brandished cane bottom chairs raised high over their heads and sought after the Rebel revelers hell-bent on tearing down their goalposts. As imaginable, many fights ensued.

As described in an article by The Memphis Commercial Appeal by Ben Hilbun, who would later become President of the Starkville campus, "The phantom of victory, that for thirteen years eluded Ole Miss, returned to the bearded Berserkers...and they won over A&M, their traditional rivals, 7-6." Ole Miss students fought for the goal posts," he added, "but were restrained." The Mississippian, Ole Miss' student newspaper, replied that the "Aggie" chair brigade which defended their goal posts "came to the field with malice after-thought...with the intent of staging a 'free for all'..."

Ole Miss and Mississippi State students, shocked by the injuries to spectators, vowed it should never happen again. The resulting agreement by the two student bodies was the "Golden Egg," a trophy that would cool the heated battle between the two bitter in-state rivals. Because the trophy was shaped in the likeness of the more standard, rounded ball of the day, it came to be called the "Golden Egg."

That initial meeting of the two schools in 1927 for the "Golden Egg" ended in a 20-12 victory for Ole Miss. Unlike during the previous year's contest, the game ended with a much-dignified ceremony celebrating the participants and the winners. As agreed upon before the game, the schools sang their alma maters. Ole Miss, the victor, sang first, followed by Mississippi State. After the serenading was complete, the two team captains, the presidents of the two student bodies, and the leaders of the two schools met on the fifty yard line. There, B.M. Walker, President of Mississippi State, presented the first "Golden Egg Trophy" to Ole Miss Captain Applewhite. Applewhite was carried off the field by a "score of students."

Today, the "Golden Egg" remains one of the most treasured prizes of either school. Symbolizing football supremacy in the State of Mississippi, the trophy is engraved annually with the score of each preceding year's game. Additionally, the trophy rests in a place of great honor at both schools. During years in which there was a tie, the trophy would return to the previous winner's school for the first half of the year, then it would go to the other school for display.

"Hotty Toddy" (popular student/fan cheer)

Are You Ready?
Hell Yes! Damn Right!
Hotty Toddy, Gosh-A-Mighty!
Who In the Hell Are We?
Hey! Flim-Flam, Bim-Bam,
Ole Miss, By Damn!

The "Hotty Toddy" cheer at Ole Miss is a unique and cherished part of the history and tradition of the university. This cheer, which makes no reference to anything hot with temperature (such as a toddy), is a corruption of "highty-tighty," an expression of the eighteenth and nineteenth centuries which was used as an exclamation or as a descriptive term like "high-falutin." A mispronunciation of hoity-toity, "highty-tighty" was the original phrase in the football cheer as required by the rhyme with "Gosh-A-Mighty." The date of the origination of the cheer is unknown for certain, but is thought to have started as early as the 1920's.

Great Bowl Games:

Delta Bowl: January 1, 1948: Ole Miss 13, Texas Christian 9

Sugar Bowl: January 1, 1958: Ole Miss 39, Texas 7

Sugar Bowl: January 1, 1960: Ole Miss 21, LSU 0

Sugar Bowl: January 1, 1963: Ole Miss 17, Arkansas 13

Liberty Bowl: December 28, 1965: Ole Miss 13, Auburn 7

Peach Bowl: December 30, 1971: Ole Miss 41, Georgia Tech 18

Motor City Bowl: December 26, 1997: Ole Miss 34, Marshall 31

Independence Bowl: December 27, 2002: Ole Miss 27, Nebraska 23

Cotton Bowl: January 2, 2004: Ole Miss 31, Oklahoma State 28

Cotton Bowl: January 2, 2009: Ole Miss 47, Texas Tech 34

Cotton Bowl: January 2, 2010: Ole Miss 21, Oklahoma State 7

BBVA Compass Bowl: January 5, 2013: Ole Miss 38, Pittsburgh 17

Fight Song:

Forward, Rebels, march to fame,
Hit that line and win this game
We know that you'll fight it through,
For your colors read and blue. Rah, rah, rah.

Rebels you are the Southland's pride,
Take that ball and hit your stride,
Don't stop till the victory's won, for you Ole Miss.
Fight, fight for your Ole Miss.

Alma Mater:

Words by Mrs. A.W. Kahle, Music by W.F. Kahle

W*ay down South in Mississippi, there's a spot that ever calls*
Where among the hills enfolded, Stand Old Alma Mater's halls.
Where the trees lift high their branches,
To the whisp'ring Southern breeze. There Ole Miss is calling,
To our hearts fond memories.
With united hearts we praise thee, All our loyalty is thine,
And we hail thee, Alma Mater, May they light forever shine;
May it brighter grow and brighter, And with deep affection true,
Our thoughts shall ever cluster 'round thee, Dear Old Red and Blue.
May thy fame throughout the nation,
Through thy sons and daughters grow,
May they name forever waken, in our hearts a tender glow,
May thy counsel and thy spirit, Ever keep us one in this,
That our own shall be thine honor, now and ever dear Ole Miss.

The Grove:

The old Rebel fan adage goes, "We may not win every game, but we never lose a party!" Such is true in the Grove, where Southern hospitality and grace is on full display for Ole Miss friend and foe alike. Seeded, aerated and fertilized annually with 4,500 pounds of tall fescue blend, the Grove is a ten-acre grassy plot in the campus center shaded by large oaks and other Southern indigenous trees. While the Grove is certainly beautiful, its undulating landscape is the revered meeting place for Rebel fans to tailgate under tent canopies prior to every home football game. The solidarity displayed on this verdant patch of Rebel land every home weekend during the fall is one of the telling indicators that the Ole Miss community is one big family. The Sporting News ranked the Grove as one of college football's greatest traditions and described it as "The Holy Grail" of college tailgating sites. The popularity of the Grove is evidenced by the amount of garbage it can create on a game day weekend. The average amount of waste collected in the Grove after a home football game is roughly 200 cubic yards, or close to 10 tons, requiring 100 to 150 man hours to clean up the hallowed grounds after each Rebel home game.

Noteworthy Ole Miss Alumni:

Mose Allison, jazz and blues pianist

Haley Barbour, Governor of Mississippi and former chairman of the NRC

Jim Barksdale, founder and former CEO of Netscape

Ron Franklin, sports broadcaster

John Grisham, best-selling novelist (Law School)

Kate Jackson, actress

Gerald McRaney, actor (Promised Land, Simon & Simon, Major Dad)

David Molpus, reporter for National Public Radio

Trent Lott, former United States Senator

Thad Cochran, United States Senator

Lt. Gen. James E. Sherrard III, Former Chief of Air Force Reserves

Shepard Smith, Fox News anchor

Larry Speakes, former press secretary to the President of the United States

Three Miss Americas, Mary Ann Mobley, 1959; Lynda Lee Mead She, 1960; and Susan Akin-Lynch, 1986

James Meredith, first black student at Ole Miss

Tate Taylor, director of "The Help"

Larry A. Thompson, film producer, talent manager

Tate Ellington, actor

2020 Ole Miss Football Schedule

Sept. 5 vs. Baylor (Houston)

Sept. 12 SE Missouri State

Sept. 19 Auburn

Sept. 26 at LSU

Oct. 3 Alabama

Oct. 10 at Vanderbilt

Oct. 17 Florida

Oct. 24 Middle Tennessee

Oct. 31 OPEN DATE

Nov. 7 at Texas A&M

Nov. 14 at Arkansas

Nov. 21 Georgia Southern

Nov. 26 Mississippi State

Texas A&M University

In 2012, Texas A&M University, the "Home of the 12th Man," like its former Southwest Conference partner, the University of Arkansas, in 1992, became a part of the nation's most powerful athletic conference. The Aggies, in true maverick fashion, did not disappoint during their inaugural season in the nation's toughest league. Led by an unlikely redshirt freshman, Texan quarterback turned Heisman Trophy winner, the fleet-footed Johnny Manziel—the Pride of Kerrville, the Aggies enjoyed a first year in the SEC that will long be remembered—especially by Alabama fans. With losses to only Florida and LSU, A&M finished 11-2, with a 41-13 Cotton Bowl thumping of former Big 12 partner, Oklahoma. However, the sweetest win of the early slate was the 29-24 road victory over #1-ranked Alabama, the defending National Champions, on their home turf in Bryant-Denny Stadium. There exists a rich coaching tradition shared between the two schools, as both Bear Bryant and Gene Stallings served as a head coach at the University of Alabama and Texas A&M University. With the tradition-rich Aggies' auspicious entrance into the nation's most competitive sub-conference, the SEC Western Division, the balance of power has unquestionably shifted toward the setting sun. A&M fans, buoyed by a new and improved Kyle Field, are counting the days until their beloved Aggies make a championship run in the nation's toughest football sub-conference. Head coach, Jimbo Fisher, a proven champ, has staked his claim in College Station, hoping to bring the Aggies back to regional and national prominence, like their rich history foretells.

Nickname: "Aggies"

An Aggie is a student at Texas A&M. Originally, the letters "A" and "M" stood for "Agricultural and Mechanical," so this is how the term Aggie came to be—it is an abbreviation of Agricultural. Since becoming a university in 1963, the "A&M" was incorporated into the official university name, but the letters no longer stand for specific words. Much like there are no "ex-Marines," there are no "ex-Aggies," only former students or cadets.

Founded:

The Agricultural and Mechanical College of Texas (A&M) was founded in 1876, as the state's first public university. The university possesses land, sea and space grant designations and holds research contracts valued at $700 million annually.

Location:

Bryan-College Station, Texas. About 90 miles northwest of Houston, this Lone Star locale is known as "Aggieland." The university is located in the Research Valley, the heart of Central Texas's Dallas, San Antonio and Houston triangle, making the area accessible to more than 14 million Texans within less than a four-hour drive. Texas A&M University is home to the George H.W. Bush Presidential Library, located on a 90-acre site on the west campus.

Population: 152,000

Enrollment: 68,603 (third largest in the country)

History: Texas A&M began as an all-male, military institution. It played its first football game in 1905. While today's membership is voluntary, the Corps of Cadets' more than 2,000 members—both male and female—form the largest uniformed body of students outside the U.S. military academies. Aside from the nation's military academies, Texas A&M commissions more officers than any other American institution of higher learning. Through the years Texas A&M has played football within many different athletic conferences. From 1894–1902, they were independent. From 1903–1908, they played within the Southern Intercollegiate Athletic Association. From 1909–1911 they were independent. From 1912–1914 they were again members of the Southern Intercollegiate Athletic Association, until 1913–1917, when they played in the Texas Intercollegiate Athletic Association. For 80 years, from 1915–1995, the Aggies were in the Southwest Conference. In 1996, they joined the Big 12 Conference where from 1996-2010 A&M competed in the Big 12 South Division. Upon the departure of Nebraska and Colorado from the Big 12, the Conference dissolved its divisions and operated as a 10-team division-less conference. Texas A&M participated in this conference arrangement for only the 2011 season. In 2012, A&M entered the Southeastern Conference, along with Missouri in the Eastern Division.

Colors: Maroon and White

The colors are a prominent part of A&M, and are referenced in the song, "The Spirit of Aggieland," written in 1925. Tied to their alma mater's pride, Aggies sing, "We've got to fight for Maroon and White." As part of a new tradition for football, certain games are designated as "Maroon-Outs" where fans are encouraged to wear maroon. In 2007, to make it easier to match the maroon color used by Texas A&M and its licensees, worldwide color authority, Pantone, Inc., created a custom "Aggie Maroon" color, Pantone 505.

Mascot: "Reveille"

Reveille, the "First Lady of Aggieland," is the official mascot of Texas A&M. Reveille first came to campus in 1931, after a group of cadets found a stray dog on the road. Reveille VIII, the current Reveille, is a full-blooded Collie and the highest-ranking member of the Corp of Cadets. "Miss Rev," as cadets address her, can be seen around campus, in class, or attending a number of planned social events.

Band name: "The Fighting Texas Aggie Band"

The Aggie Band was founded by Joseph Holick, in 1885. Holick, a migrant worker who landed in College Station, had a knack for music. Holick's musical talents did not go unnoticed by the students and professors. Holick wanted to give the growing school "more than just two tunes for its money," so he asked the commandant for permission to start a cadet band. The commandant agreed, and named Holick bandmaster. Under his tutelage and the leadership of subsequent bandmasters, the band grew from 13 members in 1894, to 75 bandsmen in 1924. Early drum majors are credited with inspiring the band's name. The first student drum major, H.A. "California" Morse, was asked to leave A&M due to fighting. Early drum majors were chosen in physical combat. Candidates were placed in a locked room. The best fighter emerged victorious and was named to the coveted position. This tradition of aggressiveness and physical combat was noted by band members, who began calling themselves, "The Fightin' Texas Aggie Band."

The nationally acclaimed Fightin' Texas Aggie Band is known for its military precision and style. Some of the band's marching maneuvers, like its signature block T, are so complex that computer programs calculate them to be impossible, figuring that two people must be in the same place at the same time. The 300-plus member band performs at all home football games and several away games. The band operates under strict military guidelines as part of the Corp of Cadets. In 2001, the John Philip Sousa Foundation presented the band with the Sudler Trophy, recognizing its long tradition of excellence.

Band Director: Dr. Timothy B. Rhea

Stadium: Kyle Field

The "Home of the 12th Man" is regarded as one of the country's most intimidating football-playing venues. Since 1905 the Aggies have won over 70 percent of their games at Kyle Field. In the fall of 1904, the stadium's namesake, Edwin Jackson Kyle, an 1899 graduate of Texas A&M and professor

of horticulture, was named president of the General Athletics Association. Kyle wanted an athletic field to promote the school's growing athletics. The university was unwilling to provide funds, so Kyle fenced off a section of the southwest corner of campus that had been assigned to him for agricultural use. Using $650 of his own money, he purchased a covered grandstand from the Bryan fairgrounds and built wooden bleachers to raise the seating capacity to 500 people. Through the years Kyle Field has seen many rounds of structural and architectural improvements, like the prestigious Bernard C. Richardson Zone that brought an additional 20,000 seats in 1999, increasing capacity to nearly 83,000. Kyle Field reverted to natural grass, from Astroturf, in 1996. On May 1, 2013, the Texas A&M Board of Regents approved a $485 million refurbishment of Kyle Field. The renovation was done in two phases, completed by the beginning of the 2015 season, bringing the official capacity to 102,733. Construction was sequenced and phased to allow the playing of regular home football games in the stadium for the 2013, 2014, and 2015 seasons. It was completed ahead of schedule and under budget. The increased seating capacity makes Kyle Field the largest stadium in the Southeastern Conference and the fourth-largest stadium in the NCAA, the fourth-largest stadium in the United States, and the fifth-largest non-racing stadium in the world. Within the state of Texas, Kyle Field has the largest seating capacity of any football stadium. Kyle Field's largest game attendance was 110,633 people when Texas A&M lost to the Ole Miss Rebels by the score of 35–20 on October 11, 2014, in front of the largest football game attendance in the state of Texas and SEC history.

Capacity: 102,733

First game: 1905

Directions to Kyle Field:

From Interstate 10 heading west, take exit 775A for Interstate 610 North. Merge onto I-610 West. Travel 12.3 miles. Take exit 13B to merge onto US-290 West toward Austin. Travel 44 miles. Exit onto TX-6N toward College Station/Bryan. Travel 39.2 miles. Take the Texas 6 Business exit on the left toward College Station. Travel .4 mile. Merge on to S Texas Ave. Travel 2.5 miles. Turn left on to George Bush Drive. Travel 1.1 miles. Turn right on to Houston Street. Travel .2 miles. The stadium is located at 1069 Houston Street.

Dining:

Verita's Wine & Bistro - Veritas presents a unique, upscale blend of contemporary decor and related cosmopolitan ambiance, inviting you to sample culinary creations focused on seasonality. A distinctive, Asian-American product; cellar features over 1800 wines. 830 University Drive East, Suite 400, College Station. 979.268.3251. 11:00 a.m. - 2:00 p.m., 5:30 p.m. - 9:30 p.m.

Cafe Eccell - Since 1989, Cafe Eccell has been has served College Station as a "fresh seafood bistro." Various seafood entrees reflect multi-regional and fusion cuisines. 11:00 a.m. – 10:00 p.m. Monday – Thursday. 10:00 a.m. – 11:00 p.m. Friday & Saturday. 101 Church Ave College Station. 979. 846.7908.

Nite Life:

Hurricane Harry's – Since 1992. Featuring live music, pretty girls and cold beer. 313 College Avenue, College Station. 979.846.3343. 9:00 p.m. - 2:00 a.m. most nights.

Fitzwilly's Bar & Grille – Since 1994. Good Food, Good Drinks, Good Times. Featuring live musical entertainment on the weekends. 303 University Drive. College Station. 979.846.8806.

Dixie Chicken – The authentic original. "College Station's Most Famous Watering Hole." Looking for a greasy burger and a cold beer in a classic, loud, fun, college-dazed atmosphere? This is where it's been happening for years. They claim to annually serve more beer per square foot than any bar in America! Find out for yourself. 307 University Drive, College Station. 979.846.2322.

Accommodations:

Rudder Jessup Bed & Breakfast – A wonderful location. A stone's throw from everything, this classic B&B is known for its hospitality and wonderful breakfast. Call ahead early and make your reservation.

115 Lee Avenue

College Station, Texas

1.866.744.2470

Hospital nearest to stadium:

College Station Medical Center

1604 Rock Prairie Rd

College Station

1.979.764.5100

Bail Bondsmen for emergencies:

Affordable Bail Bonds

114 S Main St, Bryan, TX 77803

979.822.0808

Golf Couses:

Texas A&M University Golf Course

Bizzell Street

College Station, TX 77843

979. 845.1723

Texas A&M University Golf Course II

College Station

979. 845.4511

Shopping:

Nearby historic, downtown Bryan, Texas hosts a colorful, charming array of artisan and antique shops and stores. Post Oak Mall is another retail Mecca.

National Titles: 3 (1919, 1927, 1939)

Conference Titles:

18 (17 in the Southwest Conference, 1 in the Big 12 in 1998)

All time record: 741–481–48 (.602)

Bowl Record: (18-22) .450

Great Bowl Games:

1987 Cotton Bowl – Texas A&M 35, Notre Dame 10

1990 Holiday Bowl – Texas A&M 65, BYU 14

1995 Alamo Bowl – Texas A&M 22, Michigan 20

2011 Meineke Car Care Bowl of Texas – Texas A&M 33, Northwestern 22

2012 Cotton Bowl Classic – Texas A&M 41, Oklahoma 13

2018 Gator Bowl – Texas A&M 52, North Carolina State 13

2019 Texas Bowl – Texas A&M 24, Oklahoma State 21

Texas A&M Greats:

Coaches:

Dana X. Bible **–** (1917, 1919-1928) - (72-19-9) – (.768) – A Jefferson City, Tennessee native, Dana Xenophon Bible was an American football coaching legend. Bible also coached basketball and baseball and served as a college athletics administrator. He was the head football coach at Mississippi College (1913–1915), Louisiana State University (1916), Texas A&M University (1917, 1919–1928), the University of Nebraska (1929–1936), and the University of Texas (1937–1946), compiling a career college football coaching record of 198–72–23. In addition to eleven years as football coach, Bible was the head basketball coach at Texas A&M from 1920 to 1927 and the head baseball coach there from 1920 to 1921. He also served as the athletic director at Nebraska from 1932 to 1936. Bible was inducted into the College Football Hall of Fame as a coach in 1951.

Homer Norton **–** (1934-1947) – (82-53-9) – A native of Carrollton, Alabama, Norton played four different sports at Birmingham–Southern College and played minor league baseball with the Birmingham Barons before entering coaching. He served as the head football coach at Centenary College of Louisiana from 1919 to 1921. From 1921 to 1926 he was the baseball coach at Centenary. From 1926 to 1933 he was again the Centenary football coach. From 1934 to 1947 Norton coached at Texas A&M. He compiled a career college coaching record of 143–75–18. His 1939 Aggie squad went 11–0, beat Tulane in the Sugar Bowl, and was named national champion. Norton's record at Texas A&M was 82–53–9, giving him the second most wins of any coach in Texas A&M Aggies football history. He was relieved of his duties in

1947, after his team went 3–6–1 and lost to Texas for the 8th consecutive season. He also coached baseball at Texas A&M from 1943 to 1944. Norton was inducted into the College Football Hall of Fame as a coach in 1971.

***Paul "Bear" Bryant* –** (1954-1957) - (25-14-2) – (.622) – From 1946 to 1953 Bryant led the Kentucky Wildcats to a 60-23-6 record. In 1954, Bryant accepted the head coaching job at Texas A&M University, simultaneously serving as its athletic director. Under Bryant the Aggies suffered through a grueling 1-9 initial season, beginning with the infamous training camp in Junction, Texas. Those who emerged from this brutal regimen were given the name "Junction Boys." Two years later, Bryant led the team to the Southwest Conference championship with a 34–21 victory over the University of Texas at Austin. The following year in 1957, Bryant's star running back, John David Crow won the Heisman Trophy. At the end of the 1957 season, after four years at Texas A&M, Bryant returned to Tuscaloosa to take the head coaching position, succeeding J.B. "Ears" Whitworth as head football and athletic director at his alma mater, the University of Alabama, where he became college football's most successful coach.

***Emory Bellard* –** (1972-1978) - (48-27) – (.640) – A Dana X. Bible protégé' from his playing days at the University of Texas, Bellard is remembered as one of the college game's greatest offensive innovators. The Luling, Texas native is credited with inventing the wishbone formation, an idea he derived from his experience with Homer Rice and Bill Yeoman at the University of Houston. Bellard was head coach at Texas A&M from 1972 to 1978, taking over for Gene Stallings. He had three ten-win seasons and won a Southwest Conference Championship in 1975; and was named Sporting News Coach of the Year that same year. Bellard later coached at Mississippi State University from 1979 until 1985. Bellard died on February 10, 2011, after battling Lou Gehrig's disease (ALS). Bellard is a member of the Texas Sports Hall of Fame.

***Jackie Sherrill* –** (1982-1988) – (52-28-1) – (.648) – A native of Duncan, Oklahoma, Sherrill played football under Bear Bryant at Alabama from 1962-1965, helping the Bear to two national championships. He served as the head football coach at Washington State University (1976), the University of Pittsburgh (1977–1981), Texas A&M University (1982–1988), and Mississippi State University (1991–2003), compiling a career college football record of 180–120–4. Sherrill was hired on January 19, 1982, to replace Tom Wilson, signing a record

six-year contract valued at $1.7 million. Sherrill started the tradition of the "12th Man Kickoff Team" and the Aggies won three consecutive Southwest Conference championships in 1985, 1986 and 1987. The Aggies played in the Cotton Bowl Classic at the end of each of those seasons, defeating Auburn 36–16 on January 1, 1986, and Notre Dame 35–10 on January 1, 1988. Sherrill left Texas A&M with a winning record against the Longhorns, winning his last five against The University of Texas, after losing his first two. In 1988, Sherrill's Aggies were placed on a two-year probationary period by the NCAA. Sherrill was not personally found guilty of any infractions. In December 1988, Sherrill resigned and later coached at Mississippi State where he was 75-75-2. Today, Sherrill is a studio analyst for Fox Sports college football coverage.

R.C. Slocum – (1989 – 2002) – (123-47-2) – (.721) – A native of Oakdale, Louisiana, Richard Copeland Slocum, or "R. C.," won more games as Texas A&M head football coach than anyone else in Texas A&M football history. After coaching under Vince Gibson at Kansas State and John Robinson at the University of Southern California, Slocum was hired as a receivers coach by Texas A&M head coach Emory Ballard. After Ballard left for Mississippi State, Slocum coached defensive ends and linebackers for the Aggies. In 1979, he became defensive coordinator under head coach Tom Wilson. In 1981, he was the defensive coordinator for USC. In 1982, he returned to A&M to serve as Jackie Sherrill's defensive coordinator, a post he held until Sherrill's departure in 1988. Slocum never had a losing season and won four conference championships, including the Big 12 title in 1998 and two Big 12 South Championships, in 1997 and 1998. Under him the Aggies became the first school in Southwest Conference history to post three consecutive perfect conference seasons. Those Aggie teams went four consecutive seasons without a conference loss. Slocum reached 100 wins faster than any other coach of his time. He has the best winning percentage in Southwest Conference History, ahead of the legendary Darrell Royal. Slocum was inducted into the College Football Hall of Fame as a coach in 2012.

Kevin Sumlin **–** (2012-2017) – (51-26) – (.671) – The Brewton, Alabama native and Purdue graduate forged a 35-17 head coaching record at the University of Houston from 2008-2011. Before Houston, Sumlin served as co-offensive coordinator and wide receivers coach at Oklahoma from 2003-2007. Before that he was a wide receivers coach at Texas A&M, in 2001-2002, under R.C. Slocum. Sumlin landed at A&M with great promise and hope, but his stay in College Station proved unsuccessful by program terms. Behind Heisman Trophy winner Johnny Manziel, Sumlin took Texas A&M—in their first year in the Southeastern Conference—to an 11-2 record, including victories over #1 Alabama in Tuscaloosa, and #11 Oklahoma in the AT&T Cotton Bowl. For his winning efforts, Sumlin was named the 2012 Coach of the Year in the Southeastern Conference. Over the next five seasons Sumlin failed to attain an SEC championship like A&M fans wanted. Despite never posting a losing record at A&M, Sumlin failed to reach double-digit win marks and struggled against SEC opponents—especially those in the Western Division. His bowl record was 3-2, with victories over Oklahoma, Duke and West Virginia. Sumlin was fired before the end of his sixth season. He left College Station in 2017, taking a head coaching job with the University of Arizona Wildcats where he is 9-15 after two seasons.

Jimbo Fisher **–** (2018-present) – (17-9) – (.607) - A Clarksburg, West Virginia native and graduate of Salem International University and Samford University (1989), Fisher played for Salem in 1985 and 1986. In 1987, he played for Samford, where he was the 1987 Division III National Player of the Year. In 1988, Fisher played for the Chicago Bruisers, an arena league team. Fisher attended Clemson University to play baseball before going to Salem College in Salem, West Virginia. In Salem he played quarterback for head coach Terry Bowden. When Bowden left for Samford University in Birmingham, Alabama, Fisher transferred with him to play his final season for the Bulldogs. In 1988, he assumed a position with Samford, coaching quarterbacks in a graduate assistantship. From 1991-1992 he was

Stanford's offensive coordinator and quarterbacks coach. From 1993 to 1998 he coached for Auburn as their quarterbacks coach. In 1999, he coached a year at Cincinnati as their OC/QB coach. From 2000 to 2006 he coached at LSU where he again was the OC/QB coach, under Nick Saban and Les Miles, winning a national championship in 2003. From 2007 to 2009 he served at Florida State under legendary Coach Bobby Bowden as his OC/QB coach and toward the end of Bowden's tenure he was the de facto "coach in waiting." From 2010-1017 Fisher served as head coach at Florida State University, winning the 2014 National Championship. He assumed head coaching duties at Texas A&M in 2018. Fisher is known as a crafty play caller and as a coach who knows how to create an offense based on his team's abilities. With a guaranteed ten-year, $75 million contract in College Station, he is one of college football's highest paid coaches. In his first season, Fisher led the Aggies to a record-setting, seven-overtime, 74-72 victory at home against LSU to end the regular season 9-4, 5-3 in conference play. In his second year Fisher went 8-5, 4-4, losing to eventual national champion LSU by the score of 50-7. Fisher is 9-7 in conference play.

Players:

***Jack Pardee* –** (1954-1956) – An Exira, Iowa native, Pardee is remembered as one of the toughest Aggie football players. Pardee came to A&M after starring in six-man football at a tiny school in Cristoval, Texas. One of Bear Bryant's famed "Junction Boys," Pardee was a star on both sides of the ball for the 1956 Southwest Conference Champion Aggies. He rushed for 463 yards and five touchdowns while intercepting three passes on defense. Always able to deliver the big play when needed, he was named an All-American in 1956. He was selected by the Los Angeles Rams in the second round of the 1957 NFL Draft and was named to the 1963 Pro Bowl. After his lengthy playing career, Pardee went into coaching. He coached at the University of Houston and then professionally as the head coach of the Houston Oilers. He is the only head coach to helm a team in college football, the National Football League, the United States Football League, the World Football League, and the Canadian Football League. Pardee was inducted into the College Football Hall of Fame as a player in 1986. Pardee lost a battle to cancer on April 1, 2013.

***Ray Childress* –** (1981-1984) – A Memphis, Tennessee native, Childress was one of the most dominant defensive lineman to play for Texas A&M. Childress was a two-time All-American for the Aggies in 1983 and 1984. In 1983, Childress posted 15 sacks. He added 10 as a senior, in 1984. He ranks fifth all-time at Texas A&M in both career tackles and career sacks. He was the third pick of the Houston Oilers in the first round of the 1985 NFL Draft, becoming

a five-time All-Pro player as both a defensive end and tackle. He shares the NFL record for fumble recoveries in a single game, having recovered three from the Washington Redskins on October 30, 1988. He was inducted into the Texas Sports Hall of Fame. While Childress was at Texas A&M the NCAA passed a rule disallowing schools from sending life-sized posters to recruits because Jackie Sherrill was sending life-sized posters of Childress in the mail to prospective players.

***Richmond Webb* –** (1986 – 1989) – Webb, a Dallas, Texas native, is remembered as one of the best offensive linemen to don an Aggie uniform. He was an All-Southwest Conference player in 1989, and received the Aggie Heart Award that same year. Jackie Sherrill recruited him as a defensive lineman out of Dallas' Roosevelt High School, but he switched to the offensive side of the ball at the request of the coaches and became one of the best at his position. Webb was the 9th overall selection of the 1990 NFL Draft by the Miami Dolphins and went on to participate in seven straight pro bowls. He started a team record 118 games for the Dolphins. Webb protected Hall of Fame Miami quarterback Dan Marino's blind side for much of his career and played for the Cincinnati Bengals from 2001-2002.

***Darren Lewis* –** (1987-1990) – A Dallas native, Lewis is remembered as Texas A&M's all-time leading rusher, with 5,012 yards in four years played from 1987-1990, which, at the time, was the fifth-best rushing total in NCAA history. Lewis totaled over 1,300 more yards than A&M's second-leading rusher, Curtis Dickey, who had 3,703 from 1976-79. After his senior season in which he led the nation in rushing yardage, he was named a consensus All-American and was a certain first round draft pick until he ran into personal problems stemming from illicit drug use during the NFL combine. As a result, Lewis slipped to the sixth round, with Chicago taking a chance on him late. However, a troubled Lewis lasted only two years in the league after playing sparingly for the Bears.

***Ryan Tannehill* –** (2008-2011) – A four-year starter at quarterback for the Aggies, Tannehill, a Big Spring, Texas native, is remembered as one of the Aggies most effective signal callers. Tannehill redshirted his true freshman season and then over four years threw for 5,450 yards and 42 touchdown passes. In the 2012 NFL Draft, the Miami Dolphins selected Tannehill with the 8th overall pick. He was the first quarterback selected by the Dolphins in the first round since Dan Marino in 1983. He is the third quarterback taken in the first round in franchise history, following Hall of famers Bob Griese and Dan Marino. In 2012, Tannehill set a Miami Dolphin record for passing yards by a rookie with 3,294 yards.

Johnny Manziel – (2011-2013) – As a redshirt freshman in 2012, the 6-1, 200-pound Kerrville, Texas native rewrote SEC and college football record books en route to an unforgettable, first-ever freshman Heisman-claiming, 11-2 season; punctuated by a road victory over the reigning SEC and National Champs, the University of Alabama in Tuscaloosa. In 2012, with his uncanny ability to extend plays, Manziel accounted for 47 total touchdowns, 26 rushing and 21 passing; rushing for 1,410 yards and passing for another 3,706. He finished the season with a 155.32 quarterback rating, completing 68 percent of his throws. He set the Football Bowl Subdivision (FBS) freshman record for total offense in a season with 5,116 yards. He broke Archie Manning's long-standing record for most yards of total offense in a game with 576, smashing Manning's 1969 record of 540 yards, and his own record of 557, set two weeks earlier. He broke Cam Newton's total yardage in a season record with two fewer games played. The former high school Parade All-American Player of the Year, born December 6, 1992, is also known by his nickname, "Johnny Football," a moniker he copyrighted. He is the first freshman to receive the Davey O'Brien National Quarterback Award. He won the prestigious Manning Award and was a consensus First Team All-SEC, SEC Freshman of the Year and SEC Player of the Year; and a consensus All-American. On January 4, 2013, Manziel led Texas A&M to a 41-13 victory in the 2013 Cotton Bowl Classic against Oklahoma, where he was named MVP. In 2013, his redshirt sophomore season, Manziel led the Aggies to a 9-4 season, and dropped a 49-42 game against Alabama despite throwing for 464 yards and five touchdowns. He finished fifth in Heisman voting in 2013 and entered the 2014 NFL Draft where he was the 22nd pick by the Cleveland Browns. Manziel played two disappointing years in Cleveland before being released. He also had a short stint in the Canadian Football League. Today, he is a paid endorser.

Ryan Swope – (2009-2012) – The Austin native is remembered as a fan favorite and a leader on the 2012 inaugural SEC team that featured Heisman winner Johnny Manziel. Swope attended Westlake High School, where he

was a running back. He was a regular backup receiver as a freshman in College Station, posting 19 receptions for 172 yards and a touchdown. In 2010, he evolved into the prototypical go-to receiver, starting all 13 games, and grabbing 72 passes for 825 yards and four touchdowns, including eight catches for 136 yards and a score in an upset of rival Oklahoma. Swope posted the best receiving year in school history as a junior with 89 catches for 1,207 yards. During his senior year he was reliable with 72 grabs for 913 yards. Swope was drafted in the sixth round of the 2013 NFL Draft by the Arizona Cardinals but never played due to reoccurring concussions.

Jake Matthews – (2010-2013) - A native of Missouri City, Texas where he attended Elkins High School, Matthews was a standout offensive lineman and the son of NFL Hall of Fame offensive tackle Bruce Matthews. He chose A&M over a number of schools, including Alabama and Arkansas, and started four straight years in College Station. As a freshman Matthews moved into a starting role due to an injury to a starter; he stepped in and started the final seven games, playing in a total of ten. As a sophomore he helped the Aggies offensive front that allowed only nine sacks on the season. As a junior, he was a major reason the Aggie offense outscored opponents two to one and as a senior he was again a team leader who switched from right tackle to left, demonstrating his skill and dexterity at the difficult position. His last two years were the team's first two in the Southeastern Conference. A two-time All-SEC performer, and a Walter Camp All-American, Matthews was the team's deep snapper, blocked for a freshman Johnny Manziel (Heisman) and was chosen by the Atlanta Falcons as the sixth overall pick in the 2014 NFL Draft. He is a member of the College Football Hall of Fame All-Decade Team, 2011-2019.

Myles Garrett (2014-2016) – A native of Arlington, Texas where he attended Martin High School, lettering in football, basketball and track, Garrett was a stud athlete. In football, he had 19 sacks as a senior, prompting a frenzied recruitment of his five-star rated college football services. Myles, the #2 rated player in the country, chose the Aggies, and in

doing so became the highest-rated defensive player the school signed. In his true freshman season in 2014, Garrett demonstrated superior pass-rushing abilities, notching a Texas A&M record 5.5 sacks in only six games, finishing the season with an SEC second-best 11.5. In only nine games he broke Jadeveon Clowney's SEC freshman sack record of eight. He added 53 tackles and 14 tackles for loss, ten QB hurries and a blocked kick, en route to All-SEC freshman honors. In his sophomore season Garrett led the SEC in sacks with 12. He added 57 total tackles, 18 coming at a loss. Garrett was named a Walter Camp Football All-American at the end of the season, and he won the Bill Willis Award for the nation's top defensive lineman. Although his junior year was limited by nagging injuries—he still recorded 8.5 sacks and 32 tackles, with 15 being tackles for loss. At season's end Garrett was named a consensus All-American by the Associated Press, the Football Writers Association of America and the Coaches Association. After his 41-inch vertical jump at the combine—which was the best by a lineman—Garrett was taken by the Cleveland Browns as the first overall pick in the 2017 NFL Draft.

Great Aggie Traditions:

The Legend of the 12th Man

The endearing tradition of the 12th Man speaks to the entire student body—past and present. Sprung from the selfless gesture of E. King Gill at a 1922 Dixie Classic football game in Dallas, the tradition embodies the core values held by the university. Students still show the revered 12th Man spirit at each athletic event, ready to go into the fray if needed. The story of this colorful tradition has been told and retold to generations of Aggie students, and is part of the substance that binds A&M students together forever. The 12th Man story and legend is the reason A&M students stand for each entire football game. The Late Dr. E. King Gill of Corpus Christi related the important "12th Man" A&M anecdote:

"It was in January, 1922, following the 1921 football season. The Aggies were Southwest Conference champions and were invited to play Centre College in what was then called the Dixie Classic in Dallas. I had played on the football team but was on the basketball team at that time, as those in charge felt I was more valuable to the basketball team. I was in Dallas, however, and even rode to the stadium in the same taxi with Coach Dana X. Bible. I was in civilian clothes and was not to be in uniform. Coach Bible asked me to assist in spotting players for the late Jinx Tucker, the sports editor of the Waco News-Tribune, in the press box. So, I was up in the press box, helping Jinx Tucker, when near the end of the first half, I was called down to the Texas A&M bench. There were a number of injuries. When I arrived on the field I

learned Coach Bible wanted me to put on a football uniform and be ready to play if he needed me. There were no dressing rooms at the stadium in those days. The team dressed downtown at the hotel and traveled to the stadium in taxi cabs. Me and the injured player went under the stands and he put on my clothes and I put on his uniform. I was ready to play but never was sent into the game."

A statue of E. King Gill stands to the north of Kyle Field to remind Aggies of their obligation to preserve the enduring spirit of the 12th Man.

Coach Jackie Sherrill created the "12th Man Kickoff Team" composed of non-athletic scholarship students who tried out for the team, instead of players who were recruited. Coach Sherrill wrote a book titled "No Experience Required" explaining the special kickoff team and the tradition it created. These students were placed on the roster solely for kickoffs. Each player was given the same number to wear, since at the time the NCAA did not prohibit more than one person on the field with the same number. Nicknamed "the suicide squad," many kickoff return teams feared these special walk-on students determined to leave their mark in Aggie lore. These mercenaries often had little regard for safety and were determined to make tackles. The 12th Man kickoff team was successful, holding opponents to the lowest yards-per-return average in NCAA Division I Football. Later, head coach R. C. Slocum changed the team to allow only one representative of the 12th Man on the kick off team who wears uniform number 12. The player is chosen based on the level of determination and hard work shown in practices. Under Dennis Franchione, the "12th Man Kickoff Team", entirely made up of walk-ons, was brought back, though they were rarely used.

Yell Practice

Aggies don't cheer; they yell! Thus there is always a lively spirit session held which builds enthusiasm for an upcoming athletic contest. Under the direction of the Yell Leaders, the Aggies hold Yell Practice. At practice Aggies show their support for the team by shouting the yells with spirit and singing the Aggie songs with pride. Yell Leaders are elected each year by the student body, continuing the tradition started by the five original Aggie Yell Leaders from 1907. Yell Leaders indicate each yell by a different hand signal and incoming freshmen attend "Fish Camp" to learn all the yells and corresponding hand signals. Yell Leaders operate in front of the student section at athletics events, wearing all white and encouraging their peers to show their Aggie spirit. Yell practice is held at midnight at Kyle Field before home football games. At these late night sessions Yell Leaders wearing white lead the Fightin' Texas Aggie Band, current and former students, and fans into the stadium and lead them—which sometimes numbers well above 25,000 people, through the various Aggie yells, many of which date to Texas A&M's earliest days.

Gig 'Em!

Aggies often flash a thumbs up and say "Gig 'em!" This began at Yell Practice before the 1930 TCU football game, when Aggie Pinky Downs shouted, "What are we gonna do to the Horned Frogs?" He then gave the crowd a thumbs-up, yelling the answer, "Gig 'em, Aggies!" A "gig" is a sharp, three-pronged tool used for hunting and killing frogs. The phrase and gesture identify an Aggie fan.

Silver Taps

One of the more emotional Aggie traditions, the solemn ceremony serves as a tribute and honor to an Aggie who has died. It is held in front of the Academic Building on the first Tuesday of every month at 10:30 p.m., if a student died during the preceding month. Students gather around the area, and the campus lights are dimmed, cars included. Chimes play from the Albritton Tower; a detachment from the Ross Volunteers fires three volleys; and buglers from the Aggie band play Silver Taps three times. The family members of the deceased Aggie are invited as special guests.

Muster

Muster began in 1883, when Aggies met on June 26th to "live over their college days." The early meetings were parties and banquets held during the commencement exercises. A permanent date was set — April 21 — and it became a time to pay homage to students and former students who died during the past year. At today's Muster, living comrades answer "here" to the roll call at the largest ceremony before a full house in Reed Arena, for their friends who have passed on. During World War I, groups of Aggies held Muster in trenches in Europe. In 1923, former students began holding Muster throughout Texas, the nation and numerous other parts of the world — to let Aggies remember times gone by and to meet with old friends.

Howdy

"Howdy" is the official greeting of Texas A&M. Students greeting one another, and especially visitors, with a "howdy" has earned the university a reputation as one of the friendliest campuses on the planet.

Aggie Heart Award

The coveted and cherished honor given to a Texas A&M football player, based on effort, desire, determination, competitiveness, leadership and courage.

Aggie Code of Honor

"Aggies do not lie, cheat, or steal, nor do they tolerate those who do."

The Aggie War Hymn (in lieu of a fight song)

Hullabaloo, Caneck! Caneck!
Hullabaloo, Caneck! Caneck!

First Verse

All hail to dear old Texas A&M,
Rally around Maroon and White,
Good luck to the dear old Texas Aggies,
They are the boys who show the fight.
That good old Aggie spirit thrills us.
And makes us yell and yell and yell; --
So let's fight for dear old Texas A&M,
We're goin' to beat you all to --
Chig-gar-roo-gar-rem!
Chig-gar-roo-gar-rem!
Rough! Tough!
Real stuff! Texas A&M!

Second Verse

Good-bye to Texas University.
So long to the Orange and White.
Good luck to the dear old Texas Aggies,
They are the boys who show
the real old fight.
The eyes of Texas are upon you.
That is the song they sing so well,
So, good-bye to Texas University,
We're goin' to beat you all to --
Chig-gar-roo-gar-rem!
Chig-gar-roo-gar-rem!
Rough! Tough!
Real stuff! Texas A&M!

Saw Varsity's Horns Off (normally follows War Hymn)

Saw Varsity's Horns Off!
Saw Varsity's Horns Off!
Saw Varsity's Horns Off!
Short!

Varsity's Horns are Sawed Off!
Varsity's Horns are Sawed Off!
Varsity's Horns are Sawed Off!
Short!

The Spirit of Aggieland

Some may boast of prowess bold
Of the school they think so grand,
But there's a spirit can ne'er be told
It's the spirit of Aggieland.

Chorus
We are the Aggies -- the Aggies are we.
True to each other as Aggies can be.
We've got to FIGHT boys,
We've got to FIGHT!
We've got to fight for Maroon and White.
After they' ve boosted all the rest,
They will come and join the best.
For we are the Aggies --
the Aggies so true,
We're from Texas A. M. U.

Second Chorus
T--E--X--A--S, A--G--G--I--E,
Fight! Fight! Fight! Fight! Fight!
Fight! Maroon!
White--White--White!
A--G--G--I--E, Texas!
Texas! A. M. U.
GIG 'EM AGGIES! 1! 2! 3!
FARMERS FIGHT! FARMERS FIGHT!
Fight -- fight --
Farmers, farmers, fight!

Noteworthy Alumni:

Edward Aldridge, Jr., 1960, Former United States Secretary of the Air Force

A.D. Bruce, Former President of the University of Houston, former U.S. Army Major General, founder of Fort Hood

Horace S. Carswell, Jr., 1938, Medal of Honor Recipient, namesake of Car-

swell Air Force Base, Fort Worth, Texas

Mary Beth Decker, actress and model, MTV's Road Rules

Patricia Gras, 1983, CBS TV anchor, Emmy Award winner

Rip Torn, 1952, actor

Glen McCarthy, 1931, Wildcatter

Douglas P. Stan, Pulitzer Prize recipient

Steven Swanson, 1998, NASA astronaut

Bryan Lunney, 1989, NASA Flight Director

Henry Cisneros, 1968, former Mayor of San Antonio, U.S. Housing & Urban Development, Secretary

2020 Texas A&M Football Schedule

Sept. 5 Abilene Christian

Sept. 12 North Texas

Sept. 19 Colorado

Sept. 26 vs. Arkansas (Arlington)

Oct. 3 at Mississippi State

Oct. 10 Fresno State

Oct. 17 at Auburn

Oct. 24 at South Carolina

Oct. 31 OPEN DATE

Nov. 7 Ole Miss

Nov. 14 Vanderbilt

Nov. 21 at Alabama

Nov. 28 LSU

The Art of Tailgating

Tailgating has become a practiced art among SEC football fans everywhere. The period of time prior to a gridiron contest is one in which the entire college community comes together to enjoy themselves. Southerners have long been known for their unquenchable "joie de vivre" or "joy of life" and it seems that Saturday afternoons prior to game time have become a rite of food and fun that is indicative of the way Southerners approach and enjoy life.

Like clockwork, prior to every pigskin match-up, SEC fans from near and far congregate—whether they are at the game or not, to partake in the joy of tailgating. Every family and coterie of true football fans has their own tried-and-true method for cooking up their groceries before game time. Some fans choose to barbecue ribs, chicken and spicy sausage. Some opt for jambalaya or gumbo, if the weather and inclination are right. Still other fans go as far to hire catering services to prepare a meal on their behalf for the occasion. Whatever the case, tailgating is an integral part of every SEC fan's game day experience.

The following 14 authentic, Cajun recipes have been enjoyed and tweaked by family and friends throughout the years. I grew up in South Louisiana where food is the first order of business and flavor is the key to success. Feel free to prepare and share these tasty Southern delicacies with your family and friends on fall Saturdays. Hope to see you there! Bon Appetit SEC fans! Happy Tailgating!

Tailgating...The Colorful History of America's Biggest Sporting Pastime

Tailgating—its mere mention among football fans conjures cool, leaf-blown images of the fall and football season. This anticipated weekend engagement is staged against the inviting autumn backdrop of friends, family, enemies, ice cold beer, cocktails and/or wine and of course, food. Ah yes—tailgating, the veritable game before the game, and for some fans—the more important one, is today as much a feature of the modern football experience as the forward pass. This burgeoning American cultural phenomenon is ubiquitous, and it can be witnessed prior to kickoff in the parking lot of your favorite pro stadium or on the lazy, sprawling campus of your revered alma mater. Tailgating has grown into the quintessential culinary side show of the modern sporting era; a veritable Epicurean outdoor feast that precedes the fall ritual of college and pro football games. While modern tailgating has only within the last 40 years become popular, the practice of enjoying food and football has early 20th century origins.

Early Times

In the beginning, there was only college football. Professional football did not arrive on the American sporting scene until the 1950's, while the first college football game occurred between Ivy League schools Rutgers and Princeton in New Brunswick in 1869. Twelve years later, in 1881, the first college football game south of the Mason-Dixon Line

occurred on the bluegrass at Old Stoll Field in Lexington, Kentucky. During the earliest days of the sport, food and football went hand in hand. It was customary for the fans of each team to engage in a wild fish and game supper before the contest and then to revisit the leftovers after the game and relived the on-field exploits of the daring young gridders.

And Then There Was Light

For years after the turn of the century until the advent of electric lighting and night football during the late 1920's and early 1930's, college football games were played almost exclusively during the day. Towering electric lamps and night football games brought about the practice of hosting all day football parties at fans' homes where they would congregate and leisurely hop from house-to-house as the evening kickoff approached. Night games were a critical social development since they allowed for the working man to attend, for cooler game time temperatures and for men and women to dress up for the popular pre-game parties. Women wore their best dresses adorned with team-colored corsages while men donned spiffy coats, ties, derbies and fedoras.

These festive, pre-game jaunts continued unabated for nearly 40 years until daytime college football on television pre-empted the house partiey. Along with much-needed athletic department revenue, TV coverage brought with it the dreaded day football games, which precluded the practice of party hopping around town prior to the contest. The alternative to not house partying was simple to the legions of football fans that had been weaned on pre-game football parties: Take the party to the stadium! And that they did, because today tailgating at or near the stadium is a social practice that seems to have found a continual flow of willing fall participants. Predictably, tailgating now occurs before night games and day games as college football's fan base—and their propensity to tailgate--only grows with each passing year. Tailgating has become so popular that some football fans enjoy it as much as the game itself—and that's saying something in the football-crazed American heartland!

One often-overlooked or under-studied aspect of tailgating is its name. Simple logic leads one to surmise that the term describes the practice of having an outdoor picnic on the tailgate of a truck or station wagon, and this is largely understood to be true. No official etymology of the American word exists, further reinforcing the fledgling status of this growing sporting tradition.

So this fall when you hitch up your family trickster and prepare your numerous and varied tailgating wares and eats, remember that the modern cultural ritual you are fulfilling on game day finds its humble origins during the early twentieth century. And take stock in the notion that tailgating is the last great free-for-all, and the modern counterpart of the traditional county fair—where with only a lint-filled pocket you can party with some of the most attractive, friendly and outgoing fans of American food, football and fun! That's about as good as it gets, folks! Laissez-les bon temps roulez! Happy Tailgating!

Crimson Tide Seafood Gumbo

1 cup flour
1 cup parsley chopped
1 cup oil
2 lbs. small shrimp
2 large onions
1 lb. lump crab
2 lg. bell peppers
1 lb. crawfish tails
1 bunch celery
Tony Chachere's to taste
1 lb. pork tasso
Mashed roasted garlic
1 bunch green onions
15 cloves
½ gallon water
Cayenne and salt to taste
1 cup dried shrimp
1 bay leaf
1 teaspoon Italian seasoning
Tabasco to taste
1 tablespoon sugar
1 tablespoon lemon juice
½ stick of butter
½ cup condensed milk

Crimson Tide Seafood Gumbo

In a gumbo pot on high to medium heat, mix oil and flour to make a chocolate colored roux. Add onions, peppers, celery and garlic and 137auté' well. Stir in pork tasso and cook for two minutes and then add water. Stir well and cook for one hour, seasoning occasionally to taste. Add parsley and dried shrimp during this procedure as well. Add shrimp after gumbo boils for an hour then cook additional 20 minutes. Add crawfish tails, remaining ingredients and lump crab. Cook for additional half hour. Add green onions, season again and serve! NOTE: May acquire more flavors by adding additional dried shrimp, water from boiled shrimp peelings or small gumbo crabs from the parish. Oysters would be great in this recipe as it only enhances the seafood mix. Serve over great Louisiana rice and hot, liberally-buttered French bread. Enjoy!

Razorback Jambalaya

2 lbs. of the meanest hog out there (dice pork)
2 lbs. smoked sausage
4lbs. Louisiana Rice
2 cups diced pork tasso
2 large onions, chopped
2 large peppers, chopped
½ bunch of celery chopped
1 bunch green onions
Lots of minced garlic
Tony Chachere's seasoning
Tobasco Hot Sauce to taste
3 cans chicken broth
½ cup flour
½ cup oil
Salt and pepper to taste
1 cup of parsley
1 tablespoon of lemon juice
1 cup sugar
1 stick of butter
2 tablespoons celery salt
Thyme to taste

Razorback Jambalaya

Always add ½ parts of water to rice if you are using broth! In a large black iron skillet begin browning meat on high heat. After meat is browned, remove and set aside. While skillet is still hot add rice and brown well. After your small amount of rice is browned, add celery, onions, pepper, garlic and generous seasoning. Saute' until onions are tender. Add chicken broth, water, and meat, bring all to a boil. After water begins to boil add the rest of the rice, turn heat to low and stir occasionally. Rice will begin to get fluffy after about 25 to 30 minutes. Season more if you desire while adding parsley and green onions. If rice is hard add more water and let steam again. NOTE: Flour in this recipe should be used to brown the meat in the skillet with small amounts added at a time. This will give you a lot of color for your jambalaya. If you desire a darker color add a little kitchen bouquet. 25 servings

Jordan-Hare Shrimp and Okra Stew

1 lb. fresh gulf shrimp
1 onion minced
1 can diced tomatoes with green chilis
1 green pepper chopped
1 bunch of celery chopped
Lots of mashed garlic
1 lb. fresh/frozen chopped okra
½ cup flour and ½ cup oil
Crab claws if desired
1 cup shrimp stock or boullion
Tobasco Sauce to taste
1 cup of water
1 cup dried shrimp
1 teaspoon nutmeg
Tony Chachere seasoning to taste
1 cup sugar
½ stick butter
Juice from one lemon
Gumbo file' to taste

Jordan-Hare Shrimp & Okra Stew

In a heavy pot add flour and oil; stir to make a dark roux. Add onions, peppers, celery and garlic and saute' until tender. Add okra and saute' over medium temperature to high heat for about 20 minutes. After boiling, add diced tomatoes with green chilis, and rest of ingredients. Season occasionally and add shrimp, stock and water, cook while stirring on low heat for one hour. Serve over fluffy Louisiana or brown rice. Enjoy! NOTE: Great recipe after that first shrimp boil of the season. Simply use the boiled bait shrimp that you could not eat! 12 servings.

Death Valley Crawfish Etouffee'

3 lbs. Louisiana crawfish tails
2 bell peppers
½ cup of crawfish fat (if available)
2 onions
1 cup of chopped parsley
1 bunch of celery
2 cups of green onions chopped
1 cup of flour
3 tablespoons mashed garlic
1 cup of oil
Tony Chachere's seasoning to taste
Tobasco to taste
1 tablespoon paprika
Water as needed
1 cup sugar
½ stick of butter
Juice from one lemon
1 shot of Kentucky bourbon

Death Valley Crawfish Etouffee'

Using flour and oil, make a light golden brown roux. Add chopped onion, peppers, celery and garlic. Cook until onions are tender. Add crawfish and fat. Cook for 20 minutes. Add very little water; slowly add water a little at a time. Your etouffee' should thicken. Add paprika and season to taste. Throw in chopped green onions and serve over fluffy white Louisiana rice. Enjoy! NOTE: Shrimp, lump crab, or chicken are good substitutes. Best when served on cold game days with the smell of a win in the air! If your team wins add another shot of bourbon and hand over the keys. 12-14 servings

Starkville Shrimp and Corn Soup

2 16 oz. cans of chopped kernel corn
2 large onions
½ bunch celery, chopped
1 cup of oil
2 16 oz. cans diced Rotel tomatoes
1 cup flour
Fresh Shrimp (save the shells to make stock)
Tobasco to taste
1 teaspoon onion powder
2 12 oz. cans of chicken broth
1 cup chopped parsley
2 bell peppers chopped
6 shallots chopped
Tobasco to taste
Tony Chachere's to taste

Starkville Shrimp and Corn Soup

Start with a golden brown colored roux, by heating the flower and roux in a skillet. Make sure not to burn the roux, stirring frequently on low-medium heat. In a second pot add the chicken broth and shrimp peelings with about four quarts (one gallon) of water and boil for 30 minutes. Strain into large pot, add all chopped vegetables, can corn and tomatoes. When soup has reached a boil again lower fire to lw and add roux slowly to add color and base to your soup. Add shrimp when soup returns to a low boil. Season to taste. Cook soup after shrimp are added for about 40 minutes, just in time for the game with a side piece of buttery garlic bread! 12-14 servings

Rebel Red Beans With Pork Sausage & Rice

1 ham bone or hock
Lots of finely-minced garlic
1 lb. dried red beans
½ cup chopped parsley
1 lb. of smoked pork sausage (hot)
1 bay leaf
1 lg. onion
1 lg. green pepper
1 bunch celery chopped
½ cup sweet cream
1 cup of green onion
Tony Chachere's seasoning to taste
Tobasco hot sauce
1 teaspoon of Italian seasoning
Salt and pepper to taste
½ stick of butter
1 cup of sugar
1 teaspoon Worcestershire sauce

Rebel Red Beans With Pork Sausage & Rice

Soak your beans overnight. After you bring them to a boil, add a ham bone. It adds real color and flavor that it otherwise impossible to achieve. Don't forget you ham bone or hock. They ooze fat as they cook and they are the secret to this recipe. Saute' on high heat with sausage and ham bones for five minutes. In doing so, you will retain all of that great fat that came from the sausage to cook your onions, peppers, celery and garlic. Cook on high heat while adding all beans and remaining ingredients. It is important to note: You must bring beans to a boil to cream them by mashing them to the side of the pot as they cook. Stir occasionally. Once you get the right consistency, you can add green onions and serve over your favorite Louisiana rice. NOTE: Hot fresh or homemade Southern corn bread is something you should not forget for this event! Remember to cook your beans long and slowly so you can enjoy the tailgating fun!

Texas A&M Five-Alarm Chili

3 lbs. ground beef
3 15 oz. cans of spicy chili beans
2 cans diced tomatoes
A1 6 oz. can tomato paste
1 large onion chopped
3 stalk celery chopped
1 green bellpepper, 1 red bellpepper, chopped
2 green chili peppers, seeded
¼ cup chili powder
1 tablespoon minced garlic
1 tablespoon oregano
2 tablespoons ground cumin
2 teaspoons of Tabasco
1 teaspoon dried basil
1 teaspoon salt
1 teaspoon paprika
Tony Chachere's seasoning to taste

Texas A&M Five-Alarm Tailgate Chili

Heat a large pot over medium to high heat. Brown ground beef in the pan. Cook until evenly brown and drain grease. Pour chili, beans, tomatoes and paste into pan. Add celery, onion, green and red peppers, chili peppers, etc. Blend and simmer for at least two hours. Serve with Fritos and grated cheese. Serves 12

Gainesville Alligator Sauce Piquante'

1 cup of flour
Lots of chopped garlic
1 cup of oil
½ cup of sugar
1 crushed bay leaf
Tomato sauce
1 quart diced tomatoes w/ green chilis
3 lbs. gator tail meat
1 large bell pepper chopped
3 cups celery chopped
1 bunch green onions
2 cups parsley
2 pints mushrooms sliced
Tony Chachere's to taste
Tobasco Hot Sauce to taste
1 tablespoon Italian seasoning
Salt and Pepper to taste
Seafood base or cubes (4 oz.)
1 large onion chopped
Juice from two lemons
½ stick of butter
Zucchini, thinly sliced
1 teaspoon dried oregano

Gainesville Alligator Sauce Piquante'

In a large pot, over medium to high heat, begin by adding flour and oil to make a roux. Add vegetables, tomato sauce and diced tomatoes, garlic, sugar, bay leaft, and cook for two hours. In a separate pot begin browning the alligator meat with salt and pepper. Only brown the meat; it will finish cooking in the sauce. After browning meat set aside and add after sauce has cooked for two hours. Add meat and cook another hour. Once meat is tender add mushrooms, parsley and green onions; simmer for 30-40 minutes. Serve over fluffy white Louisiana rice. NOTE: Seafood base is not required, but will add flavor to this great recipe. You may substitute turtle, chicken, rabbit, possum, armadillo, nutria or squirrel to this recipe. A crowd favorite in rural Acadiana. Ca c'est bon! 12-14 servings

Athens Redfish Courtboullion

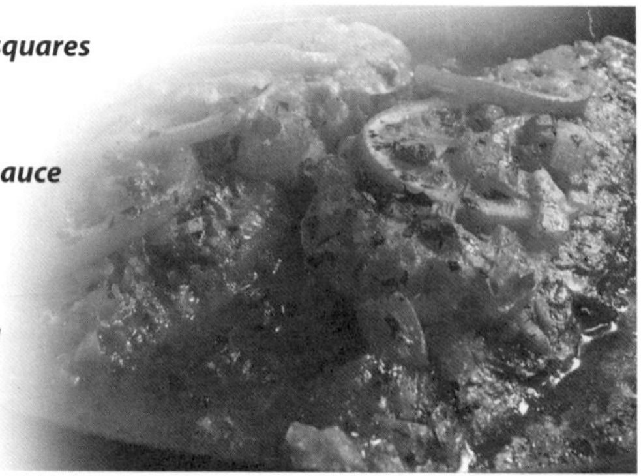

8 lbs. Redfish fillets, cut in 3-inch squares
½ bunch celery, chopped
½ cup garlic, chopped
4 tablespoons of Worcestershire sauce
2 tablespoons of sugar
1.5 cup peanut oil
2 cups water
2 bunches green onions, chopped
1 cup of flour
4 lemons
1 12 oz. Can tomato paste
salt, black-red pepper and Cajun seasonings to taste
3 large onions chopped
2 medium bell peppers, chopped
2 bunches of parsley, chopped
1 12 oz. can of diced Rotel tomatoes
5 bay leaves
2 packages of dried shrimp
Hot sauce to taste

Athens Redfish Courtboullion

Soak dried shrimp in 1 quart of warm water for 30 minutes prior to inclusion. In a large pot, combine oil and flour to make a golden colored roux. Once you have reached a golden color, begin adding all chopped vegetables and stir until onions are translucent. Slowly add stock with shrimp in it to the pot, bring to soft boil and begin adding tomato paste slowly along with the can of Rotel tomatoes. Add one quart of water and stir. Lower heat to medium and cook for 30 minutes. Your sauce should turn from dark to red to orange red, if not cook a little longer. Add sugar, lemon juice and Worcestershire sauce to pot and begin stirring in redfish cutlets. Add bay leaves, season to taste. Cook on low to medium heat for about 30 to 40 minutes, stirring occasionally. Serve over fluffy white rice. Enoy!

Kentucky Wildcat White Chicken Chili

1 lb boneless skinless chicken breasts, diced into 1/2-inch pieces (sometimes I use a rotisserie chicken to speed up the process)
1 small yellow onion, diced
1 tbsp olive oil
2 cloves garlic, finey minced
2 (14.5 oz) cans chicken broth
1 (4 oz) can diced green chilies
1 1/2 tsp cumin
3/4 tsp paprika
1/2 tsp dried oregano
1/2 tsp ground coriander
1/4 tsp cayenne pepper
salt and freshly ground black pepper, to taste
1 (8 oz) pkg Neufchatel cheese, cut into 12 slices
1 1/4 cup fresh corn (frozen works too)
2 (15 oz) cans Cannelini beans, drained and rins
1 Tbsp fresh lime juice
chopped fresh cilantro, for serving
shredded Monterrey Jack cheese, for serving
tortilla chips, for serving (optional)

Kentucky Wildcat White Chicken Chili

Heat olive oil in a 6 quart enameled dutch oven over medium-high heat. Once oil is hot add chicken and diced onion and saute until chicken is no longer pink, about 6 minutes. Add garlic and saute 30 seconds longer. Add chicken broth, green chilies, cumin, paprika, oregano, coriander, cayenne pepper and season with salt and pepper to taste. Bring mixture just to a boil then reduce heat and simmer 15 minutes. Add Neufchatel cheese and stir until melted. Stir in corn, and 1 can of Cannellini beans, then process 3/4 of the remaining beans along with 1/4 cup broth from the soup in a food processor until pureed, add bean mixture to soup along with remaining 1/4 can of beans. Simmer about 15 minutes longer. Mix in lime juice and serve with Monterrey Jack cheese, chopped cilantro and tortilla chips for dipping if desired. Serves six.

Missouri Tiger Tailgate Wings

½ cup finely chopped onion
Dash of black pepper
¼ cup Canola oil
3 teaspoons minced garlic
1 ½ cups of ketchup
½ cup cider vinegar
1/3 cup packed brown sugar
1/3 cup Worcestershire Sauce
2 teaspoons chili powder
½ teaspoons Tony Chachere's Seasoning
½ teaspoon ground cumin
Tabasco Sauce
36 wingettes
¼ cup vinegar
¼ cup olive oil
1/8 teaspoon salt, pepper

Missouri Tiger Tailgate Wings

For barbecue sauce, in large saucepan, saute' onion in oil until tender. Add garlic; cook one minute longer. Stir in the ketchup, vinegar, brown sugar, Worcestershire sauce, chili powder, cayenne and cumin. Simmer, uncovered, for 8-10 minutes, stirring often. Remove from the heat; stir in pepper sauce. Set aside 2/3 cup for serving. In a large re-sealable plastic bag, combine the vinegar, olive oil, salt and pepper; add chicken wings in batches and turn to coat. Moisten a paper towel with cooking oil; using long-handled tongs, lightly coat the grill rack. Grill wings, covered, over medium heat or broil four inches from the heat for 12-16 minutes, turning occasionally. Brush with some of the barbecue sauce. Grill, uncovered 8-10 minutes longer or until juices run clear, basting and turning several times. Serve with barbecue sauce leftover. Yield: Two and one half dozen wings

South Carolina Smoked Turkey and Andouille Gumbo

FOR THE STOCK:
3 lb. smoked turkey wings
6 scallions, roughly chopped
4 sprigs parsley
4 stalks celery, chopped
3 carrots, chopped
1 large white onion, chopped

FOR THE GUMBO:
¾ cup canola oil
1½ lb. andouille, roughly chopped
1 cup flour
3 cloves garlic, minced
1 small red onion, minced
1 small white onion, minced
1green bell pepper, minced
1red bell pepper, minced
1 tbsp. granulated garlic1 tbsp. granulated onion
2 tsp. mesquite seasoning
1 tsp. cayenne
1 tsp. ground white pepper
½ tsp. crushed red chile flakes
1½ lb. smoked turkey breast, cut into ¾" pieces
3 tbsp. Worcestershire sauce
Kosher salt, to taste
Cooked white rice, for serving

South Carolina Smoked Turkey and Andouille Gumbo

Make the stock: Bring ingredients and 1 gallon water to a boil in a large stockpot. Reduce heat to medium; simmer 4 hours, then strain stock and keep warm. Make the gumbo: Heat 2 tbsp. oil in an 8-qt. Dutch oven over medium-high. Cook andouille until fat renders, 8–10 minutes; transfer to a plate. Add remaining oil and sprinkle in flour; stir to make a dark roux. Add garlic, onions, and bell peppers; cook until soft, 10–12 minutes. Stir in granulated garlic and onion, mesquite seasoning, cayenne, white pepper, and chile flakes; cook 1 minute. Add reserved stock and andouille, the turkey breast, Worcestershire sauce, and salt; boil. Reduce heat to medium; cook, stirring occasionally, until gumbo is thickened, about 1 hour. Serve with rice.

Tennessee Spicy Short Ribs

10 lbs. Beef short ribs
2 cups sugar
½ cup salt
½ cup cayenne pepper
1 gallon BBQ sauce
12 ounces bacon fat
4 large red onions
Louisiana hot sauces
1 cup liquid smoke
1 cup garlic powder
1 cup black pepper
water
1 quart apple juice
4 large bell peppers
Tony Chachere's seasoning to taste

Tennessee Spicy Short Ribs

Fill a large pot with more than half with water. Add liquid smoke, salt and apple juice. Bring water to a boil and add ribs. Boil until somewhat tender, for about 45 minutes to an hour. Let cool and brush bacon fat on ribs. Make dry rub for ribs. Mix garlic powder, black pepper, sugar and cayenne pepper. After fat on rib cools, generously add dry rub on the ribs. This should be done before you barbecue. When barbecuing, use wood chips for best results. You should cook ribs on medium-low fire for about 1.5 hours, constantly basting with your own barbecue sauce. Your ribs should turn out sweet as candy. Cut peppers and onions and add the last 15 minutes, grill and serve as a nice touch to this delicious recipe. Enjoy!

Sweet Vandy Brisket

2 beef brisket, 5-6 pounds
2 tablespoon salt
2 tablespoon garlic powder
Cajun seasonings to taste
1 tablespoon cayenne pepper
1 tablespoon thyme
Marinade
1 cup firmly packed dark brown sugar
1 cup unsweetened pineapple juice
3 tablespoon Worcestershire sauce
½ cup cane syrup
1 ½ cup minced onion
1 cup Louisiana hot sauce
½ cup red wine vinegar
½ cup honey
3 cloves garlic minced

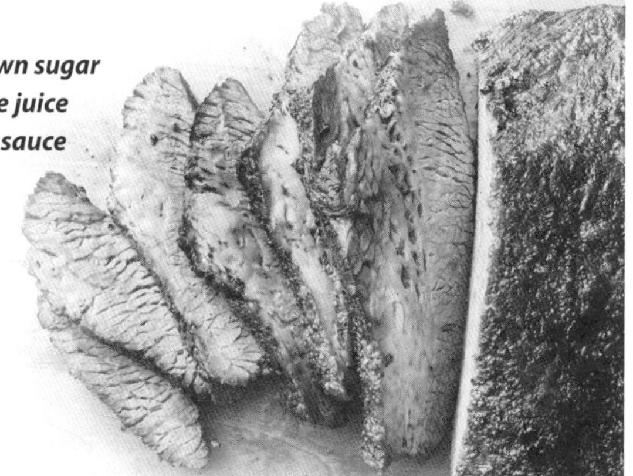

Sweet Vandy Brisket

Season the meat with seasoning mix of salt, peppers, garlic powder and thyme. Place seasoned meat in large glass-baking dish. Mix marinade and pour over brisket. Cover tightly and place in refrigerator for a maximum of 6 days and a minimum of 2 days. Rotate brisket every 12 hours during the chosen time period. Reserve marinade. Grill over coals and wood chips, until browned completely for one hour. Place in large disposable aluminum roasting pan. Pour marinade over the top. Seal pan with foil and cook over coals for an additional 2 hours. Drain marinade off, take brisket and baste with your own barbecue sauce for the last 20 minutes. Should be tender and sweet by the time you serve. Pecan wood chips are my top choice for smoking.

University of Florida

The Sunshine State is known for football, and the University of Florida is one of the main reasons for that particular claim to fame. Florida is the SEC's largest school by enrollment, and eighth-largest in the country, with over 50,000 students. During the 1990's, the Gators were the SEC's most successful football program, winning over 80 percent of their games. Florida's domination of the gridiron during the 1990's was the product of the brain trust of its most favorite football son, former Gator Steve Spurrier, the 1966 Heisman Trophy winner and two-time All-American. After Spurrier's departure, the Gators employed success under another talented football coach—Urban Meyer. Like his vaunted predecessor, Meyer led the Gators to the 2006 and 2008 National Championships. Today's lofty Florida Football expectations are born from past heroics—like with current Coach Dan Mullen, who was a member of Urban Meyer's championship staffs. One of the nation's five premier schools for combining academic and athletic achievement, the University of Florida is one of the country's finest modern-day collegiate institutions.

Founded:

In 1853, the state-funded East Florida Seminary took over the Kingsbury Academy in Ocala. The seminary moved to Gainesville in the 1860's and was consolidated with the state's land grant Florida Agricultural College, then in Lake City. In 1905, by legislative action, the college became a university and was moved to Gainesville. Classes first met with 102 students on the present site on September 26, 1906. The University of Florida opened its doors to women in 1947, and was integrated in 1958. The University of Florida is a 2,000 acre campus consisting of nearly 900 separate buildings, 160 of which contain classrooms. The northeast quadrant of the sprawling campus is an official historic district, complete with a listing on the National Register of Historic Places. The 34 residence halls on campus have a capacity of nearly 7,000 students. The campus of the University of Florida possesses the Florida Museum of National History, which ranks among the nation's top ten natural history museums.

Location:

Gainesville was named the nation's most livable city in a 1995 national ranking. The city is not only the home of the Florida Gators, it is also host to some of the most pristine, fresh-water springs in the country. Surrounded by lush state parks and other recreational facilities, Gainesville offers visitors a variety of outdoor activities in a moderate climate. If the beaches of the Sunshine State are more your cup of tea, the Gulf of Mexico and Atlantic Ocean are both an hour's drive away from the main campus. The University of Florida's influence is felt throughout the social and cultural life of the city.

Population: 124,500

Enrollment: 52,367ity)

Nickname: Gators

In 1907, Austin Miller, a law student of the University of Virginia at Charlottesville, was visited by his father, Phillip. Phillip Miller was the owner of a drug store in Gainesville, Florida, and while he was in Virginia visiting his son, he purchased pennants adorned with the University of Florida to resell to student customers back in Florida. When the manager of the shop asked for Florida's emblem, the elder Miller realized that the school did not have one. The younger Austin Miller suggested to his father that the alligator be used since no school had adopted it, and since the alligator was native to Florida. Miller's off the cuff suggestion stuck, and the first appearance of the alligator emblem was in Phillip Miller's Gainesville drug store in 1908.

Colors: Orange and Blue

The origin of the school's colors is a mystery. One explanation insists that the university acquired the colors from the two schools abolished by the Buckman Act of 1905. The University of Florida at Lake City had school colors of blue and gold and the East Florida Seminary in Gainesville used orange and black. However, there is no empirical, supporting evidence to this reasonable claim.

The first printed reference to Florida school colors appeared in the Florida Times-Union of September 27, 1906. Reporting on the opening of the school's doors, the newspaper stated that the campus buildings were draped in purple and gold. A written reference to school colors appeared in the first campus newspaper, The University News, and the colors were blue and orange. The 1911 campus YMCA calendar was not printed in blue and gold as planned, but was adorned, instead, with blue and orange edging and banners.

Mascot: Alligator

The American alligator (Alligator Mississippiensis) is one of two remaining species of alligator, a genus within the Alligatoridae family. The American alligator is native to the Southeastern portion of the United States where it is a denizen of the wetlands that intersect with human-populated areas. The American alligator is larger than its companion alligator species, the Chinese alligator. The American alligator has a large, slightly rounded body, thick, muscular limbs, a broad head and an extremely powerful tail that it uses for locomotion. Alligators generally fear humans and will avoid them as prey, and they are far less dangerous than crocodiles.

Game Mascots

The Gators have two costumed mascots who roam the sidelines during football games--Albert and Alberta, and they are both fan favorites at the University of Florida. The two characters are anthropomorphic representations of American alligators. In 1984, Jan Timmerberg, the Director of Community Relations at the University Athletic Association was assigned the job of wearing the gator costume and playing "Albert," a duty she has maintained well for many years. Timmerberg helped recreate the look of Albert in 1986 by dressing the Gator with the now-infamous orange "F" emblazoned on the blue sweater. Timmerberg also originated the idea for Alberta in 1991.

Today, eight different students collaborate to handle the demanding duties of Albert and Alberta on game day, where hot and humid Florida temperatures can range in the high 90's. The logo of the Gators athletic teams in the early 1990's was a cartoonized version of Albert. However, this was dropped in favor of a more gender-neutral Gator head logo.

Band name: The Fighting Gator Band / Pride of the Sunshine Band

The University of Florida Fighting Gator Band, also known as The Pride of the Sunshine Band plays at every home football game inside Ben Hill Griffin Stadium. Founded in 1914, the Gator Band insists it will play "anything, anytime, anywhere" representing the University of Florida.

The Fighting Gator Band was formed in 1914 by Director Pug Hamilton. The Women's Gym was used for the first band rehearsals and the first office was in Anderson Hall. The first woman of the Gator Band was Sophie Mae Mitchell in 1948. In 1972, the Gator Band was featured at the opening of Walt Disney World in Orlando, and in 1997, it participated in its 25th Anniversary celebration. The moniker, "Pride of the Sunshine Band," was coined by Dave Strickler. The voice of the Gator Band is Gerre Reynolds.

Director of Bands: Dr. David Waybright

Stadium: Ben Hill Griffin Stadium

The "Swamp" is the nickname for Ben Hill Griffin Stadium at Florida Field. It is currently the largest stadium in the entire state of Florida. Constructed in 1930, the stadium had an original capacity of 21,769. Initially, the entire stadium was constructed below ground. In 1950, over 11,000 seats were added on the west side and another 7,000 were provided by bleachers on the east side. The addition brought seating capacity to 40,116. Bleacher seats were added during the 1950's, bringing capacity to 46,164 by 1960. In December of 1965, construction added over 10,000 permanent seats on the east side as well as temporary bleachers moved from the east side to the south end zone, providing a total capacity of 62,800. The south end zone expansion in 1982, enclosed the south end of the stadium, and brought its capacity to 72,000. Later in 1991, the north end horseshoe was turned into a bowl and raised capacity to 83,000. Expanded club seats and luxury boxes raised the capacity to its current state in 2003.

The stadium's playing surface has changed through the years. In 1971, artificial turf was installed and nicknamed "Doug's Rug" for then-coach Doug Dickey. The artificial surface remained until 1990, when Steve Spurrier insisted on its removal and replacement with natural grass.

Ben Hill Griffin is a bowl stadium with some openings, but for the most part it is enclosed by seats. Possessing a steep seating angle throughout the stadium, the sound level is deafening. Florida Field also has 46 luxury skyboxes, where alcohol and food are served. In 1991, Coach Steve Spurrier commented, "The swamp is where the Gators live. We feel comfortable there, but we hope our opponents feel tentative. A swamp is hot and sticky and dangerous." The Atlanta Journal Constitution proclaimed The Swamp "the loudest, most obnoxious and notorious piece of real estate in all of college football." In 1996, the Sporting News College Football Preview ranked Florida Field among the nation's loudest stadiums.

Stadium capacity: 88,548

First game

Although the University of Florida was playing football prior to the turn of the century, official records list the school's first game in 1906, a game that the University of Florida won, defeating nearby Gainesville AC by the score of 6-0. Due to the United States' involvement in World War II, the University of Florida did not have a football team in 1943.

First game in stadium: 1930 Florida 33, Alabama 20

Record crowd: 90,916 – November 2015, against Florida State

Directions:

Coming from the North or the South on I-75: Take Exit 76 (Highway 26/Newberry Road). Head East to North-South Drive. Turn right; stadium is on left.

From North or South on 441: Go to University Avenue and head West (from the South turn left, from the North turn right). Go to North-South Drive. Turn left; stadium is on left.

Tailgating:

Like most large SEC stadiums, Ben-Hill Griffin is the epicenter of pre-game festivities. On each game day you will find thousands of revelers priming themselves for kickoff. While there is no one designated spot for tailgating, fans can be found throughout the expansive campus plying their pre-pigskin trade like the seasoned professionals they're known as. Gainesville, need we remind you—is a party town.

Nearest Hospital to Stadium:

Shands Hospital at the University of Florida

1600 SW Archer Road

Gainesville, FL 32608

1.352.265.8000

Bail Bondsman for Emergencies:

Bail Bonds Gainesville

1.352.379.0504

Golf Courses:

Mark Bostick UF Golf Course

2800 SW 2nd Ave, Gainesville, FL

1.352. 375.4866

Gainesville Country Club

7300 SW 35th Way, Gainesville, FL

1.352. 372.1458

Shopping:

Union Street Pedestrian Mall is a good start...Haile Village and Tioga Town Center are upscale possibilities. If you like antiques, you may want to venture to nearby Alachua, High Springs or Micanopy.

Dining:

David's Real Pit BBQ Restaurant - Possibly the best barbecue in central Florida as well as the largest selection of hot sauces to be found in the Gainesville area! David's also serves breakfast seven days a week. A great family atmosphere for game day. Located at Exit 390 two miles east of I-75 on 39th Avenue (Highway 222). 5121 NW 39th Avenue, Gainesville. 1.352.373.2002. Monday – Saturday, 7:00 a.m. – 9:00 p.m.; Sunday, 8:00 a.m. – 9:00 p.m.

The Swamp Restaurant – Open from late morning until early morning. Tailgaters phone ahead for "To-Go." Salads, grilled food, gourmet burgers, fried gator, quesadillas, etc. Something for everyone. 1642 West University, Gainesville 1.352.377.9267. Monday – Saturday, 11:00 a.m. – 2:00 a.m.; Sunday, 11:00 a.m. – 11:00 p.m.

Night Life

Salty Dog Saloon – Serving Gainesville since 1962! And still, the happening place! Great food with a huge selection of domestic and imported beers, draft beers, fine spirits, and wine. Next door, almost, to The Swamp Restaurant. 1712 West University Avenue, Gainesville 1.352.375.6969. Monday – Thursday, 3:00 p.m. – 2:00 a.m.; Friday and Saturday, 12:30 p.m. – 2:00 a.m.

Accommodations:

Herlong Mansion – A spacious, beautiful bed & breakfast inside a Greek-Revival mansion laden with mahogany floors and nearly a dozen fireplaces. Herlong offers six rooms, three suites, and four nearby cottages. Rates vary. Call ahead. 1.352.466.3322 or www.herlong.com.

Records:

All-Time Record: 735-420-40 (.632)

SEC Eastern Division Championships:

8 (1992, 1993, 1994, 1995, 1996, 2000, 2006, 2008, 2009, 2012, 2015, 2016

SEC Championships:

7 (1991, 1993, 1994, 1995, 1996, 2000, and 2006, 2008)

National Championships: (3) 1996, 2006, 2008

Bowl Appearances: 45

Bowl Record: 24-21 (.533)

Great Bowl Games

2002 Orange Bowl: Florida 56, Maryland 23

2005 Outback Bowl: Florida 31, Iowa 24

2006 BCS National Championship Game: Florida 41, Ohio State 14

2008 BCS National Championship Game: Florida 24, Oklahoma 14

2010 Outback Bowl: Florida 37, Penn State 24

2018 Peach Bowl: Florida 41, Michigan 15

2019 Orange Bowl: Virginia 36-28

Florida Greats:

Coaches:

Ray Graves – (1960-1969) – (70-31-4) – (.686) – Born December 31, 1918, in Rockwood, Tennessee, Graves was a coach whose decade-long tenure represented a resurgent time for the hopes of Gator football fans. During his stay in Gainesville from 1960 to 1969, Florida won 70 games, and four of five bowl games. Graves is remembered by Florida fans for his shocking upset of Alabama during his fourth year as head coach. In October 1963, Graves' Gators went to Tuscaloosa and pulled off the upset of Bear Bryant's Crimson Tide, a 10-0 shutout. The magnitude of the win grew in the following years since Bryant's boys would not lose another game at home in Tuscaloosa until 1982. Graves' best squad was his 1969 team that finished 9-1-1 and defeated Tennessee by the score of 14-13 in the Gator Bowl. That team had players like Jack Youngblood, Carlos Alvarez, and All-American quarterback John Reaves. Graves is a member of the National Football Foundation and College Football Hall of Fame.

Doug Dickey – (1970-1978) – (58-43-2) – (.573) – Born June 24, 1932, in Vermillion, South Dakota, Dickey, a Florida alumni and former football standout, returned to Gainesville from Tennessee to coach the Gators in 1970. During his nine-year Gator coaching tenure, Florida attended four bowl games, but lost all of them. He was replaced by Charley Pell for the 1979 season. Dickey

is a member of the College Football Hall of Fame.

Charley Pell – (1979-1984) – (33-26-3) – (.549) – The popular Pell, an Alabama graduate, and Bear Bryant protégé, signaled a turnaround for the Gator program in 1979, taking over the leadership of the Florida football team. Although his first year was a disastrous 0-10-1, Pell's next four seasons in Gainesville were successful, leading the Gators to four bowl games in four consecutive years. Pell's tenure was highlighted by protégé' stalwarts Wilbur Marshall and Chris Collinsworth; both would star in the NFL. Charley Pell once said, "I want players to think as positively as the 85-year old man who married a 25-year old woman and bought a five-bedroom house next to the elementary school."

Galen Hall – (1985-1989) – (40-18-1) – (.703) – In 1984, Galen Hall followed in the footsteps of Charley Pell as head coach of the Gators. Hall's first two years in Gainesville produced a record of 18-2-2, although the Gators were ineligible for post-season play due to NCAA sanctions. Emmitt Smith, one of the NFL's most talented running backs and all-time leading rusher, played during the Galen Hall years at Florida. In 1985, Florida defeated Auburn 14-10 at Jordan-Hare Stadium. The SEC win resulted in Florida being ranked number one in the nation in the AP poll for the first time in school history. NCAA investigations lasting from the previous administration cost Hall his job. He coached through game five of the 1989 season and was replaced by Gary Darnell to finish out the remainder of the season.

Steve Spurrier – (1990-2001) – (138-28-2) – (.785) – Born in Miami Beach, Florida in 1945, Spurrier is the winningest coach in University of Florida football history. A relentless adversary, Spurrier remains the modern-day coaching standard bearer for the ultra-competitive SEC. Spurrier returned to his alma mater in 1990, and implemented his unstoppable Fun N' Gun style of offense, achieving overnight success in the process. Spurrier is the only major college coach in the twentieth century to win more than 90 games in his first nine seasons and he is the only SEC coach in history to win ten or more games in six consecutive seasons (1993-98). Florida appeared in each of the first

five SEC Championship games (1992-1996), with wins in four of those games (1993-96). The Gators under Spurrier won a total of five SEC championships during the 1990's. Spurrier's teams lost only four games at home. Spurrier's dominance of the league during the 1990's, coupled with his cantankerous demeanor, led many of his SEC admirers and detractors to label him the "Evil Genius." Spurrier's 1996-1997 squad won the National Championship. Spurrier finished his 14-year career at Florida with a 132-28-2 record. His 112 victories from 1990-2000 at Florida ranks as the best win total for a major college coach in his first eleven years at a school. Spurrier achieved his 100th victory at Florida faster than any major college coach in the twentieth century (10th season, 8th game). Spurrier and Paul "Bear" Bryant are the only coaches in SEC history to win as many as four consecutive league championships (1993-96). Spurrier accomplished all he did with the 85 scholarship limit. Spurrier left Florida at the end of the 2001 season to take a short-lived head coaching position with the Washington Redskins during the 2002 and 2003 NFL seasons. Spurrier's two-year NFL coaching career record was 12-20. In 2005 Spurrier took the head coaching job at South Carolina, relieving retiring head coach Lou Holtz. He retired midseason in 2015 as the University of South Carolina's winningest football coach.

Ron Zook – (2002-2004) – (23-14) – (.621) – Born April 28, 1954, in Londonville, Ohio, Zook played defensive back for Miami University, graduating with a bachelor's degree in 1976. During the 1980's he held various assistant coaching positions at Cincinnati, Kansas, Tennessee, Virginia Tech, and Ohio State Universities. In 1991, he took the defensive coordinator job at Florida under Steve Spurrier, a post he held for three years. In 1996, Spurrier promoted Zook to defensive coordinator after Bobby Pruett left, but Zook bolted for the NFL, spending three years as the special teams coordinator for the Steelers. In 1999, he coached defensive backs for the Kansas City Chiefs. In 2001 and 2002 he was the defensive coordinator for the New Orleans Saints before taking the Gator's head coaching job in 2002 after Steve Spurrier's resignation. Zook was not a popular hire, and his assignment was as tough as his acclimation to the job, since following a legend is never easy. In three years Zook posted 8-5, 8-5, and 7-4 seasons for a 23-14 record. His ultimate downfall came after his third season in 2004, when he lost to a 1-5 Mississippi State team in Starkville. Zook was fired, but completed the season. He declined the opportunity to coach in the Gator's bowl game. In 2005, Zook was hired by the University of Illinois to replace Ron Turner.

Urban Meyer – (2005-Present) – (65-15) – (.813) – Born July 10, 1964, in Ashtabula, Ohio, Meyer led the Gators to SEC and BCS National Championships in his second season. A graduate of Saint John High School, Meyer

attended the University of Cincinnati and played defensive back, earning a psychology degree in 1986. He was selected as a shortstop by the Atlanta Braves in the thirteenth round of the Major League draft and spent two seasons playing minor league ball in their farm system. In 1988, he earned a master's degree in sports administration from Ohio State University. While studying at Ohio State, Meyer served as an administrative assistant for two years where he worked with tight ends and wide receivers. During the next 13 seasons Meyer was an assistant coach. He spent the 1988 and 1989 seasons at Illinois State where he coached linebackers, quarterbacks, and wide receivers. From 1990-1995 he coached receivers at Colorado State and from 1996-2000 he coached receivers at Notre Dame. In 2001 Meyer took his first head coaching job at Bowling Green, engineering a fantastic 17-6 turnaround in two years, earning "Mid-American Conference Coach of the Year" honors. In 2003 Meyer took the head job at Utah. In just his first season he went 10-2 and was named the Mountain West Conference Coach of the Year and The Sporting News National Coach of the Year after implementing his own brash version of the West Coast Offense. Meyer's scheme relies on short, quick passes with receivers making plays after the catch. The base offense spreads three receivers, allows for motion, and puts the quarterback in the shotgun, providing option opportunities as well. In 2004 Meyer led the undefeated Utes to an unprecedented BCS Bowl bid. Subsequently, Florida and Notre Dame both made job offers to Meyer. Meyer became Florida's coach for the 2005 season, signing a seven year contract worth $14 million. In 2005, Meyer went 9-3 with the Gators, going undefeated at home and beating Iowa in the Outback Bowl. In 2006, his second year in Gainseville, Meyer, true to form, turned the Gators into winners. They finished with a 13-1 record (8-1 in the SEC), earning SEC (Arkansas 38-28) and National Championships (Ohio State 41-14) along the way. In 2007, Meyer's team, depleted by NFL defections on defense, finished with a 9-4 record. In 2008, Meyer and the Gators repeated as National Champs with an identical 13-1 record of two seasons prior. Meyer completed his tenure in Gainesville with seasons of 13-1 and 8-5. He abruptly left Florida after the disappointing 2010 season, citing health reasons. A year later he was named the head football coach at Ohio State University where he won the 2014 National Championship with the Buckeyes.

Will Muschamp **–** (2011 – 2014) – (28-21) – (.571) - Born in Rome, Georgia but raised in Gainesville, Florida, Muschamp cut his teeth on competitive football. The former walk-on defensive back and team captain at the University of Georgia is as experienced as he is well-traveled; and the result is he has apprenticed under some of the game's best coaches. After graduating from Georgia, Muschamp was a graduate assistant at Auburn, where he worked under defensive coordinators Wayne Hall and Bill Oliver in 1995 and 1996. He earned a master's degree in education from Auburn in 1996, and spent a season each at the University of West Georgia and Eastern Kentucky University as the defensive backs coach, before becoming the defensive coordinator at Valdosta State University in 2000. Muschamp joined Nick Saban's staff at LSU as the linebackers coach in 2001, before rising to become the LSU defensive coordinator in 2002. In 2003, LSU won the BCS Championship. Muschamp left LSU with Saban after the 2004 season to join the Miami Dolphins staff as the assistant head coach and defensive coordinator. When the Auburn defensive coordinator position became available in January 2006, Muschamp took the opportunity. In January 2008, he resigned from Auburn to accept a co-defensive coordinator position with Texas. On November 18, 2008, Texas announced Muschamp would succeed Mack Brown as head football coach; but Brown stayed too long, because on December 11, 2010, UF athletic director Jeremy Foley named Muschamp to succeed Urban Meyer. In his first year he led the Gators to a 7–6 record and a 24–17 Gator Bowl victory over Ohio State. In his second season, Muschamp notched an 11–1 record with four wins over teams ranked among the top twelve of the BCS standings, including Texas A&M, LSU, South Carolina, and Florida State. The promising campaign ended with a disheartening 33-23 loss to the Louisville Cardinals in the Sugar Bowl, allowing for an 11-2 finish; setting the stage for even higher, winning expectations. Those wins never came, as Muschamp completed his last two seasons with disappointing records of 4-8 and 3-5, and his contract was terminated. He coached as Auburn's defensive coordinator in 2015, before taking over as head coach of South Carolina in 2016, after the midseason departure of Steve Spurrier. His overall coaching record is 54-46. He remains in Columbia.

Jim McElwain **–** (2015-2017) – (22-12) – (.647) - A native of Missoula, Montana, McElwain is a well-learned and well-traveled coach with mostly mixed success. He signed with Eastern Washington and played quarterback from 1980 to 1983, earning an education degree. He stayed on at Eastern and became a graduate assistant, coaching quarterbacks and receivers under head coach Dick Zornes for eight seasons, winning the Big Sky Championship in 1992. In 1995, he went to Montana State, where he was the offensive coor-

dinator for five seasons. In 2000, he took a job at Louisville under head coach John L. Smith, coaching wide receivers and special teams for three seasons. In 2003, he landed at Michigan State under John L. Smith as assistant head coach supervising receivers and special teams. In 2006, he coached quarterbacks at the Oakland Raiders for a season and took a job at Fresno State doing the same. From 2008 to 2011 he was the offensive coordinator under Nick Saban at Alabama, winning a national championship in 2009. In 2012, he took the head coaching job at Colorado State, going 4-8, 8-6 and 10-2 in three seasons. In 2015, he was hired as head coach at Florida. McElwain was considered by many as a "bad fit" in Gainesville, yet he became SEC Coach of the Year in his first season, posting a 10-4 record and winning the Eastern Division. From there it was all downhill for McElwain, as he would not again notch double digit victories. In 2016, the Gators went 9-4, won their division and dropped the championship game consecutively. In 2017, the wheels came off and the Gators posted a 3-4 record before firing McElwain prior to season's end. He finished 22-12, and his 34-game tenure as coach was the shortest by any non-interim coach at the University of Florida in over 80 years. McElwain coached wide receivers a year at Michigan and is now the head coach at Central Michigan University.

***Dan Mullen* –** (2018-present) – Mullen is regarded as an excellent quarterbacks coach and respected offensive coordinator/play caller yet to win the big time. He attended Ursinus College in Collegeville, Pennsylvania, lettering two years at tight end. He graduated in 1994 with a Bachelor's Degree in Exercise and Sport Science and went to Wagner College, where he coached wide receivers and earned a Master's Degree in Education in 1996. Before State, Mullen served as offensive coordinator at the University of Florida and served earlier alongside Urban Meyer at Utah, where he was quarterback coach of the Utes during their undefeated 2004 season. During that stint he developed quarterback Alex Smith into the number one overall pick in the 2005 NFL Draft. In his first season at Mississippi State in 2009, his team went 5–7 against one of the toughest schedules in the nation. In 2010, his Bulldog team went 9–4 overall and 4–4 in the SEC, including victories over Georgia, Florida, Kentucky, and Mississippi; and the four losses came to top-12 ranked teams. Mississippi State capped off the 2010 season by defeating traditional power Michigan in the 2011 Gator Bowl 52–14, and achieved a #15 ranking in the final AP poll. In 2011, Mullen's Bulldogs went 7-6, followed by a 2012 showing of 8-5. His 2014 team finished 10-3 and second in the SEC West. In 2017, after an 8-4 season, he left for Gainesville, where he was named head coach of the Florida Gators. Mullen's return to Gainseville was much heralded, and he did not disappoint, finishing 10-3 in 2018 and 11-2 in 2019, behind Georgia in the East and winning two bowl games.

Players:

***Steve Spurrier* –** (1963-1966) – Before he was a championship ball coach, Spurrier was a two-time All-American (1965 & 1966) and 1966 "Heisman Trophy" winner at quarterback for the Gators. During his career he broke every Florida record for game, season, and career in passing and total offense, as well as all of the league records for passing. In 1966, Spurrier led the Gators to a 9-2 mark and an Orange Bowl victory over Georgia Tech. A little known fact regarding Steve Spurrier is that he was the Gator's punter for three seasons, averaging over 40 yards per kick. Spurrier kicked field goals for the Gators as well. He was named to the College Football Hall of Fame as a player in 1986 and as a coach in 2017.

***Jack Youngblood* –** (1967-1970) – Born January 26, 1950, in Jacksonville, Florida, Youngblood was a consensus 1970 All-American. Youngblood is considered one of the top defensive ends in Gator history. A member of the All-SEC Team of the Decade in the 1970's, and also the SEC Quarter Century Team (1950-1974), he was known for a rugged style of play that intimidated Gator opponents. Following college, he was drafted in the first round of the professional draft and became an All-Pro standout for the Los Angeles Rams from 1971 to 1984. During his pro career Youngblood was twice named the NFL Defensive Player of the Year. In 1988 Jack authored his autobiography entitled, Blood, a book that outlined his competitive drive and passion for the game of football. He was named to the College Football Hall of Fame in 1992.

***Carlos Alvarez* –** (1969-1971) – An All-American in 1969, the Cuban-born Alvarez was a record-setting receiver for the Gators. An honor student who was an Academic All-American from 1969-1971, and the winner of the Post-Graduate Scholarship in 1971, Alvarez was named to the Academic All-American Hall of Fame in 1989. His 88 receptions during the 1969 season still stand as the University of Florida's single-season record and his 172 career catches still rank first in the annals of Gator football. Alvarez was drafted by Dallas in 1972 but did not sign due to knee injuries. He instead went to Duke Law School, graduating summa cum laude in 1975.

Chris Collinsworth **–** (1977-1980) – Born January 27, 1959, in Dayton, Ohio, Collinsworth was a 1980 All-American for the Gators. A high school track standout, Collinsworth was a superb multi-talented player who excelled at a number of positions in college (linebacker, receiver, and quarterback). He remains tied for one of the longest touchdown passes in college history—a 99-yard bomb. During his career at Florida he caught 120 passes for 1937 yards and 14 touchdowns. Collinsworth was a three-time All-SEC selection from 1978 to 1980 and an Academic All-American in 1980. After college, Collinsworth went on to start for the Cincinnati Bengals where he attained All-Pro status and was named NFL Rookie of the Year in 1981. Today, Collinsworth is an NFL color analyst for FOX TV.

Emmitt Smith **–** (1986-1989) – Born May 15, 1969, in Pensacola, Florida, Smith was a 1989 All-American running back for the Gators, and the SEC Player of the Year in 1989. Smith completed his junior year in college with 58 Florida records and 3,982 rushing yards, making him the school's all-time leading rusher. A first team All-SEC selection three years, from 1987 to 1989, he was selected in the first round by the Dallas Cowboys in 1990. Smith was chosen as the 1990 NFL Rookie of the Year, and was the league's leading rusher in 1991, 1992, 1993, and 1995; and was the NFL MVP in 1993. He later played for the Arizona Cardinals. Smith is a three-time Super Bowl Champion and the NFL's all-time leading rusher with 18,355 yards. As a Cowboy, Smith surpassed the legendary Walter Payton of the Chicago Bears on October 27, 2002, against the Seattle Seahawks at Texas Stadium. He is the only running back to win a Super Bowl, the NFL MVP award, the NFL Rushing Crown and the Super Bowl MVP award in the same season (1993). Smith returned to his alma mater during off-seasons and received his degree in Public Recreation from the University of Florida in May 1996. On February 5, 2005, Emmitt Smith announced his retirement from the NFL after 15 seasons. Smith was released by the Arizona Cardinals and he signed a one-day contract with the Dallas Cowboys for no compensation, and retired forever a Cowboy.

Danny Wuerffel **–** (1993-1996) – Born May 27, 1974, in Fort Walton Beach, Florida, Wuerffel was a two-time All-American for the Gators during the 1995 and 1996 seasons and the Heisman Trophy winner in 1996. He is considered one of the top college quarterbacks to ever play the game. Wuerffel's career culminated in a National Championship for the Gators in 1996, a victory earned over in-state, arch-rival Florida State. Wuerffel completed his career at Florida connecting on an amazing 798 of 1170 passes for 10,875 yards with 114 touchdown passes. His pass efficiency rating in 1995 of 178.4 was the highest recorded in college football history. After Florida, Wuerffel was selected in the fourth round of the 1997 NFL Draft by the New Orleans Saints. The son of a Lutheran chaplain in the United States Air Force, Wuerffel has made service an important aspect of his life. He maintains Desire Street Ministries, a non-profit, faith-based organization that focuses on spiritual and community development in one of New Orleans' poorest areas. For his many on and off-the-field contributions, a small stretch of the Highway 98 in Destin has been dedicated as Danny Wuerffel Way by the Florida State Legislature.

Tim Tebow **–** (2006-2009) – Timothy Richard Tebow, born August 14, 1987, in the Phillipines, was the first sophomore from Florida and the Southeastern Conference to win the Heisman Trophy. Although home schooled, Tebow played quarterback for Nease High School in Ponte Vedra Beach, Florida, where he became Florida's "Mr. Football" and was a must-have college recruit. Possessing uncommon size (6'-3", 245), speed and arm strength, Tebow was dubbed "Superman" by both admirers and detractors. A classic dual-threat quarterback, Tebow was used mainly as a "change-of-pace" quarterback for the Gators during his 2006 freshman season, playing behind senior signal

caller Chris Leak. He provided key contributions for the Gators en route to a National Championship. As a sophomore in 2007, Tebow took control of the Gator offense and posted a record-breaking season, becoming the first SEC and NCAA quarterback to both run and pass for 20 touchdowns in a season. His performance earned him consensus All-American honors, the AP Player of the Year Award, the Maxwell Award as the nation's top player, the Davey O'Brien Award as the nation's top quarterback, and of course, the Heisman Trophy, the nation's most prestigious football accolade. During his junior year Tebow guided the Gators to a second national championship in three years, and was named MVP of the National Championship Game. A bona fide Florida cult hero, and the son of former missionaries, Tebow is a vocal member of the Fellowship of Christian Athletes. The Gators again went 13–1 in 2009, Tebow's senior year, with their only loss to Alabama in the SEC Championship Game. At the conclusion of his college career, Tebow held the Southeastern Conference's all-time records in both career passing efficiency and total rushing touchdowns. He was selected in the first round of the 2010 NFL draft by the Denver Broncos. Today he is a college football analyst and maintains his charity, the Tim Tebow Foundation. He is married to a former Miss Universe, South African native and supermodel, Demi-Leigh Nel-Peters Tebow.

Vernon Hargreaves **–** (2013-2015) - A native of Manchester, Connecticut, Hargreaves attended Wharton High School in Tampa, Florida where he was a shut-down cornerback and elite track athlete. Named MVP of the 2013 Under Armour All-America Game, Vernon signed with Florida over a long list of recruiters. The elite five-star defensive back started ten of twelve games as a freshman in 2013, recording 38 tackles and three interceptions, receiving SEC All-Freshmen Team honors. As a sophomore he played in 12 games with three interceptions, 13 passes defended and two fumble recoveries to go with 50 tackles. As a junior he recorded four interceptions, a forced fumble and four passes defended on 33 tackles in 12 games. In three seasons Vernon played in 41 games, logged 121 tackles, 27 passes defended and 10 interceptions. Hargreaves, named one of three finalists for the 2015 Jim Thorpe Award and a consensus two-time First-Team All-Conference and All-American, was chosen by Tampa Bay as the eleventh pick in the first round of the 2016 NFL Draft.

Antonio Callaway **–** (2015-2017) - Callaway attended Booker T. Washington High in Miami where he was a heralded all-county and all-state player, helping his team win the 2014 Class 4A State Title over a combined 15-0 record. At Florida, like in high school, Callaway was an electric, open space player who excelled at receiving, and returning kicks and punts; unfortunately, he also had a propensity for trouble, which abbreviated an otherwise brilliant collegiate appearance. As a true freshman in 2015, he appeared in 14 games, starting in 13. His 678 receiving yards broke Florida's true freshman record held by Reidel Anthony and he had two punt returns for touchdowns—one apiece against LSU and Alabama. He was named a consensus freshman All-America. In 2016, he appeared in 12 games for the Gators and started eleven. After a rushing touchdown against Georgia and a kickoff return touchdown against Missouri, Callaway became the first player in school history and 21st FBS player since 1996 to score a rushing, receiving, passing, punt return, and kickoff return touchdown in his career. He spent his entire junior year suspended from the team due to disciplinary issues. He finished his receiving career at Florida with 89 grabs for 1,399 yards, for an average of 15.7 yards per catch. He was drafted as the 105th pick by the Cleveland Browns in the early fourth round of the 2018 NFL Draft.

***Chauncey Gardner-Johnson* –** (2016-2018)-A native of Cocoa, Florida where he attended Cocoa High, Chauncey was a standout cornerback who played in the 2016 Under Armour All-American Game in Orlando and was a USA Today All-American. As a true freshman at Florida, in 2016, Gardner-Johnson appeared in 13 games, making starts in the final three. During the Outback Bowl, he had two interceptions, one a pick-six, resulting in him being named MVP. As a sophomore, in 2017, he started in 11 games and prior to his junior season he was switched to nickel back. Before the start of his junior year, Gardner changed the name on his jersey to Gardner-Johnson in honor of his stepfather, Brian Johnson. Gardner-Johnson's biological father Chauncey Gardner, Sr. played a part in his life, but it was Johnson who raised him since infancy. One of the reasons UF claims the "DBU" namesake, Gardner-Johnson ended his collegiate career with 37 games played, nine interceptions, three of which were pick-sixes, 12 pass breakups, 161 total tackles, 15.5 tackles for loss and four sacks. Identical to his former teammate who preceded him in the previous season, Antonio Callaway, Gardner-Johnson was drafted the 105th pick by the New Orleans Saints in the early fourth round of the 2019 NFL Draft.

Traditions:

"We are the Boys of Old Florida"

It is customary at home games, between the third and fourth quarter, for Florida fans to sway side- to-side to the University of Florida fight song "We are the Boys of 'Ole Florida."

"Mr. Two Bits"

George Edmondson, an insurance salesman from Atlanta, Georgia, played his part as "Mr. Two Bits" for over forty years. During every home game Mr. Edmondson, who was a graduate of the Citadel, wandered around the stadium in a goofy yellow shirt and tie, leading cheers for the fans. One of Mr. Edmondson's favorite Florida cheers was Two-Bits, as follows: "Two-bits, four-bits, six-bits, a dollar...all for the Gators stand up and holler!" He passed away July 2, 2019. His role as unofficial fan cheerleader has been replaced by visiting celebrities and students who lead the stadium in a host of familiar cheers once sung by Edmondson.

"Gator Growl"

One great and longstanding tradition at Florida is the Gator Growl. What began as an orientation service for families and potential students in 1906, turned into a full-blown reception during the latter part of the Twentieth Century. The event was known as "Dad's Day" in the early years, and it served as the beginning of the pep rally at the University of Florida. As the custom grew, blue and orange beanie-wearing freshmen were forced to carry their weight in firewood to a bonfire constructed for the night before the big Thanksgiving football game. The event expanded its boundaries, taking on a party, skits, speakers, and singing and dancing. Today, the Gator Growl is a huge campus event, drawing crowds of 75,000 people to join in the fun where the Homecoming Queen and the senior football players are introduced to the crowd.

"The Gator Football Ring of Honor"

The Ring is Florida's alternative to retiring a player's number and pays homage to the greatest former players and coaches. Physically, it is a ring displayed on the north end zone façade of Ben Hill Griffin Stadium honoring the names of the players and coaches who contributed greatly to the Florida Gators football team and program. It was created in 2006 in commemoration of 100 years of Florida football and was revealed to the public before the Alabama game that same year. The four first inductees to the Ring of Honor were Emmitt Smith, Steve Spurrier, Danny Wuerffel, and Jack Youngblood.

"What was Once the World's Largest Outdoor Cocktail Party"

The annual game between Florida and Georgia is one of the great rivalries in college football and is officially known as the "Florida-Georgia/Georgia-Florida game, alternating annually. The game is held at Jacksonville Municipal Stadium in Jacksonville, Florida, normally on the last Saturday in October. The designated "home" team alternates from year to year, with ticket distribution split evenly between the two schools. In past years, fans from Florida and Georgia were assigned seats grouped in alternating sections of the stadium, and the contrasting colors worn by the fans created a "beach ball" visual effect in the stands. Recently the seating arrangement has split the stadium lengthwise and fans sit on the side corresponding to the sideline their team occupies.

The game was first held in Jacksonville in 1915, and has been held in Jacksonville every year since 1933, except for 1994 and 1995, when the contest was held on the respective schools' campus stadiums due to the rebuilding of Jacksonville Municipal Stadium for the Jacksonville Jaguars.

While Jacksonville is technically a neutral site, it is located only 73 miles from Gainesville, home of the Gators. Athens, Georgia, conversely, is 342 miles to the north. The crowd in the stadium is always split 50-50 between the two schools' fans. The majority of the tailgating takes place on the riverfront plaza called "The Jacksonville Landing" facing the St. Johns River. The Landing is packed with thousands of revelers each year, making it a great but crowded nightspot.

Due to sensitivity regarding alcohol consumption by college students, the match is officially known as the Florida-Georgia/Georgia-Florida game (depending on which team is the home team in a given year). In May 2006, the Southeastern Conference asked the three networks which broadcast SEC football games not to refer to the game by the moniker "World's Largest Outdoor Cocktail Party," so as not to convey an undesirable, damaging message. Legend has it that in years gone by the fans of both schools would leave the stadium at half-time for cocktails at their tailgates and return for the second half kickoff—thus the moniker, "World's Largest Cocktail Party," notwithstanding.

History

The University of Florida was the last institution of higher learning in the SEC to play football. In 1906, during its first season on the gridiron, Florida played eight games. The Gators played five with athletic clubs, two with Rollins, and one with Mercer College. By 1910, Florida had embarked on an annual, regular schedule of seven football games versus various colleges, averaging six wins and one loss per season.

Florida Songs

Orange and Blue

So give a cheer for the orange and blue, waving forever,
Forever pride of old Florida, may she droop never,

Let's sing a song for the flag today, cheer for the team to play,
On to the goal we'll fight our way for Florida!
Alma Mater
Florida our Alma Mater, thy glorious name we praise.
All thy loyal sons and daughters a joyous song shall raise.
Where palm and pine are blowing,
Where southern seas are flowing,
Shine forth thy noble gothic walls, thy lovely vine clad halls.
'Neath the orange and blue victorious, our love shall never fail.
There's no other name so glorious, all hail, Florida hail.

Noteworthy University of Florida Alumni

John Atanasoff, inventor of the electronic digital computer

Tracy Caulkins, Olympic Gold Medal swimmer

Lawton Chiles, former U.S. Senator and Governor of Florida (deceased)

Faye Dunaway, actress

Buddy Ebson, actor (deceased)

Bob Graham, U.S. Senator

Connie Mack, U.S. Senator

Jim McGee, Pulitzer Prize-winning reporter

Marshall Nirenberg, Biochemist and Geneticist, 1968 Nobel Prize Recipient

Forrest Sawyer, Emmy Award winner, former ABC News Anchor, currently a Media Strategist and Guest Lecturer

Hugh Wilson, movie producer and creator of "WKRP in Cincinnati"

James Allchin, developer Microsoft Operating Systems, former Executive

Rodney J. Bartlett, chemist, Guggenheim Fellow

Shere Hite, sex educator, feminist

Robert Grubbs, Nobel Prize, Chemistry

Andrew M. Allen, NASA astronaut

Al Rosen, former President New York Yankees, Houston Astros

Erin Andrews, reporter FOX News

Jesse Palmer, ESPN/ABC college football analyst/The Bachelor

2020 Florida Football Schedule

Sept. 5 Eastern Washington

Sept. 12 Kentucky

Sept. 19 South Alabama

Sept. 26 at Tennessee

Oct. 3 South Carolina

Oct. 10 LSU

Oct. 17 at Ole Miss

Oct. 24 OPEN DATE

Oct. 31 vs. Georgia (Jacksonville)

Nov. 7 at Vanderbilt

Nov. 14 Missouri

Nov. 21 New Mexico State

Nov. 28 at Florida State

Georgia

Football fans from the "Peach Tree State" know well the University of Georgia is one of the SEC's most successful football-playing schools. Georgia Bulldog fans, like so many in the Southeastern Conference, have enjoyed their share of the national championship experience. The University of Georgia has won the national championship on two occasions, ranking it among the SEC's elite football-playing programs. This great winning tradition can be traced to the endearing Southern school's two greatest coaches--Wally Butts and Vince Dooley. Butts brought Georgia its first national championship team in 1942, and Dooley followed his lead with his own national crown 38 years later. Regarding Dooley's championship squad--what modern-day college football fan can forget the 1980 Georgia national championship team? How could anyone who witnessed it forget the brilliance of Herschel Walker's amazing display en route to receiving college football's highest accolade, the Heisman Trophy? Today, Georgia fans have more than just the past to be proud of. Under Head Coach Kirby Smart, Georgia has made a resounding return to the forefront of competitive football in the mighty Southeastern Conference, vying annually for conference and national championships.

Founded: January, 1785

Two years after the Revolutionary War ended and four years before George Washington's first inauguration, the Georgia Legislature adopted the charter that created the University of Georgia. In founding the nation's first state university, the legislature gave birth to the American system of public higher education. The University of Georgia is listed among U.S. News & World Report's top 50 public universities in America.

Location: Athens

Known as the "Classic City," it is the home of the University of Georgia and serves as the gateway to the Antebellum Trail. Located in northeast Georgia's rolling hills, Athens is perched 65 miles east of Atlanta and surrounded by a number of tiny, quaint townships. Northeast Georgia is famous for its natural beauty. Miles of farmland, forests, lakes and rivers surround the Athens area, making it an enclave for outdoor enthusiasts. Popular local spots include the Oconee National Forest, Lake Hartwell, Lake Oconee, the State Botanical Garden and the Oconee River, which runs through the town. In addition to its rustic magnetism, Athens is a dense mixture of music haunts, restaurants, bars, sports, college students, intellectuals, bands, football weekends, art, and culture. Popular music groups like R.E.M., Widespread Panic, and the B-52s made their meteoric starts in Athens.

Population: (Clarke County) 127,000

Enrollment: 37,606

Colors:

Although red and black have served as the official school colors since 1887, their beginnings are nebulous. According to Bulldog lore, "Turf wars" involving Georgia and its ancient rival, Georgia Tech, began with the first football game in the series. The effect of the opponent's underhanded ploy in that inaugural 1893 contest resulted in the University of Georgia removing the color gold (or yellow) from its official school colors. In short, Georgia's colors relate directly to good, clean, old-fashioned hate.

In the December 1891 issue of Georgia's literary magazine, the editors, who were selected members of the Demosthenian and Phi Kappa literary societies, proclaimed those colors to be "old gold, black, and crimson." This selection extended an earlier custom of each class selecting its colors and publishing them in the yearbook. However, Dr. Charles H. Herty, the faculty member, father of intercollegiate athletics' at Georgia, and her first football coach, saw "yellow," as he called it, instead of gold, when he viewed the hues on the cover of The Georgia University Magazine.

The 24-year-old doctorate from Johns Hopkins led initial efforts to stimulate and harness school spirit, organized the school's first Athletic Association, and saw to it that yellow was eliminated from the colors. "Speaking with student leaders, we all agreed we didn't want yellow around Georgia athletics," reflecting extreme distaste for anything "yellow", or cowardly. Further, during those early years, the "crimson" evolved into "good ole" Georgia "red."

A mailed glove, however, was laid across the face of Georgia athletics that day the heated rivalry commenced. It was the "somebody-stole-my-gal" maneuver perpetrated by "the Teckity Techs" of 1893. During that season the

Techs chose white and gold as their colors. They nicely dressed 200 young ladies from all-girl Lucy Cobb Institute in those white and gold colors to cheer on Tech's varsity at old Herty Field. "These are our girls!" Their fans cheered. The Georgia fans fumed. Today, when a Georgia Bulldog smells out a Georgia Tech "Yellow Jacket," he fittingly sees "good ole Georgia red."

Nickname: "Bulldogs"

Many alumni claim Georgia acquired the nickname, "Bulldogs," because of the strong ties with Yale, whose nickname is also Bulldogs. Georgia's first President, Abraham Baldwin, was a Yale graduate, and the early buildings on campus were designed from blueprints of the same buildings at Yale. Regardless of the obvious connection to Yale, Morgan Blake, a reporter for the Atlanta Journal, wrote on November 3, 1920, about school nicknames, "The Georgia 'Bulldogs' would sound good because there is a certain dignity about a bulldog, as well as ferocity." After a 0-0 tie with Virginia in Charlottesville On November 6, 1920, the Atlanta Constitution writer Cliff Wheatley used the name "Bulldogs" in his story five times. The name has been used since.

Mascot: English Bulldog

The English Bulldog is small in stature, but wide and compact, with a thick, massive head. Its head and shoulders are broad with cheeks that extend to the sides of its eyes. The skin on the skull and forehead falls in dense folds, making it particularly appealing. Its muzzle is short and pug; its nose, broad and black with large nostrils. Its upper lip is pendent and its lower jaw is undershot. Its round eyes are far apart and dark, giving it a sullen look, that all humans—especially Georgia fans—find irresistible.

Mascot Name: "Uga"

"Uga" is a bulldog from a long line owned by the Frank W. (Sonny) Seiler family of Savannah, Georgia. Uga I was born on December 2, 1955, beginning the line that still represents the University of Georgia at all football games. A solid white English bulldog, he hailed from Columbus, Georgia, and was at birth named "Hood's Ole Dan."

Georgia's Uga V, was featured on the cover of Sports Illustrated on April 28, 1997 when Uga was honored by the magazine as the best mascot in the country. SI spoke highly of Uga in the feature, stating, "If you can't appreciate the swaggering gait and Churchillian physiognomy of Uga V, the Bulldog's bulldog, you must be a cat lover." Uga is so revered in Georgia that he has even visited the Georgia House of Representatives and the Senate Chamber in the State Capitol upon invitation by the Speaker of the House. He once had his picture taken with Governor Joe Frank Harris while standing on the

Governor's desk. The current Uga is Uga X, serving since 2015.

Band: "Georgia Redcoat Band"

Founded in 1905, as a section of the University of Georgia Military Department, the Redcoat Band has grown in the last 100 years from 20 military cadets to over 350 men and women covering almost every university major. The band's first non-military performance was not at a football game, but the 1906 Georgia-Clemson baseball game! For the first 25 years of its existence, the band members split time between their studies, their military drill, the band, and the athletic events they were required to entertain. It was during this time that the fight song "Glory Glory to Old Georgia," composed by former bandsman and future head of the Music Department, Hugh Hodgson, made its debut. At a Georgia Tech game in the late 1900s, a reporter for the Atlanta Journal, not knowing the new Georgia fight song, complained of "the incessant playing of 'John Brown's Body' the main Georgia fight song many remember as modeled after "The Battle Hymn of the Republic."

The early Redcoat Band was a mainstay at the many parades held in the city of Athens, among them the 1915 Woodmen of the World Convention parade, as well as a parade signaling America's entry into World War I. Throughout the 1920s and 30s, the band, still under the Military Department, expanded modestly in size by allowing non-military musicians to join their ranks, spurred by the introduction of band scholarships. During this time, the band made short trips with the football team when financing was available. In preparing for a major match-up with Auburn in Columbus, Georgia, the band needed $700 to make the train ride. They raised the funds by holding a "tag sale" among the students at the school, which was made more successful by the fact that the female students, which had only recently arrived on campus, were able to raise the most money. Not only did they make the money needed to go to Columbus, they had some left over for needed repairs.

During the 1935 football season, an event took place that brought the need for a larger, more "appropriate" marching band. In November, Georgia was scheduled to play Louisiana State University. The Louisiana Governor made special plans to take the "Golden Band from Tigerland," by then one of the largest marching bands in the nation. Upon seeing the small Georgia band against the massive LSU band, movements among the alumni and athletic association began to fund and equip the band with more instruments and members. While the number dwindled during World War II, the band maintained a moderate size until 1955, when everything changed.

In 1955, the Redcoat Band we know today was formed by the arrival of Roger Dancz and his wife Phyllis, who was to become the Director of the Auxiliaries.

Before Roger's arrival, the band was known as the Georgia Marching Band. There are several stories as to how the Redcoats got their name. One version has an Atlanta reporter writing about a joint concert among the bands of Georgia and Georgia Tech. While the Tech band was known as the "yellow-jacketed band," the reporter found it necessary to dub UGA's band as "the red-coated band." The name stuck and by the time Roger and Phyllis arrived, the University of Georgia Dixie "Redcoat Band" was conceived.

Director of Bands: Dr. Cynthia Johnston Turner

Stadium: Sanford Stadium

Georgia's famed football stadium is named for Dr. Steadman Vincent Sanford, who joined the faculty of the University of Georgia in 1903. Sanford was one of the most popular men on campus at the university during the early years of the twentieth century. Founder of the Henry W. Grady School of Journalism in 1921, Sanford served as University Dean from 1927-32, and held the post of University President and Chancellor until 1935. Sanford was a guiding force behind the construction of Sanford Stadium in 1929, and was termed many times as "the best friend of the athletic." Sanford is responsible for persuading the Bulldogs of Yale to make their first trip south of the Mason-Dixon Line to play the dedication game of Sanford Stadium in 1929. The venue is referred to as "Between the Hedges," a reference to Sanford Stadium that dates to the early 1930's. The famous English privet hedges that surround Sanford's playing field were only one foot high when the stadium was dedicated in 1929, and were protected by a wooden fence. Southern sportswriter Grantland Rice observed that "...The bulldogs will have their opponent between the hedges."

Sanford Stadium has been augmented several times over the years. Built in 1929, it held only 30,000 at the onset. To fund his vision, Dr. Sanford had an idea that members of the athletic association would sign notes guaranteeing a bank loan to fund the construction. In turn, those guarantors would be granted lifetime seats. The response was overwhelming, and in 1928 a loan of $150,000 supported by fans and alumni allowed construction to begin on a stadium whose total cost was $360,000.

Sanford Stadium saw additions completed in 1949, '64, '67, '81, '84, '91, and 1994, when deluxe luxury skyboxes were installed. In 2003, another upper deck was added to the north side. This added 5,500 new seats at a cost of $25 million, bringing capacity to 92,058. Most of these "upper-upper deck" seats are reserved for the fans of the visiting team. In 2005, installation of a new video display on the West End zone was completed. The stadium reached its current capacity of 92,746 in 2004, when 27 SkySuites were added to the North side of the stadium at a cost of $8 million. Sanford Stadium is unique in that it is situated in the middle of campus. It is considered an architectural gem in that throughout its numerous expansions it has maintained its historic look and feel as one of the country's most breathtaking football-playing venues.

Vince Dooley Field:

In May 2019, university officials announced the playing surface of Sanford Stadium would be named in honor of former Bulldog head coach and athletic director Vince Dooley. Official dedication of Dooley Field took place in a pregame ceremony at the Bulldogs' 2019 home opener on September 7.

Stadium capacity: 92,746

Record crowd: On September 21, 2019, Sanford Stadium set an attendance record of 93,246 in the Bulldogs victory against seventh-ranked Notre Dame.

First game: January 30, 1892. Georgia played Mercer College. On February 20th, Georgia and Auburn met at Atlanta's Piedmont Park, marking the inaugural game of what became the South's oldest college rivalry.

Georgia's First Interstate Game:

"Atlanta will be the scene Saturday of the first interstate intercollegiate football game. Both teams have been practicing for weeks."
- Atlanta Journal, February 17, 1892

Alabama Polytechnic and Mechanical School at Auburn defeated Georgia in that game 10-0, marking the beginning of the South's oldest football rivalry.

First game in stadium: November 12, 1929; Georgia 15, Yale 0 (30,000+ attendance)

First night game in stadium:

October 26, 1940; Georgia 7, Kentucky 7

Blackout Game: On November 10, 2007, Georgia fans of the 92,746 attending, wore black, and the football team wore black jerseys for the first time as the Bulldogs defeated Auburn 45-20.

Directions:

Coming from Atlanta via I-20 E: Take I-20 to the Conyers Exit (Exit 42 Hwy. 138). Turn left. Continue for approximately 20 miles where highway 138 will merge into Hwy. 78 East. Continue on 78 East for 18 miles and turn right onto Hwy. 316. Continue approximately 4 miles to the Athens Bypass (Loop 10) southbound. Take College Station Road Exit and turn left.

Coming from Augusta via I-20 W: Take I-20 and exit at Hwy. 78 N (west) to Athens. Continue on 78 to Athens. Turn left onto the Athens Bypass (Loop 10) southbound. Take College Station Road exit and turn left.

Coming from Greenville via I-85 S: Take I-85 S to the Carnesville Exit-Hwy. 106. Continue to Athens. The road changes to Danielsville Road, then North Ave., then Thomas St. and the East Campus Road.

Dining:

Fresh Air Barbecue – A local favorite with two locations. Chopped pork, as tender as it is tasty, is served with a vinegar-based sauce. The bar-b-cue chicken is a must-try for first-timers. Order the dry-rubbed ribs. Tailgate specials available. 1110 Hull Road. Athens 706.546.6060. Open seven days a week. 11:00 a.m. – 8:00 p.m.

Five Star Day Café – Gourmet Southern soul food; no, this is not an oxymoron! Staples like fried green tomatoes, collard greens, corn bread muffins, pot roast, meatloaf...as good as your grandma's. Plenty of options for vegetarians; and, all the sides are meat-free. Don't miss the home-style banana pudding. Country-style breakfast also served. Two locations: 229 East Broad Street, Athens, 1.706.543.8552. 2230 Barnett Shoals Road, Athens, 1.706.613.1001. Monday thru Friday 7:00 a.m. – 10:00 p.m. and 11:00 p.m. on Friday. On Saturday and Sunday, opens at 9:00 a.m., closes at 11:00 p.m. on Saturday and 10:00 p.m. on Sunday.

The Varsity – An Athens tradition! Serving Bulldogs and their friends for over 75 years! As you enter, expect to hear, "What'll 'Ya Have?" It is the server's typical greeting. Known as the "World's Largest Drive-In Restaurant," The Varsity puts the comfort in comfort food. Delicious chili cheese dogs, nine different hamburgers, 12 different sandwiches, salads, onion rings...good stuff! 1000 West Broad, Athens. 1.706.548.6325. Sunday – Thursday 10:00 a.m. to 10:00 p.m.; Friday and Saturday; 10:00 a.m. to 12:00 a.m.

Night Life:

The city that gave birth to R.E.M., the B-52's and Widespread Panic is a club mecca. There are nearly 40 taverns within walking distance of the campus where one can find drinks that are dirt cheap and where the music is always blaring.

General Beauregard's – Referred to by regulars as, "The General." Pre-Civil War-themed décor matches perfectly with the beverages offered, including shots of classic Kentucky and Tennessee bourbons. Derby Day mint juleps are refreshing pre-game and post-game treats. Music is a mix of popular tunes. 164 East Clayton Street, Athens. 1.706.543.8201

Radio: 750 AM WSB

Accommodations:

Gameday Luxury Suites – Furnished one, two and three bedroom suites available. Restaurants on premises and located within walking distance of the university. 250 West Broad Street, Athens. 1.706.583.4500.

Magnolia Terrace Bed & Breakfast – Located near the Old North Campus, this circa 1902 bed and breakfast is a step back into a simpler Victorian era. Eight guest rooms with spacious, private baths ornately adorn this modern antiquity. Some rooms come equipped with fireplaces. Room rates vary. 277 Hill Street 706.548.3860.

Nearest Hospital to Stadium:

Athens Regional Medical Center

1199 Prince Avenue, Athens, Georgia 30601

Bail Bondsman for Emergencies:

Bond, James Bond, Inc., Athens, Georgia

1.706.613.0007

Golf Course:

University of Georgia Golf Course

2600 River Bend Road, Athens, Georgia 30605

(706) 369-5739

Shopping:

Athens' unique shopping has won accolades in Southern Living and Lucky Magazine. Downtown, Five Points, Colonial Beechwood Promenade, Geor-

gia Square Mall and Prince Avenue/Normaltown are all wallet drainers.

All-Time Record: 831–425–54 (.655)

Bowl Appearances: 53

Georgia has been to more different bowl games than any other school, 17.

Bowl Record: 32–21–3 (.598)

Eastern Division Champs: (2002, 2003, 2005, 2007, 2012, 2017, 2018, 2019)

SEC Championships:

12 (1942, 46t, 48, 59, 66t, 68, 76t, 80, 81t, 82, 2002, 2005, 2012, 2017)

National Championships: Two Georgia teams have been consensus national champions--1942 and 1980. Three others have been declared national champions by at least one poll at season's end--1927, 1946, and 1968.

Great Bowl Games:

1981 Sugar Bowl: Georgia 17, Notre Dame 10

1984 Cotton Bowl: Georgia 10, Texas 9

1989 Gator Bowl: Georgia 34, Michigan State 27

1993 Florida Citrus: Georgia 21, Ohio State 14

1998 Peach Bowl: Georgia 35, Virginia 33

2003 Sugar Bowl: Georgia 26, Florida 13

2004 Capital One Bowl: Georgia 34, Purdue 27 (Overtime)

2005 Outback Bowl: Georgia 24, Wisconsin 21

2006 Chick-Fil-A Bowl: Georgia 31, Virginia Tech 24

2008 Sugar Bowl: Georgia 41, Hawaii 10

2013 Capital One Bowl: Georgia 45, Nebraska 31

2017 Rose Bowl: Georgia 54, Oklahoma 48

2019 Sugar Bowl: Georgia 26, Baylor 14

Georgia Greats:

Coaches:

Glen "Pop" Warner - (1895-96) – (7-4) – (.636) – Born April 5, 1871 in Springville, New York; a Cornell graduate, Warner took a job coaching for the University of Georgia in 1895 for the salary of $34 a week for ten weeks during his first season and for $40 a week during his second season. Warner led the Bulldogs to a 7-4 record in two years and later started the largest and most successful youth football league in the country that is still operating today, Pop Warner Football. He died December 7, 1954.

Harry Mehre - (1928-1937) – (59-34-6) – (.595) - A Huntington, Indiana native and graduate of Notre Dame, Mehre arrived at Georgia upon recommendation of Notre Dame's Knute Rockne. Mehre assumed head coaching duties in 1928 and led Georgia to a 59-34-6 record in his ten years as head coach. Known as a master motivator, Mehre is perhaps known best for his smashing 15-0 defeat of Yale in the 1929 dedication game of Sanford Stadium. Mehre was the only coach in the country at the time to have beaten Yale five straight times at the height of their football existence. Mehre left Athens in 1937 to assume the head coaching position at Ole Miss, where he remained in that capacity for eight more seasons before retiring to a 22-year career as a football analyst for the Atlanta Journal. He died September 27, 1978.

Wally Butts **-** (1939-1960) – (140-86-9) – (.595) – Born February 7, 1905 in Milledgeville, Georgia and a graduate of Mercer, Butts coached the Bulldogs over 22 seasons to six bowl games, four SEC championships, a consensus national championship in 1942, and another national title recognized by polls in 1946. Known affectionately by Georgia fans far and wide as "Little Round Man', Butts was one of the greatest football coaches of his era. An advocate of the passing game when passing had not yet gained equal footing with the run as a means for moving the football, Butts resigned his head coaching position in 1960, so he could become the Athletic Director at Georgia, a post he held until his retirement in 1963. The Butts-Mehre Heritage Hall on the Georgia campus is named in his honor. He died December 17, 1973 in Athens.

Vince Dooley **-** (1964-1988) – (201-77-10) – (.715) – A native of Mobile, Alabama where he attended Magill Institute, Dooley is considered one of the greatest college coaches. An Auburn grad, Dooley coached the Bulldogs for 25 years, leading Georgia to a consensus national championship in 1980 and another national title recognized by one poll in 1968, six SEC championships (1966, 68, 76, 80, 81, 82) and 20 bowl games. His 201

career victories made him only the ninth coach in Division 1-A (FBS) history to win 200 or more games. Dooley is a seven-time SEC Coach of the year and was named the National Coach of the Year in 1980. He is a 1997 inductee to the National College Football Hall of Fame and served as the Athletic Director at Georgia before retiring in 2004. Dooley won the "Paul Bear Bryant Award" for the nation's top coach in 1980, and the Amos Alonzo Stagg Award in 2001.

Jim Donnan **–** (1996-2000) – (40-19) – (.678) – A Laurens, South Carolina native and North Carolina State graduate, Donnan got his head coaching start at Marshall in 1990, after holding the position of offensive coordinator for Oklahoma from 1985-89. Donnan coached Marshall to the Division I-AA championship in 1992 with a 31-28 win over Youngstown St. He took over the reigns at Georgia in 1996 and over five years led the Bulldogs to four straight winning seasons. At the time of his departure from UGA Donnan's career coaching record was an impressive 104-40. Donnan may have had trouble beating Georgia's traditional rivals, but he never had trouble winning bowl games. Donnan was the first coach in school history to lead Georgia to four straight postseason victories.

Mark Richt **–** (2001- 2015) – (145-51) – (.740) - During a 15-year tenure Mark Richt was one of Georgia's most successful football coaches. Born February 18, 1960 in Omaha, Nebraska, Richt graduated from Boca Raton High School in Florida, where he was a standout quarterback. He attended the University of Miami, backing up former NFL Hall of Fame quarterback Jim Kelly. In 2001, Mark Richt was hired as head coach of the Georgia football program to replace embattled coach Jim Donnan. Prior to taking the Georgia job Richt was an offensive coordinator for East Carolina and Florida State University for head coach Bobby Bowden. Richt had a keen offensive mind and was a good recruiter. He won many games but failed to bring home the hardware Georgia fans most covet. He won two SEC Championships (2002 & 2005), five SEC Eastern Division Championships (2002, 2003, 2005, 2011, 2012), two Sugar Bowls (2003 & 2008), an Outback Bowl (2005), a Chik-Fil-A Bowl (2006) and a Capital One Bowl (2004). Richt was 9-5 in bowl games. He left Georgia in 2015 and coached three seasons at the University of Miami, his alma mater, from 2016-2019, posting a 26-13 (.666) record.

Kirby Smart **–** (2016-present) – (44-12) – (.785) – Smart is a young, experienced and pedigreed coach who has had much success, having cut his teeth as a long-time assistant in the conference. Recently his Bulldogs have sniffed multiple national championships—and he's still in the hunt. Born December 23, 1975 in Montgomery, Alabama, Smart played at Georgia, under head coaches Ray Goff and Jim Donnan, from 1995 to 1998, where he was a defensive back. His expertise is defense, particularly defensive backs, and he is in every way a Nick Saban protégé, having worked with Saban for many years at more than one stop. In 1999, he served as an administrative assistant at Georgia. In 2000, he coached defensive backs at Valdosta State. In 2001, he served at Valdosta as defensive coordinator. In 2002-2003, he was Florida State's Graduate Assistant and in 2004 coached defensive backs at LSU under Nick Saban. In 2005 he coached running backs at Georgia and in 2006 he followed Saban to Miami, where he coached safeties for a season. In 2007, he followed Saban to Alabama, serving as assistant head coach and defensive backs coach. From 2008 to 2015 he was Alabama's defensive coordinator. In 2016, he took the head coaching job at Georgia. After a rough first season (8-4) that claimed a Liberty Bowl victory, Smart and the Bulldogs won the Eastern Division three straight years (2017-2019), claiming the SEC Championship in 2017. During the 2017 season, Smart led the Bulldogs to a 9–0 start. At season's end SEC-Champion Georgia, ranked No. 3, was set to play No. 2 Oklahoma in the Rose Bowl on New Year's Day as part of the College Football Playoff. Georgia rallied from a 31–14 first-half deficit, defeating Oklahoma 54–48 in double overtime, completing the largest comeback in Rose Bowl history. In 2018, Georgia completed the regular season with an 11-1 record and earned a spot in the 2018 SEC Championship game as the Eastern Division Champions. Georgia would play the Western Division Champions, the Alabama Crimson Tide, losing 35-28. In 2019, after losing to eventual national champion LSU in the SEC Championship Game, Georgia defeated the Baylor Bears 26-14 in the Rose Bowl, finishing the season 12-2.

Players:

Frank Sinkwich **–** (1940-1942) – Born October 10, 1920, Sinkwich remains one of Georgia's brightest football stars and an American great. A fantastic athlete, he was the 1942 Heisman Trophy recipient. During his senior season, Sinkwich was a unanimous All-American selection at quarterback after setting the SEC total offense record of 2,187 yards (792 yards rushing, 1,392 passing). That same year, Sinkwich led Georgia to an 11-1 record and scored the Bulldogs' only touchdown in a 9-0 win over UCLA in that Rose Bowl. After college he served in the Merchant Marines in World War II and played for the Detroit Lions in the NFL where he was the 1944 Most Valuable Play-

er. He starred for the New York Yankees (football) and the Baltimore Colts. Sinkwich died October 20, 1990 at 70. He is a member of the Georgia Circle of Honor and the College Football Hall of Fame. Sinkwich is of Croat origin, born in Starjak, Croatia. His family moved after World War I to Youngstown, Ohio when he was two years old, joining his father Ignatius, who operated a grocery store. His surname was originally spelled Sinković. He said he grew to appreciate the value of competitiveness on the streets of Youngstown's west side. "I learned early in neighborhood pickup games that I had the desire to compete...When people ask why I succeeded in athletics, I always tell them that I didn't want to get beat."

***Fran Tarkenton* -** (1958-1960) - Born February 3, 1940, in Richmond, Virginia, Tarkenton is considered Georgia's most famous, if not its most successful, quarterback. Known as the "Peerless Pilot" the 1960 All-American went on to an All-Pro career with the Minnesota Vikings, as well as the New York Giants. During his senior season, Tarkenton threw for 1,189 yards and seven touchdowns for the Bulldogs. After football, Tarkenton enjoyed a successful television career, where he was a commentator on Monday Night Football and a co-host of the popular weekly TV show, "That's Incredible!" Tarkenton founded Tarkenton Software, a computer-program generator company, serving as president, until selling the company to Sterling Software in 1994. Tarkenton on the topic of leadership: "Leadership must be demonstrated, not announced."

***Patrick Dye* -** (1957-1960) – Born November 6, 1939, in Blythe, Georgia, Patrick Fain Dye is remembered as a great player and coach. Dye played high school football at Richmond Academy where he was selected All-American and All-State while leading the team to the 1956 3A state championship as team captain. Following this success, the Atlanta Journal Constitution selected Dye as Georgia's 3A Lineman of the Year for 1956 before being recruited to play for the Georgia Bulldogs. Known for his toughness, Dye was a second team All-SEC guard in 1959 and first team in 1960. He played for coach Wallace Butts, leading the way for the "Peerless Pilot," Frank Tarkenton. After a stellar senior season in 1960, Dye played in the annual post-season Blue-Gray game between all-star players from various schools representing the North and the South. Upon graduation from Georgia, Dye played three years of professional football as a linebacker for the Edmonton Eskimos in the Canadian Football League. Of course, Dye is also remembered as the head coach of Auburn University, from 1981 to 1992.

Herschel Walker - (1980-1982) - Born March 3, 1962, Walker is remembered as Georgia's most dominating and prolific offensive player. Walker played for the Johnson County High School Trojans in Wrightsville, Georgia from 1975-1979 and was valedictorian of his senior class. In 1979, he rushed for 3,167 yards, helping the Trojans to their only state championship. He was awarded the first Dial Award for the National High School Scholar-Athlete of the Year in 1979. Herschel's brilliance as a running back transcended the college game. He won the Heisman Trophy in 1982 after placing as runner-up in 1981, and finishing third as a freshman in 1980. Walker led Georgia to the National Championship (1980), three consecutive SEC titles (1980, 1981 and 1982), a three-year record of 33-3, and three consecutive Sugar Bowl appearances. A three-time consensus All-American, Herschel said, "I never get tired of running. The ball ain't that heavy." In 1980, as a freshman, Walker in one game carried the football 23 times for a staggering 283 yards-an average of 12.3 yards a clip. Walker finished his three-year career at Georgia as the SEC's All-Time leading rusher, with 5,259 yards on 994 carries. After his junior season, Herschel, the maverick, left Athens with a year of eligibility remaining and played for the New Jersey Generals in the now-defunct USFL and later for the Dallas Cowboys, the Philadelphia Eagles, Minnesota Vikings and the New York Giants, proving to be a durable and effective professional commodity. Herschel has performed sparingly as a semi-professional mixed martial artist. Shortly after his retirement from football in 1997, Herschel was diagnosed with multiple personality disorder, or D.I.D., which he manages through professional help.

Kevin Butler – (1981-1984) – Born July 24, 1962 in Savannah, Georgia, Butler etched his place in the record books as one of the greatest Georgia kickers and one of the greatest in college history. Butler connected on 78.6 percent of his attempts at Georgia even though over 20 percent of them were from over 50 yards. During his final game for the Dawgs, Butler nailed field goals from 57, 50, and 34 yards and added an extra point, which was his 72nd straight. Butler made five of seven from beyond 50 yards as a senior, including a 60-yarder against Clemson and he left UGA with 13 school records, seven SEC records and four national marks, including the highest percentage

of field goals made from 50 yards and beyond. After Georgia, Butler played for the Chicago Bears and the Arizona Cardinals.

***Hines Ward* - (**1995-1998) - Born March 8, 1976 in Seoul, South Korea, Ward attended Forest Park High School in Forest Park, Georgia where he was a gifted quarterback, scholar-athlete and two-time Clayton County Offensive Player of the Year. Born to a Korean mother and an African-American father, he is remembered as one of the University of Georgia's best all-around athletes. The speedy, heady Ward starred as a wide receiver for the Bulldogs, but he saw spot duty at quarterback and tailback, leading him to 3,870 all-purpose yards, second in program history behind the great Herschel Walker. As a receiver, he made 144 career receptions for 1,965 yards, good for second in school history. Ward was All-SEC First Team as a senior. When he finished his college career it was discovered that he was missing an ACL in his left knee, which he lost as the result of a childhood biking accident. Nevertheless, Ward was still highly regarded and was drafted by the Pittsburgh Steelers in Round Three of the 1998 NFL Draft (92nd pick overall). In the grand ranks of the National Football League, Hines Ward performed as a quintessential pro. Having earned three MVP selections (Super Bowl XL), he is a five-time consecutive NFL Pro Bowl selection (2001-2005). Today he is an offensive assistant coach for the New York Jets.

***David Greene* - (**2001-2004) - Born June 22, 1982 in Snellville, Georgia, Greene grew up, along with his teammate David Pollack, with dreams of one day being a Georgia Bulldog. Those dreams came true as the two enjoyed All-American careers in Athens, with Green becoming the winningest quarterback in college football history with 42 wins, eclipsing Peyton Manning's mark. Greene attended South Gwinnett High School where he was a two-sport athlete, excelling in football at quarterback and at baseball, where he was an outfielder. After a redshirt year and the departure of Quincy Carter, Greene was named the 2001 starter. That year he was remembered for his now-infamous "hobnail boot" game at Tennessee, when play-by-play announcer Larry Munson was quoted after a successful Green screen pass for a touchdown, "We just stepped on their face with a hobnail boot and broke their nose. We just crushed their face!" He was named the 2001 SEC Offensive Rookie of the Year and was the 2002 SEC Offensive Player of the Year, highlighted by leading his team to an SEC Championship and a 2002 Sugar Bowl victory. In 2004, Greene completed 59 percent of his passes for 2,508 passing yards and twenty touchdowns with only four interceptions and led Georgia to its first victory over Florida since 1997. Drafted by the Seattle Seahawks in the third round (85th pick) of the 2005 NFL draft, after two years in Seattle he was picked up by Kansas City.

David Pollack **-** (2001-2004) - Born June 19, 1982 in New Brunswick, New Jersey, Pollack attended Shiloh High School in Snellville, Georgia where he was a three-sport letterman. He signed with Georgia where he was a standout All-American defensive end and one of the most active and popular Bulldogs to ever don the silver britches. A college roommate of teammate David Greene, Pollack became only the second Bulldog in history to thrice be named an All-American (2002, 2003, 2004) and a two-time SEC MVP (2002, 2004). Known for a "motor that never quit," Pollack played in 50 games for the Bulldogs, starting 44. His 36 career sacks are a Georgia mark, and fourth on the All-Time SEC list. If there was ever a play by Pollack that personified his collegiate career, it was one during his sophomore year in 2002. Pollack knocked down a pass from South Carolina quarterback Corey Jenkins in the Gamecock end zone and managed to catch the ball before it hit the ground, giving him a pass deflection and a 0-yard interception return for a touchdown. A team captain as a senior, he managed altogether 283 tackles, 36 sacks, 58.5 tackles for loss, 117 quarterback hurries, 18 passes defended, four interceptions, seven forced fumbles three fumble recoveries, three blocked punts and a blocked field goal. A winner of the Chuck Bednarik Award 92004), the Lott Trophy (2004), the Lombardi Award (2004) and twice the Ted Hendricks Award (2003, 2004), he was drafted by the Cincinnati Bengals in the first round (17th pick) of the 2005 NFL draft. He suffered a career-ending injury in the second game of his second professional season. Today he is a college football television analyst.

Matthew Stafford **–** (2007-2009) – Remembered as one of Georgia's most successful passers, Stafford was a prolific three-year quarterback for the Bulldogs, throwing for almost 3,500 yards his junior year and 7,731 overall during his abbreviated career in Athens. After defeating Michigan State 24–12 and winning MVP honors in the 2009 Capital One Bowl, Stafford finished his three years at Georgia with a 3–0 record in bowl games and a 6–3 record in rivalry games (1–2 against Florida, 3–0 against Auburn, and 2–1 against Georgia

Tech). Stafford chose to forgo his senior season and enter the 2009 NFL Draft. NFL analyst Mel Kiper predicted Stafford's number one slot in the draft, as he was chosen first overall, going to the Detroit Lions. In 2011 Stafford became only the fourth NFL quarterback to throw for 5,000 yards in a season.

Aaron Murray **–** (2009-2013) - A native Floridian, Murray attended Plant High School after transferring from Jesuit High School in Tampa, Florida, where he played quarterback and was All-State and a Parade All-American. Aaron participated in the U.S. Army All-American Bowl and chose Georgia and Coach Mark Richt over 52 other scholarship offers. Murray was one of Georgia's greatest quarterbacks—a prolific passer and scorer and a more than adequate runner, when necessary. After redshirting in 2009, Murray, who wore #11, was a rare four-year starter for the Bulldogs, etching his name in the conference record books, going an incredible 921 for 1,478—to 41 different players, for a staggering 13,166 yards, 121 touchdowns—to 23 different players, 41 interceptions and a career quarterback rating of 158.5. As a junior he set a single-season Georgia passing record with 3,893 yards and 36 touchdowns. He is the only SEC quarterback to have four 3,000-plus yard seasons. His eleven 300-yard games and 16 rushing touchdowns are school records. His 121 career touchdowns are a conference record. Murray was selected 163rd overall by the Kansas City Chiefs in the 5th round of the 2014 NFL Draft.

Todd Gurley **–** (2012–2014) - Gurley attended Tarboro High School in Tarboro, North Carolina, where he excelled at football, basketball and track. The all-region running back and sprinter committed to the Bulldogs and Coach Mark Richt. In 2012, during his freshman season in Athens, he started 12 of 14 games and rushed for 1,385 yards on 222 carries with 17 touchdowns. When healthy, Gurley was unstoppable, as he possessed incredible quickness for someone his size. A blur at 6-1, 235 pounds, he became only the second freshman in Georgia history to rush for 1,000 yards—the other being the great Herschel Walker. In the spring of 2013, Gurley ran track for Georgia and ran the 60-yard dash at 8.12 seconds, the seventh-fastest time in school history. In ten games in the fall he rushed for 989 yards on 165 carries with 10 touchdowns, earning second team All-SEC honors. In October 2014, Gurley, a junior, was suspended by Georgia over an alleged NCAA rules violation—that he had received $3,000 for signing autographs. He was suspended for four games and returned against Auburn only to tear his ACL, ending his Georgia Football career. In three seasons, his last abbreviated by injury, Gurley rushed 510 times for 3,285 yards for a 6.4 yard average and 36 touchdowns. The consensus All-SEC honoree was the tenth overall pick by the St. Louis Rams in the first round of the 2015 NFL Draft.

Nick Chubb – (2014-2017) - A native of Cedartown, Georgia, Chubb attended Cedartown High School where he was a star running back and track athlete, rushing for 6,983 yards and 102 touchdowns, while running the 100 meters, long jump and throwing the shot put; foreshadowing what would prove to be a productive college gridiron career that will long be remembered by Georgia and SEC football fans. In 2013, Chubb signed with Coach Mark Richt and Georgia, spurring one of college football's greatest rushing careers. An uncanny blend of size, strength and speed epitomized the college game displayed by Chubb, who in his first start as a Bulldog in 2014 rushed for 143 yards on 38 carries against Missouri. Chubb began the season backing up starter Todd Gurley, but assumed a starting role after Gurley was suspended for charging for signed autographs. He finished the season with 1,547 yards on 219 carries, second in the SEC, despite starting only eight games. On October 3, 2015, Nick tied Herschel Walker with 13 consecutive 100-yard games. Just days later, on October 10th, Chubb suffered a horrific knee injury against the Tennessee Vols, preventing him from beating the record. He missed the rest of the season but returned in 2016 under new head coach Kirby Smart. In his first game of the 2016 season, against a ranked North Carolina team, he rushed for 222 yards and two touchdowns. Chubb sprained his ankle three weeks later and Georgia went 1-4 over a five week period, the only win coming from an injured Chubb's 121 yards against South Carolina. He split carries with Sonny Michel for the remainder of the season but played in the Liberty Bowl, finishing with 142 yards and a game-sealing touchdown against TCU. Chubb surprised everyone by returning for his senior year. In 2017, he shared carries with Sonny Michel and still rushed for 1,345 yards on 223 carries. The two led Georgia to a 12-1 record and an SEC title. In a double-overtime victory over Oklahoma in the Rose Bowl in the College Football Playoff Semifinal, Chubb had 145 yards on 14 carries and a game-tying two-yard run with time running out in regulation. In the National Championship Game, Alabama's impenetrable defense held Chubb to only 25 yards on 18 carries in a 26-23 overtime loss. In four seasons Chubb rushed for 4,769 yards on 758 carries for a 6.3 yard average, and 44 touchdowns. He was drafted 35th by the Cleveland Browns in the early second round of the 2018 NFL Draft.

History:

Atlanta developed as a burgeoning transportation crossroads that became a city in 1845. However, with the start of the Civil War in 1861, Georgia's progress came to a halt. During the war, in 1863, William Tecumseh Sherman's Union forces marched across Georgia, destroying and burning nearly everything in their path. After the Civil War, Georgia's cities prospered and her economy slowly recovered, buoyed by the growth of the manufacturing, banking and railroad industries.

Beginnings of football at Georgia:

In the beginning, it was a 24-year-old University of Georgia Chemistry Professor, Dr. Charles Herty, who introduced the sport to his alma mater. During the fall of 1891, Herty introduced the game of "football," a new style of rugby developed by Walter Camp, to the Georgia students. During that fall of 1891, Herty brought to the University of Georgia a Walter Camp rule book and a penchant for the new contest played on a gridiron; it was a game he learned while playing it at Johns Hopkins University. Herty was instrumental in laying out the first football field at Georgia, as well as organizing and coaching its first team. Although there were no opponents for the fledgling Georgia squad in that first fall of 1891, the students at nearby Mercer agreed to organize a team and play Georgia following Christmas. The Mercer team was organized and as a result, Georgia played its first football game on January 30, 1892. According to Dr. John F. Stegeman, the game was the first in the Deep South, a contention he makes at the opposition of Auburn, which also claims the noteworthy distinction of being the first school to play the game. The final score of the Georgia-Mercer contest was Georgia 50, Mercer, 0. Professor Herty's name was memorialized on the home arena of the University of Georgia, "Herty Field" until Sanford Field was constructed in the 1920's.

Traditions:

The Georgia "G" Helmet:

The Georgia football helmet featuring the oval "G" has become a tradition that is known across the country as the logo of the Georgia Bulldogs. The helmet's design originated when Vince Dooley became head coach in 1964. Dooley was impressed with the Green Bay Packers' helmet, which featured the oval "G" in a different color pattern. Dooley liked the black oval "G" accompanied by a white oval background on each side of the helmet. The design has remained the same since, although a smaller black stripe was added inside the white stripe over the top in 1996, by head coach Jim Donnan.

The Arch:

The historical arch which sits on the edge of northern campus was installed in 1864. For years, freshmen were forbidden to walk under the Arch. Violators risked punishment from upperclassmen. Once rigidly enforced, the tradition of hazing freshmen became old hat. However, many freshmen, learning of the tradition during orientation or from other sources, still choose to honor the century-old tradition.

Silver Britches:

Silver Britches were the brain trust of Coach Wally Butts, who took over as head coach in 1939. The silver pants, complemented by a bright red jersey, made for a striking uniform. Through the years the fans referred to the Bulldogs' silver britches in their chants and on banners, but the phrase really caught on in the early fifties with a cheer, banners, and colorful vests that proclaimed "Go You Silver Britches."

Ringing of the Chapel Bell:

The ringing of the chapel bell after a Georgia victory is a tradition that continues even though freshmen are no longer ordered to perform the chore. In the 1890's the football field was located a stone's throw away from the Chapel and first year students were compelled to ring the bell until midnight in celebration of a Bulldog victory. Today, students, alumni and townspeople still rush to the Chapel to ring the bell after a Georgia gridiron victory.

Clean, Old-Fashioned Hate:

The ominous label is the nickname given to the rivalry between the Georgia Bulldogs and the Georgia Tech Yellow Jackets. The two schools are separated by a paltry 70 miles and have been bitter rivals since 1893.

The "Circle of Honor":

The Circle is considered the highest tribute to former Bulldog athletes and coaches. This honor was created in 1996 with the induction of Frank Sinkwich, Charley Trippi and other Bulldog greats.

"How 'Bout Them Dogs":

Although this is a slogan that has been recently employed by Bulldog fans, it is one that has become a vintage battle cry of the Georgia faithful. The yell started in the mid 1970's when the Bulldogs became known for pulling out unlikely victories in close games. The phrase caught on fully in 1980 when Georgia won its second national championship.

Fight Song:

Georgia's fight song, Glory, Glory, which is sung to the tune of the Battle Hymn of the Republic, was sung at Georgia games as early as 1890. The song in its current form was rearranged by Georgia musician-composer Hugh Hodson in 1915.

Glory

Glory, glory to old Georgia!
Glory, glory to old Georgia!
Glory, glory to old Georgia!

G-E-O-R-G-I-A
Glory, glory to old Georgia!
Glory, glory to old Georgia!
Glory, glory to old Georgia!
G-E-O-R-G-I-A

Alma Mater:

From the hills of Georgia's northland, Beams thy noble brow,
And the sons of Georgia rising, Pledge with sacred vow.
"Neath the pine tree's stately shadow, Spread thy riches rare,
And thy sons, dear Alma mater, Will they treasure share.
And thy daughters proudly join thee, Take their rightful place,
Side by side into the future, Equal dreams embrace.
Through the ages, Alma Mater, Men will look to thee;
Thou the fairest of the Southland Georgia's Varsity.
Chorus:
Alma Mater, thee we'll honor, True and loyal be,
Ever crowned with praise and glory, Georgia, hail to thee.

Noteworthy Georgia Alumni:

Zell Miller, United State Senator

Saxby Chambliss, United States Senator

Bill Anderson, country music recording artist

Robert Benham, first person of color appointed to Georgia Supreme Court

D.W. Brooks, presidential advisor to seven presidents

Mike Edwards, senior writer, National Geographic

Phil Gramm, United States Senator (Texas)

Lewis Grizzard, author, humorist (deceased)

Dewey Grantham, historian

W. Randall "Randy" Jones, founder of Worth Magazine

Julie Moran, former ABC sports reporter, host Entertainment Tonight

Philip Lee Williams, author

Stuart Woods, author

Charlyne Hunter Gault, journalist

John Huey, Editor-in-Chief, Time Inc.

Raymond Huges, Chorus Master, Metropolitan Opera

Jason Aldean, country musician

A.E. Stallings, poet

Jack Davis, cartoonist for Mad Magazine

Bill Goldberg, pro football player, pro wrestler, actor

R.E.M. , All four members attended

2020 Georgia Football Schedule

Sept. 7 vs. Virginia (Atlanta)

Sept. 12 East Tennessee State

Sept. 19 at Alabama

Sept. 26 ULM

Oct. 3 Vanderbilt

Oct. 10 Auburn

Oct. 17 at Missouri

Oct. 24 OPEN DATE

Oct. 31 vs. Florida (Jacksonville)

Nov. 7 at South Carolina

Nov. 14 Tennessee

Nov. 21 at Kentucky

Nov. 28 Georgia Tech

University of Kentucky

When SEC fans think of the University of Kentucky, they think of bluegrass—and the school's longtime winning basketball tradition. Although Kentucky has dominated the indoor game on the hardwood developed by Dr. James Naismith, it has had shining moments on the gridiron. Past Wildcat greats like Paul "Bear" Bryant, Blanton Collier, Howard Schnellenberger, George Blanda, Jeff Van Note, Tim Couch, Randall Cobb and Benny Snell, Jr. are reminders to the Kentucky faithful that basketball is not the Wildcats' only sport—as they have had much football success in the Southeastern Conference. Kentucky has a noble tradition of famous firsts in college football in the South. It holds the distinction of being the first college to play football in the Lower Mason-Dixon, as well as the first Southeastern Conference member school to sign a black athlete to play football, Nat Northington, in 1965, forever changing society and the beloved game.

Founded: 1865

Designated a land-grant institution in 1865, the 673-acre campus is located south of downtown Lexington. The University of Kentucky grew from the vision of one man, John Bowman. In 1865, after gaining financial support through the federal Morrill Land-Grant College Act, along with private donations, Bowman saw the realization of his dream with the inauguration of the state's new Agricultural and Mechanical College. Originally, courses were offered at Ashland, the Henry Clay estate. Three years later, James Kennedy Patterson became the first president of the land grant university and the first degree was awarded. In 1876, the university began to offer graduate degrees. Two years later, A&M withdrew from Kentucky University, which is now Transylvania University. For the new institution, Lexington donated a 52-acre park and fairground, which became the core of the university's present campus. The school was renamed the University of Kentucky in 1916. It was first a male-only institution, but allowed women in 1880.

Location: Lexington

Lexington is thoroughbred country. It has rightly been called the "Horse Capital of the World." Some of the finest race horses in the country can be found in and around Kentucky's capital city. Kentucky is known as the "bluegrass state," for the beautiful blue tint that mysteriously shades the indigenous rolling fields and knolls. Lexington is the second-largest city in the state (Louisville). After its founding in 1782 it became a cultural and financial focal point in the Alleghenies. Today, Lexington remains one of Kentucky's most progressive cities, serving as the location for the state's flagship university, the University of Kentucky, in addition to the Kentucky Horse Park, the Keeneland race course, and the Red Mile race course.

Population: (Lexington-Fayette) 321,959

Student Enrollment: 28,000

History:

In 1881, the University of Kentucky was the first Southeastern Conference member to introduce football. During that inaugural year Kentucky Agricultural and Mechanical College (later the University of Kentucky) played Kentucky University (later Transylvania) and won, 2 goals to 1. During World War II in 1943, like many other American colleges and universities, Kentucky did not play football.

Nickname: Wildcats

The nickname "Wildcats" became synonymous with the University of Kentucky after a 6-2 football road win over Illinois on October 9, 1909. Commandant Carbusier, then head of the military department at old State University, told a group of students in a chapel service following the game that the Kentucky football team had "fought like Wildcats." The name Wildcats became popular among UK followers and media members, and was adopted by the university.

Colors: Blue and White

Kentucky adopted blue and white as its official colors in 1892. Students decided on blue and yellow prior to the Kentucky-Centre football game on December 19, 1891. A random student asked the question, "What color blue?" The students decided on the hue of royal blue from the color adorning the tie of future football player Richard C. Stoll, who lettered on the 1893-94 teams. Stoll answered the question after he removed his tie and held it into the air. The students replaced the yellow with white the following year.

Mascot: Wildcats

The University of Kentucky has three official mascots. There is "Blue," a live Bobcat, or Wildcat. He lives at the state-operated Salato Wildlife Education Center near the state capital of Frankfort. Unlike the school's two costumed mascots, Blue never attends games, because Bobcats are shy by nature and do not react well with large crowds.

The Bobcat (Lynx rufus), is a North American mammal of the cat family, Felidae. With twelve recognized subspecies, it ranges from southern Canada to northern Mexico, including most of the continental United States. The Bobcat or Wildcat is an adaptable predator that inhabits wooded areas, as well as semi-desert, urban edge, and swampland environments. With a gray to brown coat, whiskered face, and black-tufted ears, the Bobcat resembles the other species of the mid-sized Lynx genus. It is smaller than the Canadian Lynx, with which it shares parts of its range, but is twice as large as the domesticated cat. It has distinctive black bars on its forelegs and a black-tipped, stubby tail, from which it derives its name.

In addition to Blue, there is "The Wildcat," a costumed student. The Wildcat made his debut during the 1976-1977 school year and has since been a fan favorite. If Blue and "The Wildcat" weren't enough to represent the beloved Kentucky mascot, in recent years the University of Kentucky has added "Scratch," who is a more child-friendly version of "The Wildcat."

Band: Wildcat Marching Band

The first marching band at UK was an unofficial "Cadet Band" led by Herman Trost, a bandleader in Sherman's Army in the Civil War and a close friend of John Philip Sousa (Marine Corps Hymn) and was part of a group of immigrants from Germany and Prussia called the Forty-Eighters. Informally affiliated with military training, the band existed by 1893, and as early as 1889.

In 1903, Captain George Byroade, Commandant of the Military Science department, appointed Professor Rucker as band director, creating the first official marching band at UK. In the fall of 1920, Sergeant John J. Kennedy was hired as band director, and under his direction it became known as "The Best Band in Dixie."

The UK Band was honored during this time to perform at the 1969 Presidential Inauguration of Richard M. Nixon. It has participated in bowl games, a World Series, and performed more than once for the Cincinnati Bengals.

Director of Bands: Dana Biggs, 2017- present

Stadium: Commonwealth Stadium at C. M. Newton / Kroger Field

Prior to the construction of Commonwealth Stadium, the Wildcats played their ball at Old Stoll Field/McLean Stadium. Stoll Field/McLean Stadium was home to Kentucky football for 56 years (1916-1972). The seating capacity of the stadium was 37,000 when Kentucky played its final game there in 1972, defeating the Vanderbilt Commodores 14-13 on November 11th. Stoll Field was dedicated October 14, 1916 in honor of the late Judge Richard C. Stoll, a generous alumnus and benefactor. McLean Stadium was dedicated on November 1, 1924, in memory of Price Innes McLean, a center on the 1923 UK team who passed away from injuries sustained during the Kentucky-Cincinnati contest on November 6, 1923.

Commonwealth Stadium is named for the Commonwealth of Kentucky. The field is named C.M. Newton Field in honor of past UK athletic director and former baseball and basketball player, C.M. Newton, who died in 2018. Built in 1973, it is the newest football stadium in the Southeastern Conference, as measured by date of original construction. The original capacity for the stadium was 57,800. In Commonwealth's first game, played on September 15, 1973, the Wildcats defeated the Virginia Tech Hokies 31-26.

In 1999, the stadium ends were enclosed and 40 suites were added, ten in each corner. The total cost of the expansion was $27.6 million. During the 1999 season, Kentucky's average home attendance for football games was 67,756. Attendance for the Tennessee game that year was 71,022, which remained the record until the Wildcats' 2007 game against Florida drew 71,024. The stadium underwent a $110 million renovation in 2015. The renovation included a new press box, loge box seats, club seats, recruiting room, suites, concourses, bathrooms, lights, and exterior facade while reducing capacity to around 61,000.

On May 1, 2017, UK along with marketing partner JMI Sports, announced the stadium's name change to Kroger Field, part of a 12-year, $1.85 million per year naming rights deal with Cincinnati-based retailer Kroger. The agreement made the University of Kentucky the first school in the Southeastern Conference to enter into a corporate partnership for the naming rights to their football stadium.

First Game

On April 9, 1881, football in the Southeast made its debut at Old Stoll Field at the University of Kentucky, then known as Kentucky A&M. Kentucky served as host to two visiting teams-Transylvania College and Centre College. Transylvania prevailed 13 ¾ to 0. The Lexington Daily Transcript reported on the event: "An estimated 500 ladies and gentlemen watched the game, which was like "...the head-on explosion of Spanish bulls crashing into one another." Kentucky A&M was enamored. It formed its own squad and issued a chal-

lenge to Transylvania for a best-of-three series slated for November 1881. Kentucky won the first game, but lost the second two. By 1895, ten colleges from today's SEC were playing intercollegiate football.

First Forward Pass

The first forward pass was thrown on October 13, 1906, by quarterback Earl Stone during a game against Eminence Athletic Club. Kentucky records do not indicate whether or not the first pass was completed. The newly-formed NCAA that same year legalized the forward pass.

First Night Game

UK was one of the first schools to play at night. On October 5, 1929, at Stoll Field, Kentucky defeated Maryville 40-0 under the lights. Thereafter, Kentucky played one home night game per season until 1946.

First game in stadium: September 15, 1973: Kentucky 31, Virginia Tech 26

Directions

Coming from the airport or from Bluegrass Parkway: Head east on Highway 60 (Versailles Road). Take a right on Mason Headley Road. Mason-Headley will change to Waller Avenue, then Cooper Drive. Commonwealth Stadium is at the intersection of Cooper Drive and University Avenue.

From I-75 South, take exit 110 (Winchester Road) and go west into Lexington. Head south on Highway 4 (New Circle Road). Take Alumni Drive exit and turn right. Stay on Alumni Drive. The stadium will be on the right.

From I-75 North, take exit 115 and turn right onto Newtown Road. Head 1.8 miles and turn right onto Highway 4 (New Circle Road). Stay on New Circle and exit east on Versailles Road, toward Lexington. Turn right on Mason-Headley Road.

Dining

AZUR Restaurant & Patio – Contemporary elegance at its best! This is the place for a celebration with family and/or other fans. Gourmet menu is varied. 3070 Lakecrest Circle in Beaumont Centre, Lexington. 1.859.296.1007.

Billy's Bar-B-Q Restaurant – Dang near perfect bar-b-que with years of practice. Voted best bar-b-que in the Blugrass by the Lexington Herald Leader. Paul Harvey gave Billy's a "10 out of 10" on his once-syndicated radio show. Billy's has food for every family member. Tailgaters phone ahead to pick-up bulk orders for the game! 101 Cochran Road, Lexington. 1.859.269.9593.

Columbia Steakhouse – A Lexington tradition; in business since 1946 makes the Columbia the oldest restaurant in central Kentucky. Famous for their

"Nighthawk" special. The Columbia offers a broad selection. Try their Kentucky Silk Pie. 201 North Limestone Street (Downtown), 1.859.253.3135; 2750 Richmond Road, 1.859.268.1666; and Columbia Steak Express, 125 Southland Drive, 1.859.313.5300; all locations in Lexington.

Night Life

Austin City Saloon – Woodsy bar & music joint hosting local & touring country-western bands in convivial digs. Great if you like country music. 2350 Woodhill Drive, Lexington 1.859.266.6891 Wednesday – Saturday, 6:00 p.m. – 2:00 a.m.

Accommodations

The Sire Hotel Lexington by Hilton / Formerly Gratz Park Inn – Once the first medical clinic west of the Allegheny Mountains, this historic structure offers 44 guest rooms and six suites. Guests are greeted by a welcoming library; and are enchanted by one of Lexington's favorite Five Star Restaurants, Jonathan at Gratz Park Inn. This fancy abode has earned its reputation as a timeless, classic luxury boutique inn. Located in downtown Lexington, the stylish and elegant Gratz Park Inn has been synonymous with gracious living for ages. Call for your reservation early. 859.231.1777.

Nearest Hospital to Stadium:

Central Baptist Hospital

1740 Nicholson Road, Lexington, KY 40503 859.260.6100

Bail Bondsman for Emergencies:

A1 Bail Bonds: 513.732.1900

Golf Courses:

University Club of Kentucky

4850 Leestown Road, Lexington, KY 859. 381.8585

Spring Valley Golf Club

2300 Sandersville Road, Lexington, KY 859.272.3428

Shopping:

Choose a destination: Fayette Mall, The Mall at Lexington Green, The Shops at Lexington Center or Turfland Mall.

Records

All-Time Record: 623–626–44 (.499)

SEC Championships: 2 (1950, 1976 tie)

Bowl Appearances: 19

Bowl Record: 10-9 (.526)

Kentucky Greats

Coaches

Paul "Bear" Bryant **–** (1946-1953) – (60-23-5) – (.710) – A native of Cleveland County, Arkansas, and University of Alabama graduate, Bryant coached at Kentucky from 1946-53 and led the Wildcats to eight consecutive winning seasons and four bowl games. He led the Wildcats to their greatest victory in program history in the 1951 Sugar Bowl. The Wildcats scored early and held on for a 13-7 win over the defending National Championship Oklahoma squad. Before the game, the Sooners had won 31 straight. Bryant is the most successful coach in Kentucky history. The sixty wins are the most by any Kentucky football coach. The story behind Bear's departure from Kentucky to Texas A&M is that Adolph Rupp, the legendary Wildcat basketball coach, received a Rolls Royce after winning the SEC Championship, whereas Bryant, in stark contrast, received a money clip. Had Kentucky treated the Bear differently, he may have instead worn a blue and white houndstooth hat. Bryant also coached at Texas A&M, and for his alma mater.

Blanton Collier **–** (1954-1962) – (41-36-3) – (.533) – A Millersburg, Kentucky native, Collier followed in the large footsteps of Paul Bryant, coaching Kentucky for eight seasons from 1954 to 1962. Collier found immediate success in Lexington, leading the Wildcats to a 7-3 mark during his first campaign. For that he was named SEC Coach of the Year by the Nashville Banner. After serving in the Navy in World War II, Collier coached the Cleveland Browns in 1946 as an assistant coach under Paul Brown. After leaving the Browns to coach Kentucky, Collier migrated back to the Browns organization where he coached them to an impressive 76-34-2 record, which included an NFL title in 1964. Kentuckians best remember Collier for posting an impressive 5-2-1 record against its most hated nemesis, Tennessee. Collier's 1959 coaching staff was one of the most capable ever assembled. The young apprentices of Collier that year were: Ed Rutledge, Howard Schnellenberger, Ermal Allen, Don Shula, John North, Bob Cummings, and Bill Arnsparger. He died March 22, 1983 in Houston, Texas.

Mark Stoops **–** (2013 – present) – (44-44) – (.500) - The Youngstown, Ohio native attended Cardinal Mooney High School and is a brother of Oklahoma head coach Bob Stoops. He is a tough, defensive leader who has brought stability and respectability to the program. He played college ball for the Iowa Hawkeyes from 1986–1988 and was a grad assistant at Iowa from 1989–1991. He became A.D. and defensive backs coach at Nordonia High School in Macedonia, Ohio (1992–1995). In 1996, when Kansas State assistant Jim Leavitt was hired as the head coach for the South Florida Bulls, he hired Stoops as defensive backs coach. He was the defensive backs coach for the University of Wyoming Cowboys from 1997–1999, under head coach Dana Dimel. When Dimel was hired at the University of Houston, he took Stoops along. Stoops was the Cougars' co-defensive coordinator and safeties coach in 2000. In February 2001, he was named the defensive backs coach for the University of Miami Hurricanes, replacing Chuck Pagano. Mike Stoops was hired as the head coach of the Arizona Wildcats for the 2004 season. Mike hired his brother Mark to his staff. On December 11, 2009, Mark Stoops accepted the defensive coordinator job at Florida State University. On November 27, 2012, he was hired as head coach of the University of Kentucky, replacing Joker Phillips. Like his predecessors, Stoops took over a difficult position. He has succeeded in every measurable way, as the Wildcats are no longer just a basketball school. Stoops' teams always fight, and he has built a respectable program, posting winning records in four straight seasons, with him being named SEC Coach of the Year in 2018 for a 10-3 record, culminating with a victory over Penn State in the Citrus Bowl. The 9-3 regular season record was one of four nine-win seasons in Kentucky history. 2019 was a challenge. After a 2-3 start in which they lost every scholarship quarterback to injury, Kentucky turned to receiver Lynn Bowden Jr. for leadership. With a revamped offense, Stoops and the Wildcats finished the year 7-5, beating Louisville 45-13. Kentucky capped the season with a climactic victory over Virginia Tech in the Belk Bowl. The Wildcats scored the go-ahead touchdown with 15 seconds left for an 8-5 finish. Stoops is 2-2 in bowl games. He is closing in on Bryant's 60 wins.

Players

George Blanda **–** (1945-1948) – Born September 17, 1927, in Youngwood, Pennsylvania, Blanda, nicknamed "the fossil" for his longevity, was a fantastic all-around player, serving as quarterback, punter and kicker for the Wildcats. Blanda threw for over 1,400 yards and twelve touchdowns in his final two seasons in Lexington. In 1947, he helped lead Kentucky to their first bowl

game. After completing 26 pro seasons with the Chicago Bears, Houston Oilers, and Oakland Raiders, he is the leading scorer in NFL history (first player to score 2,000 points), and a member of the NFL Hall of Fame in Canton, Ohio. He died December 27, 2010.

Bob Gain – (1947-1950) – A native of Akron, Ohio, Gain was a two-time (1949 & 50) first-team All-American and the 1950 Outland Trophy winner, the first from the SEC to win the prestigious award. He also received the Jacobs Blocking Trophy. As a talented tackle and place kicker, Gain was a three-time All-SEC selection. Kentucky was 33-10-2 during his playing days under Coach Bryant. He was a first-round draft choice by the Packers in 1951 and played in the Canadian Football League. He died in 2016 in Willoughby, Ohio.

Howard Schnellenberger – (1952-1956) – Born March 16, 1934, in St. Meinrad, Indiana, Shcnellenberger is considered one of Kentucky's greatest players and coaches. Although he was never a head coach at Kentucky, he was one of the Wildcats' best – both on the field and on the sidelines. He played two years as a standout tight end under Paul Bryant and two years under Blanton Collier, earning four varsity letters as an offensive and defensive lineman. In 1955, he was named a first team All-American, and during his Kentucky career the Wildcats notched a 25-12-4 record. Schnellenberger started his coaching career as an assistant at Kentucky (1959-60) under Head Coach Blanton Collier, his former mentor. From there, he headed to Alabama, where he coached from 1961-1965 under his other former Kentucky mentor, Paul Bryant. At Alabama he was responsible for recruiting Joe Namath. Schnellenberger coached professional football under George Allen with the Dolphins from 1970-72; and again from 1975-79. For two years (1973-74) he served as head coach of the Baltimore Colts and in 1983, he led the Miami Hurricanes to a national championship. Later he became head coach at Louisville, Oklahoma and Florida Atlantic. His HC coaching record is 158-151-3.

Nat Northington – (1965-1967) – A native of Louisville, Northington was the first black football player to sign with a Southeastern Conference school, in December of 1965. In Lexington, in 1967, he became the first black player to play in an SEC game where two SEC teams met head-to-head (Ole Miss). Northington became the first man to officially break the league color barrier on the field, but that watershed event did not come without pain. During an August practice in 1967, the Wildcats executed on the practice field a pursuit drill that they had done hundreds of times. The drill was elementary: One player had the football and the eleven defenders chased him and each hit the ball carrier once and then backed off. Greg Page, a defensive end, was the ball carrier on this particular drill, and when the defenders cleared out, Page was motionless. Page remained that way—forever. Completely paralyzed, he required a respirator. He died 38 days later. Northington, a receiver, was Page's roommate. Although he became the first black player to participate in an SEC game when he logged several minutes in Kentucky's 26-13 loss to Ole Miss in Lexington, he appeared in only three more games before leaving the team, distraught over his friend's death. Northington remains the forerunner of race and football in the Southeastern Conference.

Jeff Van Note **–** (1966-68) – Born February 7, 1946, in South Orange, New Jersey, Van Note was a three-year letterman at defensive end and Kentucky's Most Valuable Player in 1968. Recruited as a fullback for the Cats, he ended his career as a standout SEC defensive player. Van Note played in six NFL Pro Bowls during an 18-year career with the Atlanta Falcons. Van Note was an eleventh round draft choice and played center for his 18 years with the Falcons. He was named All-Pro in 1982 and served as a radio analyst.

Art Still **– (**1974-1977) – Born December 5, 1955 in Camden, New Jersey, Still was a four-year letterman and 1977 first team All-American defensive end for the Wildcats. Still broke the Kentucky record for tackles behind the line with 22 in 1977. A two-time All-SEC player in 1976 and 1977, he was honored by the Columbus, Georgia Touchdown Club as the SEC's "Most Outstanding Player" in 1977. He finished his career in Lexington with 327 tackles and was selected the second overall pick in the first round of the 1978 NFL draft by the Kansas City Chiefs. He played professionally for twelve years.

Jim Kovach **–** (1974-1978) – Born May 1, 1956, in Parma Heights, Ohio, Kovach is one of the most prolific tacklers in SEC and college football history, and one of its noted scholars. A fantastic linebacker who gobbled up running backs, quarterbacks, and receivers, Kovack is Kentucky's All-Time tackles leader with 521, totaling 164 during the 1978 football season. A four-year letterman who received a medical hardship ruling in 1977 because of a shoulder injury, Kovach was a consensus first-team All-American in 1978. The recipient of the 1979 NCAA Post-Graduate scholarship, he was an Academic All-American. A fourth-round choice by the New Orleans Saints in the 1979 NFL draft, Kovach played seven seasons in the NFL, six with the Saints and one year with the San Francisco 49ers. Kovach completed his medical degree at Kentucky and earned a law degree from Stanford.

Derrick Ramsey **–** (1975-1977) – Born December 23, 1956, in Hastings, Florida, Ramsey was a 1977 first team All-SEC standout, and third team All-Amer-

ican. He was named Outstanding SEC Quarterback his senior year by the Birmingham Touchdown Club. He guided the Wildcats to consecutive 9-3 and 10-1 seasons as a junior and a senior, including a 21-0 victory over North Carolina in the 1976 Peach Bowl. He ranks third in school career rushing touchdowns with 25. Ramsey was selected in the 5th round of the 1978 NFL Draft by the Oakland Raiders and played tight end for three different teams (New England, and Detroit) over a ten year pro career.

Craig Yeast **–** (1995-1998) – Born November 20, 1976, in Danville, Kentucky, Yeast was one of Kentucky's most electric receivers. Benefiting from the arm talent of quarterback Tim Couch, he earned unanimous first-team All-SEC honors while setting Kentucky season records with 85 catches, 1311 yards, and 14 touchdowns in 1998. Yeast averaged 29.3 yards on 14 kickoff returns, including a 100-yarder (tie for school record) for a touchdown versus Florida in 1998. Upon graduation, Yeast was the all-time leader in career receptions in the history of the SEC, with 208 catches, and was second in career receiving yards with 2,899. As a senior he was a third-team All-American and a semi-finalist for the Biletnikoff Award. Yeast was drafted in round four of the 1999 NFL Draft by the Cincinnati Bengals. After a stint with the New York Jets, he played in the Canadian Football League for the Hamilton Tiger Cats.

Tim Couch **–** (1996-1998) – A Hyden, Kentucky, native, Couch was born July 31, 1977 and attended Leslie County High School. An All-American quarterback at Kentucky as a junior and a senior under Head Coach Hal Mumme, Couch led the Wildcats to a winning season and a bowl appearance in 1998. The first pick of the 1999 NFL draft, he holds many University of Kentucky passing records. Couch finished his abbreviated college career (he went pro after his junior year) as one of college football's most successful quarterbacks. Despite playing in only twenty-four games as a starter, Couch shattered Kentucky's career passing records, completing 795 of 1184 attempts for 8835 yards in total offense. These totals eclipsed the old Kentucky all-time mark of 5456 yards by Bill Ransdell (1983-86). He placed fourth in voting for the Heisman, pacing the nation with 400 completions (on 553 attempts) while ranking second in pass completion percentage (72.3), yards (4,275), and touchdowns (36). He threw for at least 300 yards with one touchdown in every game he played. Couch ended his three-year career the holder of seven NCAA records, 14 SEC records and 26 Kentucky records. Couch played for the Cleveland Browns from 1999-2003.

Derek Abney **–** (2001-2004) – Born December 19, 1980, in Minot, North Dakota, Abney was raised in Mosiness, Wisconsin. He redshirted his first year at Kentucky but started every game thereafter as a receiver and return man. During his career Abney established numerous Kentucky, SEC, and NCAA records for his incredible punt and kick return skills. Possessing an uncommon fearlessness coupled with great speed and the uncanny ability to quickly change direction, Abney was an electric kick returner for the Wildcats, and arguably their best. Kentucky records held by Abney include: most all-purpose yards in a career (5,856); most yards-per all-purpose play (14.8); most kickoff return yards in a career (2,313); most kickoff returns in a career (96). Drafted in round seven of the 2004 NFL Draft by the Baltimore Ravens, he was released without playing a game. Chicago picked him up in 2005, but again, he never played professionally.

Randall Cobb **–** (2008-2010) – Remembered as a versatile quarterback, receiver and return man, during his freshman year Cobb was named to the SEC All-Freshmen team at QB, playing in eleven games and starting four at quarterback. He scored two throwing, two receiving, and seven rushing touchdowns during his freshman year. As a sophomore, he played wide receiver and in the offense/special teams by returning kicks, place kick holding, receiving, and playing the quarterback role in the "Wildcat" formation. He scored four receiving, one returning, and ten rushing touchdowns during the 2009 season. As a junior, on October 9, 2010, Cobb scored four touchdowns against an undefeated Auburn team, tying the Kentucky school record for career touchdowns at 32. He was the first player to score a rushing, passing, and receiving touchdown in the same game for the University of Kentucky since Shane Boyd in 2003. An All-SEC performer as a sophomore and a junior, and a consensus All-American as a senior, Cobb was the 64th overall pick by the Green Bay Packers during the 2nd round of the 2011 NFL Draft.

Benny Snell, Jr. **–** (2016-2018) – Benny attended Westerville Central in Westerville, Ohio where he rushed for over 2,000 yards his junior season and combined for an additional 2,000+ yards his senior year. A three-star recruit, Snell became one of the league's best backs, joining some of the SEC's greatest runners. During his freshman year Snell rushed for 1,091 yards, breaking Moe Williams' record. As a sophomore, he rushed for 1,333 yards and scored 19 touchdowns, becoming the first Wildcat to rush for 100 yards in ten or more games before his junior season, and

was 2nd Team All-SEC. As a junior in 2018, Snell rushed for 1,449 yards and scored 16 touchdowns, becoming one of only four backs to rush for 1,000 yards in three seasons—Herschel Walker, Darren McFadden and Alex Collins. With 3,873 yards on 737 carries, Snell averaged 5.3 yards per rush with 48 touchdowns. He is Kentucky's all-time rushing leader, surpassing the 43-year old record held by Sonny Collins—broken in just three seasons by Snell. At the close of his junior year he was named a consensus First-Team All-SEC player. He was drafted 122nd by the Pittsburgh Steelers in the fourth round of the 2019 NFL Draft.

Great Bowl Games

1947 Great Lakes Bowl: Kentucky 24, Villanova 14

1951 Sugar Bowl: Kentucky 13, Oklahoma 7

1952 Cotton Bowl: Kentucky 20, TCU 7

1976 Peach Bowl: Kentucky 21, N. Carolina 0

1983 Hall of Fame Bowl: Kentucky 20, Wisconsin 19

2006 Music City Bowl: Kentucky 28, Clemson 20

2007 Music City Bowl: Kentucky 35, Florida State 28

2018 Citrus Bowl: Kentucky 27, Penn State 24

2019 Belk Bowl: Kentucky 37, Virginia Tech 30

Radio Commentator: Tom Leach, 2007-present

Kentucky Wildcats Radio Broadcast Stations: 98.1 FM WBUL 630 AM WLAP

The Immortals

Known as "The Immortals," the 1898 University of Kentucky football team remains the only undefeated, untied, and unscored upon team in school history. During that magical season the Wildcats went a perfect 7-0-0, squashing their seven opponents by a scoring margin of 180-0. The closest of the games was a victory of 6-0 over Centre College. Rosco Severs was the team captain that fabled year under Coach W.R. Bass.

The Year

Considered the greatest year in sports for the University of Kentucky, it transpired in Lexington during the 1977-1978 school calendar. The 1977 football team went 10-1, finishing top five with victories over North Carolina (10-7), West Virginia (28-13), Penn State (24-20), LSU (33-13), Georgia (33-0), Florida (14-7), and Tennessee (21-17). On the basketball court, Joe B. Hall and the

Wildcats sealed the institution's fifth NCAA title by defeating Duke 94-88.

British Pub

Prince Charles of Wales witnessed Kentucky beat Georgia in Athens on October 22, 1977. All-American Art Still and company blanked the Bulldogs on that day 33-0. At halftime Prince Charles was greeted by the 6'-6" Still. Prince Charles told Still, "You're a tall one aren't you?"

Traditions

The Bourbon Barrel

The "Bourbon Barrel" is the trophy presented to the winner of the Kentucky-Indiana football game. The teams met as early as 1893. The trophy, or keepsake, is a half-barrel that lists all the scores of the series. A blue stripe is painted in the background for a Kentucky win and a red stripe for an Indiana victory. The Bourbon Barrel game is the third-longest series in the Southeastern Conference, as it trails only the Auburn-Georgia series (102 consecutive games) and the Mississippi-Mississippi State series (95). The "Beer Barrel" is the trophy that is given to the winner of the Kentucky-Tennessee game.

Horse-Drawn Homecoming

Homecoming games at UK are highlighted by the Homecoming Queen and her court being presented in horse-drawn carriages.

Fight Song

On on, U of K, we are right for the fight today,
Hold that ball and hit that line;
Ev'ry wildcat start will shine;
We'll fight, fight, fight, for the blue and white
As we roll to that goal, Varsity,
And we'll kick, pass and run, 'til the battle is won,
And we'll bring home the victory.

Alma Mater

Hail Kentucky, Alma Mater!
Loyal sons and daughters sing;
Sound her praise with voice united;
To the breeze her colors fling;
To the blue and white be true;
Badge triumphant age on age;
Blue, the sky that o'er us bends; White,
Kentucky's stainless page.

Noteworthy Alumni

Harry Monroe Caudill, author, lawyer, historian, activist, legislator

Thomas Clark, former Secretary, Organization of American Historians

Ernest Fletcher, U.S. House of Representative from Kentucky (1998 to now)

Ashley Judd, actress

William Kirwan, former Ohio State President; Chancellor of U of Maryland

Pat Riley, NBA coach

Sam Abell, National Geographic photographer

George Akin, scientist on the Manhattan Project

Emily Cox, Miss Kentucky 2008

Nick Dimango, Editor Maxim Magazine

Tom Hammond, sportscaster

Beverly Perdue, former Governor of North Carolina

2020 Kentucky Football Schedule

Sept. 5 Eastern Michigan

Sept. 12 at Florida

Sept. 19 Kent State

Sept. 26 South Carolina

Oct. 3 at Auburn

Oct. 10 Eastern Illinois

Oct. 17 Vanderbilt

Oct. 24 at Missouri

Oct. 31 OPEN DATE

Nov. 7 at Tennessee

Nov. 14 Mississippi State

Nov. 21 Georgia

Nov. 28 at Louisville

The University of Missouri

A revered stalwart of the "Show Me" State, in 2012 the University of Missouri was introduced to the ultra-competitive world of Southeastern Conference Football, through its Eastern Division, along with Texas A&M in the Western Division, rounding out an unprecedented, new-and-improved league of 14 premier Southern football-playing universities. Columbia, Missouri possesses a storied Big 12 gridiron tradition, and it has served as a proud and welcome host to first-time traveling SEC fans, competing amongst the league's best. Mizzou in its short SEC tenure has twice played in the league championship game (2013 & 2014). It has produced noteworthy NFL signal callers and is credited with holding the first "Homecoming" game in 1911, a revered cultural tradition since copied by every American high school, college and university. Missouri Tiger fans, longing for the glory days of Tiger coaching greats Faurot, Devine and Pinkel have pinned their winning hopes on the sleeves of its newest field general, Eliah Drinkwitz, a pedigreed up-and-comer bent on returning pigskin pride to the Southeastern Conference's newest eastern division upstart.

Nickname:

"Tigers" is the moniker for Missouri's athletic teams. Its origin can be traced to the Civil War. Plundering Confederate guerilla bands habitually raided small Missouri towns, and Columbia's citizens constantly feared an attack. Temporary "home guards" and vigilance companies banded together to counter these possible threats. The town's preparedness discouraged guerilla activity, and the protecting organization disbanded in 1854. However, it was rumored that a guerilla band, led by the notorious Bill Anderson, intended to sack the town. Quickly organized was an armed guard of Columbia citizens, who built a blockhouse and fortified the old courthouse in the center of town. This brave company was called "The Missouri Tigers." The marauders never showed. The reputation of the intrepid "Tigers" forced Anderson's gang to detour around Columbia, thereby avoiding a fight. Soon after Missouri's first football team was organized in 1890, the athletic committee adopted the nickname "Tigers" in official recognition of the intrepid Civil War defenders; it has since remained.

Founded: 1839

Location: Columbia, Missouri

The County Seat of Boone County, Columbia is home to the University of Missouri, or "Mizzou." The college town has been called "The Athens of Missouri" and "College Town USA." Settled in Pre-Columbian times by mound-build-

ing Native Americans of the Mississippi region, in 1818, a group incorporated the area under the Smithton Land Company and purchased over 2,000 acres, establishing the Village of Smithton near today's downtown Columbia. In 1821, the settlers moved and renamed the settlement Columbia. The founding of the University of Missouri in 1839, established the city as a center of education and research. Located amidst tributary valleys of the Missouri River, Columbia is equidistant from St. Louis and Kansas City. Greater St. Louis is 70 miles to the East, and the Kansas City Metropolitan Area is 100 miles to the West.

Population: 121,717

Enrollment: 29,866

History:

The University of Missouri, whose motto is: "Let the welfare of the people be the supreme law," began in 1839, when 900 citizens of Boone County pledged $117,921 in cash and land to win the bid to locate the new state university in Columbia. This investment in the promise of a better future for all through public higher education made MU the first public university west of the Mississippi River. It was also the first of Thomas Jefferson's Louisiana Purchase Territory. University cultural life began in 1842, with the formation of two literary societies, the Union Literary and the Athenaean Society. The first department of art was directed by George Caleb Bingham, the famous Missouri artist. In 1849, the first course in civil engineering west of the Mississippi River was taught at MU. The "Normal College," now the College of Education, was established in 1867, to prepare teachers for Missouri public schools. It also enrolled the university's first female students. Women were admitted to all academic classes in 1871. The real impetus for growth occurred in 1870, when MU was awarded land-grant status and the College of Agriculture and Mechanic Arts, later renamed the College of Agriculture, Food and Natural Resources, opened its doors. The Missouri Agricultural Experiment Station began operation in 1888. During those early years, MU added law and medical schools. Undaunted by a disastrous fire in 1892, the university rebuilt the remnants of its first academic building, erecting six prominent, iconic columns that symbolize public higher education in Missouri.

Missouri has played football for different conferences through the years. From 1890 to 1892 they were independent. From 1892 to 1897 they were members of the Western Interstate University Football Association. From 1898-1906 they were independent. From 1907-1963 they were members of the Missouri Valley Intercollegiate Athletic Association (MVIAA). From 1964 to 1995 they became members of the Big Eight when the MVIAA changed its name. From 1996 to 2011 they were members of the Big 12 Conference, competing in the North Division. In 2012, Missouri entered the Southeastern Conference Eastern Division, in concert with Texas A&M in the Western Division.

First game: Thanksgiving Day, 1890

Mizzou's first football team was formed in 1890, by the sophomore class of the "Academic School," which is today the College of Arts and Sciences. A team of engineering students in April that same year, upon the encouragement of Dr. A. L. McRea, a university professor, organized a playing squad. Interest in the sport grew among the students, professors and administrators, and a Foot Ball Association was formed at a meeting on October 10, 1890. The first intercollegiate game for the university took place on Thanksgiving Day, 1890, when Missouri played Washington University before a crowd of 3,000 people in St. Louis, Missouri. The Washington University team, which had been playing for several years, defeated the fledgling University of Missouri team by a score of 28–0.

Colors: Black & Gold

Early historical references note the use of crimson and gold as Mizzou's colors. Nevertheless, all true Tiger fans know that the official colors for Mizzou are black and gold, in keeping with the natural colors of the Bengal Tiger.

Mascot:

Truman the Tiger was introduced as the school's mascot against the Utah State Aggies, in 1986, receiving his name from former U.S. President Harry S Truman, a Missouri native. Truman has thrice been named the "Nation's Best Mascot."

Band name: Marching Mizzou (M2)

Beginning with 12 members in 1885, the Marching Mizzou is today a proud organization of over 300 strong, making it the largest student organization. The band performs at every home game and features a signature drill called "Flip Tigers," which is a fan favorite and staple of their pre-game warm-up.

In this formation Marching Mizzou makes straight lines while playing Every True Son. After, they chant: "Hit It! Hooray! Hurrah! Mizzou! Mizzou! Hooray! Hurrah! Mizzou! Mizzou! Hooray! Hurrah -- and a Bully for Ole Mizzou RAH! RAH! RAH! Mizzoooou-RAH! Mizzoooou-RAH! Mizzoooou-RAH! TIGERS!" The band forms the word "MIZZOU" and plays Fight Tiger. After this song, the band chants "T-I-G-E-R-S-TIGERS-GO!" while moving to spell "TIGERS" in just eight beats. This formation is floated off of the field to the South Endzone before forming a tunnel for the football players to run through.

During pregame Marching Mizzou forms a Block "M" and "waltz-steps" down the field while playing the first part of the "Missouri Waltz." During this portion of the song, the crowd waves its arms back and forth to the song's beat. At the "cut time" portion of the song, the band changes from "waltz step" to a "high step" as they continue to float the "M" to mid-field.

Band members wear black hats with gold trim; a Tiger emblem; 14-inch plumes; black overalls; gloves; shoes with white jackets with black, gold striped collars; and a large, gold, tilted 'M,' part of which runs down the right arm, creating a gold sleeve. Marching Mizzou has a full color guard, two featured twirlers and four drum majors. These drum majors serve as the top student leaders in M2, assisting in practices and with show design. Further, the Golden Girls, a coquettish, baton-twirling unit, works with the bands' leaders and attend daily practices with Marching Mizzou.

M2's shows at pregame and halftime offer a marked contrast between traditional and conservative marching styles. Before the game the band is led on the field by the head drum major; who, upon reaching midfield, tips his hat to the Faurot Field crowd and performs many of the school's favorite tunes. During the playing of "Old Missouri," the school's alma mater, the crowd links arms and sways, adding fist pumps and emphasis during the lines "here's a HEALTH! to thee" and "thy high FAME! shall last." For the Missouri Waltz, the band plays the first half of the song as a slow waltz, with fans waving their arms to the beat. At the song's midpoint, Marching Mizzou changes to cut time, playing the remainder of the song at a fast clip. During the game, the band sits in the south end of Faurot Field.

Band Director: Amy M. Knopps

Stadium:

Faurot Field in Columbia is where the Missouri Tigers play their home football games. Nicknamed the "Zou," it can be unfriendly to opposing teams. In 1972, Memorial Stadium's gridiron was named Faurot Field in honor of longtime coach, Don Faurot. The stadium is of horseshoe-shape, with seating added in the "open" endzone. The horseshoe is completed by a grass berm in the curved end, which is used for general admission on game days. The berm behind the endzone is known for the giant block "M" made of painted white stones.

Fundraising started in 1921, for a "Memorial Union" and a "Memorial Stadium." The projects were a tribute to Mizzou alumni who lost their lives in service during World War I. In 1925, ground was broken at the site of the stadium, a sizeable natural valley between twin bluffs south of the campus. Original plans were for the stadium to seat 25,000, with later stages of expansion to seat 35,000, 55,000, 75,000 and 95,000. Legend has it that an industrial rock crusher and a truck were buried there during initial blasting, and that they remain buried underneath the field.

Memorial Stadium was dedicated on October 2, 1926, to the memory of 112 alumni and students who lost their lives in World War I. That first October game against Tulane was marred by rainstorms that washed out a bridge into Columbia coming from the western side of Missouri. While the game sold out, the field could not be sodded due to the wet conditions. Instead, a surface of sawdust and tree bark was used, and the Tigers and Green Wave played to what was called "a scoreless, mudpie tie," by sportswriter Bob Broeg. Grass was used thereafter, until the 1980's.

The recognizable rock 'M' of the northern end zone debuted on October 1, 1927, to a 13-6 victory over Kansas State. The monument was built by members of the freshman class using leftover rocks from the original stadium construction. The 90-foot wide by 95-foot high 'M' has remained intact and an integral start of the Faurot Field experience. When full, Faurot Field is the ninth-largest city in the State of Missouri.

The playing surface of Faurot Field was grass from 1926 to 1984 and 1995 to 2002. Omniturf was used from 1985 to 1994 and Field Turf was installed in 2003; and is still being used today. The stadium's current capacity came as a result of renovations and expansions through the years. Renovations oc-

curred in 1978, 2003 and 2012 and expansions took place from 1949-1950, 1961-1963, 1971, 1978, 1996, 2003 and 2009.

Stadium capacity: 71,004

Directions to Faurot Field:

From the East: Traveling on Interstate 70 (I-70), turn south on Highway 63 and exit at Stadium Blvd. South, turn west (right) on Stadium Boulevard.

From the South: Traveling on Highway 63 north, exit at Stadium Boulevard. Turn west (left) on Stadium Boulevard.

From the West: Traveling on Interstate 70 (I-70) to Stadium Boulevard, turn south (right) on Stadium Boulevard.

From the North: Traveling on Highway 63 south, exit at Stadium Boulevard. Turn west (right) on Stadium Boulevard.

Dining:

Shakespeare's Pizza – Using the freshest, high-grade ingredients, these hand-tossed pizzas made from scratch are the real deal. "It's about the pizza, stupid. And maybe the beer. Everything else can go fly." Downtown, 225 S. Ninth Street, Columbia 1.573.449.2454. Sunday – Thursday: 11:00 a.m. – 10 p.m. Friday – Saturday: 11:00 a.m. – 11:00 p.m.

Café Berlin – Original, hand-crafted, farm-sourced gourmet breakfast, lunch and dinner. Breakfast served all day...try a pancake burrito, omelet, chicken or tuna salad. This place will fill you up! 220 North 10th at Park. Columbia 1.573.441-0400.

Flat Branch Pub & Brewing – A local favorite. Several local, fresh beers available on tap. Inside Columbia Magazine's 2013 Best of Columbia Readers Poll cited FBP&B as Best Overall Restaurant, Best Al Fresco Dining, and Best Beer Menu. Open 11:00 a.m. to midnight daily. 115 South 5th Street, Columbia 573.499.0400.

Nite Life:

Harpo's: Established in 1971, this world-famous bar is a Mizzou Tiger tradition. A favorite of the ESPN College Game Day crew when they visit Columbia. Try the pizza, and of course, the beer! 29 South 10th Street, Columbia 573.443.5418.

The Blue Note: Since, 1980, it has been the featured spot for great live music in Columbia. Specializing in all genres--from jazz to blues, from reggae to rock. Music devotees have experienced R.E.M., Johnny Cash, Jack Johnson, Wilco, and Dave Matthews in an intimate setting unlike any other. 17 N.

Ninth Street, Columbia, 573.874.1944.

Accommodations:

The Tiger Hotel: An historic refurbishment located in the heart of downtown, within walking distance of the mainstays. 23 South 8th St, Columbia, MO 65201 573.875.8888.

Hospital nearest to stadium:

University of Missouri Hospital, 1 Hospital Drive, Columbia, 573.882.4141

Bail Bondsmen for emergencies:

M.U. Bail Bonds - 1200 Rogers Street, Columbia 573.442.5311

Golf:

A.L. Gustin Golf Course

University of Missouri

18 Stadium Boulevard, Columbia 573. 882.6016

University of Missouri - Rolla Golf Course

1001 West 10th Street, Rolla, Missouri 65409 573. 341.4217

Shopping:

Columbia Mall, Forum Shopping Center, The District, or the North Village Arts Districts are sure bets for effective retail therapy.

All-time record: 678–560–52 (. 546)

Bowl record: 15-18 (.454)

Conference Championships:

Mizzou last won a conference championship in the Big Eight, in 1960, under Dan Devine. They also claim 14 other conference championships, eleven from 1909 to 1960 in the MVIAA and three in the WIUFA from 1893 to 1895. Missouri claims three Big 12 North Division titles from 2008 to 2010. In 2013 and 2014 they won the Eastern Division of the SEC and played in the conference championship game in Atlanta.

Missouri greats

Coaches:

Don Faurot – (1935-1942)-(1946-1954)-(101-79-10-(.531) - Faurot is remembered as Mizzou's most successful football coach. Despite losing two fingers on his right hand in a farming accident as a young boy, Faurot developed

into a fine athlete. Born June 23, 1902, in Mountain Grove, Missouri, Faurot lettered in three sports at the University of Missouri from 1922 to 1924. He played halfback in football, basketball and baseball. Faurot was the head football coach at the Northeast Missouri State Teachers College, now Truman State University, from 1926 to 1934 and at the University of Missouri from 1935 to 1942 and again from 1946 to 1956, compiling a 101-79-10 record at Mizzou during that span. During World War II, Faurot coached the Iowa Pre-Flight Seahawks in 1943 and the football team at the Naval Air Station in Jacksonville in 1944. He was the head basketball coach at the Northeast Missouri State Teachers College from 1925 to 1934, tallying a mark of 92–74. Faurot is credited with conjuring the split-T formation. He was inducted into the College Football Hall of Fame as a coach in 1961. The playing surface as Missouri's Memorial Stadium was named Faurot Field in his honor in 1972. Faurot passed away October 19, 1995.

***Dan Devine* –** (1958-1970) – (93-37-7) – (.704) - Born December 22, 1924, in Augusta, Wisconsin, Devine served as the head football coach at Arizona State University from 1955 to 1957, the University of Missouri from 1958 to 1970, and Notre Dame from 1975 to 1980, compiling a college coaching record of 173–56–9. His Missouri record of 93–37–7 included four bowl victories, and his winning percentage of .704 eclipsed Don Faurot's, the coaching legend who preceded him. An interesting side note is that a young Frank Broyles served as the interim head football coach at Mizzou in 1957—for one year, between the long tenures of Faurot and Devine. Devine is second on Missouri's all-time wins list, behind only Faurot. Devine served as Mizzou Athletic Director from 1967 to 1970 and was also the head coach of the National Football League's Green Bay Packers from 1971 to 1974, tallying a mark of 25–27–4. His 1977 Notre Dame team won a national championship after beating Texas in the Cotton Bowl. Devine was inducted into the College Football Hall of Fame as a coach in 1985. He died May 9, 2002.

***Gary Pinkel* –** (2001-2015) – (90-61) – (.677) - Born in 1952, the Akron, Ohio native served as the head football coach at the University of Missouri for 15 seasons. Pinkel is remembered as a solid coach who did more with less in terms of talent, taking over a Missouri team that had two winning seasons in 17 years

prior. From 1991 to 2000, Pinkel was the head football coach at the University of Toledo, where his team won a Mid-American Conference championship, in 1995. He was an assistant at the University of Washington, where he worked under Don James as his offensive coordinator. Pinkel graduated from Kent State with an education degree in 1973, where he played tight end under Coach James and roomed with Alabama Head Coach Nick Saban. Pinkel took over Toledo in 1991, when Saban left to become defensive coordinator for the Cleveland Browns. His other roommate at Kent State was Pittsburgh Steelers great, Jack Lambert. In 2012, Pinkel led the Tigers to a 5-7 record in their first year of Southeastern Conference Football. In 2013, he won the Eastern Division with a 12-2 record, and a win in the Cotton Bowl. In 2014, he and the Tigers again won the Eastern Division, this time claiming an 11-3 record and a Citrus Bowl victory and Pinkel being named SEC Coach of the Year. The next year was a repeat of Pinkel's first season in the SEC, 5-7, and it proved to be his last in Columbia. Pinkel retired after the season, announcing he had Non-Hodgkins Lymphoma. Pinkel took the Tigers to ten bowl games in 14 seasons, winning six. From 2002-2015, he placed 26 players in the NFL. His overall head coaching record is: 163–98–3 (.625).

Eliah Drinkwitz **–** (2019 – present) – (0-0) - Born April 12, 1983, Drinkwitz is a native of Norman, Oklahoma. He attended Arkansas Tech, graduating in 2004. In 2005, he coached at Alma High School in Alma, Arkansas. From 2006 to 2009 he coached at Springdale High School in Springdale, Arkansas under Coach Gus Malzahn. Drinkwitz is known as a heady play caller and an up-and-coming coach with a solid offensive pedigree. In 2010, he went to Auburn, where he was in charge of quality control for two seasons, helping Gene Chizik to a national championship with Cam Newton. In 2012, after two seasons on the Plains, Drinkowitz became the running backs coach and special teams coordinator at Arkansas State. He was co-offensive coordinator at Arkansas State in 2013 under Bryan Harsin, after Malzahn vacated for Auburn. In 2016, Drinkwitz became offensive coordinator at the University of North Carolina, helping the Tarheels to back-to-back winning bowl games. Hired by Appalachian State in December 2018, Drinkwitz led the Mountaineers to a 12-1 record and a Sun Belt Conference championship in his first season as a head coach in 2019, posting road wins over two Power 5 teams, North Carolina and South Carolina, and giving him a career head coaching record of 12-1. He was hired by

Mizzou in December 2019, to replace a departing Barry Odom, who followed Pinkel and finished 25-25 in four seasons, 13-19 in conference play.

Players:

Johnny Roland – (1962-1965) – The Corpus Christi, Texas native is remembered as one of Mizzou's best early running backs and a pioneering black athlete. In 1962, Roland rushed for 830 yards, which was seventh best in the nation, and scored 78 points, good for ninth in the nation. This rushing total included 155 yards against Oklahoma State University and 104 against Iowa State University. In his first varsity game he rushed for 171 yards and three touchdowns. That season, Roland earned his first All-Big Eight Conference honor. Shortly after, he was accused of stealing a pair of tires, and was forced to leave the team and the school during the 1963 season while he worked in Kansas City. He was welcomed back to the team in 1964, and was moved to the defensive back position. He led his team to a 6-3-1 record and was again chosen as an All-Big Eight player. In 1965, Roland led the Tigers to an 8-2-1 record and a victory in the 1966 Sugar Bowl over the University of Florida, 20-18. That season, he was named the team's captain, was voted a College All-American, and was again named to the All-Big Eight team. By being named the captain of the 1965 team, Roland was the first African-American to serve as the captain for any University of Missouri athletic team. Roland's jersey, #23, was retired by Missouri and he was inducted to the College Football Hall of Fame in 2005. He was drafted in the fourth round of the 1965 NFL Draft by the St. Louis Cardinals and was named UPI NFL-NFC Rookie of the Year in 1966.

Kellen Winslow – (1976-1978) - The East Saint Louis, Illinois native caught 71 passes for 1,089 yards and ten touchdowns from 1976-78, earning all-Big Eight honors in 1977 and 1978, and consensus all-American accolades as a senior. He played in the East-West Shrine and Senior Bowls before being a first-round pick by the San Diego Chargers in the NFL draft. At San Diego, from 1979-88, he caught more passes than any tight end in National Football League history. A member of the Pro Football Hall of Fame, he is one of the greatest tight ends in history. In 1999, he was named to the Sporting News Top 100 NFL Football Players at #71. His son, Kellen Winslow, Jr., plays professionally for the Cleveland Browns, the team the Chargers traded with to draft Winslow Sr. back in 1979.

Chase Coffman – (2005-2008) – At Mizzou, Coffman, a Peculiar, Missouri native, was one of college football's top tight ends. During his freshman year in 2005, he had one of the best seasons for a tight end. He finished with 47 receptions for 503 yards and 4 touchdowns, and earned First-Team Freshman

All-American honors. In 2006, Coffman led Big 12 tight ends with 58 catches for 638 yards and nine touchdowns, all of which were Missouri records. He was awarded First-Team All-Big 12 and was a finalist for the John Mackey Award. He had a great 2007 season finishing with 52 receptions for 531 yards and 7 touchdowns. As a senior in 2008, he was named a consensus All-American and he won the John Mackey Award, given annually to the nation's best tight end, becoming the first Missouri player to win the award; en route logging 90 receptions for 987 receiving yards and 10 touchdowns. Coffman was a third round pick by the Cincinnati Bengals in the 2009 NFL Draft. In 2012, he signed with the Atlanta Falcons, after a brief stint with Tampa Bay.

Chase Daniel **–** (2006-2008) - A three-year starter for the Tigers, Daniel is remembered as a great leader and Mizzou's most productive offensive player, with 13,256 total yards, surpassing Brad Smith's previous mark of 13,088. As a sophomore in 2006, Daniel started all 13 games and threw for 3,527 yards and 28 touchdowns, earning Second Team All-Big 12 honors. In 2007, he threw for 4,306 yards with a 68.2% completion rate and 33 touchdowns, with only 11 interceptions in 14 games. He rushed for a net 253 yards and four touchdowns for a total offense of 37 touchdowns and 4,559 yards, or 326 total yards per contest. Mizzou finished the season 12-2 with a 38-7 victory over Arkansas in the Cotton Bowl. For his contributions, Daniel was named 2007 Big 12 Player of the Year, and he finished fourth in the Heisman balloting. In 2008, his senior year, Daniel was a preseason favorite to win the Unitas Award. He broke all of Mizzou's passing records that season, and during a two-week span against Southeast Missouri State and Nevada, he threw more touchdowns—seven, than he did incompletions—6. Due to size and speed concerns, Daniel was not drafted in the 2009 NFL Draft. Instead, he was signed as a free agent by the Washington Redskins. He was soon waived by the Redskins and was picked up by the New Orleans Saints, where he won a Super Bowl, in 2010. Daniel was with New Orleans through March 2013, when he signed a contract with the Kansas City Chiefs.

Blaine Gabbert **–** (2008-2010) – The Ballwin, Missouri native and graduate of Parkway West High School was a standout signal caller and five-star recruit who had two productive passing years in Columbia before leaving early for the NFL. In 2009 and 2010 Gabbert started every game, amassing 6,822 yards on 568 completions and 40 touchdowns. During his junior season he had 3,186 passing yards, 16 passing touchdowns, nine interceptions, 232 rushing yards, and five rushing touchdowns. He bypassed his senior year and was the 10th overall pick by the Jacksonville Jaguars in the 2011 NFL Draft. He played for the San Francisco 49ers, Arizona Cardinals, and Tennessee Titans.

Charles Harris **–** (2013-2016) - Harris attended Lincoln College Prep Academy in Kansas City where he was a standout football and basketball player. He committed to Mizzou and redshirted his true freshman season. After redshirting in 2013, Harris appeared at defensive end in all 14 games as a redshirt freshman in 2014, recording 19 tackles and two sacks. Harris started in 2015 and had 56 tackles and seven sacks. In 2016, Harris finished second on the team with 61 tackles (35 solo) while leading the team in tackles for loss with 12, nine sacks, ten quarterback hurries, a pair of forced fumbles, one fumble recovery and two pass break-ups. He finished his career with 18 sacks and 34.5 tackles for loss. Harris was named to the Nagurski, Hendricks, Lombardi and Bednarik Award Watch lists prior to his junior year. He skipped his senior year and went pro, resulting in a first round selection (22nd pick) by the Miami Dolphins in the 2017 NFL Draft.

Drew Lock **-** (2015-2018) - A native of Columbia, Missouri, Lock attended Lee's Summit High School in Lee's Summit, MO, where he was the sixth-ranked quarterback coming out of high school in the 2015 class. As a senior in 2014, he was named the Kansas City Star's All-Metro Player of the Year. Highly recruited, possessing a cannon arm, he chose his home town team, the Mizzou Tigers over a number of league suitors, proving to be one of the greatest signal callers and team captains in school and conference history, playing in an incredible 50 games and starting 46. Lock started the final eight games of his freshman year, in 2015, going 129 of 263 for 1,332 yards and four touchdowns. In 2016, after a sophomore season that saw him play in 12 games, Drew ranked first in the SEC in passing yards with 3,399 and 23 touch-

downs. In 2017, during his junior year, he improved greatly over 13 games, connecting on 242 of 419 attempts for 3,964 yards and 44 touchdowns. He finished the season first-team All-SEC. As a senior, in 2018, over 13 games he completed 275 of 437 passes for 3,498 yards. Over his career he was 883 of 1553 for 12,193 yards (57%) and 99 touchdowns. A consensus First-Team All-SEC performer his senior year, he was selected 42nd by the Denver Broncos in the early second round of the 2019 NFL Draft.

Great Bowl Games:

1998 Insight.com Bowl Missouri 34, West Virginia 31

2005 Independence Bowl Missouri 38, South Carolina 31

2008 Cotton Bowl Classic Missouri 38, Arkansas 7

2008 Alamo Bowl Missouri 30, Northwestern 23 (OT)

2011 Independence Bowl Missouri 41, North Carolina 24

2013 Cotton Bowl Missouri 41, Oklahoma State 31

2014 Citrus Bowl Missouri 33, Minnesota 17

Fight song:

"FIGHT TIGER"
Fight, Tiger, fight for old Mizzou,
Right behind you, everyone is with you.
Break the line and follow down the field,
And, you'll be, on the top, upon the top.
Fight, Tiger, you will always win,
Proudly keep the colors flying skyward.
In the end, we'll win the victory,
So Tiger, fight for Old Mizzou!

Alma mater:

The Alma Mater for the University of Missouri is "Old Missouri." Written in 1895, it is sung to the tune of "Annie Lisle" and has two verses. Before and after athletic events, sometimes only the first verse is sung. The first and second verses are more commonly sung together at student orientation and at commencement/graduation ceremonies. Both verses are followed by the chorus.

First Verse:
Old Missouri, fair Missouri
Dear old varsity.

Ours are hearts that fondly love thee
Here's a health to thee.
Chorus:
Proud art thou in classic beauty
Of thy noble past
With thy watch words honour, duty,
Thy high fame shall last!

Second verse:
Every student, man and maiden
Swells the glad refrain.
'Till the breezes, music laden
Waft it back again.

Traditions:

The First Homecoming

The first homecoming was born at Mizzou in 1911, when the Mizzou football coach and Director of Athletics, Chester Brewer, invited alumni to "come home" to Columbia for the annual football game against the University of Kansas. The fans responded, swelling the crowd at Rollins Field in Columbia to more than ten thousand. The NCAA, Trivial Pursuit, and Jeopardy agree this game in 1911 was the first homecoming game. While this tradition has spread across the country, Mizzou still boasts the largest student-run Homecoming in the nation. The annual events include a parade, blood drive, talent competition and tailgate. The 2010 edition of the University of Missouri Homecoming included its first-visit by ESPN College GameDay.

Big MO

The original Big MO is a 6-foot, 150-pound bass drum that was employed at Mizzou football games. Big MO is handled by University of Missouri alumni rather than student members of the Marching Mizzou. Big MO is used to lead fans in the traditional MIZ-ZOU cheer. The drum has been a Mizzou football tradition since 1981, when it was acquired by a Mizzou athletic booster club known as the St. Louis Quarterback Club. The club donated $5,000 to purchase the original drum, which was built by Ludwig Drums in Chicago. Painted red with gold flakes, the drum was brought back from Chicago strapped in the back of a pickup truck. When it arrived in Columbia, it was repainted black and presented to the university a week before the first 1981 football game at an event known as the Tiger Fall Rally. Responsibility for Big MO was transferred to the Mizzou chapters of Kappa Kappa Psi and Tau Beta Sigma in 1993. The original Big MO is the third largest bass drum in the United States, behind Big Bertha at the University of Texas and the Purdue Big Bass Drum. In April 2011, the Mizzou chapters of Kappa Kappa Psi and Tau Beta Sigma kicked off a fundraising campaign to replace Big MO, which had deteriorated over several decades of use. A new Big MO was commissioned--one weighing 800-plus-pounds, with a nine-foot diameter and a 54-inch width, making it the largest collegiate bass drum, and the largest bass drum in the United States. It was built by Neil Boumpani of Boumpani Music Company, in Barnesville, Georgia. The new record-setting Big MO debuted as Mizzou entered Southeastern Conference play in 2012.

Harpo's Goal Post Tradition

Since 1971, when the goal posts are torn from the turf of Faurot Field they have landed in the same place: Harpo's Bar and Grill at 29 South Tenth Street in Columbia. Following the 2005 season, removable goal posts were installed, which are lowered at the close of each home game. In 2010, the goal post tradition was revived following the victory against BCS #1 ranked Oklahoma. Thousands of fans swarmed the field before the final play ended. Although event staff and highway patrol were present, security was unable to prevent fans from storming the field and removing the north end zone goal post from the stadium.

The Columns

The Columns are the remains of Academic Hall, the first and main building on campus until it burned on January 9, 1892. The Columns were deemed unsafe and were slated for demolition, but a rally in their defense preserved them as an endearing symbol of the university

Noteworthy Alumni:

Robin Luke, Ph.D., Marketing Professor, Missouri State University, previously a popular singer, best known for the 1958 hit, "Susie Darlin"

Stephen Morehouse Avery, Hollywood screenwriter

Neal E. Boyd, 2008 "America's Got Talent" winner

Carl Edwards, NASCAR driver

Kate Capshaw, 1975, Actress

Sheryl Crow, 1984, musician

Richard Matheson, 1949, author, screenwriter

Brad Pitt, actor, one credit short of graduation

SallyAnn Salsano, producer, creator of Jersey Shore

Tennessee Williams, playwright

George C. Scott, actor

Brendan Fournie, goalkeeper, U.S. National Soccer Team

John Hamm, 1993, actor, Don Draper, Mad Men

Elizabeth Vargas, American journalist, 20/20 anchor

Stan Utley, professional golfer

Andrew Cherng, Co-founder, Panda Express

2020 Missouri Football Schedule

Sept. 5 Central Arkansas

Sept. 12 Vanderbilt

Sept. 19 at South Carolina

Sept. 26 Eastern Michigan

Oct. 3 at Tennessee

Oct. 10 at BYU

Oct. 17 Georgia

Oct. 24 Kentucky

Oct. 31 OPEN DATE

Nov. 7 at Mississippi State

Nov. 14 at Florida

Nov. 21 Louisiana

Nov. 28 Arkansas

University of South Carolina

Whether it be the legend of Heisman Trophy winner George Rogers, the allure of the one-of-a-kind Cock-A-Boose Railroad, or the elevated grandeur of the University of South Carolina's Williams-Brice Stadium, the reasons to be a die-hard "Fighting Gamecock" fan are various and sundry, to say the least. The University of South Carolina is a relative newcomer to the SEC ranks. They were added to the mix of SEC East schools by way of the ACC in 1990, and began playing in 1992. The Palmetto State's football fans are known to be among the country's most loyal enthusiasts, evidenced by the fact that regular attendance for the Gamecocks' home games in Columbia are among the league's highest annual percentage totals. The Gamecocks have been blessed with great coaches, consecutive gridiron legends like Lou Holtz and Stephen Orr Spurrier, South Carolina's most successful football coach. Great coaching brings great expectations, and it is no exception for Carolina's current head coach, Will Muschamp, who's followed greatness his entire career.

Founded: Chartered in 1801, as South Carolina College

The University of South Carolina was the first state university to be supported annually by state funding. The pre-Civil War USC campus included Longstreet Theatre and the buildings in the vicinity known today as the Horseshoe, with the exception of McKissick Museum. During the Civil War, the campus was forced closed and used by the Confederacy as a hospital. By the time William Tecumseh Sherman reached Columbia in 1865, the hospital contained Union soldiers.

Since its humble beginnings at the original campus blocks from the South Carolina State House in Columbia, the university has expanded to include eight separate campuses throughout the state. The modern Columbia campus, the state's flagship institution, radiates from the historic Horseshoe, the original site of its predecessor, the South Carolina College campus. With its buildings restored to their natural nineteenth century ambiance, the Horseshoe is the university's heart and soul, while the rest of the 242-acre campus offers a stark architectural contrast of styles.

Location: Columbia

As South Carolina's capital city, Columbia serves as the focal point. Nearby Hilton Head Island is a famous resort area that has in the past served as host to a number of championship sporting events. Darlington Raceway, one of NASCAR's most storied race tracks, and home of the TransSouth 500, is located an hour away. USC's teeming downtown campus is home to thousands of college students who keep this historical city hopping. Just a two-hour ride in either direction (west or east) leads to the Blue Ridge Mountains or to the sandy beaches of the Atlantic Ocean.

Population: 133,114

Enrollment: 34,731

Colors: Maroon (Garnet) and Black

The two colors were adopted at the turn of the nineteenth century as the official colors of the athletic teams of the University of South Carolina. The colors are dominant of the gamecock, the school's official mascot.

Mascot: Gamecock

The University of South Carolina is the only major college athletic program in the country using "Fighting Gamecocks" as its official nickname and mascot. In the 1890's during the early, formative years of football at the University of South Carolina, the team was commonly, yet informally referred to by friend and foe alike as "Game Cocks." In 1903, the student newspaper on campus, The State, shortened the moniker to one word, Gamecock, and the athletic teams of South Carolina have been referred to as such ever since. A gamecock is a feisty, fighting rooster known for its spirit, its courage and its capacity to fight to the end. Cockfighting, although illegal in certain states, was a popular sport during the nineteenth century. A famed guerrilla fighter in the Revolutionary War, General Thomas Sumter, was known as the "Fighting Gamecock."

Mascot name: "Cocky"

The official mascot of the University of South Carolina is "Cocky." The garnet and black plumage-adorned fan favorite can be seen on the sidelines of South Carolina football games. Introduced in 1980, as his father's (Big Spur) replacement, Cocky won number one mascot honors in 1986 and 1994.

History:

South Carolina fielded its first football team in 1892, and for the first three seasons no head coach was designated. The all-time won-lost-tie records include those three seasons. No football was played in 1893, and in 1906 the trustees abolished the sport for one season.

Stadium: Williams-Brice Stadium

Expanded in 1996, to seat more than 80,000 spectators (80,250), Williams-Brice stadium is an architectural gem and one of the premier Southern venues to witness a college football game. Originally constructed in 1934, by the Works Progress Administration (WPA), as Columbia Municipal Stadium, it held 17,600. It replaced Melton Field, an aging wooden structure located where USC's Thomas Cooper Library currently exists. All USC home football games, sans the annual Thanksgiving matchup with Clemson, were played at Melton Field. The Clemson game was played at the South Carolina fairgrounds at the location that would become the site for Williams–Brice Stadium. In 1941, the stadium was deeded to USC and renamed Carolina Stadium. The facility has undergone changes through the years, with the largest prior to the early eighties coming during the years of 1971-1972. A special bequest by the estate of Mrs. Martha Williams-Brice boosted the capacity from 43,000 to over 54,000.

Mrs. Brice's husband, Mr. Thomas H. Brice, was a Gamecock football letterman from 1922-1924, and her family managed the Williams Furniture Company in nearby Sumter. Mrs. Brice left a considerable fortune amassed from her furniture business to her nephews, Thomas W. and Phillip Edwards (much of which they have passed on to the university), and included a bequest for the stadium expansion project.

The name of the stadium was changed from Carolina Stadium to Williams-Brice Stadium in dedication ceremonies during the September 9, 1972, home opener with Virginia. The field is sodded with Bermuda grass, having at one time entertained artificial turf. Through the years, other improvements to the facility have been made in the form of new locker rooms, a weight room expansion; as well as new meeting areas and training rooms. In 1982, the east grandstands were double-decked, increasing capacity to 72,400.

During the 1983–84 offseason, at the urging of new coach Joe Morrison, the university removed the AstroTurf and replaced it with natural grass. Over the last 10 years, renovations and improvements have taken place at Williams–Brice Stadium, bringing the official capacity to 80,250. Williams-Brice Stadium has been nicknamed "The Cockpit" by Gamecock fans and local media, although the nickname is unofficial. Coach Steve Spurrier suggested "The Barnyard," due to the stadium's proximity to the State Farmers Market.

Stadium capacity: 80,250

Record crowd:

85,199 October 6, 2012 versus Georgia, Cocks win 35-7

First Game:

December 24, 1893 vs. Furman at Charleston, SC lost 44-0.

First Victory:

November 8, 1895 vs Furman at Columbia (14-10)

First game in stadium:

October 6, 1934 South Carolina 22 Virginia Military Institute 6

Directions:

Coming from the airport: Take Aviation Way to Highway 302. Take a left and head 4 miles to Knox Abbot Drive. Merge onto Knox Abbott and go 3 miles to Assembly Street. Take a right on Assembly. The Visitor's Center is located one mile on the right.

Coming from I-20 and I-26 (east bound): Take Columbia exit and continue onto Elmwood Avenue. Continue for 1.5 miles and turn right onto Assembly Street. Follow Assembly approximately 4 miles. Visitor's Center is on the left.

Coming from I-26 (west bound): Take I-77 exit and go 4 miles. Take Shop Rd. exit. Continue past one light and merge onto George Rogers Boulevard/Assembly St. The Visitor's Centre is on your left at the fifth light.

Dining:

Blue Marlin Seafood **–** Specializing in creative seafood dishes with a Low-country kick. Hand cut steaks, popular shrimp and grits from across the street at Adluh Flour, crab cakes and fresh grilled fish, like the Firecracker Flounder served with jalapeno salsa. Voted best area seafood! Lunch & dinner. 1200 Lincoln Street. 1.803.799.3838.

Little Pigs Barbecue – Serving Columbia since 1963! The best barbecue in Columbia! Tasty all-you-can-eat country style buffet. Call ahead for tailgater's specials to pick up before the game. Or, have Little Pigs cater for you. 4927 Alpine Road, Columbia. 1.803.788.8238. Order off the menu or have the country-style buffet. Wednesday: 11:00 a.m – 2:00 p.m. Thursday – Saturday: 11:00 a.m. – 9:00 p.m.

Nightlife:

Liberty Taproom and Grill – You'll find an array of ales, lagers, stouts, porters and more on tap. Fun and relaxed atmosphere! Wash your beer down with favorites like burgers, steaks, wings, salads and barbecue chicken. 828 Gervais Street, Columbia. 1.802.461.4677. Monday – Wednesday: 11:00 a.m. – 10:00 p.m.; Thursday – Saturday: 11:00 a.m. – 11:00 p.m.; Sunday, 10:00 a.m. for brunch.

The Art Bar - Underground club with live music & an artsy vibe has a dance floor, lounge & full bar plus karaoke. 1211 Park Street, Columbia. 803.929.0198. Opens at five.

Five Points Area - During the evening, football fans can enjoy elegant dining and quaint sidewalk cafes, clubs and live bands. During the day the area becomes a unique shopping village with a tree-lined street and many specialty shops and galleries.

Accommodations:

Graduate Columbia – Hip, vintage-style hotel offers vibrant quarters, a cafe/bar & a 24-hour gym, plus loaner bikes. 1619 Pendleton Street. 803.779.7779.

Golf Course:

Cobblestone Park

Blythewood, SC 29016 1.803.714.2620

Shopping:

Downtown Columbia offers malls, specialty shops and flea markets. Look for the Five Points and the Congaree Vista shopping districts.

Radio: 106.7 FM WTCB, 1320 AM WISW

All-Time Record: 613–585–44 (.511)

Bowl Appearances: 23

Bowl Record: 9-14 (.391)

SEC Championships:

None (Entered into the league in 1990 with Arkansas, began play in 1992.) South Carolina was formerly a member of the Atlantic Coast Conference, where they won a league championship under coach Paul Dietzel in 1969.

Great Bowl Games:

1995 Carquest Bowl: South Carolina 24 West Virginia 21

2001 Outback Bowl: South Carolina 24 Ohio State 7

2002 Outback Bowl: South Carolina 31 Ohio State 28

2006 Liberty Bowl: South Carolina 44 Houston 36

2012 Capital One: South Carolina 30 Nebraska 13

2013 Outback Bowl: South Carolina 33 Michigan 28

2017 Outback Bowl: South Carolina 26, Michigan 19

South Carolina Greats:

Coaches:

Paul Dietzel **–** (1966-1974) – (42-53-1) – (.437) - A native of Mansfield, Ohio, Paul Dietzel served as Athletic Director and Head Coach at South Carolina. He led the Gamecocks to their first and only conference championship, a 1969 Atlantic Coast Conference Title and subsequent berth in the Peach Bowl in Georgia. For his efforts, Coach Dietzel was awarded ACC Coach of the Year honors. Dietzel is best known for his 1958 National Championship season at LSU, a feat he accomplished at the age of 34. After Dietzel left LSU, he spent four seasons at the United States Military Academy, before finally settling in at South Carolina in 1966. He later returned to LSU and served as athletic director. He died September 24, 2013 in Baton Rouge, Louisiana, at the age of 89.

Joe Morrison **–** (1983-1988) – (39-28-2) – (.565) - A native of Lima, Ohio, Morrison was named the 1984 National Coach of the Year. Having coached at UT-Chattanooga and New Mexico, Morrison led the Gamecocks to three bowl games (1984 Gator Bowl, 1987 Gator and the 1988 Liberty) and his 1984 team posted a school-best 10-2 record. Morrison was also named the All-South Independent Coach of the Year in 1984. Nicknamed as "Old Dependable" for his reliable, all-around coaching ability, Morrison enjoyed an outstanding 14-year career in the NFL with the New York Giants. Following Morrison's retirement from the game in 1972, the seven-time team captain was granted the ultimate honor as a player when his number 40 was forever retired by the Giants organization. Morrison was the victim of a sudden and fatal heart attack on February 5, 1989, in Columbia. He was 52.

Lou Holtz **–** (1999-2004) – (33-37) – (.471) - Lou Holtz is one of the most successful college football coaches in American history. The Follansbee, West Virginia native attended Kent State University prior to making a name for himself in coaching with William & Mary, then North Carolina State, the University of Arkansas, Notre Dame and finally at South Carolina. A veteran of 32 years of experience, Holtz surprised many when he took over the reins of a hapless Gamecock program in 1999, only to go winless (0-11) during his first gridiron campaign. The undaunted Holtz motivated his squad to an amazing turnaround in 2000, won 8 games and defeated Ohio State 24-7 in the Outback Bowl. The 2000 season was impressive because prior to that the Gamecocks and their fan base had endured a 21-game losing streak. In 2001, Holtz repeated his magic by leading the Gamecocks to a 9-3 record and a thrilling 31-28 comeback victory again against Ohio State in the Outback Bowl. The two-year run by Holtz was unprecedented in Carolina Gamecock football history. It was the first time a South Carolina team finished in the top 20 two seasons in a row (19th in 2000 and 13th in 2001.) 2002 and 2003 were difficult, losing seasons for Holtz, but he came back in 2004 and finished with a respectable 6-5 season, which proved to be the last of his Gamecock and coaching career. His career coaching record is 249-132-7. Holtz is the only coach in NCAA history to lead six different schools to bowl games and he is the only coach to guide four different programs to final Top 20 rankings. Holtz was replaced at South Carolina by Steve Spurrier. On May 1, 2008, he was named to the College Football Hall of Fame. He is a noted motivational speaker, magician, comedian and ESPN college football analyst.

Steve Spurrier **-** (2005-2015) – (86-49) – (.637) – Born April 20, 1945 in Miami Beach, Florida, Stephen Orr Spurrier, nicknamed "The Ole Ball Coach," took over the South Carolina Football Program in 2005, after an unsuccessful two-year stint in the NFL with the Washington Redskins. Prior, he coached his alma mater, the University of Florida, from 1990-2001 where he was the 1966 Heisman Trophy recipient, posting a 122-27-1 record. He played a decade of pro football as a quarterback and punter after being drafted in 1967 by the San Francisco 49ers. Spurrier, already a legend, replaced another, Lou Holtz, after his retirement in November, 2004. In 2005, his

first season in Columbia, Spurrier achieved notable victories. The Gamecocks shocked everyone, reeling off five straight conference wins for the first time in school history. Among those was the program's first victory at Tennessee, 16-15, and against 12th-ranked Florida, 30-22—the program's first win over the Gators since joining the SEC in 1992. Spurrier continued the tradition of excellence established by Lou Holtz. From 2005 to 2010 Spurrier won 44 games, averaging more than seven wins a season. In 2011, 2012 and 2013 he had identical eleven-win seasons (11-2) and won three consecutive bowl games, the Capital One, the Outback, and Capital One. In 2014, the team went 7-6; and there were ominous signs. In 2015, Spurrier coached the Gamecocks to a 2-4 record and resigned; abruptly ending the season and his coaching career on a mysterious, somber note. In eleven seasons in Columbia Spurrier compiled an 86-49 record, going 5-4 in bowl games. His son, Steve Spurrier, Jr. is an assistant on Mike Leach's Mississippi State staff, coaching wide receivers. In 2012, Spurrier became South Carolina's winningest head football coach, surpassing Rex Enright's previous mark of 64 head coaching victories. He is also the University of Florida's winningest coach. His overall coaching record is 228-89-2 (.719).

Will Muschamp **–** (2016-present) – (26-25) – (.509) - Born in Rome, Georgia and raised in Gainesville, Florida, Muschamp cut his teeth on competitive football. The former walk-on defensive back and team captain at the University of Georgia is as experienced as he is well-traveled; and the result is that he has apprenticed under some of the game's best coaches. Taking over for a legend is never easy; Muschamp followed Steve Spurrier and Urban Meyer at Florida; and Steve Spurrier at South Carolina. After Georgia, Muschamp became a grad assistant at Auburn, where he worked under defensive coordinators Wayne Hall and Bill Oliver in 1995 and 1996. He earned a master's in education from Auburn in 1996, then spent a season each a West Georgia and Eastern Kentucky as the defensive backs coach, before becoming the defensive coordinator at Valdosta State University in 2000. Muschamp joined Nick Saban's staff at LSU as linebackers coach in 2001, before becoming the LSU defensive coordinator in 2002. In 2003, LSU won the BCS Championship. Muschamp left LSU with Saban after the 2004 season to join the Miami Dolphins staff as the assistant head coach and defensive coordinator. When the Auburn defensive coordinator position became available in January 2006, Muschamp capitalized. In January 2008, he

resigned from Auburn to accept a co-defensive coordinator position with Texas. On November 18, 2008, the University of Texas announced Muschamp would succeed Mack Brown as head football coach; but Brown stayed too long. On December 11, 2010, UF Athletic Director Jeremy Foley named Muschamp to succeed Urban Meyer as Gators head coach. In his first year he led the Gators to a 7–6 record and a 24–17 Gator Bowl victory over Ohio State. In his second season, Muschamp led the Gators to an 11–1 regular season with four wins over teams ranked among the top twelve of the BCS standings, including Texas A&M, LSU, South Carolina, and Florida State. The promising season ended with a disheartening 33-23 loss to the Louisville Cardinals in the Sugar Bowl, allowing for an 11-2 finish, setting the stage for even higher, winning expectations. Those wins never came, as Muschamp finished his last two seasons with disappointing records of 4-8 and 3-5, and his contract was terminated. He coached as Auburn's defensive coordinator in 2015, before taking over as head coach of South Carolina in 2016, after the midseason departure of Steve Spurrier. On December 6, 2015, Muschamp was introduced as the 34th head coach of the Gamecocks. He inherited from Spurrier a 3–9 team and managed a 6–7 record in 2016, his first year. In his second season, 2017, the Cocks improved to 9–4, including a 26–19 win over Michigan in the Outback Bowl. South Carolina's 5–3 conference record marked the program's first winning record in conference play since 2013 under Steve Spurrier. In year three, 2018, Muschamp led South Carolina to a 7–5 regular season record, and dropped the bowl game. In 2019, South Carolina finished his fourth season 4–8, the only bright spot being an upset of #3 Georgia between the hedges. Muschamp is 26-25 in Columbia. His 25 losses through his first four seasons are the most among Gamecock head football coaches.

Players:

***Steve Wadiak* –** (1948-1951) – Born January 8, 1926 in Chicago, Illinois, Wadiak was a four-year letterman and All-American running back in 1951. Named All-Southern in 1950 and 1951, Wadiak played in the 1951 Blue-Gray Classic and the 1952 Senior Bowl. He holds the school record for the longest run from scrimmage, 96 yards versus George Washington in 1950. Wadiak ranks third on the all-time career rushing list at South Carolina with 2,878 yards. His number 37 was retired by the South Carolina Athletic Department. He died March 9, 1952 in Richmond County, Georgia.

***Tommy Suggs* –** (1967-1970) - A native of Lamar, South Carolina, Suggs was a standout quarterback who set numerous South Carolina passing records during his career. He led the Gamecocks to the 1969 Atlantic Coast Conference Championship and a subsequent Peach Bowl berth. Throwing for more than 200 yards or more on eight occasions during his career, Suggs complet-

ed 355 of 672 passes for 4,916 yards and 34 touchdowns. Named South Carolina football's Most Valuable Player in 1970, Suggs shares the Gamecock record for the most touchdowns ever scored in a game, five. Suggs was also named as the 1970 Blue-Gray game's Most Valuable Player. As a quarterback, Suggs never lost to Clemson during his time in Columbia. Suggs served as the color analyst on the Gamecock Football radio network for more than 40 years.

Dan Reeves – (1962-1964) - Born January 19, 1944, in Rome, Georgia, Reeves was a standout letterman in football for the Gamecocks in 1962, 1963 and 1964, playing quarterback under head coach Marvin Bass. Over eight seasons in the NFL with the Dallas Cowboys, Reeves collected 1,990 rushing and 1,693 receiving yards. His best year came in 1966, when he rushed for seven touchdowns, good for second in league totals. Reeves threw a touchdown pass in the Cowboys' losing effort in the notorious "Ice Bowl," the 1967 Championship Game against the Green Bay Packers. The Cowboys made the playoffs every year of Reeves's playing days, reaching the Super Bowl twice, realizing a 24-3 victory over the Miami Dolphins in 1971. Reeves served as head coach of the Denver Broncos from 1981-1993, and the New York Giants from 1993-1996. He was also the head coach of the Atlanta Falcons from 1997-2003. Dan's brother, Don "Butch" Reeves was also a gamecock-lettering three years in football at South Carolina. Dan Reeves was inducted into the South Carolina Athletic Hall of Fame in 1977.

George Rogers – (1977-1980) - A native of Deluth, Georgia, Rogers was born December 8, 1958, and was the recipient of the 1980 Heisman Trophy. Rogers was a consensus All-America selection his senior year when he led the country in rushing with 1,894 yards. Rogers holds many South Carolina records, including most career rushing yards (5,204); most yards rushing in a single season (1,894); and he is tied with Harold Green for most career touchdowns (33). The stout Rogers rushed for 100 or more yards in 27 of his 46 games at South Carolina. Rogers rushed for over 200 yards in a single game on three occasions. His single game high total was a 237-yard performance against Wake Forest on November 18, 1978. Rogers is the only player to have his jersey (#38) retired while he was still playing as a Gamecock. Rogers was the first pick chosen in the 1981 NFL Draft. He later won Rookie of the Year honors for the New Orleans Saints. Rogers played for the 1988 Super Bowl Champion Washington Redskins. A two-time Pro Bowler, Rogers was elected to the College Football Hall of Fame in 1997.

Rick Sanford **–** (1975-78) – Born January 9, 1957, in Rock Hill, South Carolina, Sanford was an All-American defensive back in 1978. Sanford played for Coach Jim Carlen and wore number 25 for the Gamecocks. Sanford finished his career with nine interceptions, four during his senior year. Sanford went on to play for six years in the NFL with the New England Patriots, and one year with the Seattle Seahawks. Sanford was inducted into the South Carolina Athletic Hall of Fame in 1998.

James Seawright **–** (1981-1984) - A native of Simpsonville, South Carolina, Seawright was named first team All-American in 1984 as a linebacker. Seawright is remembered as the leader and leading tackler of the 1984 "fire ant" and "black magic" defense at South Carolina. During the 1984 season, Seawright tallied a 133 tackles, finishing his Gamecock career with 369 tackles. Once, during a game against North Carolina State in 1984, he made 29 tackles. Seawright logged 384 career tackles and wore number 45 for the Gamecocks. He was elected to the Gamecocks Hall of Fame in 2003. He lost a battle with cancer in 2014. He was 53.

Steve Taneyhill **–** (1992-1995) - Quarterback Steve Taneyhill, an Altoona, Pennsylvania native, made his mark at South Carolina as much for his flashy style as for his enormous talent. He led the Gamecocks to five of six victories his freshman year. More importantly, he notched the team's first win over Tennessee after joining the Southeastern Conference. Taneyhill accomplished this after earning the starting job midway through his rookie season. Fans loved his long hair that blocked his name on the back of his jersey and his brazen attitude. Because of the image, Taneyhill was always a favorite among autograph-seeking Gamecock fans. Taneyhill led the Gamecocks to their first bowl victory, a 24-21 win over West Virginia in the 1995 Carquest Bowl. He holds several South Carolina records, including 473 yards passing in a game and 62 career touchdown passes. After football, he coached at Union County High School. Today he is a businessman in Columbia, South Carolina.

Sterling Sharpe **–** (1983) - (1985-1987) – Born April 6, 1965 in Chicago, Illinois, Sharpe attended Glenville High School in Glenville, Georgia where he was a standout wide receiver. He chose to play for the University of South Carolina and was an All-America Wide Receiver in 1987. He ranks as the top receiver in Gamecock history and holds many South Carolina's receiving records, including career marks for receptions (169) receiving yardage (2,497) and single season records for most receptions (74), receiving yardage (1,106)

and touchdown receptions (10). Sharpe caught at least one ball in 34 consecutive contests. He was the seventh player chosen in the 1988 NFL draft, by the Green Bay Packers. An All-Pro with the Packers, Sharpe retired as Green Bay's All-time career receptions leader. Today he's a studio analyst for the NFL Network. Sharpe wore number two for the Gamecocks.

Duce Staley **–** (1995-1996) - Born February 27, 1975 in Tampa, Florida, Staley was a transfer player from Itawamba, Mississippi Junior College. After growing up in Columbia, Staley was partial to the Gamecocks, and transferred there to play college ball. He is remembered as one of South Carolina's most impressive running backs. Staley was one of college football's best all-around runners in 1996 when he was ranked 13th in the country with 1,116 rushing yards en route to earning First-Team All-SEC honors. Staley finished his two-year college career ranked 13th on Carolina's all-time rushing list with 1,852 yards and 17 touchdowns on 345 carries. A versatile back, the Duce reeled in 59 passes for 489 yards and two touchdowns and returned 26 kickoffs for 566 yards while at South Carolina. After his Carolina playing days ended Staley was drafted by the Philadelphia Eagles where he proved to be one of the league's toughest and most prolific runners. He played for the Pittsburgh Steelers from 2004-2006, before retiring. During his decade-long NFL career Staley rushed for 5,785 yards caught passes for 2,587 yards and scored 24 touchdowns with a 4.0 yard-per-carry average. He was a member of the XL Super Bowl Championship team while in Pittsburgh.

Sidney Rice **-** (2006-2007) - Born September 1, 1996, Rice, a Gaffney native, is remembered as one of South Carolina's brightest yet briefest stars. The gifted receiver redshirted in 2004, but the next year he shook up the SEC with a marvelous debut—70 catches for 1,143 yards and 13 touchdowns, earning him Freshman All-SEC and All-America honors while setting the South Carolina single-season plateau for receiving yards and touchdowns. The following year, as a consensus preseason All-American, he caught 72 passes for 1090 yards and 10 touchdowns, prompting an early entry into the professional ranks. Rice was drafted in the 2nd Round of the 2007 NFL Draft, 44th overall by the Minnesota Vikings.

Alshon Jeffery **–** (2009-2011) – The St. Matthews, South Carolina native is remembered as one of South Carolina and Steve Spurrier's most dynamic receivers. Jeffrey was a consensus first-team Freshman All-SEC and first-team Freshman All-American. As a sophomore, in 14 games, Jeffery made 88 catches totaling 1,517 yards and nine touchdowns, including eight games with 100 yards or more receiving. Jeffery was named a Biletnikoff Award finalist and an All-American after helping lead the Gamecocks to their first SEC Championship Game. In the 2012 Capital One Bowl, Jeffery caught 4 passes for 148 yards and a touchdown and was named the Capital One Bowl MVP. Jeffery bypassed his senior year to enter into the 2012 NFL Draft where he was the 45th pick (2nd Round) by the Chicago Bears.

Jadeveon Clowney - (2011-2014) – A Rock Hill, South Carolina native, Clowney was born February 14, 1993. He graduated from South Pointe High School, where he was highly recruited as Mr. Football in South Carolina and the consensus #1 recruit in the nation. He is remembered as the prototype college defensive end, and a terror to opposing quarterbacks. As a sophomore in 2012, Clowney set school records in quarterback sacks (13) and tackles for a loss (23.5) while earning SEC Defensive Player of the Year honors. Clowney was selected first overall by the Houston Texans in the 2014 NFL Draft. He played five seasons, making three Pro Bowls before being traded to the Seahawks before the 2019 season.

Melvin Ingram – (2007-2011) - Ingram was born and raised in Hamlet, North Carolina. He attended Richmond Senior High School in Rockingham, North Carolina and signed with Coach Steve Spurrier to play linebacker for the Gamecocks before switching to defensive end. The athletic Ingram played on special teams as a freshman and was used as a kick returner. He redshirted in 2008 after a foot injury. In 2009, Ingram played sparingly. As a junior in 2010, he led the team with nine sacks. In 2011, Ingram registered 10 sacks, 15 tackles for loss, and two interceptions. He also scored three touchdowns. Two of his touchdowns came against Georgia in a 45–42 victory in Athens, including a 68-yard fake-punt for a touchdown. Ingram's strong senior campaign helped propel the Gamecocks defense to a final #4 national poll ranking, and he was a first-team All-Southeastern Conference (SEC) selection, and was recognized as a consensus All-American. He was selected by the San Diego Chargers with the 18th overall pick in the 1st round of the 2012 NFL Draft. He remains with the Chargers, although now based in Los Angeles.

Cooper Pharoh – (2013-2015) - A native of Havelock, North Carolina, Pharoh was a defensive back before moving to wide receiver prior to the start of his freshman Gamecock season, playing in 11 of 13 games in 2013. He had three receptions for 54 receiving yards, 202 rushing yards, one rushing touchdown and made two of three pass attempts for 29 yards and a touchdown. Against Tennessee as a sophomore in 2014, Cooper set the school single-game

receiving yards record with 233. In the 2014 Independence Bowl against Miami he had nine catches for 170 yards and a touchdown and was named Most Valuable Player. For the season, Cooper appeared in all 13 games and was named first team All-SEC after recording 69 receptions for 1,136 yards and nine touchdowns. He ran for 200 yards with two touchdowns and passed for 78 yards and two TDs. As a junior in 2015, Cooper had 873 receiving yards along with 111 rushing yards with 9 total touchdowns. He had 55 return yards on 12 punt return opportunities. He was All-SEC in 2014 & 2015. In 2016, he was a fourth round choice by the LA Rams. He played for the Chiefs and the Bengals before returning to the Chiefs, in time for the 2020 Superbowl.

Traditions:

2001-A Space Odyssey:

At the beginning of every home contest, in a rendition the movie theme song from "2001--A Space Odyssey" is blared over the PA system at Williams-Brice Stadium. In synchronization with the music, the Gamecocks storm the field.

Cockaboose Railroad:

South Carolina can boast of a unique, and revered Southern tailgating tradition. This treasure is a veritable party on wheels. The Cockaboose Railroad consists of 22 lavishly-restored stationary cabooses lined on a small, off-track section, just south of Williams-Brice Stadium. Each authentic caboose contains modern tailgating amenities like running water, cable television, air conditioning and heating, as well as luxurious home furnishings.

Black Hats:

South Carolina has worn "eggshell" helmets since 2004, a white lid with black and garnet stripes down the middle. Some South Carolina fans await the return of the black helmets displayed during Lou Holtz's final season, last worn in Holtz's final game, marred by a brawl with Clemson.

Palmetto Bowl:

South Carolina's arch-rival is Clemson. The Gamecocks have played Clemson every year since 1909. Clemson holds a 71-42-4 edge all time, but South Carolina won five straight games from 2009-13 before Clemson snapped the streak.

Forever to Thee:

Once the final whistle sounds in all games, the team heads toward the band — win or loss — to sing the alma mater, which ends with the fans and team "raising a health" to the school, in perfect solidarity.

Gamecock Fight Song:

Hey, Let's give a cheer, Carolina is here,
The Fighting Gamecocks lead the way.
Who gives a care, If the going gets tough,
And when it is rough, that's when the 'Cocks get going.
Hail to our colors of garnet and Black,
In Carolina pride have we.
So, Go Gamecocks Go –FIGHT!
Drive for the goal –FIGHT!
USC will win today – GO COCKS!
SO, let's give a cheer, Carolina is here.
The Fighting Gamecocks All The Way!

About the Fight Song:

The tune is from the musical "How Now, Dow Jones" and the original is titled "Step to the Rear" composed by Elmer Bernstein with lyrics by Carolyn Leigh. The sheet music is copyrighted to Carwin music, Incorporated in 1967. The music was chosen as USC Fight Song by former football coach and Athletic Director, Paul Deitzel. Mr. Deitzel also wrote the lyrics to this USC Fight Song.

Alma Mater:

We hail thee, Carolina, and sing they high praise
With loyal devotion, remembering the days
When proudly we sought thee, thy children to be:
Here's a health, Carolina, forever to thee!
Since pilgrims of learning, we entered thy walls
And found dearest comrades in they classic halls
We've honored and love thee as sons faithfully;
Here's a health, Carolina, forever to thee!
Generations of sons have rejoiced to proclaim
They watchword of service, thy beauty of fame;
For ages to come shall their rallying cry be:
Here's a health, Carolina, forever to thee!
Fair shrine of high honor and truth, though shalt still
Blaze forth as a beacon, thy mission fulfill,
And crowned by all hearts in a new jubilee:
Here's a health, Carolina, forever to thee!

About the Alma Mater:

The alma mater was written in 1911 by George A. Wauchope, an English professor at the University, and set to the music of Robert Burns' "Flow Gently,

Sweet Afton." It was written as a result of the need for this type of school song. A March 1911 issue of the Gamecock reported that a year or two earlier the faculty, "realizing we should have a stirring alma mater," offered a prize of $50. Songs submitted were placed in a songbook and sung at chapel. Although it was several years before the song written by Dr. Wauchope became known as the Alma Mater of the university, it was the most popular as soon as it came out. Over the years the custom of raising the right hand, with fingers cupped, when "Here's A Health, Carolina" occurs, as if offering a toast.

Notable South Carolina Alumni:

Leeza Gibbons – TV host, "Entertainment Tonight"

"Hootie & the Blowfish" Darius Rucker, M. Bryan, J. Sonefeld & D. Felber

Charles Jones, Jr. – journalist

Floyd D. Spence – U.S. House of Representatives

Brigadier General Charles M. Duke, Jr. – USAF retired

William Price Fox – author, screenwriter, columnist

Charles Frazier, author "Cold Mountain"

Patrick Tyler, chief correspondent, New York Times

Amos Lee, singer/songwriter, folk artist

Courtney Hope Turner, Miss South Carolina 2011, Miss USA 2011

Bruce Littlefield, author, lifestyle expert

Jenilee Harrison, actress

Ainsley Earhardt, news anchor

Kathryn Dennis, model

Robert F. Furchgott, chemist

America Ferrera, actress

Mark Dantonio, football coach

Wade Boggs, baseball player

Chazwick Bundick, aka Toro Y Moi, musician

Amanda Baker, actress, General Hospital

Lauren Michelle Hill, Playboy Playmate of the month, February 2001

2020 South Carolina Football Schedule

Sept. 5 Coastal Carolina

Sept. 12 East Carolina

Sept. 19 Missouri

Sept. 26 at Kentucky

Oct. 3 at Florida

Oct. 10 Tennessee

Oct. 17 OPEN DATE

Oct. 24 Texas A&M

Oct. 31 at Vanderbilt

Nov. 7 Georgia

Nov. 14 at LSU

Nov. 21 Wofford

Nov. 28 at Clemson

University of Tennessee

Shortly up the Tennessee River from Chattanooga stands Knoxville, Tennessee, home of the University of Tennessee. Knoxville is the heart of "The Volunteer State," and the people of this football hotbed, Volunteer fans, are some of most devoted football enthusiasts among the Southeastern Conference schools. Claiming a tradition that is rivaled only by the University of Alabama, Tennessee is one of the SEC's most successful football programs. Tennessee's gridiron legacy has been built on the shoulders of coaching virtuoso and patriot, General Robert Neyland and a string of talented successors named Barnhill, Wyatt, Dickey, Battle and Majors. Phil Fulmer made his own lasting, championship mark on the SEC, and the national record books, following in the heavy footsteps of his great military predecessor. Overall, the University of Tennessee has won twelve SEC Championships, and has claimed two national titles since the league's inception in 1933, making it one of the traditional standard bearers of Southeastern Conference gridiron excellence. After an outlier 20-year hiatus of winning football, fiery new head coach Jeremy Pruitt has rekindled the pride of past Volunteer Football, filling the old bowl in Knoxville with legions of faithful fans bent on returning to the gridiron glory of yesteryear.

Founded: 1794

The University of Tennessee is the state's largest and oldest university, as well as one of the preeminent public academic institutions of higher learning in the United States. A full land grant institution and a comprehensive research university, the University of Tennessee, which can trace its beginnings to the inception of Blount College in 1794, celebrated its 200th birthday in 1994.

Location: Knoxville

Situated in the center of the East Tennessee Valley, Knoxville serves as the urban pathway to the Smoky Mountains. Surrounded by what is referred to as "The Great Lakes of the South," Knoxville is a teeming metropolitan area with a population of over 700,000, making it one of the largest cities among the Southeastern Conference. In early spring, a fifty mile trail of blooming dogwoods transforms the city into a sea of pink and white.

Population: 187,347

Enrollment: 28,321

History

The University of Tennessee began playing football in 1891. The one game the Volunteers played that year was against Sewanee (University of the South). Players and fans of Tennessee traveled to Chattanooga by train to take part in and witness the contest. In 1892, Tennessee began a regular football schedule with games against Maryville, Vanderbilt twice, and Sewanee twice. The first game between Vanderbilt and Tennessee was the first played on Dudley Field in Nashville, which was called Curry Field when Dudley Stadium was built in 1922.

Born March 23, 1886, in Scott County, Virginia, Dr. Nathan W. Dougherty is the founding father of University of Tennessee Athletics. Dougherty, an associate professor of Civil Engineering and former football Hall of Famer was named interim chairman of the University's Athletic Council in 1917, and held this "temporary" position for the next 39 years. During this time, he designed Shields-Watkins Field, helped create the Southeastern Conference, and hired a football coach whose name would become synonymous with Tennessee football – General Robert Reese Neyland. Dr. Dougherty's book, "Educators and Athletes," was the inspiration for this book. He died in Knoxville, May 18, 1977.

Nickname: Volunteers

Known as "The Volunteer State," the State of Tennessee garnered its nickname in the early nineteenth century when General Andrew Jackson mustered large armies from his home state to fight the Indians and later the British at the "Battle of New Orleans." The name "Volunteers" became even more popular subsequent to the Mexican-American War when Governor Aaron V. Brown issued a call for 2,800 men to tangle with Santa Ana; and over 30,000 volunteered. The dragon uniform donned by Tennessee regulars during that conflict can still be seen adorning the color guard at UT athletic events.

Colors: Orange and White

The colors of orange and white were selected by Charles Moore, a member of the first football team in 1891 and adopted by a vote of the student body. The colors were those of the common American daisy which grew in profusion on The Hill, although Tennessee players did not appear in the now-famous orange jerseys until the season opener in 1922. Coach M.B. Banks led the Vols over Emory and Henry in that game by a score of 50-0.

The orange color is distinct to the school, dubbed "UT Orange," and has been offered for sale as a paint, licensed by the university. Home games at Neyland Stadium have been described as a "sea of Orange" due to the large number of fans wearing the school color; the moniker Big Orange, as in "Go Big Orange!" comes from the usage of UT Orange. The color is spot color PMS 151, as described by the University.

Mascot: Smokey X

After a student poll revealed a desire to select a live mascot for the University, the UT Pep Club held a contest in 1953 to select a coon hound, a native breed of the state, as the school mascot. Announcements for the contest in local newspapers read, "This can't be an ordinary hound. He must be a 'Hound Dawg' in the best sense of the word." The late Reverend W.C. Brooks entered his prize-winning blue tick coon hound, Smokey, in the contest. At halftime of a game in 1953, the dogs were lined up on the old cheerleaders' ramp at Neyland Stadium. Each dog was introduced over the loud-speaker and the student body cheered for their favorite. Smokey was the last hound introduced. When his name was called out, he barked. The students cheered and Smokey threw his head back and howled. This kept going and soon the whole stadium was in a roar and UT had found its mascot. Reverend Brooks supplied UT with the line of canines until his death in 1986, when his wife Mrs. Mildred Brooks and family friends took over the canine caretaking role.

The dogs have lived exciting lives. Smokey II was dognapped by Kentucky students in 1955, and survived a confrontation with the Baylor Bear at the 1956 Sugar Bowl. Smokey VI, who suffered from heat exhaustion in 140 degree temperatures at the 1991 UCLA game, was listed on the Vols injury report until he returned later in the season. Smokey III (1965-77) was the winningest dog with a 105-39-5 record and two SEC championships. Smokey VIII, who passed away in 2007, had the highest winning percentage with a mark of .805 with two SEC championships and the 1998 national championship. One of the most beloved figures in the state, Smokey is famous for leading the Big Orange out of the giant "T" prior to each home game. The present Smokey, Smokey X, carries on the banner of the Smokey lineage. Taken care of by members of the Alpha Gamma Rho Fraternity, he is one of the SEC's most loveable mascots.

Game Mascot: Smokey

A costumed "Smokey" performs at Tennessee football games and other athletic events. In January 2008 at the Universal Cheerleaders Association's National Championships in Orlando, Florida, Smokey was selected as the National Mascot Champion. In addition to the costumed "Smokey," there is a

Volunteer on the UT game day sidelines. This live undergraduate dresses in Volunteer garb replete with a coon skin hat and accompanying rifle.

Band: The Pride of the Southland Band

The University of Tennessee band was organized after the Civil War when the University was reopened. Since, enrollment has grown to more than 300 students in all college bands. The band program is divided into different units. The most famous of these is the marching band, "The Pride of the Southland Band," which appears at all home football games and three out-of-town games annually.

Director of Bands: Dr. Donald Ryder

Stadium: Neyland Stadium

The Tennessee Volunteers football team first played at Baldwin Park, which was located between Grand Avenue and Dale Avenue, north of Fort Sanders. From 1908 to 1920, the team played at Wait Field, located where the Walters Life Science Building now stands. Neyland Stadium, Shields-Watkins Field saw its beginning in 1919. Colonel W.S. Shields, President of Knoxville's City National Bank and a Trustee of the University, provided the initial capital to prepare and equip the field, completed in March 1921, named Shields-Watkins Field, in honor of the donor and his wife, Alice. The stadium came to bear its own distinguished name: Neyland Stadium. It was named in 1962 for the man most responsible for the growth and development of Tennessee football, General Robert R. Neyland, who served as head coach from 1926 to 1952. After retiring from coaching, General Neyland served as athletic director at Tennessee until his death in 1962. Neyland served as the guiding force behind additions to the stadium's capacity and is the one most responsible for the winning tradition that Volunteer fans have learned to expect through the years. Neyland Stadium is the third-largest football-playing venue in the country, behind Michigan Stadium and Beaver Stadium (Penn State). Since 1921, it has been expanded fourteen times. Neyland Stadium also holds the impressive Tom Elam Press Box, which contains seven different levels of luxurious skyboxes and suites.

Stadium Capacity:

106,538 (average); 102,037 (official)

First game:

November, 1891 - Sewanee 24, Volunteers 0

First game in stadium:

September 21, 1921 - Tennessee 27, Emory & Henry 0

Record crowd:

109,061 - September 18, 2004 - Tennessee 30, Florida 28

In 2004, the stadium set a national college football record for the most people to ever attend a college football game with 109,061. Neyland Stadium is the largest college football stadium in the South, the fourth-largest stadium in the United States and among the largest in the world.

The Volunteer Navy

In 1962, former Volunteer broadcaster George Mooney found a quicker and more exciting way to get to Neyland Stadium other than fighting the notorious Knoxville traffic–via the Tennessee River! While other Vol fans employed more traditional modes of transportation, Mooney navigated his way to Tennessee football games by boat. Mooney cruised his little runabout down river to the stadium and spawned what would later become "The Volunteer Navy." Today, approximately 200 boats of all shapes and sizes make up this extremely unique, giant floating tailgate party, also known as the "Floatilla." In the United States, only the University of Washington has a stadium adjacent to a water body like does Tennessee.

Checkerboard End Zones:

A trademark of the Tennessee program since the 1960's, the practice was reinstated in 1989. The colorful and popular end zones were a part of Tennessee football until 1968, when the natural sod was removed and artificial turf was put in its place. Natural grass has since returned to Shields-Watkins Field.

Directions:

Coming from the airport, head north on U.S. 129 leaving airport. Following the Tennessee River Bridge, exit on U.S. 11/70 (Cumberland Avenue). Turn right at the bottom of the ramp and then right again at the second light onto Volunteer Boulevard. Follow this route to the stadium.

From I-40 East (Nashville): Exit at U.S. 129 South. Take 129 South to U.S.

11/70 exit (Cumberland Avenue). Turn left off of ramp and turn right at third light onto Volunteer Boulevard. Follow this route to stadium.

From I-40 West (Asheville): Exit to the left at James White Parkway. Follow the Parkway to Neyland Drive (Highway 153) to stadium area on the right.

From I-75 South (Lexington): Exit onto I-275 South. Follow I-275 to I-40 East. Exit I-40 East to the left at James White Parkway. Follow James White Parkway to Neyland Drive (stadium on right hand side).

Tailgating:

The atmosphere outside Neyland Stadium on game day is always buzzing with excitement, and there are opportunities for Volunteer fans to tailgate. Some arrive by boat and tie off to other boats on the nearby Tennessee River, creating a unique pre-game experience. Another unique aspect of Tennessee tailgating is the "railgate party" that occurs on the Three Rivers Rambler, a vintage steam engine train operating a 90-minute ride through the rolling hills of Knoxville. However, for the "railgate party," the train remains stationary on its tracks at the base of the hill below Neyland Stadium. The serving line is inside one of the train's cars and the food can be consumed on the open, adjoining platform car. All tailgating outside Neyland—whether it be on water, rail or land outside the stadium—usually involves real Tennessee barbecue. Ribs, juicy chicken breasts and generous homemade fixings.

Nearest Hospital to Stadium:

Fort Sanders Regional Medical Center

1901 W Clinch Ave, Knoxville, TN 865.541.1111

Bail Bondsman for Emergencies:

Smokey Mountain Bail Bonds

Knoxville, TN 865.691.1919

Golf Courses:

Knoxville Municipal Course

3925 Schaad Road, Knoxville, TN

865.691.7143

William Creek Golf Course

2351 Dandridge Avenue, Knoxville, TN

865.546.5828

Shopping:

Try the trendy Market Square District. It has a variety of shops and boutiques to suit your every whim and fancy.

Dining:

Calhoun's – Ideal for the entire family, its signature hickory smoked baby-back ribs won the title of "Best Ribs in America" at the National Rib Cook-Off. Four locations. Calhoun's on the Tenn. River, 400 Neyland Dr., 865.673.3399; Calhoun's Turkey Creek, 625 Turkey Cove, 865.288.1600; Calhoun's Microbrewery atop Bearden Hill, 6516 Kingston Pike, 865.673.3377; and Calhoun's Kingston Pike at Pellissippi Parkway, 865.673.3444. Mon-Thurs, 11 am-10:30 pm; Fri-Sat 11 am-11pm; Sun, 11 am-10 pm

Parkside Grill – Broad menu for all family members. Soups, salads, half-pound burgers, specialty sandwiches, hand-cut steaks, fresh seafood, martinis, wines, and desserts. 338 North Peters Road, Knoxville 865.862.5358. Monday – Thursday, 11am-10pm; Fri & Sat, 11 am-11pm; Sun, 11 am-9 pm.

Night Life:

Downtown Grill & Brewery – Located one block north of the historic Tennessee Theater on Gay Street. Downtown Knoxville's favorite gathering place with its copper and mahogany bar, tempting menu, and craft-brewed beers. 424 South Gay Street, Knoxville 1.865.633.8111. Sun– Thurs, 11 am–10 pm- full menu, bar open until Midnight; Friday and Saturday, 11 am – 11 pm. full menu, bar open until 3:00 am. Serving Sunday Jazz Brunch.

Preservation Pub - Live music, pub food & beer served on 2 stories with a speakeasy vibe & a rooftop garden deck. 28 Market Square, Knoxville. Opens at noon. 865.524.2224.

Accommodations:

The Maple Hurst Inn: The Inn is a 90-year old mansion in historic Maplehurst Park in downtown Knoxville, Tennessee. It is located near the University of Tennessee and Neyland Stadium, the convention center and fine restaurants. Unique accommodations blend 18th century charm and modern amenities. Enjoy a bottle of wine from the Penthouse Jacuzzi Suite overlooking the Tennessee River. 800 West Hill Avenue, Knoxville. 865.523.7773.

Records:

All-Time Record: 846–395–53 (.674)

SEC Championships: 13 (1938, '39 tie, '40, '46 tie, '51 tie, '56, '67, '69, '85, '89 tie, '90, '97, and '98)

National Championships: 2 (1951, 1998)

Bowl Appearances: Tennessee ranks second behind Alabama in all-time college bowl appearances with 48; and fourth with victories at 26.

Bowl Record: 29-24 (.547)

Great Bowl Games:

1971 Sugar Bowl: January 1, 1971 Tennessee 34, Air Force 13

1986 Sugar Bowl: January 1, 1986 Tennessee 35, Miami 7

1990 Cotton Bowl: January 1, 1990 Tennessee 31, Arkansas 27

1991 Sugar Bowl: January 1, 1991 Tennessee 23, Virginia 22

1999 Fiesta Bowl: January 4, 1999 Tennessee 23, Florida State 6

(Philip Fulmer led Tennessee to its second National Championship)

2002 Citrus Bowl: Tennessee 45 Michigan 17

2008 Outback Bowl: Tennessee 21, Wisconsin 17

2016 Outback Bowl: Tennessee 45, Northwestern 6

2019 Gator Bowl: Tennessee 23, Indiana 22

Tennessee Greats:

Coaches:

Z.G. Clevenger – (1911-1915) – (26-15-2) – (.600) – A former Muncie, Indiana native and player, Clevenger coached the 1914 Tennessee Volunteer football team to the SIAA Championship game in which they defeated an undefeated Vanderbilt team, a feat no other Volunteer coach accomplished until the Neyland era. Clevenger's 1914 team went 9-0 en route to the title of SIAA Champions. He died November 24, 1970.

John Bender – (1916-1920) – (18-5-4) – (.670) – A Sutton, Nebraska native, Bender was a former 1905 Nebraska player who came to Tennessee via Kansas State. Bender installed a short punt scheme at Tennessee and was successful as head coach. However, his tenure there was interrupted by World War I in 1917-1918. Bender returned to Knoxville in 1920 to post a 7-2 record. He died July 24, 1928 at the age of 46.

M.B. Banks – (1921-1925) – (27-15-3) – (.490) – A Breesport, New York native born June 5, 1883, Banks came to Tennessee during the initial year of the Southern Conference. A former player for Syracuse University, and a former coach at Duke University, Banks was successful at employing various and sun-

dry offenses for the Volunteers, although his most favored mode of attack was the universal winged-T. Banks became too sick to continue his duties in 1925 and resigned. He died January 12, 1970 at age 86.

General Robert Reese Neyland – (1926-1934), (1936-1940), (1946-1952) – (173-31-12) – (.800) – Born in Greenville, Texas in 1892, General Neyland is Tennessee's biggest football legend and a great patriot who served his country when needed. A graduate of the United States Military Academy at West Point, Neyland coached 21 years in three separate stints at Tennessee and rose to the rank of brigadier general in the United States Army. Twice Neyland left his position as head football coach to serve his country in active military duty. His first nine year span as head coach of the Vols produced a 76-7-5 record, while enjoying undefeated runs of 33 and 28 games, as well as winning 14 straight games. Neyland used the vaunted single-wing to capture SEC championships in 1927 and 1932. His teams won an impressive 173 games and during a span of seven years, they lost two games. Neyland's Volunteers held opponents scoreless for 71 consecutive quarters, which is nearly two complete seasons. They battled through eight seasons without recording a regular season loss. Neyland left his beloved Volunteers, and in the volunteer spirit, served his country in the Panama Canal Zone in 1934. During his year-long absence in 1935, Neyland's head coaching duties were assumed by W.H. Britton. Britton coached the Vols to a 4-5 record until Neyland's return from active duty in 1936. Upon his return from active duty in 1936, Neyland retooled his football machine in Knoxville by replenishing with young talent. What resulted were a jubilant three years of perfect football in Tennessee from 1938-1940. Neyland's 1939 team was the last in NCAA history to be unscored upon during regular season play. In 1941, Neyland returned to active military duty, serving in World War II. John Barnhill served as an admirable replacement during Neyland's five year hiatus. Neyland returned in 1956, retired from military service. This allowed him to concentrate on claiming a national championship. After his return in 1946, Neyland led the Vols to three straight major bowl appearances and the 1951 National Championship. Declining health forced Neyland to retire to the position of athletic director, a post he held until his passing in 1962. In 1956, for his coaching achievements, and for his many contributions to the collegiate game of football, Neyland was inducted into the College Football Hall of Fame. General Neyland passed away on March 28, 1962.

John Barnhill **–** (1941-45) – (32-5-2) – (.820) – Born February 23, 1903, in Savannah, Tennessee, Barnhill was a valued associate of General Douglas McArthur. Coach Robert Neyland volunteered for duty during World War II and served in the Panama Canal fighting zone. In Neyland's absence, Barnhill assumed the position of head coach for the Vols. A former Volunteer, Barnhill posted a most solid record of wins versus losses during his short tenure as football coach. However, during 1943, no football was played at Tennessee due to the war effort. In 1946, Barnhill was hired by the University of Arkansas as its football coach and athletic director. The former Arkansas men's basketball facility and current women's facility is named after Barnhill. He died October 21, 1973.

Bowden Wyatt **–** (1952-1962) – (49-29-4) – (.600) – Born October 4, 1917 in Kingston, Tennessee, Wyatt was a legend on the Tennessee playing fields. Wyatt returned to his alma mater after claiming coaching championships at Wyoming and Arkansas and serving as an assistant at Mississippi State. In just his second season with the Volunteerss he was awarded National Coach of the Year honors for leading Tennessee to the SEC Championship. His overall coaching record was 99-56-5. Coach Wyatt is a member of the College Football Hall of Fame as both a player (1972) and coach (1997). He died January 21, 1969. He was 51.

Doug Dickey **–** (1964-1969) – (46-15-4) – (.710) – Born June 24, 1932, the Vermillion, South Dakota native, grew up in Gainesville, Florida and is an alumnus of the University of Florida. He was originally hired from the University of Arkansas staff by Tennessee Athletic Director Bob Woodruff. Dickey was tapped to rebuild a stagnant Tennessee program. Dickey reversed the Volunteers' football fortunes by guiding the Orange to SEC titles in both 1967 and 1969. He was named the SEC Coach of the Year in 1965 and 1967. The former Gator signal-caller returned to his alma mater in Gainesville (1954) following the 1969 season. His career head coaching record is 104-58-6. Dickey returned to Knoxville in 1984 in an administrative capacity and served as the Tennessee athletic director from 1986 through 2002. Dickey is a member of the Tennessee Sports Hall of Fame and the College Football Hall of Fame.

Bill Battle **–** (1970-1976) – (59-22-2) – (.710) – The Birmingham, Alabama native and University of Alabama graduate was touted as the youngest head coach in the nation when he assumed the position of head coach for the Volunteers at 28. A Bear Bryant protégé, Battle was undeniably precocious. With poise uncharacteristic of someone his age, he led the Big Orange to five straight bowl games (1970-1974) and three of Battle's teams finished in the top ten nationally. Battle presided as head coach of the Volunteers during

Tennessee's first-ever night game at Neyland Stadium, a contest Tennessee won over the Nittany Lions of Penn State 28-21 on September 23, 1972. Battle is founder and chairman of The Collegiate Licensing Company ("CLC"). In 1981, while working for Golden Eagle Enterprises in Selma, Alabama, Battle signed Coach Paul "Bear" Bryant to a licensing agreement, making the University of Alabama CLC's first client. In 1983, Battle moved CLC from Selma to Atlanta, Georgia.

Johnny Majors **–** (1977-92) – (116-62-8) – (.620) – Born May 21, 1935 in Lynchburg, Tennessee, Majors became an All-American tailback for the Volunteers during the 1950's. A triple-threat tailback for the Vols, Majors was one of the last collegiate quarterbacks to use the single wing formation rather than the emerging T formation. He was a consensus 1956 All-American, Heisman runner-up and later played professionally for the Montreal Alouettes of the Canadian Football League. Majors returned to his alma mater to coach after he coached at Iowa and then he led the Pittsburgh Panthers to a national championship in 1976. Three of Majors' squads won SEC championships. His 1985 team went 9-1-2, with a crushing defeat of Miami by a score of 35-7 in the Sugar Bowl in New Orleans. His 1989 team finished 11-1-0 with a Cotton Bowl victory over Arkansas in Dallas by the score of 31-27. Majors' 1990 team went 9-2-2 with a close victory over Virginia in the Sugar Bowl by the score of 23-22. In 1992 Majors had heart bypass surgery and was replaced by Coach Phillip Fulmer. In an interesting aside, actor Lee Majors of The Six Million Dollar Man fame, borrowed Majors' last name as his stage name. Apparently Lee, whose real name was Harvey Lee Yeary, in his youth met Majors while he was a football player at Tennessee, and became a fan.

Phillip Fulmer **–** (1992-2008) – (152-52) – (.745) – Born September 1, 1950, in Winchester, Tennessee, Fulmer enrolled at UT in 1968 and joined the football team as an offensive guard. The Vols went 30-5 from 1969-1971 with Fulmer's help, and the direction of coaches Doug Dickey and Bill Battle. The Vols captured the

SEC title in 1969 and won the Sugar Bowl the following year. In 1971, they were the Liberty Bowl champions after notching a 10-2 record. As a young coach Fulmer served the Vols as a linebacker and defensive coordinator for the freshman team in 1973 before moving to Wichita State in 1974. He spent five years at Wichita, where he coached the offensive line and linebackers. He followed the Wichita years with a lone season at Vanderbilt, where he was an aide to Commodore Head Coach George MacIntyre, in 1979. In 1980, he was named an assistant at Tennessee. In 1989, he became the Volunteers' offensive coordinator, lasting three years before taking over for an ill Johnny Majors in 1992. Known for his ability to recruit, Fulmer won the 1998 SEC and National Championships with quarterback Tee Martin and was named National Coach of the Year for his efforts. Philip Fulmer Way is a street on the Tennessee campus. He was inducted into the College Football Hall of Fame in 2012.

***Butch Jones* –** (2013-2017) - (34-27) – The Saugatuck, Michigan native played college ball at Ferris State University in Big Rapids, Michigan. As a senior, Jones interned for the Tampa Bay Bucs and became a defensive assistant at Rutgers University, in 1990. Two years later, he became the offensive coordinator at Wilkes University. In 1995, he returned to Ferris State as the offensive coordinator. He arrived at Central Michigan University in 1998, coaching tight ends for one year, running backs for two more, and called plays on offense from 2002 to 2004. He left in 2005 to work for Rich Rodriguez coaching wide receivers at West Virginia. Jones returned to Central Michigan as head coach in 2007. He left CMU with a 27–13 overall record and 20–3 MAC record. On December 16, 2009, Jones was named head coach at the University of Cincinnati. He replaced Brian Kelly, who left to become head coach at Notre Dame; Jones replaced Kelly at Central Michigan. Jones led the Bearcats to records of 4–8 in 2010 and 10–3 in 2011, including a Big East championship, a Liberty Bowl victory (31–24 over Vanderbilt), and he was named Big East Coach of the Year. He led the Bearcats to a 9–3 record in 2012. Twenty days prior to the bowl game, on December 7, 2012, Jones announced he accepted the head coaching job at the University of Tennessee, declining offers from Colorado, Purdue, and others. Jones was never a perfect fit in Knoxville, and he did not blaze a trail; but he came close to turning the program around—before losing it. After going 5-7 his first year, he followed with a 7-6 season, capping it with a Taxslayer Bowl victory. 2015 and 2016 were back-to-back 9-4 seasons with bowl wins in the Outback and Music City, respectively. The Volunteers finished second in the East both seasons. 2017 proved to be Jones' last, as the talent ran out and the team went a hapless 4-6, 0-6 in the SEC, prior to his early firing.

Jeremy Pruitt **–** (2018-present) – (13-12) - A native of Rainsville, Alabama, Pruitt is a seasoned coach who has worked with some of the SEC's most successful coaches. He played defensive back at Middle Tennessee in 1993 and 1994 and at Alabama in 1996. In 1997, Pruitt began his career like many former players—at the school he last played for—Alabama, as a graduate assistant, under DB Coach Curley Hallman. In 1998, he coached defensive backs at Plainview HS and in 1999 he coached DB's at West Alabama. In 2000 he went back to Plainview as their defensive coordinator and from 2001-2003 he was an assistant at Fort Payne High School. From 2004-2006 he coached at Hoover High as their defensive coordinator. In 2007, he was hired by Alabama as an assistant in the role of player development. He was named defensive backs coach at Alabama in 2010, after the Tide's 2009 National Championship. During his first season Pruitt's secondary led the SEC in passing efficiency. The 2011 Tide secondary led the nation in pass defense and efficiency. In 2013, Pruitt took the defensive coordinator position at Florida State under Jimbo Fisher. There Pruitt's defense allowed 12 points per game, helping the Seminoles to a National Championship. In 2014, Pruitt joined the Georgia staff as the defensive coordinator, and his unit finished 14th nationally. Pruitt returned to Alabama in 2016, as Defensive coordinator, replacing Kirby Smart, who vacated the position to become head coach at Georgia. His 2016 defense led the nation in scoring and rushing defense and in 2017 his unit finished second in total defense. In 2018 he took the head coaching position at the University of Tennessee. Bent on winning, Pruitt is an experienced, pedigreed coach, and an undeniable disciple of Nick Saban. On October 13, 2018, against #21 Auburn, Pruitt coached the Volunteers to their first victory over a SEC West team since 2010, despite going 5-7 on the season. The 2019 season began with setbacks—a shocking loss to Georgia State and another in overtime to BYU. The Volunteers dropped consecutive games against Florida and Georgia. Things looked bleak. But, they clawed their way back with victories over Mississippi State, South Carolina, Kentucky, Missouri and Vanderbilt and a thrilling, come-from-behind victory in the Gator Bowl against Indiana, 23-22, to finish the season 8-5, creating great expectations for Volunteer fans pining for a triumphant return to winning football in Knoxville.

Players:

John (Johnny) T. Majors – (1954-1956) – An All-American tailback in 1956, Majors was also the runner-up to the Heisman Trophy winner, Paul Hornung, a Notre Dame star. Majors later coached at Tennessee, where he was the "1976 Coach of the Year." Majors is originally from Huntland, Tennessee. He is a member of the College Football Hall of Fame and is considered one of the greatest college players. Actor Lee Majors of "Six Million Dollar Man" fame took his stage name after Majors.

Bob Johnson – (1965-1967) – A Gary, Indiana native, Johnson was a two-time All-American center for the Vols. In July of 1997 Johnson was named to the GTE Academic All-American All-Time Team for his earned B+ grade point average in Industrial Engineering. Johnson played at Tennessee under Volunteer Coach Doug Dickey and went on to a 12-year career in the National Football League with the Cincinnati Bengals. Johnson was the last original Bengal to retire, and his uniform number was retired by the team—the only jersey the organization retired. In 1989, Johnson was inducted into the College Football Hall of Fame.

Reggie White – (1981-1984) – Born December 19, 1961, in Chattanooga, Tennessee, White was a consensus All-American defensive tackle for the Vols in 1983, and became one of pro football's all-time greats, as well as one of the game's biggest personalities. White set records in Knoxville, including most sacks in a career (32), season (15), and a single game (4). White was voted the SEC's Most Outstanding Player in 1983, by the Atlanta and Birmingham Touchdown Clubs. Nicknamed the "Minister of Defense" for his gridiron greatness, and for his noted Evangelical ministry, during his final season in Knoxville he was also one of four finalists for the Lombardi Award, given to the nation's outstanding college lineman. White went on to an All-Pro career with the Philadelphia Eagles and the Green Bay Packers. He was selected by the Memphis Showboats (USFL) in the early first round of the draft. He played with Memphis for only two seasons before the league went defunct. Thereafter, he played for Phil-

adelphia from 1985-1992 and for Green Bay from 1993-1998. He retired, played for Carolina in 2000 for one season, and retired again. Reggie White died on December 26, 2004 of cardiac arrhythmia. He was 43.

Leonard Little **–** (1995-1997) – Born October 19, 1974, in Asheville, North Carolina, Little, a ferocious defensive end and linebacker, was a 1997 team Co-Captain, as well as an AP, Football News, and Walter Camp All-American who was the "SEC's Defensive Player of the Year." Little and quarterback Peyton Manning led the Volunteers to the 1997 SEC Championship, a goal they attained with a victory over the Auburn Tigers in the Georgia Dome, 30-29. Little was chosen by the St. Louis Rams in the 3rd round of the 1998 NFL draft. He was a 2003 All-Pro selection.

Peyton Manning **–** (1994-1997) – Born March 24, 1976, Manning is remembered as Tennessee's greatest quarterback. Manning holds nearly every statistical passing record for the Vols. Revered by Tennessee fans for his unselfish decision to complete his eligibility at Tennessee instead of opting for millions of pro dollars, Peyton proved to be what the Volunteers needed in 1997. A consensus All-American, Davey O'Brien National QB Award and Sullivan Award winner, Peyton won every post-season accolade possible for a player, except the Heisman, in which he finished second. From New Orleans' Isadore Newman High School, Peyton is the son of former Ole Miss great, Archie Manning, who played for the Saints, and the brother of Super Bowl MVP, Eli Manning, of the NY Giants, who also played at Ole Miss. Peyton received academic awards during his career, including the National Football Foundation Scholar Athlete Award and the NASDAQ Scholar Athlete Award. Peyton ran and threw for 11,020 yards during his four-year career in Knoxville. Peyton Manning Pass, named in his honor, is a Tennessee campus street. Peyton was drafted first by the Indianapolis Colts in the first round of the 1998 NFL Draft. He holds NFL records for consecutive seasons with over 4,000 yards passing and the most seasons with 4,000 or more passing yards. He is the all-time passing leader for the Colts Franchise and a 12-time Pro Bowl selection. He was named the "Super Bowl XLI MVP" after the Colts defeated the Chicago Bears 29-17 on February 4, 2007. Manning maintains a charitable organization, the Peyback Foundation. He retired in 2015, a member of the Denver Broncos organization, where he played his last four years in the league.

Tamaurice Nigel "Tee" Martin **–** (1996-1999) – A Mobile native, Martin followed Peyton Manning and guided Tennessee to the 1998 National Championship. As a junior Martin led the Volunteers to a 13-0 record and a national championship over Florida State University. During his last season in Knoxville, Martin made All-Southeastern Conference as the Volunteers went 9-3, losing to Nebraska in a return trip to the Fiesta. Martin holds the Volunteer record for the most rushing touchdowns by a quarterback (17). In 2000, he was drafted in the fourth round by the Pittsburgh Steelers. In 2001, he left Pittsburgh to play for the Rhein Fire in NFL Europe. In 2003, he went to the Oakland Raiders before playing with the Winnipeg Blue Bombers for a season. Tee Martin Drive is a street on the Tennessee campus.

Jamal Lewis – (1997-1999) **–** A native of Atlanta, Georgia, Lewis attended Douglass High School. The "MVP" of the Florida-Georgia All-Star Game, he is remembered as one of Tennessee's most explosive running backs, and a key reason why the Vols won the first BCS National Championship Game in 1998. In his abbreviated, three-year career in Knoxville Lewis rushed for 2,677 yards and accounted for 3,161 all-purpose yards. He is third on the university's list of all-time rushers. As a freshman Lewis ran for 1,364 yards and seven touchdowns, earning him freshman All-American honors. The following year he helped Tennessee win the national championship over the Florida State Seminoles. Lewis was the fifth pick overall by the Baltimore Ravens in the 2000 NFL Draft. In his rookie season he rushed for over 1,000 yards. In Super Bowl XXXV, Lewis rushed for 103 yards and scored a touchdown, becoming only the second rookie to rush for over 100 yards in a Super Bowl. In 2003, he was named the AP NFL Offensive Player of the Year.

John Henderson **–** (1998-2001) – A Nashville, Tennessee native, "Big John" Henderson was one of the most dominant defensive linemen to wear the Volunteer orange. A natural at the defensive line position, Henderson was blessed with a rare combination of raw power and quickness to complement a sturdy, imposing 6' 7" frame. He finished his college career with 165 tackles (130 solo and 39 for loss) and 20.5 sacks, seven pass deflections, four forced fumbles, and five fumble recoveries. One of the most decorated players in Tennessee history, Henderson was an All-American and the Outland Trophy winner in 2000, a consensus First Team All-American in 2001 and a first round pick (9th overall) by the Jacksonville Jaguars in the 2002 NFL Draft.

Donte' Stallworth **–** (1999-2001) –A Sacramento, California native, who attended Grant Union High School, the gifted Stallworth excelled at track and field and football. He chose Tennessee over a litany of college callers and became one of the school's all-time receiving greats. Stallworth became a full-time starter as a junior for the Volunteers, tallying 99 catches for 1,747

yards for a 17.6 yard-per-catch average and thirteen touchdowns. The All-SEC receiver entered the professional draft with a year of eligibility remaining. He was selected by the New Orleans Saints with the 13th pick of the first round of the 2002 NFL Draft. In 2006, he played with the Philadelphia Eagles and in 2007 signed with the New England Patriots. He played for Cleveland, Washington and Baltimore before making a last stop in New England in 2012.

Alex Walls **–** (1999-2002) – A native of Bristol, Virginia, Walls was a four-year starter as place kicker for the Vols. An All-SEC and All-American, Walls was a Lou Groza Award finalist in 2000, scoring ninety-three points on 18 of 20 field goals and 39 extra points without a miss. In 2001, Walls tied a career long with a 51-yard field goal in the SEC Championship game in Atlanta, which was also an SEC Championship game record. Walls scored 292 points in his career at Tennessee, connecting on 53 of 68 field goals (77.9%) and 133 of 137 extra point attempts. His 53 field goals rank third on the all-time Volunteer list.

Jason Witten **–** (2000–2002) – An Elizabethton, Tennessee native, Witten attended Elizabethton High School and was one of the University of Tennessee's greatest tight ends. In his first of three seasons in Knoxville, Witten switched from defensive end to a standout tight end due to a team need, and became a superstar in the process, posting school records for receptions (39) and receiving yards (493). In the 2003 NFL Draft Witten was chosen as the 69th overall pick (third Round) by the Dallas Cowboys. He is an eleven-time Pro Bowl selection (2004-10, 2012-2014, 2017) and holds the Cowboys' career receptions record and is still on the active roster, after 16 seasons.

Cordarrelle Patterson – (2012) - Patterson attended Northwestern High School in Rock Hill, South Carolina, where he starred in football and basketball, and ran track. His time in Knoxville was as bright as it was brief. He attended junior college in Hutchinson, Kansas, where he in 2010 and 2011 he was an All-American and the 2011 Jayhawk Conference Offensive Player of the year. In 2012, he signed with the Volunteers, where he made an immediate impact with rare rushing, receiving and return skills. In 2012, he rushed for 308 yards on 25 carries for a 12.3 yard average, caught 46 passes for 778 yards for a 16.9 yard average, and 29 returns for 772 yards for a 26.6 yard average. He was the 29th overall pick by the Minnesota Vikings in the first round of the 2013 NFL Draft. In a game against the Green Bay Packers in 2013, Patterson tied the NFL record for longest play and set the NFL record for longest kick return with 109 yards, the longest possible.

Derek Barnett **–** (2014-2016) - A native of Nashville, Barnett attended Brentwood Academy in Brentwood, Tennessee. Barnett was the first true freshman defensive lineman to start a season opener for the Vols. Barnett played in all 13 games and made 10 starts in the 2014 season, finishing with records of 10 sacks and 20.5 tackles for loss. In his true sophomore season he duplicated the effort, with 10 sacks and 12.5 tackles for loss. In the New Year's Day 2016 Outback Bowl he had a sack in the Vols' 45-6 win over Northwestern. During his junior year he notched 13 sacks and 19 tackles for loss. On December 30, 2016, in the Music City Bowl, Barnett broke the UT sack record held by UT legend Reggie White, with 33. Barnett was the 14th overall pick by the Philadelphia Eagles in the first round of the 2017 NFL Draft.

Alvin Kamara **–** (2015-2016) – Kamara's mother was from Liberia. He attended Norcross High in Norcross, Georgia where he was named the 6-A Player of the Year and Georgia's Mr. Football by the Atlanta Journal Constitution. In 2013, Kamara signed with Alabama and Coach Nick Saban and redshirted during the 2013 behind a logjam of talented runners. Injuries and what the staff revealed as "behavior issues" forced a transfer to Hutchinson Community College in Kansas, in 2014. At Hutchinson Kamara rushed for 1,211 yards with 18 touchdowns and again became a hot commodity, signing with Tennessee over Georgia before the 2015 season. In 2015, Kamara eased into the Tennessee offense with 698 total yards and seven touchdowns, averaging 6.5 yards per rush, which was third best in the league. In 2016, he added 596 yards and 9 touchdowns for 5.8 yards per carry. After receiving the highest Wonderlic Test score at the combine, he was selected by the Saints as the 67th pick in the early 3rd round of the 2017 NFL Draft, and the fifth running back selected. He was the 2017 NFL Rookie of the Year.

Traditions:

The Formation "T"

Since 1964, the team has entered the stadium through a giant "T" formed on the field by the Pride of the Southland Marching Band. Bob Neyland's "63" team began this tradition which continued under Doug Dickey's command and subsequent repositioning of the "T." It continues today in its present form, from north to south. It is sometimes formed at away games but does lose some of its pizzazz without the 107,000 fans.

The Helmet "T"

The famed letter "T" debuted on Tennessee's helmets in the fall of 1964 as Doug Dickey assumed the head coaching reins. Prior to 1964 the helmets had been white with an orange stripe down the middle. There have been exceptions. In Coach Bowden Wyatt's final season in 1962, the Vols had orange numerals on the sides of their helmets. In 1963, Coach Jim McDonald stuck with the numbers on the helmets, but changed the numerals' color to black. When Johnny Majors was named head coach in 1977, he had the "T" redesigned and the orange stripe widened.

"The Vol Walk"

The team takes this stroll from Gibbs Hall to the field down Yale Avenue two hours prior to every home game at Neyland Stadium. Smokey, the Vols' own blue tick coon hound usually makes the stroll, as this newer tradition has become a fan favorite since its inception in the early 1990's.

"Tennessee Tradition"

According to the Tennessee Media Guide, Tennessee Tradition is defined as:

"...the wave of orange across the 102,854-seat Neyland Stadium...It's tailgating in the parking lots and hearing John Ward's pregame show at the base of the Hill near Alumni Gym...It's hearing public address announcer Bobby Denton say, 'Please pay these prices and please pay no more.'"

"Rocky Top"

Copyright 1967 by House of Bryant Publications
Post Office Box 120608, Nashville, Tennessee 37212

Wish that I was on old Rockytop Down in the Tennessee hills.
Ain't no smoggy smoke on Rockytop Ain't no telephone bills.
Once I had a girl on Rockytop Half bear, the other half cat,
Wild as a mink, but sweet as soda-pop I still dream about that.

Chorus: Rockytop, you'll always be Home sweet home to me.
Good old Rockytop, Rockytop, Tennessee. Rockytop, Tennessee.

Once two strangers climbed old Rockytop
Lookin' for a moonshine still.
Strangers ain't come down from Rockytop, Recon they never will.
Corn won't grow at all on Rockytop – Dirt's too rocky by far.
That's why all the folks on Rockytop Get their corn from a jar.
Repeat Chorus

I've had years of cooped up city life, Trapped like a dog in a pen.

All I know is it's a pity life Can't be simple again.

Repeat Chorus

Notes on Rocky Top: "Rocky Top" is one of seven official Tennessee songs as well as the unofficial fight song for the Volunteers of the University of Tennessee. The two best-known versions of the song are by the Osborne brothers and Lynn Anderson. The Osborne brothers first had a regional hit with the song in 1967; however, it was Anderson's rendition that was a country chart-topper in 1970.

Alma Mater:

On a hallowed hill in Tennessee Like a beacon shining bright

The stately walls of old UT Rise glorious to the site

So here's to you, old Tennessee Our alma mater true

We pledge in love and harmony Our loyalty to you

What torches kindled at that flame Have passed from hand to hand

What hearts cemented in that name Blind land to stranger land.

O, ever as we strive to rise

On life's unresting stream Dear Alma Mater, may our eyes

Be lifted to that gleam.

Noteworthy Tennessee Alumni:

Albert Zachary Baker, former president of Rotary International (deceased)

Howard Baker Jr., former United States Senator, former Senate Majority Leader

Samuel E. Beall III, founder of Ruby Tuesday restaurants

James Buchanan, Nobel Prize winner in economics

Deana Carter, country music artist

John Cullum, Tony Award winning actor

Charles Ergen, started EchoStar Communications Corporation in 1980

John Dickson Harper, former president of ALCOA (deceased)

James A. Haslam II, chairman of the board and president of Pilot Corporation; in 2006, he and his wife, Natalie, made a $32.5 million gift to UT

Charles O. "Chad" Holliday, chairman and CEO of DuPont

Cormac McCarthy, novelist

Lamar Alexander, Tennessee Governor, UT President, U.S. Senator

Guy Bailey, former President, University of Alabama

Dolly Parton, honorary doctorate 2009

Dave Ramsey, financial peace guru

Ann Taylor, NPR newscaster

2020 Tennessee Football Schedule

Sept. 5 Charlotte

Sept. 12 at Oklahoma

Sept. 19 Furman

Sept. 26 Florida

Oct. 3 Missouri

Oct. 10 at South Carolina

Oct. 17 OPEN DATE

Oct. 24 Alabama

Oct. 31 at Arkansas

Nov. 7 Kentucky

Nov. 14 at Georgia

Nov. 21 Troy

Nov. 28 at Vanderbilt

Vanderbilt University

Through the years Vanderbilt University has established itself as the SEC's most prestigious academic institution. Although it is known throughout the country and the world for its success in the classroom, Vanderbilt has enjoyed its share of success on the gridiron. During the formative years of the Southeastern Conference, Vanderbilt was one of the nation's most feared football-playing schools. The legend and lore of those early squads led by Coach Dan McGugin, serve as reminders of the proud Commodore tradition and the rightful place it holds in the annals of SEC football. Vanderbilt Football continues to build on that lasting, winning tradition. At Vanderbilt, a charter member school of the powerful Southeastern Conference, student athletes receive the best of both worlds. They compete in one of the finest athletic conferences and in some of the nation's most challenging classrooms, against the exciting backdrop of Nashville's music scene.

Nickname: Commodores

Founded: 1873

Vanderbilt University was founded in 1873, when successful steam boater and railroad baron Commodore Cornelius Vanderbilt gave one million dollars to erect an institution of higher learning, one that in his words, would "contribute to strengthening the ties that should exist between all sections of our common country." A year earlier, in 1872, a charter for the constitution of a "Central University" was set forth in Nashville, but a lack of monetary resources stymied the effort. Commodore Vanderbilt's generous donation allowed for the establishment of the school that today bears his name. At the time of its inception, the City of Nashville had 40,000 residents. The 316-acre campus rested within an existing cornfield and the stone wall enveloping the campus served to keep neighboring cows off the school's grounds. Vanderbilt University first opened for classes in October 1875, with an enrollment of 192 students. In 1966, the Peabody campus was named a registered National Historic Landmark.

Location: Nashville, Tennessee

Possessing a metropolitan population of close to two million people, Nashville can stake its claim as the largest urban hometown of any SEC member institution. Despite its recent growth spurt, Nashville retains a small-town feel to those who know it. Positioned midway between the north and south boundaries of the United States, Nashville is the capital of Tennessee as well as the cultural and entertainment Mecca of the mid-South. Popularly known as "Music City USA" and home to the Grand Ole Opry, and Music Row, Nash-

ville is a city whose music preferences vary from country to rock n' roll to gospel to American folk, blues, funk and Jazz. Singer-songwriters from across the country find themselves looking for fame and success on the streets of Nashville, peddling their music to anyone who will listen. Located two miles from the center of the downtown entertainment district, is the thriving urban campus of Vanderbilt University.

History:

Vanderbilt began playing football on Thanksgiving Day, November 27, 1890. The Commodores played the University of Nashville, which became the George Peabody College for Teachers. According to Fred Russell, the following is an account of what Elliot R. Jones, coach and captain of the first Commodore team from 1890-1892, remarked about the beginning of Vanderbilt football.

"In November 1890, a letter was received from the University of Nashville challenging Vanderbilt to a football game on the holiday of Thanksgiving Day. Upon receipt of the communication, the President of the Athletic Association for the Commodores, Dr. William Dudley, called forthwith a meeting of the Executive Committee. The matter was considered serious by the committee, so serious that a mass meeting of the student body was called. An impressive 150 students assembled at four o'clock the next day in the campus gymnasium, two weeks before Thanksgiving Day. The students voted to accept the challenge of the University of Nashville and the game was played. Vanderbilt prevailed in the rout, 40-0.

In 1893, 1894, 1897, 1904 and 1905 Vanderbilt was crowned the Southern Intercollegiate Athletic Association Champions.

In 1906, the Atlanta Journal wrote of the Vanderbilt Commodore football program:

"Vanderbilt is the best team in the South and one of the best in the nation. No Southern team, recruited by any means, has classed with it. This team was secured by honest athletic methods. No inducements are held out for athletes to go to Vanderbilt. The team has been built up by methods above criticism and it proves one thing; that honesty pays in college athletics as well as elsewhere."

Vanderbilt won national championships in 1906 and 1911 under the old Billingsley System Ratings. Vanderbilt, an eleven-time champion of the Southern Intercollegiate Association, won the Southern Conference Championship, in 1922 and 1923.

Population: 691,243

Enrollment: 12,686

*Vandy has the smallest enrollment of the SEC schools. Ole Miss, the second smallest, has twice as many undergraduates enrolled as their Eastern Division counterpart.

Colors: Old Gold and Black

The origins of old gold and black are nebulous. Some at Vanderbilt say the original colors were orange and black, given to the university by Judge W.L. Granbery of Princeton. Others say Livingfield More offered the colors of his eastern prep school. Others contend Commodore Vanderbilt's legacy was called upon to develop school colors for the university that bears his name: black for the magnate's control of coal and gold for his money. When questioned by an early 1940's writer, most members of the 1890 football team could not recall why they appeared in Old Gold and Black. It is believed that the student body may have formally voted on the school's colors of Old Gold and Black in the mid-teens (1910's), but no such record corroborates that assertion.

Mascot Name: Commodores

The name "Commodore" comes from university founder Cornelius Vanderbilt's affinity for steamboats, as he built a vast shipping fortune. The term commodore was used by the Navy during the mid-to-late-nineteenth century. A commodore was the commanding officer of a task force of ships, and therefore higher in rank than a captain, but lower in rank than an admiral. The closest parallel to this now-defunct rank is rear-admiral lower half.

In the Royal Navy, the designation of commodore was applied to the commanding officer of a convoy in World War II. Since the term was used during the latter nineteenth century and because it was then that Cornelius received his nickname, Vanderbilt's mascot is always portrayed as a naval officer from the 1880's, replete with sideburns, cutlass, and nineteenth-century naval regalia.

Stadium: Vanderbilt Stadium, Dudley Field

Dr. William L. Dudley was the Dean of the Vanderbilt Medical College from 1895 to 1914. Dr. Dudley helped found the Southern Intercollegiate Athletic Association, which later became the SEC and the ACC. In 1906, he was instrumental in the inception of the NCAA. He is remembered as the "Father of Clean Athletics." Dudley Field at Vanderbilt Stadium is named after him.

Stadium Capacity: 40,550

Stadium History:

Vanderbilt Stadium at Dudley Field was constructed in 1922, as the first stadium in the South to be used exclusively for college football. At that time the venue seated 20,000. In 1960, capacity was increased to 34,000, with the addition of the south stands connecting the horseshoe and the north end zone bleacher stands.

In 1963, President John F. Kennedy spoke there to a crowd of 33,000. The first game played at Dudley Field was between the Commodores and the Michigan Wolverines. A late 4th quarter goal line stand by the Commodores preserved a 0-0 tie. Most of the stadium was razed between 1980 and 1981, with the remaining stands on each sideline elevated ten feet through the use of 22 hydraulic jacks. The stadium's maximum capacity was reached after the 1980–81 renovation. In 1998, a JumboTron video screen was installed, and the stadium served as the site for the Music City Bowl and also was the home field for the Tennessee Oilers. n 2004, Vanderbilt officials removed the unpopular wooden bleachers from the north end zone and replaced them with a visitors' concourse that offers fans a field-level, up-close experience with the playing surface. In 2012, Vanderbilt unveiled a new artificial turf, new lighting and 52x72 foot High Definition Jumbotron TV for replays.

First Game:

1890 - Vanderbilt defeated Nashville on the Vanderbilt campus, 40-0

First Game at Dudley Field:

October 14, 1922 – Vanderbilt 0, Michigan 0

First Night Game in Stadium:

September 25, 1954 - Vanderbilt 19, Baylor 25

First Game in the Renovated Stadium:

September 12, 1981 - Vanderbilt 23, Maryland 17

Record crowd: 41,523

September 5, 1996 - Notre Dame 14, Vanderbilt 7

Directions:

Coming from the South: Take I-65 North to Exit 2098 (Broadway-West End). Then turn left and go west on Broadway. Broadway splits. Keep right to enter West End Avenue. Continue past University and turn left on Natchez Trace. Take the first right and make a sharp right onto 28th Avenue.

Coming from the North: Take I-65 South to I-265 to Exit 209B (Broadway-West End). Go right and then west on Broadway. Then follow the above "Coming from the South" directions.

Coming from the East: Take I-40 West to Exit 209B (Broadway-West End). Turn left on Broadway heading west. Then follow the above "Coming from the South" directions.

Coming from the West: Take I-40 East to Exit 209B (Broadway-West End). Turn right and go west on Broadway. Then follow the above "Coming from the South" directions.

Coming from Chattanooga: Take I-24 West until it merges with I-40 West. Continue on I-40 until Exit 209B (Broadway-West End). Turn right and go west on Broadway. Then follow the above "Coming from the South" directions.

Band: "Spirit of Gold Marching Band"

The band forms the core of the student section at Vanderbilt Stadium on game days and performs at all Vanderbilt Commodores home football games, as well as a select number of away games. The "Spirit of Gold" has developed revered game day traditions. It leads a parade through campus before games and provides music for pre-game and in-game spirit. The band plays the university's fight song, "Dynamite", throughout the game and provides a halftime show for every home game, performing from a variety of musical genres. Past performances have featured music from Lady Gaga, The Blues Brothers, the Backstreet Boys, and Bon Jovi. The last halftime performance of the year is traditionally a completely student-run, student-organized show.

Band Director: Dr. Douglas Morin

Dining:

Pancake Pantry - 1796 21st Avenue, Nashville 1.615.383.9333. One of Nashville's most popular breakfast spots, near Music Row in the likeable Hillsboro Village District. If it is a late on a Saturday morning, expect a line! Open daily, 6:00 a.m. – 5:00 p.m.

Prince's Hot Chicken Shack – Hot chicken! Really hot chicken! The hottest in Tennessee, folks claim...don't order the hot—or it will be a long, long weekend! A Nashville tradition. 123 Ewing Drive, Nashville. 1.615.226.9442.

Night life:

The Bluebird Café – Open since 1982, it is one of Nashville's true treasures. Located in a strip mall, don't let its non-descript appearance fool you. Garth Brooks, Vince Gill and Kathy Mattea honed their skills on its small stage. Offers original music by singer/songwriters, seven nights a week. Traditional grill open to all! 4101 Hillsboro Road, Nashville. 1.615.383.1461.

Tootsie's Wild Orchid Lounge – Named after the famed "Tootsie" Bess, a lover of songwriters and song, this world-famous honky tonk lounge and stage has seen many rising young country stars perform live, including Kris Kristoferson, Willie Nelson, Patsy Cline and Waylong Jennings, among many others. 422 Broadway. 9 am – 2 pm 7 days a week. 615.726.0463.

The Wildhorse Saloon – The #1 destination for night life in the Music City! A three-level historic warehouse turned into a honky tonk! 66,000 square feet. A restaurant, bar, concert hall, dance venue and TV studio. A full menu, centered around its award-winning barbecue and some of the best fried pickles east of the Mississippi. 120 2nd Avenue North, Nashville. 615.902.8200.

Country Music Destinations:

Country Music Hall of Fame - 4 Music Square East, Nashville. 1.615.416.2001. Personal possessions of the stars, video clips, and music; admission includes trolley tour of Music Row and RCA's historic Studio B.

Grand Ole Opry - 2808 Opryland Drive, Nashville. 1.615.889.3060. A 4000-plus-seat theater and museum, staging old-timers like Dolly Parton, as well as today's young chart toppers. Reservations recommended.

Opryland - Theme park nine miles northeast of downtown on Briley Parkway, just off the I-40 E loop. Over twenty rides, paddle steamer trips and of course, live music. 1.615.889.6700

Radio: 650 AM and 95.5 FM WSM

Accommodations:

Daisy Hill Bed & Breakfast: This beautifully furnished Tudor style home sits on 2816 Blair Boulevard and is a short walk from the university. Daisy Hill contains three guest rooms, a conservatory and a screened porch. Rooms vary. 1.800.239.1135.

Golf Course:

Vanderbilt Legends Club

1500 Legends Club Lane, Franklin, TN 37069 (615) 791-8100

Shopping:

The Hillsboro Village Area near the intersection of 21st Avenue South and Blakemore Avenue, near the southeast corner of Vanderbilt, has a nice mix of clothing shops and boutiques. Look to the West End area for more.

All-Time Record: 609–629–50 (.492)

Bowl Appearances:

1955 Gator Bowl: Vanderbilt 25, Auburn 13

1974 Peach Bowl: Vanderbilt 6, Texas Tech 6

1982 Hall of Fame Bowl: Vanderbilt 28, Air Force 36

2008 Music City Bowl: Vanderbilt 16, Boston College 14

2011 Liberty Bowl: Vanderbilt 24, Cincinnati 31

2012 Music City Bowl: Vanderbilt 38, North Carolina State 24

2013 BBVA Compass Bowl: Vanderbilt 41, Houston 24

Bowl Record: 4-4-1 (.444)

Vanderbilt Greats:

Coaches:

Dan McGugin - (1904-1917, 1919-1934) - (197-55-19) – (.730) – Born July 29, 1879, in Tingley, Iowa, McGugin is a member of the College Football Hall of Fame. McGugin's teams during his 33-year reign won 197 games, including four undefeated seasons. He was one of the greatest college coaches of his time. McGugin left football temporarily in 1918, to serve his country in World War I. In his first year as Vanderbilt's head coach, McGugin posted a 9-0-0 record. His three

other undefeated campaigns were in 1919, 1921, and 1922. His 1906 and 1911 teams were consensus National Champions. McGugin won ten conference titles as head coach at Vanderbilt. McGugin compiled a 30-0 record (24 shutouts) in season opening games in his career, outscoring opponents 1,302 to 40 in those contests. Between 1904 and 1909 he compiled a 34-0-1 record versus Southern opposition. During his career, McGugin was 18-8-4 versus their in-state arch nemesis, the University of Tennessee. McGugin once remarked to his players, "Don't live on the fading memories of your forefathers. Go out and make your own records, and leave some memories for others to live by." McGugin personified the "Golden Era" of Vanderbilt football (1890-1934), which were the Commodores' most successful football-playing years. In 1924, McGugin prepared his team to play Minnesota in Minneapolis. The Gophers, at the time, were a team to be reckoned with, having handed Illinois' Red Grange his first collegiate loss. McGugin, a master motivator, inspired his team with the following immortal words: "Men, those people in the stands out there haven't heard of Southern football. When they think about the South, they think – they think about pain, suffering, and death. Many people have no idea of what Southern manhood is all about. Today we can show them. When your mothers looked on you sleeping in your cradles twenty years ago, they wondered when the time would come when you could bring honor the South. That time has arrived!"

The Commodores, subsequent to the moving speech, defeated the favored Gophers in a 16-0 shutout. McGugin died on Jan. 23, 1936 in Memphis.

Red Sanders - (1943-1948) - (36-22-2) – (.600) – The Asheville, North Carolina native is given credit as being head coach during the war-torn years from 1943-1945, but Sanders was on active duty in the military for World War II. Sanders led the Commodores to a respectable record of 36-22-2 (10-9-1 in SEC play) during his stint in Nashville. Sanders was the quintessential competitor. He once stated, "The only thing worse than finishing second is to be lying on the desert alone with your back broken. Either way, nobody ever finds out about you." But he is more famously known for: "Winning isn't everything, it's the only thing." The 1953 saying often attributed to Coach Sanders, according to Bartlett's Familiar Quotations, sixteenth edition (1992).

James Franklin – (2011-2013) - (24-15) – (.615) - Franklin was born in Langhorne, Pennsylvania on February 2, 1972. He attended college at East Stroudsburg University where he was a four-year starter at quarterback, earning a psychology degree in 1995. That year he was hired as a wide receivers coach at Kutztown University of Pennsylvania. The following season, he took over as secondary coach for his alma mater, East Stroudsburg. That year, he was also the offensive coordinator for the Roskilde Kings of the Danish American Football Federation. In 1997, he became wide receivers coach at James Madison. The following year he became tight ends coach at Washington State. In 1999, he served as wide receivers coach at Idaho State. In addition to coaching, Franklin held internships at several NFL franchises. In 2000, he coached wide receivers in Maryland. In 2003, he was recruiting coordinator. In 2005, Franklin left Maryland to serve as the wide receivers coach for the Packers. From 2006 to 2007, he worked at Kansas State as the offensive coordinator and quarterbacks coach. Franklin returned to Maryland for the 2008 season as the offensive coordinator, implementing the West Coast offense at Maryland and on February 6, 2009, Maryland designated Franklin as head coach-in-waiting. On December 17, 2010, after firing a 2-10 Robbie Caldwell, Vanderbilt announced Franklin was hired as its new head coach. Franklin was the first person of color to be head coach of a major sport at Vanderbilt, and the third to be a head football coach in the Southeastern Conference (Sylvester Croom, at Mississippi State, and former Kentucky head coach Joker Phillips). Franklin led Vanderbilt to a bowl game in each of his three seasons. Vanderbilt had never played in bowl games in consecutive seasons. In his second season, 2012, the Commodores finished 9–4 and were ranked in both the Associated Press and USA Today end-of-season coaches' Top 25 for the first time since 1948. It was the first ranking in any week since 2008, and the third nine–win season in school history. Vanderbilt's 15 combined wins in Franklin's first two years were the Commodores' highest total since 1926–1927. The Commodores ended the season with a win at home in the Music City Bowl. In 2013, Franklin again won nine games, leading the Commodores to another post-season victory in the BBVA Compass Bowl. After the season he took the head coaching position at Penn State, following Joe Paterno's retirement. He remains in Happy Valley.

Derek Mason **–** (2014-present) – (27-47) – (.364) - Born September 29, 1969 in Phoenix, Arizona, Mason played cornerback at Northern Arizona. A seasoned defensive mind, Mason always has his troops prepared, and when he has the right mix of athletes, he is one of the toughest coordinators to scheme against. He began coach-

ing receivers at Mesa Community College in 1994. From 1995 to 1998 he coached wide receivers and defensive backs at Weber State. He made stops at Bucknell, Utah and St. Mary's, where he was the Assistant Head Coach and Defensive Coordinator, and at New Mexico (2004)and Ohio (2005) where he coached wide receivers. In 2007, he coached defensive backs with the Minnesota Vikings and left to do the same for Stanford in 2010. From 2011 to 2013 he was the assistant head coach at Stanford, as well as their defensive coordinator. In 2014, he took the Vanderbilt job. After six seasons, Mason has yet to post a winning record; the closest being two 6-7 seasons in 2016 and 2018. In 2019 the Commodores went 3-9.

Players:

Owsley Manier **–** (1904-1906) – A Nashville native, Manier was a 1906 third team All-American. As the Commodore's top rushing weapon at fullback, Manier was the first Commodore to receive All-American accolades. In 1906, in the opener against Kentucky, Manier rushed for 3 touchdowns as Vanderbilt gained 630 yards in a 28-0 win. Two games later, Manier scored 5 times as Vanderbilt thrashed Alabama 78-0. That season, in the 37-6 win over Georgia Tech in Atlanta, Manier galloped for five scores. Vanderbilt's 1906 Manier-led squad lost only to Michigan by the score of 10-4, and scored 278 points while allowing 16. He died in Nashville on September 1, 1956.

Irby Rice Curry **–** (1913-1916) - Captain of the 1916 Vanderbilt Commodores, "Rabbit" Curry, as he was affectionately known, scored two touchdowns in the fourth quarter of the 1915 game with Sewanee to lead the Commodores to a climactic, come-from-behind victory and a 9-1 season. Curry was named third team All-American in 1916 and was also an All-Southern selection in both 1915 and 1916. He quarterbacked the 1916 Commodores to a 7-1-1 record and to one of the biggest victories in school history - an 86-0 thrashing of the University of Southwestern Louisiana, now the University of Louisiana at Lafayette. Tragically, Irby Rice "Rabbit" Curry was killed in action serving his country during World War I on August 10, 1918.

Jess Neely **-** (1920-1922) - During his 40 years as a coach at Southwestern Tennessee from 1924-1927, Clemson from 1931-1939, and Rice from 1940-1966, Neely's record was 207-176-19. A member of the College Football Hall of Fame, Neely, a Smyrna, Tenn. native, was the Captain of the 1922 Vanderbilt Southern Conference Championship team. Neely was 20-3-3 as a Vanderbilt player and was a perfect 3-0 against the Volunteers. Neely was named Vanderbilt Athletic Director Emeritus in 1967, and had the honor of tossing the coin at the rededication of Vanderbilt Stadium in 1981. He died April 9, 1983.

Bob Werckle – (1947, 1949-1951) - An All-American Offensive/Defensive Tackle, Werckle was known for his blocking and tackling skills. Early in his career, he battled culture shock, since he was from Brooklyn, New York. As a team captain and All-SEC selection in 1951, he recalled, "I felt like a Yankee and a stranger when I first came here, but I guess I've been reconstructed. Vanderbilt is the greatest thing that ever happened to me." He played professionally for Detroit and served as a Marine Corps officer in the Korean War. He died August 25, 2005.

George Deiderich – (1956-1958) - An All-American Guard in 1958, Deiderich, a Pittsburgh native, garnered first team All-American honors by the Associated Press, the Nation's Coaches, and the Football Writers Association of America. A two-time All-SEC selection, Deiderich played offensive and defensive line for the Commodores, with defense being his specialty. Deiderich was a standout track athlete, setting a Vanderbilt record in the 120 yard high hurdles with a time of 14.46 seconds. He scored in four varsity events for the Vanderbilt track team: the shot put, discus, long jump, and low hurdles. In 1960, Deiderich was drafted by the CFL's Montreal Alouettes, where he played for two seasons. He was known by his teammates as "Lu-Lu." He died July 9, 1999 in Gallatin, Tenn.

Bob Asher – (1967-1969) - A 1969 All-American Offensive Tackle and native of Falls Church, Virginia, Asher was named first team All-American by the Associated Press and played in the College All-Star Game, the Senior Bowl, the North-South Shrine Game and the Canadian-American Bowl. Asher started every game of his three year career at Vandy, serving as an impenetrable pass blocker. In 1970, he was drafted by the Dallas Cowboys and played on the 1971 Super Bowl team. Asher completed his professional football career in Chicago, where he started for the Bears from 1972-1975. In 1995, Asher was honored as a "Living Legend of SEC Football" at the SEC Championship game in Atlanta.

Chris Gaines – (1984-1987) – A homegrown product of Nashville's DuPont High, Gaines was selected as a first team Kodak All-American at linebacker. During his senior season for the Commodores, Gaines set a SEC single-season record for tackles with 214. Tennessean sports columnist Larry Woody once described Gaines as "...sort of a Rambo on a leash." In the annual post-season Blue-Gray

game, Gaines led the Gray to a 12-10 victory and was named Most Valuable Player, tallying 18 tackles. Against Tulane he registered 37. He was selected in the fifth round of the 1987 NFL draft by the Phoenix Cardinals and had brief NFL runs with the Miami Dolphins and Tampa Bay Bucs before heading to Canada to play for the Argonauts. Gaines set the Argo's single-season record for tackles with 117 in 1990, and he led the team in special teams tackles in addition to six interceptions. In 1991, he helped lead Toronto to the Grey Cup Championship. Gaines returned to Nashville as the Commodores' strength and conditioning coach in 1995, and was promoted to linebackers coach in 1997.

***Bill Marinangel* –** (1993-1996) - A 1996 All-American Punter, Marinangel was named first team All-American by the Sporting News in 1996. That same year, Marinangel won the NCAA punting championship with an average of 46.6 yards. Subsequent to the completion of the regular season, he was tabbed to play in the annual Blue-Gray All-Star Game. Marinangel is remembered for one heroic play in his senior year. During the season's second game, against Alabama in Tuscaloosa, Marinangel surprised everyone--including the Tide's special teams unit, as he took the snap from center and proceeded to scamper 81 yards for a touchdown. The run from scrimmage was the longest in the SEC in 1996.

***Jamie Duncan* –** (1995-1997) – An All-American Linebacker in 1997, Duncan was a dominating Commodore linebacker. Born July 20, 1975 in Wilmington, Delaware, Duncan was an outstanding defender of both the run and the pass, and he possessed an uncanny knack of causing turnovers and making big plays. At the end of the 1997 season, Duncan was named a first team All-American by the Football Writers Association of America. Duncan finished his career in Nashville with 425 tackles and was named SEC Defensive Player of the Year by the Mobile Press Register. Duncan was chosen in the third round by the Tampa Bay Buccaneers in the 1997 NFL Draft (84th overall).

***Jamie Winborn* –** (1997-2000) - A three year starter at Vanderbilt, the Wetumpka, Alabama native finished his college career with 377 tackles (236 solo), 16.5 sacks and 45 tackles for loss. Winborn was an All-American Dream Team selection by Sports Xchange as a junior and he was selected as a second team All-American by Football News and was a first team All-SEC pick as a sophomore. In 1998, after a redshirt year in 1997, Winborn was tabbed as a freshman All-American by Sporting News and Football News. Winborn left Vandy for the pros in 2001, when he was drafted the 47th pick in the second round of the NFL Draft by the San Francisco 49ers.

Jay Cutler **–** (2002-2005) - Born in Santa Claus, Indiana on April 23, 1983, Cutler is remembered as the most prolific signal caller in Commodore history. Cutler was a three-time captain and four-year starter, setting school career records for total offense (9,953 yards), touchdown passes (59), passing yards (8,697), pass completions (710), pass attempts (1,242), and combined touchdowns (76). A product of Heritage Hills High School in Lincoln City, Indiana, he started three years at quarterback and notched a 26-1 record his last two years. In 2002, as a freshman he set school records for passing and rushing yards and rushed for more yards than any SEC quarterback. As a junior he completed 61 percent of his passes—another school record, while throwing for 1,844 yards and ten touchdowns. Cutler broke out as a senior in 2005. Starting eleven games he registered 273 completions in 462 attempts (59.1%) for 3,073 yards, 21 touchdowns and nine interceptions, as he became the first Vanderbilt player to win the SEC Offensive Player of the Year award since Bob Goodridge in 1967. A consensus All-SEC pick, In his last Vanderbilt game Cutler led the Commodores to victory over Tennessee, 28-24, with a thrilling, last-second touchdown pass to Earl Bennett. The win was Vanderbilt's first over the Volunteers since 1982, the year preceding Cutler's birth. Jay Cutler was drafted in the first round as the 11th overall pick of the 2006 NFL draft.

Earl Bennett **–** (2005-2007) - Born March 23, 1987, in Birmingham, Alabama, Bennett is remembered as Vanderbilt's and the Southeastern Conference's most prolific receiver with 236 receptions for 2,852 yards and 20 touchdowns. He was the first SEC receiver to catch 75 passes in three consecutive seasons (2005-79, 2006-82, 2007-75) earning him three-time All-SEC honors in the process. During his first season with Vanderbilt he had the good fortune of working with quarterback Jay Cutler, an eventual first-round draft pick, and the two made the most of their time together, connecting 79 times for 876 yards. Bennett's 223 receiving yards against the Richmond Spiders is a Vanderbilt record, as is his 2,126 receiving yards after two years; which is another conference mark. With little left to accomplish at the collegiate level, Bennett opted to go pro early and forego his senior year. He was draft-

ed the 70th pick overall in the early third round of the 2008 NFL Draft by the Chicago Bears.

Jordan Matthews **–** (2010-2013) – A native of Huntsville, Alabama, Matthews attended Madison Academy, where he starred as a receiver, posting 181 catches for 3,218 receiving yards and 32 touchdowns. A three-star recruit, Matthews signed with Vanderbilt after receiving offers from Kansas, Tulane, Arkansas State and Jacksonville State. In 2010, as a true freshman, Matthews had 15 catches for 181 yards. As a sophomore he had 41 receptions for 778 yards and five scores. As a junior, in 2012, he was named All-SEC, finishing with 94 grabs for 1,323 yards and eight touchdowns. In 2013, as a senior, he set the all-time SEC record for career receptions and career receiving yards, eclipsing the marks of former Gamecock Earl Bennett. He finished the season with 112 receptions for 1,477 yards and seven touchdowns. Matthews' 112 receptions in 2013 set the SEC record for most receptions in a single season. In his final college game, he was the MVP of the 2014 BBVA Compass Bowl, recording five catches for 143 yards and two touchdowns. For his career, Matthews had 262 receptions for 3,759 yards, both SEC and school records. His 24 career touchdowns are the best in school history. Matthews graduated from Vanderbilt with a degree in economics. He was the 42nd pick by the Philadelphia Eagles in the second round of the 2014 NFL Draft.

Zach Cunningham **–** (2013-2016) – A native of Pinson, Alabama, Cunningham played high school ball at Pinson Valley High, where he was a standout linebacker, totaling 448 tackles, 194 as a senior. After a redshirt season he played in 11 games in 2014, posting 67 tackles and 1.5 sacks. As a redshirt sophomore in 2015, he played in 12 games with nine starts, finishing with 103 tackles and 4.5 sacks and was named first team All-SEC. In December 2016, Cunningham led the league in tackles with 119 and became the first unanimous All-American in Vanderbilt history. He was a consensus first-team All-SEC player and was named first team defensive All-American by the American Football Coaches Association, becoming the seventh Commodore to earn the consensus All-American honor for Vanderbilt. The last consensus All-American for Vanderbilt was punter Ricky Anderson in 1984. Cunningham was the 57th overall pick by Houston in the second round of the 2017 NFL Draft.

The Horn:

The nautical theme spawned by the University's founder, Cornelius Vanderbilt, continues with the sounding of a large ship's horn mounted on the press box at high points in the game.

Rivalries:

Vanderbilt's primary rival in nearly every sport is the University of Tennessee. A rivalry exists with the University of Mississippi, since the two schools play each other every year as SEC cross-division permanent opponents. Wake Forest, like Vanderbilt, is a private school which is the smallest in its conference, the Atlantic Coast Conference, and uses the same black and old gold as its colors.

V-U Hand Sign:

Formed by extending the thumb, index, and middle fingers of the hand, the resulting shape forms a "V" and "U". This is a recent development compared to other Vanderbilt traditions.

Game Day Traditions:

Vanderbilt has a number of football traditions: the "Commodore Creed" in the football locker room; the "Corridor of Captains" that honors Vanderbilt's athletics history; the "Star Walk" with fans, cheerleaders, and the Spirit of Gold Marching Band; the "Star V," an on-field formation by the marching band; the "Touchdown Foghorn" from a U.S. Navy battleship that sounds when Vanderbilt scores; "Mr. Commodore," the mascot; "Freshman Walk" by first-year students rushing the football field before kickoff of each season's home open; and the "Victory Flag" that is raised over Dudley Field after home wins.

The Vanderbilt Commodore Mission Statement:

"As an integral part of a private research university and a charter member of the Southeastern Conference, we are committed to setting and achieving standards of excellence in education and athletics by developing the full potential of our student-athletes and staff. Individually and together, we are accountable for placing the highest value on people, integrity and winning."

Alma Mater:

(Text by Robert F. Vaughn, 1907)
On the city's western border
Reared against the sky
Proudly stands our Alma Mater
As the years roll by.

Forward ever be thy watchword, Conquer and Prevail.
Hail to thee our Alma Mater, Vanderbilt, All Hail!

Cherished by thy sons daughters,
Mem'ries sweet shall throng
Round our hearts, O Alma Mater,
As we sing our song.

Fight Song: "Dynamite"
(Fight song written by Francis Craig in 1924)

Dynamite, Dynamite
When Vandy starts to fight

Down the field with blood to yield
If need be, save the shield.

If vict'rys won when battle's done
Then Vandy's name will rise in fame.

But, win or lose, The Fates will choose,
And Vandy's game will be the same.

Dynamite, Dynamite,
When Vandy starts to fight!

Noteworthy Vanderbilt Alumni:

Bettie Page, model

James Patterson, novelist

John Ingram, President of Ingram Distribution Holdings

Roseanne Cash, songwriter/entertainer

Marshall Chapman, entertainer

James Dickey, novelist and poet, author of Deliverance (deceased)

Grantland Rice, considered the greatest sportswriter of the 20th century

Amy Grant, entertainer

Dinah Shore, entertainer

Lamar Alexander, Tennessee Governor, U.S. Senator, U.S. Secretary of Education

Skip Bayless, syndicated newspaper columnist

John Bloom, humorist, journalist, and actor

Roy Blount, author and humorist

Alfred Hume, chancellor, University of Mississippi, 1924-30, 1932-1935

Ann S. More, Chairperson/CEO, Time, Inc.

Dierks Bentley, country musician

Randy Brooks, songwriter, "Grandma Got Runned Over By a Reindeer"

Roseanne Cash, singer-songwriter

Molly Sims, supermodel, actress

Robert Penn Warren, literary critic, novelist

Amy Ray, singer-songwriter

2020 Vanderbilt Football Schedule

Sept. 5 Mercer

Sept. 12 at Missouri

Sept. 19 at Kansas State

Sept. 26 Colorado State

Oct. 3 at Georgia

Oct. 10 Ole Miss

Oct. 17 at Kentucky

Oct. 24 OPEN DATE

Oct. 31 South Carolina

Nov. 7 Florida

Nov. 14 at Texas A&M

Nov. 21 Louisiana Tech

Nov. 28 Tennessee

Bibliography

Barber, Phil and Didinger, Ray. Football America: Celebrating our National Passion. 1996, Turner Publishing, Atlanta, Georgia.
Barner, William G. The Egg Bowl: Mississippi State Vs. Ole Miss. University of Mississippi Press, 2010.
Brewer, Jim. Arkansas Football: Yesterday & Today. Publisher's International. Ltd., 2000.
Broeg, Bob. Ol Mizzou: A Story of Mizzou Football. Strode Publishing, 1974.
Clark, Brooks & Heller, Robert. More Than a Game. Sports Publishing, 2002.
Danzig, Allison. The History of American Football. Prentice-Hall, 1956.
Daugherty, Nathan W. Educators and Athletes. University of Tennessee, 1976.
Davis, Jerry. Roll Tide: The Alabama Crimson Tide Story. Creative Education, 1999.
Evans, Wilbur. The Twelfth Man: A Story of Texas A&M Football. Strode, 1974.
Finney, Peter. The Fighting Tigers, 1893-1993: One Hundred Years of LSU Football. LSU Press, 1993.
Foley, Larry. Hog Calls: 100 Years of Arkansas Razorback Football. Longstreet, 1994.
Garbin, Patrick. About Them Dawgs! Georgia's Memorable Teams and Players. Scarecrow Press, 2008.
Gold, Eli. Crimson Nation. Thomas Nelson, Inc., 2006.
Griffin, John Chandler. The First Hundred Years: A History of Carolina Football. 1992. Longstreet Press.
Groom, Winston. The Crimson Tide, An Illustrated History. The University of Alabama Press, 2000.
Gruenfelder, M.H. A History of the Origin and Development of the Southeastern Conference. B.S. Thesis, University of Illinois.
Hemphill, Paul; & Dooley, Vince. A Tiger Walk Through History: The Complete Story of Auburn Football. Pebble Hill Books, 2008.
Hester, Wayne. The Centennial History of Auburn Football. Seacoast Publishing, Inc., 1991.
Hollis, Dan. Auburn Football: The Complete History. Auburn Sports Publications, 1988.
Irwin, Joseph & Michael. Cathedrals of College Football. 1998. Alliance Press.
Jacobs, Homer. The Pride of Aggieland: Spirit and Football at a Place Like No Other. Silver Lining Books, 2002.
McCallum, John D. Southeastern Conference Football, 1980.
McCarthy, Kevin. Fightin' Gators: A History of the University of Florida. Arcadia Publishing, 2000.
Moorman, Dave. Fighting Tiger Handbook. Wichita Eagle & Beacon Publishing, 1996.
Mule, Marty. A Hundred Years of LSU Football. Longstreet, 1993.
Official Southeastern Conference Football Handbook. BellSouth Advertising and Publishing, 1998.
Orville, Henry. Razorbacks: The Story of Arkansas Football. University of Arkansas Press, 1996.
Rice, Russell. The Wildcats: A Story of Kentucky Football. Strode, 1980.
Scott, Richard. SEC Football: 75 Years of Pride and Passion. MVP Books, 2008.
Sellers, James B. History of the University of Alabama. University of Alabama Press, 1953.
Sorrels, William. The Maroon Bulldogs: Mississippi State Football. Strode Publishing, 1986.
Stegeman, John. The Ghosts of Herty Field. University of Georgia Press, 1966.
Stewart, Mark. The Georgia Bulldogs. Norwood House, 2010.
Sugar, Burt Randolph. The SEC: A Pictorial History of Southeastern Conference Football, 1979.
Traughber, Bill. Vanderbilt Football: Tales of Commodore Gridiron History. The History Press, 2011.
Walsh, Christopher. Tennessee Football Guide & Record Book. Triumph Books, 2009.

In addition to the aforementioned, content was gleaned from the respective media guides from the 14 member schools, as well as each school's official academic and athletic websites, and other reputable primary and secondary sources, web pages, news agencies and the like.

About the Author:

A native of New Iberia, Louisiana, Chris Warner is a double graduate of Louisiana State University in Baton Rouge and of the University of New Orleans, where he received a doctorate in 2002. He is the author of over 20 books, his first being "A Tailgater's Guide to SEC Football," in 2000. A former radio and television host, high school teacher and college professor, he has appeared on the History Channel, CBS College Sports Television, James Carville's 60-20 With Luke Russert and the Paul Finebaum Radio Show. He lives in Perdido Key, Florida. He is a noted speaker on the History of College Football in the South, the history of the SEC and the history of tailgating.

Other books by Chris Warner, you may also enjoy:

Bushwhacked at the Flora Bama – A Character-laden history and tales from the Last Great American Roadhouse on the Alabama and Florida state line at the Gulf of Mexico; with founder, Joe Gilchrist.

SEC Sports Quotes Compendium – A collection of adages, aphorisms, quips, maxims and pronouncements from players, coaches, sportswriters and observers of the nation's toughest athletic conference.

The Wagon to Disaster – The untold story of the HealthSouth scandal; with Aaron Beam, former founder and CFO; Featured on American Greed and 60 Minutes; a cautionary tale of greed you won't forget, along with its dark character, Richard Marin Scrushy, an unlikely opportunist with a G.E.D. and a respiratory therapy certificate who makes $900 million building a Fortune 500 company...only to lose it.

Professional Bone – A novel set in Birmingham, Alabma, inspired by the HealthSouth scandal.

Santa & Sam – A heartwarming Christmas novella set in Madison, Wisconsin; with Larry Bielat.

The Tiger Among Us – A terrorism novel set at LSU in 1990; with Daniel Mark Waghelstein. POTUS sends a lone Recon Marine, Michael Stein, to LSU to locate, exploit and eliminate two Arab students and a Mediterranean Restaurant owner, in the name of national security. Michael falls in love with a Cajun girl and has a host of pitfalls he must overcome in order to fulfill his mission in a thrilling climax.

The Ulysses Long Story – A Louisiana prison inmate at Angola, Ulysses Long, is pardoned by Governor Edwin Edwards at the request of LSU Basketball Coach Dale Brown. This is his unbelievable, true story of faith, determination, hope and love.

Saved at the Alabama-Florida Line – A novel set in Perdido Key, Florida. Johnny Glass has had it with Nashville. He meets a beautiful girl at Flora-Bama and finds a regular gig playing music. Her father is a senator and he doesn't take kindly to musicians...and uses his political connections to do the unthinkable: shutter the beach bar for good. Musicians and locals unite to save the bar from ruin.

They Met at the Alabama-Florida Line – A second novel set in Perido Key, Florida. Baton Rouge Frat brothers meet girls from Alabama who look better than them. One is a preacher's daughter with a fake I.D. She and the alpha male are arrested by the Orange Beach cops. The loveable owner must save the kids from the legal jam and the reputation of the Flora-Bama from Jewish filmmakers. A third novel set in Perido Key is in the works... "Trouble at the Alabama-Florida Line."

Food N' Fun at the Flora-Bama – Food and drink recipes by the owners, musicians, songwriters, locals and bartenders. Easy-to-make recipes and a Flora-Bama patron favorite.

If the Walls Could Talk – Graffiti from the hallowed walls of the Noted Pump House on the Line.

Find out more about Chris and his books and speaking availability at his facebook page and website: Southern Beach Reads by author and speaker Chris Warner.